STUDENT HELP TECHNOLOGY OVERVIEW

STUDENT COMPANION WEBSITE

BigIdeasMath.com

ONLINE PUPIL EDITION

INTERACTIVE GLOSSARY
English, Spanish, Haitian Creole

SKILLS REVIEW HANDBOOK

LESSON TUTORIALS

BIG IDEAS
MATH.

RED

Ron Larson
Laurie Boswell

Erie, Pennsylvania
BigIdeasLearning.com

Big Ideas Learning, LLC
1762 Norcross Road
Erie, PA 16510-3838
USA

For product information and customer support, contact Big Ideas Learning
at **1-877-552-7766** or visit us at ***BigIdeasLearning.com***.

Printed in the U.S.A.

ISBN 13: 978-1-60840-014-0
ISBN 10: 1-60840-014-X

2 3 4 5 6 7 8 9 10 WEB 13 12 11 10 09

AUTHORS

Ron Larson is a professor of mathematics at Penn State University in Erie, Pennsylvania where he has taught since receiving his Ph.D. in mathematics from the University of Colorado in 1970. Dr. Larson is well known as the lead author of a comprehensive program for mathematics that spans middle school, high school, and college courses. His high school and Advanced Placement books are published by Holt McDougal. Dr. Larson's numerous professional activities keep him in constant touch with the needs of students, teachers, and supervisors. Dr. Larson and Laurie Boswell began writing together in 1992. Since that time, they have authored over two dozen textbooks. In their collaboration, Dr. Larson is primarily responsible for the pupil edition and Laurie is primarily responsible for the teaching edition of the text.

Laurie Boswell is a mathematics teacher at the Riverside School in Lyndonville, Vermont. She is a recipient of the Presidential Award for Excellence in Mathematics Teaching. Laurie has taught math to students at all levels, elementary through college. In addition, Laurie was a Tandy Technology Scholar, and served on the NCTM Board of Directors from 2002 to 2005. She currently serves on the board of NCSM, and is a popular national speaker. Along with Dr. Larson, Laurie has co-authored numerous math programs.

ABOUT THE BOOK

This book is brand new! It is not a revision of a previously published book.

When the NCTM released its new *Curriculum Focal Points* for mathematics for grades 6–8, we were delighted. The traditional mile-wide and inch-deep programs that have been followed for years have clearly not worked. Middle school students need something new . . . fewer topics with deeper coverage.

- **DEEPER**   Each section is designed for 2–3 day coverage.
- **DYNAMIC**   Each section begins with a full class period of active learning.
- **DOABLE**   Each section is accompanied by full student and teacher support.
- **DAZZLING**   How else can we say this? This book puts the dazzle back in math!

Ron Larson

Laurie Boswell

TEACHER REVIEWERS

Aaron Eisberg
Napa Valley Unified School District
Napa, CA

Gail Englert
Norfolk Public Schools
Norfolk, VA

Alexis Kaplan
Lindenwold Public Schools
Lindenwold, NJ

Lou Kwiatkowski
Millcreek Township School District
Erie, PA

Marcela Mansur
Broward County Public Schools
Fort Lauderdale, FL

Bonnie Pendergast
Tolleson Union High School District
Tolleson, AZ

Tammy Rush
Hillsborough County Public Schools
Tampa, FL

Patricia D. Seger
Polk County Public Schools
Bartow, FL

Elizabeth Wright
Pinellas County Schools
Largo, FL

STUDENT REVIEWERS

Ashley Benovic

Vanessa Bowser

Sara Chinsky

Kaitlyn Grimm

Lakota Noble

Norhan Omar

Jack Puckett

Abby Quinn

Victoria Royal

Madeline Su

Lance Williams

CONSULTANTS

Patsy Davis
Educational Consultant
Knoxville, Tennessee

Deb Johnson
Differentiated Instruction Consultant
Missoula, Montana

Mark Johnson
Mathematics Assessment Consultant
Raymond, New Hampshire

Ryan Keating
Special Education Advisor
Gilbert, Arizona

Michael McDowell
Project-Based Instruction Specialist
Scottsdale, Arizona

Sean McKeighan
Interdisciplinary Advisor
Midland, Texas

Bill Setzer
Retired Mathematics Supervisor
Roanoke County, Virginia

Bonnie Spence
Differentiated Instruction Consultant
Missoula, Montana

A Focal Points Curriculum

Chapter Coverage for Focal Points and Connections

①—②—③—④—⑤—⑥—⑦—⑧—⑨

Focal Point   Develop an understanding of and apply proportionality, including similarity.

- Distinguish between situations that are proportional or not proportional and use proportions to solve problems.
- Solve percent problems, including problems involving discounts, simple interest, taxes, tips and percents of increase or decrease.
- Solve problems involving similar figures.
- Graph proportional relationships and identify the unit rate as the slope of the related linear function.
- Distinguish direct variation from other relationships, including inverse variation.
- Apply proportionality to measurement in multiple contexts, including scale drawings and constant speed.

①—②—③—④—⑤—⑥—⑦—⑧—⑨

Focal Point   Develop an understanding of and use formulas to determine surface areas and volumes of three-dimensional shapes.

- Justify and apply formulas for surface area and volume of pyramids, prisms, cylinders, and cones.
- Use formulas to find surface areas and volumes of three-dimensional composite shapes.

①—②—③—④—⑤—⑥—⑦—⑧—⑨

Focal Point   Develop an understanding of operations on all rational numbers and solving linear equations.

- Use and justify the rules for adding, subtracting, multiplying, dividing, and finding the absolute value of integers.
- Add, subtract, multiply, and divide integers, fractions, and terminating decimals, and perform exponential operations with rational bases and whole number exponents including solving problems in everyday contexts.
- Formulate and use different strategies to solve one-step and two-step linear equations, including equations with rational coefficients.
- Use the properties of equality to represent an equation in a different way and to show that two equations are equivalent in a given context.

Connection — Geometry and Measurement

1 2 3 4 5 6 7 8 9

- Determine how changes in dimensions affect the perimeter, area, and volume of common geometric figures and apply these relationships to solve problems.
- Predict the results of transformations and draw transformed figures, with and without the coordinate plane.
- Identify and plot ordered pairs in all four quadrants of the coordinate plane.
- Compare, contrast, and convert units of measure between different measurement systems (US customary or metric (SI)), dimensions, and derived units to solve problems.

Connection — Number and Operations

1 2 3 4 5 6 7 8 9

- Express rational numbers as terminating or repeating decimals.
- Solve non-routine problems by working backwards.

Connection — Data Analysis

1 2 3 4 5 6 7 8 9

- Evaluate the reasonableness of a sample to determine the appropriateness of generalizations made about the population.
- Construct and analyze histograms, stem-and-leaf plots, and circle graphs.

Connection — Probability

1 2 3 4 5 6 7 8 9

- Determine the outcome of an experiment and predict which events are likely or unlikely, and if the experiment is fair or unfair.
- Determine, compare, and make predictions based on experimental or theoretical probability of independent or dependent events.

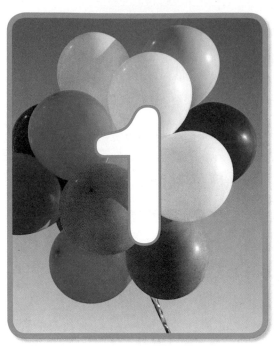

Unit 1
Chapters 1 and 2

Rational Numbers and Linear Equations

Operations with Integers

"I love my math book. It has so many interesting examples and homework problems. I have always liked math, but I didn't know how it could be used. Now I have lots of ideas."

Rational Numbers and Equations

"I like starting each new lesson with a partner activity. I just moved to this school and the activities helped me make friends."

Proportions and Variation

"I like having the book on the Internet. The online tutorials help me with my homework when I get stuck on a problem."

Percents

"I love the cartoons. They are funny and they help me remember the math. I want to be a cartoonist some day."

Similarity and Transformations

"I like how I can click on the words in the book that is online and hear them read to me. I like to pronouce words correctly, but sometimes I don't know how to do that by just reading the words."

Unit 3 Surface Area and Volume
Chapters 6 and 7

Surface Areas of Solids

"I really liked the projects at the end of the book. The history project on ancient Egypt was my favorite. Someday I would like to visit Egypt and go to the pyramids."

Volumes of Solids

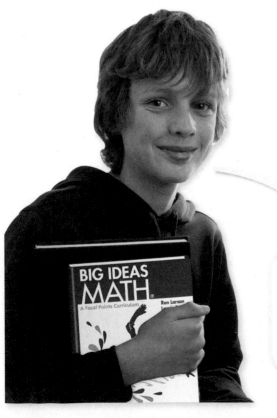

"I like how the glossary in the book is part of the index. When I couldn't remember how a vocabulary word was defined, I could go to the index and find where the word was defined in the book."

Data Analysis and Samples

"I like the practice tests in the book. I get really nervous on tests. So, having a practice test to work on at home helped me to chill out when the real test came."

Probability

"I like the review at the beginning of each chapter. This book has examples to help me remember things from last year. I don't like it when the review is just a list of questions."

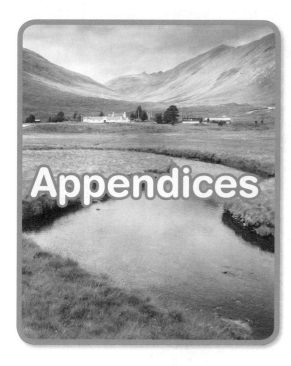

Appendix A: My Big Ideas Projects

Appendix B: Exploring Equations and Functions

"I like the workbook (Record and Practice Journal). It saved me a lot of work to not have to copy all the questions and graphs."

How to Use Your Math Book

● Read the **Essential Question** in the activity.

   Work with a partner to decide **What Is Your Answer?**

   Now you are ready to do the **Practice** problems.

● Find the **Key Vocabulary** words, **highlighted in yellow**.

   Read their definitions. Study the concepts in each **Key Idea**.
   If you forget a definition, you can look it up online in the

    Multi-Language Glossary at BigIdeasMathcom.

● After you study each **EXAMPLE**, do the exercises in the ● **On Your Own**.

   Now You're Ready to do the exercises that correspond to the example.

   As you study, look for a **Study Tip** or a **Common Error !** .

   ● The exercises are divided into 3 parts.

      ✓ **Vocabulary and Concept Check**

      Practice and Problem Solving

      Fair Game Review

   If an exercise has a **①** next to it, look back at
   Example 1 for help with that exercise.

   More help is available at .

   ● To help study for your test, use the following.

      Quiz   **Study Help**

      Chapter Review   **Chapter Test**

SCAVENGER HUNT

Use this *Scavenger Hunt* to find where things are in **Chapter 1**.

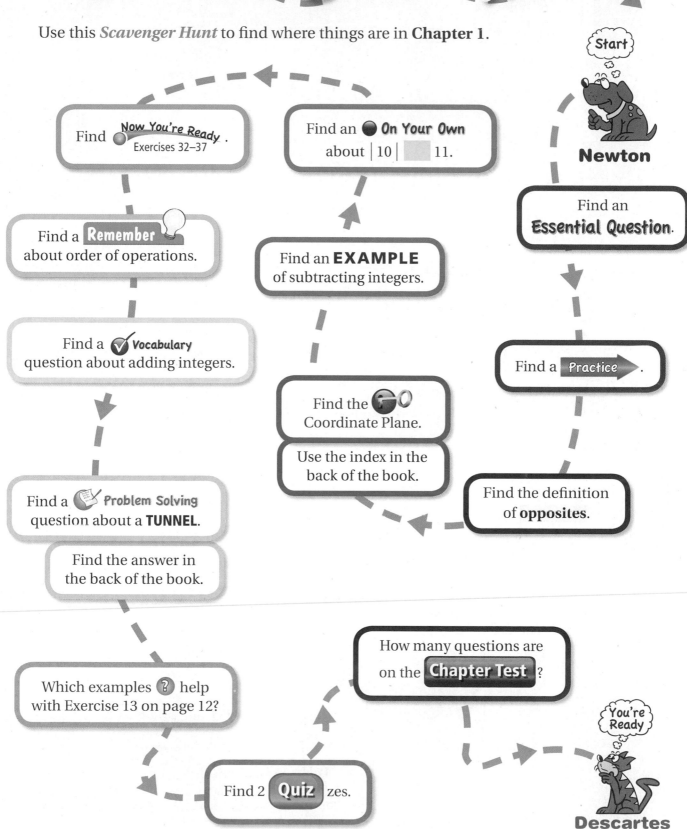

Start

Newton

Find an **Essential Question**.

Find an ● **On Your Own** about | 10 | 11.

Find ● Now You're Ready .
Exercises 32–37

Find a **Remember** about order of operations.

Find a ✓ **Vocabulary** question about adding integers.

Find an **EXAMPLE** of subtracting integers.

Find a **Practice** .

Find the ⚷O Coordinate Plane.

Find the definition of **opposites**.

Use the index in the back of the book.

Find a **Problem Solving** question about a **TUNNEL**.

Find the answer in the back of the book.

How many questions are on the **Chapter Test** ?

You're Ready

Which examples ❓ help with Exercise 13 on page 12?

Find 2 **Quiz** zes.

Descartes

1 Operations with Integers

"Look, subtraction is not that difficult. Imagine that you have five squeaky mouse toys."

$5 + (-1) = 4$

"After your friend Fluffy comes over for a visit, you notice that one of the squeaky toys is missing."

$4 - (-1) = 5$

I'm going to count my toys

"Now, you go over to Fluffy's and retrieve the missing squeaky mouse toy. It's easy."

"Dear Sir: You asked me to 'find' the opposite of −1."

That's not the only thing that is missing.

"I didn't know it was missing."

What You Learned Before

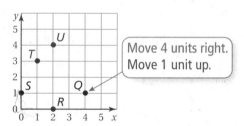

"I liked it because it is the opposite of the freezing point on the Fahrenheit temperature scale."

Ordering Integers

Example 1 Order 0, −1, 2, 5, and −6 from least to greatest.

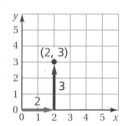

Try It Yourself

Order the integers from least to greatest.

1. −10, 15, 4, −2, −12

2. 7, −5, 3, −3, 1

Plotting Points

Example 2 Plot the point (2, 3).

Example 3 Write an ordered pair corresponding to Point Q.

Move 4 units right.
Move 1 unit up.

The ordered pair (4, 1) corresponds to Point Q.

Try It Yourself

Use the graph in Example 3 to write an ordered pair corresponding to the point.

3. Point S **4.** Point T **5.** Point U **6.** Point R

Using Order of Operations

Example 4 Evaluate $6^2 \div 4 - 2(9 - 5)$.

First:	Parentheses	$6^2 \div 4 - 2(9 - 5) = 6^2 \div 4 - 2 \cdot 4$
Second:	Exponents	$= 36 \div 4 - 2 \cdot 4$
Third:	Multiplication and Division (from left to right)	$= 9 - 8$
Fourth:	Addition and Subtraction (from left to right)	$= 1$

Try It Yourself

Evaluate the expression.

7. $15\left(\dfrac{8}{4}\right) + 2^2 - 3 \cdot 7$ **8.** $5^2 \cdot 2 \div 10 + 3 \cdot 2 - 1$ **9.** $3^2 - 1 + 2(4(3 + 2))$

Essential Question How are velocity and speed related?

On these two pages, you will investigate vertical motion (up or down).

- Speed tells how fast an object is moving, but does not tell the direction.
- Velocity tells how fast an object is moving and also tells the direction.

    If velocity is positive, the object is moving up.

    If velocity is negative, the object is moving down.

1 EXAMPLE: Falling Parachute

You are gliding to the ground wearing a parachute. The table shows your height at different times.

Time (seconds)	0	1	2	3
Height (feet)	45	30	15	0

a. **How many feet do you move each second?**

b. **What is your speed? Give the units.**

c. **Is your velocity positive or negative?**

d. **What is your velocity? Give the units.**

a. For each 1 second of time, your height is 15 feet less.

b. You are moving at 15 feet per second.

c. Because you are moving down, your velocity is negative.

d. Your velocity is -15 feet per second. This can be written as -15 ft/sec.

2 ACTIVITY: Rising Balloons

Work with a partner. The table shows the height of a group of balloons.

Time (seconds)	0	1	2	3
Height (feet)	0	4	8	12

a. How many feet do the balloons move each second?

b. What is the speed of the balloons? Give the units.

c. Is the velocity positive or negative?

d. What is the velocity? Give the units.

ACTIVITY: Finding Speed and Velocity

Work with a partner. The table shows the height of a firework's parachute.

Time (seconds)	Height (feet)
0	480
1	360
2	240
3	120
4	0

a. How many feet does the parachute move each second?

b. What is the speed of the parachute? Give the units.

c. Is the velocity positive or negative?

d. What is the velocity? Give the units.

Inductive Reasoning

4. Copy and complete the table.

Velocity (feet per second)	−14	20	−2	0	25	−15
Speed (feet per second)						

5. Find two different velocities for which the speed is 16 feet per second.

6. Which number is greater: −4 or 3? Use a number line to explain your reasoning.

7. One object has a velocity of −4 feet per second. Another object has a velocity of 3 feet per second. Which object has the greater speed? Explain your answer.

What Is Your Answer?

In this lesson, you will study **absolute value**. Here are some examples:

Absolute value of −16 = 16   Absolute value of 16 = 16
Absolute value of 0 = 0   Absolute value of −2 = 2

8. **IN YOUR OWN WORDS** How are velocity and speed related?

9. Which of the following is a true statement? Explain your reasoning.

  a. Absolute value of velocity = speed

  b. Absolute value of speed = velocity

Practice

Use what you learned about absolute value to complete Exercises 4–11 on page 6.

Check It Out
Lesson Tutorials
BigIdeasMath.com

The following numbers are **integers**.

$$\ldots, -3, -2, -1, 0, 1, 2, 3, \ldots$$

Key Vocabulary
integer, *p. 4*
absolute value, *p. 4*

Key Idea

Absolute Value

Words The **absolute value** of an integer is the distance between the number and 0 on a number line. The absolute value of a number a is written as $|a|$.

Numbers $|-4| = 4$ $\qquad$ $|4| = 4$

EXAMPLE 1 Finding Absolute Value

Find the absolute value of 2.

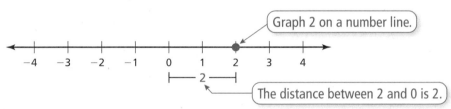

Graph 2 on a number line.

The distance between 2 and 0 is 2.

So, $|2| = 2$.

EXAMPLE 2 Finding Absolute Value

Find the absolute value of -3.

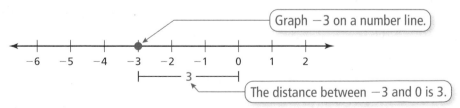

Graph -3 on a number line.

The distance between -3 and 0 is 3.

So, $|-3| = 3$.

On Your Own

Now You're Ready
Exercises 4–19

Find the absolute value of the integer.

1. 7 $\qquad$ **2.** -1 $\qquad$ **3.** -5 $\qquad$ **4.** 14

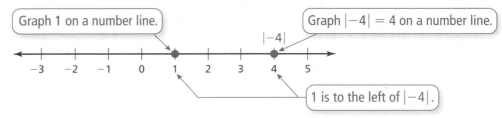

EXAMPLE 3 — Comparing Values

Compare 1 and $\left| -4 \right|$.

Remember

A number line can be used to compare and order integers. Numbers to the left are less than numbers to the right. Numbers to the right are greater than numbers to the left.

Graph 1 on a number line.

Graph $|-4| = 4$ on a number line.

$|-4|$

$-3 \quad -2 \quad -1 \quad 0 \quad 1 \quad 2 \quad 3 \quad 4 \quad 5$

1 is to the left of $|-4|$.

So, $1 < \left| -4 \right|$.

On Your Own

Now You're Ready
Exercises 20–25

Copy and complete the statement using $<$, $>$, or $=$.

5. $\left| -2 \right|$ [ ] -1

6. -7 [ ] $\left| 6 \right|$

7. $\left| 10 \right|$ [ ] 11

8. 9 [ ] $\left| -9 \right|$

EXAMPLE 4 — Real-Life Application

Substance	Freezing Point (°C)
Butter	35
Airplane fuel	−53
Honey	−3
Mercury	−39
Candle wax	55

The *freezing point* is the temperature at which a liquid becomes a solid.

a. Which substance in the table has the lowest freezing point?

b. Is the freezing point of mercury or butter closer to the freezing point of water, 0°C?

a. Graph each freezing point.

Airplane fuel −53 Mercury −39 Honey −3 Butter 35 Candle wax 55

$-60 \quad -50 \quad -40 \quad -30 \quad -20 \quad -10 \quad 0 \quad 10 \quad 20 \quad 30 \quad 40 \quad 50 \quad 60$

Airplane fuel has the lowest freezing point, $-53°C$.

b. The freezing point of water is 0°C, so you can use absolute values.

Mercury: $\left| -39 \right| = 39$ **Butter:** $\left| 35 \right| = 35$

Because 35 is less than 39, the freezing point of butter is closer to the freezing point of water.

On Your Own

9. Is the freezing point of airplane fuel or candle wax closer to the freezing point of water? Explain your reasoning.

Vocabulary and Concept Check

1. **VOCABULARY** Which of the following numbers are integers?

$$9, 3.2, -1, \frac{1}{2}, -0.25, 15$$

2. **VOCABULARY** What is the absolute value of an integer?

3. **WHICH ONE DOESN'T BELONG?** Which expression does *not* belong with the other three? Explain your reasoning.

$$|6| \qquad 6 \qquad -6 \qquad |-6|$$

 Practice and Problem Solving

Find the absolute value of the integer.

4. 9   **5.** -6 **6.** -10 **7.** 10

8. -15 **9.** 13   **10.** -7 **11.** -12

12. 5   **13.** -8 **14.** 0   **15.** 18

16. -24 **17.** -45 **18.** 60   **19.** -125

Copy and complete the statement using <, >, or =.

20. $2 \quad \boxed{} \quad |-5|$ **21.** $|-4| \quad \boxed{} \quad 7$ **22.** $-5 \quad \boxed{} \quad |-9|$

23. $|-4| \quad \boxed{} \quad -6$ **24.** $|-1| \quad \boxed{} \quad |-8|$ **25.** $|5| \quad \boxed{} \quad |-5|$

ERROR ANALYSIS Describe and correct the error.

26.

✗ $|10| = -10$

27.

✗ $|-5| < 4$

28. **SAVINGS** You deposit $50 in your savings account. One week later, you withdraw $20. Write each amount as an integer.

29. **ELEVATOR** You go down 8 floors in an elevator. Your friend goes up 5 floors in an elevator. Write each amount as an integer.

Order the values from least to greatest.

30. $8, |3|, -5, |-2|, -2$ **31.** $|-6|, -7, 8, |5|, -6$

32. $-12, |-26|, -15, |-12|, |10|$ **33.** $|-34|, 21, -17, |20|, |-11|$

Simplify the expression.

34. $|-30|$ **35.** $-|4|$ **36.** $-|-15|$

37. **PUZZLE** Use a number line.

 a. Graph and label the following points on a number line: $A = -3$, $E = 2$, $M = -6$, $T = 0$. What word do the letters spell?

 b. Graph and label the absolute value of each point in part (a). What word do the letters spell now?

38. **OPEN-ENDED** Write a negative integer whose absolute value is greater than 3.

REASONING Determine whether $n \geq 0$ or $n \leq 0$.

39. $n + \left| -n \right| = 2n$

40. $n + \left| -n \right| = 0$

14 feet

18 feet

41. **CORAL REEF** Two scuba divers are exploring a living coral reef.

 a. Write an integer for the position of each diver relative to sea level.

 b. Which integer in part (a) is greater?

 c. Which integer in part (a) has the greater absolute value? Compare this with the position of the diver farther from sea level.

42. **VOLCANOES** The *summit elevation* of a volcano is the elevation of the top of the volcano relative to sea level. The summit elevation of the volcano Kilauea in Hawaii is 1277 meters. The summit elevation of the underwater volcano Loihi in the Pacific Ocean is −969 meters. Which summit is closer to sea level?

43. **MINIATURE GOLF** The table shows golf scores, relative to *par*.

 a. The player with the lowest score wins. Which player wins?

 b. Which player is at par?

 c. Which player is farthest from par?

Player	Score
1	+5
2	0
3	−4
4	−1
5	+2

True or False? Determine whether the statement is *true* or *false*. Explain your reasoning.

44. If $x < 0$, then $\left| x \right| = -x$.

45. The absolute value of every integer is positive.

Fair Game Review What you learned in previous grades & lessons

Add. *(Skills Review Handbook)*

46. $19 + 32$

47. $50 + 94$

48. $181 + 217$

49. $1149 + 2021$

50. **MULTIPLE CHOICE** Which value is *not* a whole number? *(Skills Review Handbook)*

 Ⓐ −5   Ⓑ 0   Ⓒ 4   Ⓓ 113

Essential Question
Is the sum of two integers *positive*, *negative*, or *zero*? How can you tell?

1 **EXAMPLE: Adding Integers with the Same Sign**

Use integer counters to find $-4 + (-3)$.

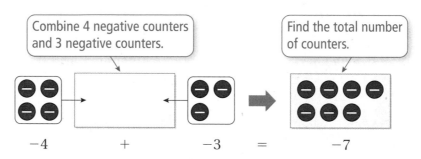

Combine 4 negative counters and 3 negative counters.

Find the total number of counters.

$$-4 \qquad + \qquad -3 \qquad = \qquad -7$$

∴ So, $-4 + (-3) = -7$.

2 **ACTIVITY: Adding Integers with Different Signs**

Work with a partner. Use integer counters to find $-3 + 2$.

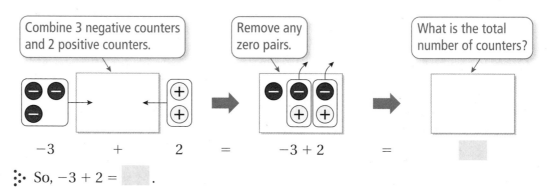

Combine 3 negative counters and 2 positive counters.

Remove any zero pairs.

What is the total number of counters?

$$-3 \qquad + \qquad 2 \qquad = \qquad -3 + 2 \qquad =$$

∴ So, $-3 + 2 = \boxed{}$.

3 **EXAMPLE: Adding Integers with Different Signs**

Use a number line to find $5 + (-3)$.

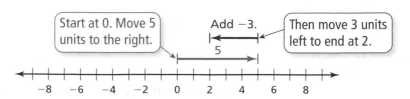

Start at 0. Move 5 units to the right.

Add -3.

Then move 3 units left to end at 2.

5

∴ So, $5 + (-3) = 2$.

4 ACTIVITY: Adding Integers with Different Signs

Work with a partner. Write the addition expression shown. Then find the sum.

Start at 0. Move 7 units to the right.

Add −10

Then move 10 units left to end at −3.

7

Inductive Reasoning

Work with a partner. Use integer counters or a number line to complete the table.

	Exercise	Type of Sum	Sum	Sum: Positive, Negative, or Zero
①	**5.** −4 + (−3)	Integers with the same sign		
②	**6.** −3 + 2			Negative
③	**7.** 5 + (−3)		2	
④	**8.** 7 + (−10)	Integers with different signs		
	9. 2 + 4			
	10. −6 + (−2)			
	11. −5 + 9			
	12. 15 + (−9)			
	13. −10 + 10			
	14. −6 + (−6)			
	15. 12 + (−12)			

What Is Your Answer?

16. IN YOUR OWN WORDS Is the sum of two integers *positive*, *negative*, or *zero*? How can you tell?

17. Write general rules for adding (a) two integers with the same sign, (b) two integers with different signs, and (c) an integer and its opposite.

Practice

Use what you learned about adding integers to complete Exercises 8–15 on page 12.

Key Vocabulary 🔊
opposites, *p. 10*
additive inverse, *p. 10*

🔑 Key Idea

Adding Integers with the Same Sign

Words   Add the absolute values of the integers. Then use the common sign.

Numbers $2 + 5 = 7$ $-2 + (-5) = -7$

EXAMPLE **1**   **Adding Integers with the Same Sign**

Find $-2 + (-4)$. Use a number line to check your answer.

$$-2 + (-4) = -6 \qquad \text{Add } |-2| \text{ and } |-4|.$$

Use the common sign.

⋮• The sum is -6.

Check

The Meaning of a Word

Opposite

When you sit across from your friend at the lunch table, you sit **opposite** your friend.

⬤ On Your Own

Add.

1. $7 + 13$ **2.** $-8 + (-5)$ **3.** $-20 + (-15)$

Two numbers that are the same distance from 0, but on opposite sides of 0, are called **opposites.** For example, -3 and 3 are opposites.

🔑 Key Ideas

Adding Integers with Different Signs

Words   Subtract the lesser absolute value from the greater absolute value. Then use the sign of the integer with the greater absolute value.

Numbers $8 + (-10) = -2$ $-13 + 17 = 4$

Additive Inverse Property

Words   The sum of an integer and its **additive inverse,** or opposite, is 0.

Numbers $6 + (-6) = 0$ $-25 + 25 = 0$

🔊 Multi-Language Glossary at BigIdeasMath✓com.

EXAMPLE **2** **Adding Integers with Different Signs**

a. Find 5 + (−10).

$$5 + (-10) = -5$$

$|-10| > |5|$. So, subtract $|5|$ from $|-10|$.

Use the sign of −10.

∴ The sum is −5.

b. Find −3 + 7.

$$-3 + 7 = 4$$

$|7| > |-3|$. So, subtract $|-3|$ from $|7|$.

Use the sign of 7.

∴ The sum is 4.

c. Find −12 + 12.

$$-12 + 12 = 0$$

The sum is 0 by the Additive Inverse Property.

−12 and 12 are opposites.

∴ The sum is 0.

On Your Own

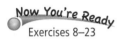
Now You're Ready
Exercises 8–23

Add.

4. $-2 + 11$

5. $13 + (-8)$

6. $9 + (-10)$

7. $-8 + 4$

8. $7 + (-7)$

9. $-31 + 31$

EXAMPLE **3** **Adding More than Two Integers**

The list shows four bank account transactions in July. Find the change *C* in the account balance.

JULY TRANSACTIONS	
Deposit	**$50**
Withdrawal	**-$40**
Deposit	**$75**
Withdrawal	**-$50**

Find the sum of the four transactions.

$C = 50 + (-40) + 75 + (-50)$ Write the sum.

$= 10 + 75 + (-50)$ Add 50 and −40.

$= 85 + (-50)$ Add 10 and 75.

$= 35$ Add 85 and −50.

∴ Because $C = 35$, the account balance increased $35 in July.

On Your Own

Now You're Ready
Exercises 28–33

10. WHAT IF? In Example 3, the deposit amounts are $30 and $55. Find the change *C* in the account balance.

Vocabulary and Concept Check

1. **WRITING** How do you find the additive inverse of an integer?

2. **NUMBER SENSE** Is $3 + (-4)$ the same as $-4 + 3$? Explain.

Tell whether the sum is *positive*, *negative*, or *zero* without adding. Explain your reasoning.

   3. $-8 + 20$ 4. $50 + (-50)$ 5. $-10 + (-18)$

Tell whether the statement is *true* or *false*. Explain your reasoning.

   6. The sum of two negative integers is always negative.

   7. An integer and its absolute value are always opposites.

 Practice and Problem Solving

Add.

 8. $6 + 4$ 9. $-4 + (-6)$ 10. $-2 + (-3)$ 11. $-5 + 12$

12. $5 + (-7)$ 13. $8 + (-8)$ 14. $9 + (-11)$ 15. $-3 + 13$

16. $-4 + (-16)$ 17. $-3 + (-4)$ 18. $14 + (-5)$ 19. $0 + (-11)$

20. $-10 + (-15)$ 21. $-13 + 9$ 22. $18 + (-18)$ 23. $-25 + (-9)$

ERROR ANALYSIS Describe and correct the error in finding the sum.

24.
$$\bcancel{}\quad 9 + (-6) = -3$$

25.
$$\bcancel{}\quad -10 + (-10) = 0$$

26. **TEMPERATURE** The temperature is $-3°F$ at 7 A.M. During the next four hours, the temperature increases $21°F$. What is the temperature at 11 A.M.?

27. **BANKING** Your bank account has a balance of $-\$12$. You deposit $\$60$. What is your new balance?

Add.

28. $13 + (-21) + 16$ 29. $22 + (-14) + (-35)$ 30. $-13 + 27 + (-18)$

31. $-19 + 26 + 14$ 32. $-32 + (-17) + 42$ 33. $-41 + (-15) + (-29)$

Tell how the Commutative and Associative Properties of Addition can help you find the sum mentally. Then find the sum.

34. $9 + 6 + (-6)$ 35. $-8 + 13 + (-13)$ 36. $9 + (-17) + (-9)$

37. $7 + (-12) + (-7)$ 38. $-12 + 25 + (-15)$ 39. $6 + (-9) + 14$

ALGEBRA Evaluate the expression when $a = 4$, $b = -5$, and $c = -8$.

40. $a + b$ **41.** $b + c$ **42.** $|a + b + c|$

43. OPEN-ENDED Write two integers with different signs that have a sum of -25. Write two integers with the same sign that have a sum of -25.

MENTAL MATH Use mental math to solve the equation.

44. $d + 12 = 2$ **45.** $b + (-2) = 0$ **46.** $-8 + m = -15$

47. FIRST DOWN In football, a team must gain 10 yards to get a first down. The team gains 6 yards on the first play, loses 3 yards on the second play, and gains 8 yards on the third play. Which expression can be used to decide whether the team gets a first down?

$$10 + 6 - 3 + 8 \qquad 6 + (-3) + 8 \qquad 6 + (-3) + (-8)$$

48. DOLPHIN Starting at point A, the path of a dolphin jumping out of the water is shown.

  a. Is the dolphin deeper at point C or point E? Explain your reasoning.

  b. Is the dolphin higher at point B or point D? Explain your reasoning.

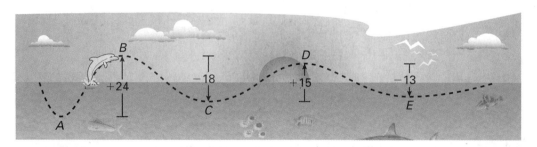

49. **Puzzle** According to a legend, the Chinese Emperor Yu-Huang saw a magic square on the back of a turtle. In a *magic square*, the numbers in each row and in each column have the same sum. This sum is called the magic sum.

Copy and complete the magic square so that each row and each column has a magic sum of 0. Use each integer from -4 to 4 exactly once.

Fair Game Review What you learned in previous grades & lessons

Subtract. *(Skills Review Handbook)*

50. $69 - 38$ **51.** $82 - 74$ **52.** $177 - 63$ **53.** $451 - 268$

54. MULTIPLE CHOICE What is the range of the numbers below? *(Skills Review Handbook)*

  12, 8, 17, 12, 15, 18, 30

  Ⓐ 12 Ⓑ 15 Ⓒ 18 Ⓓ 22

1.3 Subtracting Integers

Essential Question How are adding integers and subtracting integers related?

1 EXAMPLE: Subtracting Integers

Use integer counters to find 4 − 2.

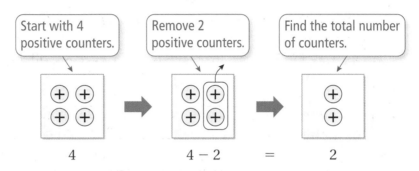

Start with 4 positive counters.

Remove 2 positive counters.

Find the total number of counters.

4   4 − 2   =   2

So, 4 − 2 = 2.

2 ACTIVITY: Adding Integers

Work with a partner. Use integer counters to find 4 + (−2).

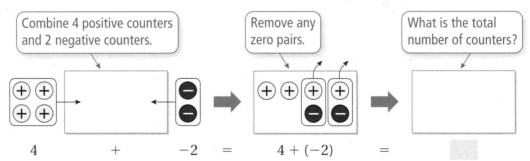

Combine 4 positive counters and 2 negative counters.

Remove any zero pairs.

What is the total number of counters?

4   +   −2   =   4 + (−2)   =

3 EXAMPLE: Subtracting Integers

Use a number line to find −3 − 1.

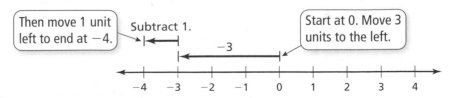

Then move 1 unit left to end at −4.

Subtract 1.

Start at 0. Move 3 units to the left.

−3

So, −3 − 1 = −4.

4 ACTIVITY: Adding Integers

Work with a partner. Write the addition expression shown.
Then find the sum.

Then move 1 unit left to end at −4.

Add −1.

−3

Start at 0. Move 3 units to the left.

Inductive Reasoning

Work with a partner. Use integer counters or a number line to complete the table.

	Exercise	Operation: Add or Subtract	Answer
1	**5.** $4 - 2$	Subtract 2	2
2	**6.** $4 + (-2)$	Add −2	2
3	**7.** $-3 - 1$	Subtract 1	−4
4	**8.** $-3 + (-1)$	Add −1	−4
	9. $3 - 8$		
	10. $3 + (-8)$		
	11. $9 - 13$		
	12. $9 + (-13)$		
	13. $-6 - (-3)$		
	14. $-6 + (3)$		
	15. $-5 - (-12)$		
	16. $-5 + 12$		

What Is Your Answer?

17. IN YOUR OWN WORDS How are adding integers and subtracting integers related?

18. Write a general rule for subtracting integers.

Practice

Use what you learned about subtracting integers to complete Exercises 8–15 on page 18.

Check It Out
Lesson Tutorials
BigIdeasMath com

Key Idea

Subtracting Integers

Words To subtract an integer, add its opposite.

Numbers $3 - 4 = 3 + (-4) = -1$

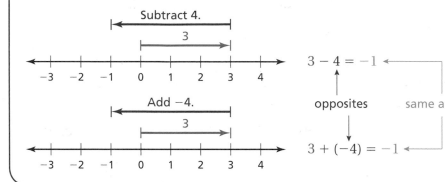

Subtract 4.
3

$3 - 4 = -1$

Add −4.
3

opposites   same answer

$3 + (-4) = -1$

EXAMPLE 1 **Subtracting Integers**

a. **Find 3 − 12.**

$$3 - 12 = 3 + (-12) \qquad \text{Add the opposite of 12.}$$
$$= -9 \qquad \text{Add.}$$

∴ The difference is −9.

b. **Find −8 − (−13).**

$$-8 - (-13) = -8 + 13 \qquad \text{Add the opposite of } -13.$$
$$= 5 \qquad \text{Add.}$$

∴ The difference is 5.

c. **Find 5 − (−4).**

$$5 - (-4) = 5 + 4 \qquad \text{Add the opposite of } -4.$$
$$= 9 \qquad \text{Add.}$$

∴ The difference is 9.

On Your Own

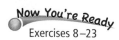

Now You're Ready
Exercises 8–23

Subtract.

1. $8 - 3$
2. $9 - 17$
3. $-3 - 3$
4. $-14 - 9$
5. $9 - (-8)$
6. $-12 - (-12)$

EXAMPLE 2 Subtracting Integers

Evaluate $-7 - (-12) - 14$.

$$
\begin{aligned}
-7 - (-12) - 14 &= -7 + 12 - 14 && \text{Add the opposite of } -12. \\
&= 5 - 14 && \text{Add } -7 \text{ and } 12. \\
&= 5 + (-14) && \text{Add the opposite of } 14. \\
&= -9 && \text{Add.}
\end{aligned}
$$

So, $-7 - (-12) - 14 = -9$.

On Your Own

Now You're Ready
Exercises 27–32

Evaluate the expression.

7. $-9 - 16 - 8$

8. $-4 - 20 - 9$

9. $0 - 9 - (-5)$

10. $0 - (-6) - 8$

11. $15 - (-20) - 20$

12. $13 - 18 - (-18)$

EXAMPLE 3 Real-Life Application

Which continent has the greater range of elevations?

	North America	Africa
Highest Elevation	6198 m	5895 m
Lowest Elevation	−86 m	−155 m

To find the range of elevations for each continent, subtract the lowest elevation from the highest elevation.

North America

range $= 6198 - (-86)$

$= 6198 + 86$

$= 6284$ m

Africa

range $= 5895 - (-155)$

$= 5895 + 155$

$= 6050$ m

Because 6284 is greater than 6050, North America has the greater range of elevations.

On Your Own

13. The highest elevation in Mexico is 5700 meters, on Pico de Orizaba. The lowest elevation in Mexico is -10 meters, in Laguna Salada. Find the range of elevations in Mexico.

Vocabulary and Concept Check

1. **WRITING** How do you subtract one integer from another?

2. **OPEN-ENDED** Write two integers that are opposites.

3. **DIFFERENT WORDS, SAME QUESTION** Which is different? Find "both" answers.

Find the difference of 3 and -2.	What is 3 less than -2?
How much less is -2 than 3?	Subtract -2 from 3.

MATCHING Match the subtraction expression with the corresponding addition expression.

4. $9 - (-5)$ 5. $-9 - 5$ 6. $-9 - (-5)$ 7. $9 - 5$

A. $-9 + 5$ B. $9 + (-5)$ C. $-9 + (-5)$ D. $9 + 5$

 ## Practice and Problem Solving

Subtract.

 8. $4 - 7$ 9. $8 - (-5)$ 10. $-6 - (-7)$ 11. $-2 - 3$

12. $5 - 8$ 13. $-4 - 6$ 14. $-8 - (-3)$ 15. $10 - 7$

16. $-8 - 13$ 17. $15 - (-2)$ 18. $-9 - (-13)$ 19. $-7 - (-8)$

20. $-6 - (-6)$ 21. $-10 - 12$ 22. $32 - (-6)$ 23. $0 - (20)$

24. **ERROR ANALYSIS** Describe and correct the error in finding the difference $7 - (-12)$.

$$✗ \quad 7 - (-12) = 7 + (-12) = -5$$

25. **SWIMMING POOL** The floor of the shallow end of a swimming pool is at -3 feet. The floor of the deep end is 9 feet deeper. Which expression can be used to find the depth of the deep end?

$$-3 + 9 \qquad -3 - 9 \qquad 9 - 3$$

26. **SHARKS** A shark is at -80 feet. It swims up and jumps out of the water to a height of 15 feet. Write a subtraction expression for the vertical distance the shark travels.

Evaluate the expression.

27. $-2 - 7 + 15$ 28. $-9 + 6 - (-2)$ 29. $12 - (-5) - 8$

30. $8 + 14 - (-4)$ 31. $-6 - (-8) + 5$ 32. $-15 - 7 - (-11)$

MENTAL MATH Use mental math to solve the equation.

33. $m - 5 = 9$ **34.** $w - (-3) = 7$ **35.** $6 - c = -9$

ALGEBRA Evaluate the expression when $k = -3$, $m = -6$, and $n = 9$.

36. $4 - n$ **37.** $m - (-8)$

38. $-5 + k - n$ **39.** $|m - k|$

40. PLATFORM DIVING The figure shows a diver diving from a platform. The diver reaches a depth of 4 meters. What is the change in elevation of the dive?

11 m

41. OPEN-ENDED Write two different pairs of negative integers, x and y, that make the statement $x - y = -1$ true.

42. TEMPERATURE The table shows the record monthly high and low temperatures in Anchorage, AK.

	Jan	Feb	Mar	Apr	May	Jun	Jul	Aug	Sep	Oct	Nov	Dec
High (°F)	56	57	56	72	82	92	84	85	73	64	62	53
Low (°F)	-35	-38	-24	-15	1	29	34	31	19	-6	-21	-36

   a. Find the range of temperatures for each month.

   b. What are the all-time high and all-time low temperatures?

   c. What is the range of the temperatures in part (b)?

REASONING Tell whether the difference between the two integers is *always*, *sometimes*, or *never* positive. Explain your reasoning.

43. Two positive integers   **44.** Two negative integers

45. A positive integer and a negative integer   **46.** A negative integer and a positive integer

 Number Sense For what values of a and b is the statement true?

47. $|a - b| = |b - a|$ **48.** $|a + b| = |a| + |b|$ **49.** $|a - b| = |a| - |b|$

 Fair Game Review What you learned in previous grades & lessons

Add. *(Section 1.2)*

50. $-5 + (-5) + (-5) + (-5)$ **51.** $-9 + (-9) + (-9) + (-9) + (-9)$

Multiply. *(Skills Review Handbook)*

52. 8×5 **53.** 6×78 **54.** 36×41 **55.** 82×29

56. MULTIPLE CHOICE Which value of n makes the value of the expression $4n + 3$ a composite number? *(Skills Review Handbook)*

   (A) 1   (B) 2   (C) 3   (D) 4

You can use an **idea and examples chart** to organize information about a concept. Here is an example of an idea and examples chart for absolute value.

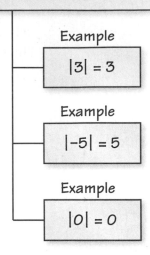

Absolute Value: the distance between a number and O on the number line

Example
$|3| = 3$

Example
$|-5| = 5$

Example
$|0| = 0$

On Your Own

Make an idea and examples chart to help you study these topics.

1. integers

2. adding integers

   a. with the same sign

   b. with different signs

3. Additive Inverse Property

4. subtracting integers

After you complete this chapter, make idea and examples charts for the following topics.

5. multiplying integers

   a. with the same sign   b. with different signs

6. dividing integers

   a. with the same sign   b. with different signs

7. quadrants

8. plotting ordered pairs

"I made an idea and examples chart to give my owner ideas for my birthday next week."

Check It Out
Progress Check
BigIdeasMath **✓**com

Copy and complete the statement using <, >, or =. *(Section 1.1)*

1. $\left| -8 \right|$ ⬜ 3

2. 7 ⬜ $\left| -7 \right|$

Order the values from least to greatest. *(Section 1.1)*

3. $-4, \left| -5 \right|, \left| -4 \right|, 3, -6$

4. $12, -8, \left| -15 \right|, -10, \left| -9 \right|$

Simplify the expression. *(Section 1.2 and Section 1.3)*

5. $-3 + (-8)$

6. $-4 + 16$

7. $3 - 9$

8. $-5 - (-5)$

Evaluate the expression when $a = -2$, $b = -8$, and $c = 5$.
(Section 1.2 and Section 1.3)

9. $4 - a - c$

10. $\left| b - c \right|$

11. EXPLORING Two climbers explore a cave. *(Section 1.1)*

   a. Write an integer for the depth of each climber relative to the surface.

   b. Which integer in part (a) is greater?

   c. Which integer in part (a) has the greater absolute value?

12. SCHOOL CARNIVAL The table shows the income and expenses for a school carnival. The school's goal was to raise $1100. Did the school reach its goal? Explain. *(Section 1.2)*

Games	Concessions	Donations	Flyers	Decorations
$650	$530	$52	−$28	−$75

13. TEMPERATURE Temperatures in the Gobi Desert reach $-40°F$ in the winter and $90°F$ in the summer. Find the range of the temperatures. *(Section 1.3)*

Essential Question Is the product of two integers *positive*, *negative*, or *zero*? How can you tell?

1 EXAMPLE: Multiplying Integers with the Same Sign

Use repeated addition to find 3 · 2.

Recall that multiplication is repeated addition. 3 · 2 means to add 3 groups of 2.

Now you can write
$3 \cdot 2 = 2 + 2 + 2 = 6$.

So, $3 \cdot 2 = 6$.

2 EXAMPLE: Multiplying Integers with Different Signs

Use repeated addition to find 3 · (−2).

3 · (−2) means to add 3 groups of −2.

Now you can write
$3 \cdot (-2) = (-2) + (-2) + (-2)$
$= -6$.

So, $3 \cdot (-2) = -6$.

3 ACTIVITY: Multiplying Integers with Different Signs

Work with a partner. Use a table to find −3 · 2.

Describe the pattern in the table. Use the pattern to complete the table.

2	· 2	=	4
1	· 2	=	2
0	· 2	=	0
−1	· 2	=	
−2	· 2	=	
−3	· 2	=	

Notice the products decrease by 2 in each row.

So, continue the pattern.

$-1 \cdot 2: 0 - 2 = $

$-2 \cdot 2: -2 - 2 = $

$-3 \cdot 2: -4 - 2 = $

So, $-3 \cdot 2 = $.

4 ACTIVITY: Multiplying Integers with the Same Sign

Work with a partner. Use a table to find $-3 \cdot (-2)$.

Describe the pattern in the table. Use the pattern to complete the table.

-3	$\cdot$	3	$=$	-9
-3	$\cdot$	2	$=$	-6
-3	$\cdot$	1	$=$	-3
-3	$\cdot$	0	$=$	
-3	$\cdot$	-1	$=$	
-3	$\cdot$	-2	$=$	

Notice the products increase by 3 in each row.

So, continue the pattern.

$-3 \cdot 0$: $-3 + 3 =$

$-3 \cdot -1$: $0 + 3 =$

$-3 \cdot -2$: $3 + 3 =$

So, $-3 \cdot (-2) = $.

Inductive Reasoning

Work with a partner. Complete the table.

	Exercise	Type of Product	Product	Product: Positive or Negative
1	**5.** $3 \cdot 2$	Integers with the same sign		
2	**6.** $3 \cdot (-2)$	Integers with different signs		
3	**7.** $-3 \cdot 2$	Integers with different signs		
4	**8.** $-3 \cdot (-2)$	Integers with the same sign		
	9. $6 \cdot 3$			
	10. $2 \cdot (-5)$			
	11. $-6 \cdot 5$			
	12. $-5 \cdot (-3)$			

13. Write two integers whose product is 0.

What Is Your Answer?

14. IN YOUR OWN WORDS Is the product of two integers *positive*, *negative*, or *zero*? How can you tell?

15. Write general rules for multiplying (a) two integers with the same sign and (b) two integers with different signs.

Practice

Use what you learned about multiplying integers to complete Exercises 8–15 on page 26.

Lesson

Key Ideas

Multiplying Integers with the Same Sign

Words The product of two integers with the same sign is positive.

Numbers $2 \cdot 3 = 6$ $-2 \cdot (-3) = 6$

Multiplying Integers with Different Signs

Words The product of two integers with different signs is negative.

Numbers $2 \cdot (-3) = -6$ $-2 \cdot 3 = -6$

EXAMPLE ① **Multiplying Integers with the Same Sign**

Find $-5 \cdot (-6)$.

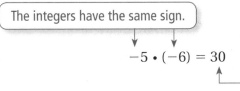

The integers have the same sign.

$$-5 \cdot (-6) = 30$$

The product is positive.

∴ The product is 30.

EXAMPLE ② **Multiplying Integers with Different Signs**

Multiply.

   a. $3(-4)$ **b.** $-7 \cdot 4$

The integers have different signs.

$$3(-4) = -12 \qquad -7 \cdot 4 = -28$$

The product is negative.

∴ The product is -12.   ∴ The product is -28.

On Your Own

Now You're Ready
Exercises 8–23

Multiply.

1. $5 \cdot 5$ **2.** $4(11)$

3. $-1(-9)$ **4.** $-7 \cdot (-8)$

5. $12 \cdot (-2)$ **6.** $4(-6)$

7. $-10(6)$ **8.** $-5 \cdot 7$

EXAMPLE 3 **Using Exponents**

Study Tip

Place parentheses around a negative number to raise it to a power.

a. Evaluate $(-2)^2$.

$$(-2)^2 = (-2) \cdot (-2) \qquad \text{Write } (-2)^2 \text{ as repeated multiplication.}$$

$$= 4 \qquad \text{Multiply.}$$

b. Evaluate -5^2.

$$-5^2 = -(5 \cdot 5) \qquad \text{Write } 5^2 \text{ as repeated multiplication.}$$

$$= -25 \qquad \text{Multiply.}$$

c. Evaluate $(-4)^3$.

$$(-4)^3 = (-4) \cdot (-4) \cdot (-4) \qquad \text{Write } (-4)^3 \text{ as repeated multiplication.}$$

$$= 16 \cdot (-4) \qquad \text{Multiply.}$$

$$= -64 \qquad \text{Multiply.}$$

On Your Own

Now You're Ready
Exercises 32–37

Evaluate the expression.

9. $(-3)^2$ **10.** $(-2)^3$ **11.** -7^2 **12.** -6^3

EXAMPLE 4 **Real-Life Application**

Taxis in Service

The bar graph shows the number of taxis a company has in service. The number of taxis decreases by the same amount each year for four years. Find the total change in the number of taxis.

The bar graph shows that the number of taxis in service decreases by 50 each year. Use a model to solve the problem.

| Total change | = | Change per year | · | Number of years |

$$= -50 \cdot 4$$

Use -50 for the change per year because the number *decreases* each year.

$$= -200$$

The total change in the number of taxis is -200.

On Your Own

13. A manatee population decreases by 15 manatees each year for 3 years. Find the total change in the manatee population.

✓ Vocabulary and Concept Check

1. **WRITING** What do you know about the signs of two integers whose product is (a) positive and (b) negative?

2. **WRITING** How is $(-2)^2$ different from -2^2?

Tell whether the product is *positive* or *negative* without multiplying. Explain your reasoning.

3. $4(-8)$

4. $-5(-7)$

5. $-3 \cdot (12)$

Tell whether the statement is *true* or *false*. Explain your reasoning.

6. The product of three positive integers is positive.

7. The product of three negative integers is positive.

Practice and Problem Solving

Multiply.

① ② 8. $6 \cdot 4$

9. $7(-3)$

10. $-2(8)$

11. $-3(-4)$

12. $-6 \cdot 7$

13. $3 \cdot 9$

14. $8 \cdot (-5)$

15. $-1 \cdot (-12)$

16. $-5(10)$

17. $-13(0)$

18. $-9 \cdot 9$

19. $15(-2)$

20. $-10 \cdot 11$

21. $-6 \cdot (-13)$

22. $7(-14)$

23. $-11 \cdot (-11)$

24. **JOGGING** You burn 10 calories each minute you jog. What integer represents the change in your calories after you jog for 20 minutes?

25. **WETLANDS** About 60,000 acres of wetlands are lost each year in the United States. What integer represents the change in wetlands after 4 years?

Multiply.

26. $3 \cdot (-8) \cdot (-2)$

27. $6(-9)(-1)$

28. $-3(-5)(-4)$

29. $-7(-3)(-5)$

30. $-6 \cdot 3 \cdot (-6)$

31. $3 \cdot (-12) \cdot 0$

Evaluate the expression.

③ 32. $(-4)^2$

33. $(-1)^3$

34. -8^2

35. -6^2

36. $-5^2 \cdot 4$

37. $-2 \cdot (-3)^3$

ERROR ANALYSIS Describe and correct the error in evaluating the expression.

38.

✗ $-2(-7) = -14$

39.

✗ $-10^2 = 100$

ALGEBRA Evaluate the expression when $a = -2$, $b = 3$, and $c = -8$.

40. ab

41. $\left| a^2 c \right|$

42. $ab^3 - ac$

NUMBER SENSE Find the next two numbers in the pattern.

43. $-12, 60, -300, 1500, \ldots$

44. $7, -28, 112, -448, \ldots$

45. GYM CLASS You lose four points each time you attend gym class without sneakers. You forget your sneakers three times. What integer represents the change in your points?

46. AIRPLANE The height of an airplane during a landing is given by $22{,}000 + (-480t)$, where t is the time in minutes.

  a. Copy and complete the table.

  b. Estimate how many minutes it takes the plane to land. Explain your reasoning.

Time	5 min	10 min	15 min	20 min
Height				

47. INLINE SKATES In June, the price of a pair of inline skates is $165. The price changes each of the next three months.

  a. Copy and complete the table.

Month	Price of Skates	
June	165	= $165
July	165 + (−12)	= $____
August	165 + 2(−12)	= $____
September	165 + 3(−12)	= $____

  b. Describe the change in the price of the inline skates for each month.

  c. The table at the right shows the amount of money you save each month to buy the inline skates. Do you have enough money saved to buy the inline skates in August? September? Explain your reasoning.

Amount Saved	
June	$35
July	$55
August	$45
September	$18

48. Reasoning Two integers, a and b, have a product of 24. What is the least possible sum of a and b?

Fair Game Review   What you learned in previous grades & lessons

Divide. *(Skills Review Handbook)*

49. $27 \div 9$

50. $48 \div 6$

51. $56 \div 4$

52. $153 \div 9$

53. MULTIPLE CHOICE What is the prime factorization of 84? *(Skills Review Handbook)*

  Ⓐ $2^2 \times 3^2$

  Ⓑ $2^3 \times 7$

  Ⓒ $3^3 \times 7$

  Ⓓ $2^2 \times 3 \times 7$

1.5 Dividing Integers

Essential Question

Is the quotient of two integers *positive*, *negative*, or *zero*? How can you tell?

1 EXAMPLE: Dividing Integers with Different Signs

Use integer counters to find $-15 \div 3$.

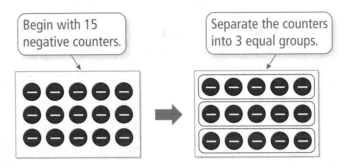

Begin with 15 negative counters.

Separate the counters into 3 equal groups.

∴ Because there are five negative counters in each group, $-15 \div 3 = -5$.

2 ACTIVITY: Rewriting a Product as a Quotient

Work with a partner. Rewrite the product $3 \cdot 4 = 12$ as a quotient in two different ways.

First Way

12 is equal to 3 groups of   .

∴ So, $12 \div 3 = $.

Second Way

12 is equal to 4 groups of   .

∴ So, $12 \div 4 = $.

3 EXAMPLE: Dividing Integers with Different Signs

Rewrite the product $-3 \cdot (-4) = 12$ as a quotient in two different ways. What can you conclude?

First Way

$12 \div (-3) = -4$

Second Way

$12 \div (-4) = -3$

∴ In each case, when you divide a positive integer by a negative integer, you get a negative integer.

4 EXAMPLE: Dividing Negative Integers

Rewrite the product $3 \cdot (-4) = -12$ as a quotient in two different ways. What can you conclude?

First Way

$-12 \div (-4) = 3$

Second Way

$-12 \div (3) = -4$

∴ When you divide a negative integer by a negative integer, you get a positive integer. When you divide a negative integer by a positive integer, you get a negative integer.

Inductive Reasoning

Work with a partner. Complete the table.

	Exercise	Type of Quotient	Quotient	Quotient: Positive, Negative, or Zero
1	**5.** $-15 \div 3$	Integers with different signs		
2	**6.** $12 \div 4$			Positive
3	**7.** $12 \div (-3)$		-4	
4	**8.** $-12 \div (-4)$	Integers with the same sign		Positive
	9. $-6 \div 2$			
	10. $-21 \div (-7)$			
	11. $10 \div (-2)$			
	12. $12 \div (-6)$			
	13. $0 \div (-15)$			
	14. $0 \div 4$			

What Is Your Answer?

15. IN YOUR OWN WORDS Is the quotient of two integers *positive*, *negative*, or *zero*? How can you tell?

16. Write general rules for dividing (a) two integers with the same sign and (b) two integers with different signs.

Practice Use what you learned about dividing integers to complete Exercises 8–15 on page 32.

Key Ideas

Dividing Integers with the Same Sign

Words   The quotient of two integers with the same sign is positive.

Numbers $8 \div 2 = 4$ $-8 \div (-2) = 4$

Dividing Integers with Different Signs

Words   The quotient of two integers with different signs is negative.

Numbers $8 \div (-2) = -4$ $-8 \div 2 = -4$

EXAMPLE ① **Dividing Integers with the Same Sign**

Find $-18 \div (-6)$.

> The integers have the same sign.

$$-18 \div (-6) = 3$$

> The quotient is positive.

∴ The quotient is 3.

EXAMPLE ② **Dividing Integers with Different Signs**

Divide.

   a. $75 \div (-25)$ **b.** $\dfrac{-54}{6}$

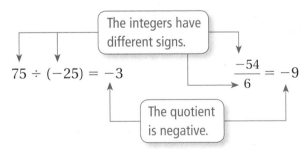

> The integers have different signs.

$$75 \div (-25) = -3 \qquad \frac{-54}{6} = -9$$

> The quotient is negative.

∴ The quotient is -3.   ∴ The quotient is -9.

On Your Own

Now You're Ready
Exercises 8–23

Divide.

1. $14 \div 2$ **2.** $-32 \div (-4)$ **3.** $-40 \div (-8)$

4. $0 \div (-6)$ **5.** $\dfrac{-49}{7}$ **6.** $\dfrac{21}{-3}$

EXAMPLE **3** **Evaluating Expressions**

Evaluate $10 - x^2 \div y$ when $x = 8$ and $y = -4$.

$$10 - x^2 \div y = 10 - 8^2 \div (-4) \qquad \text{Substitute 8 for } x \text{ and } -4 \text{ for } y.$$
$$= 10 - 8 \cdot 8 \div (-4) \qquad \text{Write } 8^2 \text{ as repeated multiplication.}$$
$$= 10 - 64 \div (-4) \qquad \text{Multiply 8 and 8.}$$
$$= 10 - (-16) \qquad \text{Divide 64 and } -4.$$
$$= 26 \qquad \text{Subtract.}$$

Remember

Use order of operations when evaluating an expression.

On Your Own

Now You're Ready
Exercises 28–31

Evaluate the expression when $a = -18$ and $b = -6$.

7. $a \div b$ 　　　　**8.** $\dfrac{a + 6}{3}$ 　　　　**9.** $\dfrac{b^2}{a} + 4$

EXAMPLE **4** **Real-Life Application**

You measure the height of the tide using support beams of a pier. Your measurements are shown in the picture. What is the mean hourly change in the height?

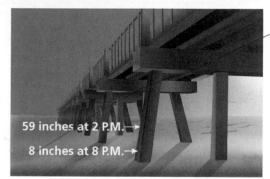
59 inches at 2 P.M.→
8 inches at 8 P.M.→

Use a model to solve the problem.

$$\text{Mean hourly change} = \frac{\text{Final height} \ - \ \text{Initial height}}{\text{Elapsed Time}}$$

$$= \frac{8 - 59}{6} \qquad \text{Substitute. The elapsed time from 2 P.M. to 8 P.M. is 6 hours.}$$

$$= \frac{-51}{6} \qquad \text{Subtract.}$$

$$= -8.5 \qquad \text{Divide.}$$

∴ The mean change in the height of the tide is -8.5 inches per hour.

On Your Own

10. The height of the tide at the Bay of Fundy in New Brunswick decreases 36 feet in 6 hours. What is the mean hourly change in the height?

1.5 Exercises

✓ Vocabulary and Concept Check

1. **WRITING** What can you tell about two integers when their quotient is positive? negative? zero?

2. **VOCABULARY** A quotient is undefined. What does this mean?

3. **OPEN-ENDED** Write two integers whose quotient is negative.

4. **WHICH ONE DOESN'T BELONG?** Which expression does *not* belong with the other three? Explain your reasoning.

$$\frac{10}{-5} \qquad \frac{-10}{5} \qquad \frac{-10}{-5} \qquad -\left(\frac{10}{5}\right)$$

Tell whether the quotient is *positive* or *negative* without dividing.

5. $-12 \div 4$

6. $\dfrac{-6}{-2}$

7. $15 \div (-3)$

 ## Practice and Problem Solving

Divide, if possible.

 8. $4 \div (-2)$

9. $21 \div (-7)$

10. $-20 \div 4$

11. $-18 \div (-6)$

12. $\dfrac{-14}{7}$

13. $\dfrac{0}{6}$

14. $\dfrac{-15}{-5}$

15. $\dfrac{54}{-9}$

16. $-33 \div 11$

17. $-49 \div (-7)$

18. $0 \div (-2)$

19. $60 \div (-6)$

20. $\dfrac{-56}{14}$

21. $\dfrac{18}{0}$

22. $\dfrac{65}{-5}$

23. $\dfrac{-84}{-7}$

ERROR ANALYSIS Describe and correct the error in finding the quotient.

24.
✗ $\dfrac{-63}{-9} = -7$

25.
✗ $0 \div (-5) = -5$

26. **ALLIGATORS** An alligator population in a nature preserve in the Everglades decreases by 60 alligators over 5 years. What is the mean yearly change in the alligator population?

27. **READING** You read 105 pages of a novel over 7 days. What is the mean number of pages you read each day?

ALGEBRA Evaluate the expression when $x = 10$, $y = -2$, and $z = -5$.

28. $x \div y$

29. $\dfrac{10y^2}{z}$

30. $\left| \dfrac{xz}{-y} \right|$

31. $\dfrac{-x^2 + 6z}{y}$

Find the mean of the integers.

32. $3, -10, -2, 13, 11$

33. $-26, 39, -10, -16, 12, 31$

Evaluate the expression.

34. $-8 - 14 \div 2 + 5$

35. $24 \div (-4) + (-2) \cdot (-5)$

36. **PATTERN** Find the next two numbers in the pattern $-128, 64, -32, 16, \ldots$. Explain your reasoning.

37. **SNOWBOARDING** A snowboarder descends a 1200-foot hill in 3 minutes. What is the mean change in elevation per minute?

38. **THE MASTERS** In 1997, at the age of 21, Tiger Woods became the youngest golfer to win the Masters Tournament. The table shows his score for each round.

Scorecard	
Round 1	-2
Round 2	-6
Round 3	-7
Round 4	-3

    a. Tiger set the tournament record with the lowest total score. What was his total score?

    b. What was his mean score per round?

39. **TUNNEL** The Detroit-Windsor Tunnel is an underwater highway that connects the cities of Detroit, Michigan, and Windsor, Ontario. How many times deeper is the roadway than the bottom of the ship?

40. **AMUSEMENT PARK** The regular admission price for an amusement park is $72. For a group of 15 or more, the admission price is reduced by $25. How many people need to be in a group to save $500?

41. Write five different integers that have a mean of -10. Explain how you found your answer.

 Fair Game Review What you learned in previous grades & lessons

Graph the values on a number line. Then order the values from least to greatest. *(Section 1.1)*

42. $-6, 4, |2|, -1, |-10|$

43. $3, |0|, |-4|, -3, -8$

44. $|5|, -2, -5, |-2|, -7$

45. **MULTIPLE CHOICE** What is the value of $4 \cdot 3 + (12 \div 2)^2$? *(Skills Review Handbook)*

    (A) 15   **(B)** 48   **(C)** 156   **(D)** 324

1.6 The Coordinate Plane

Essential Question
How can you use ordered pairs to locate points in a coordinate plane?

Share Your Work at... My.BigIdeasMath.com

1 EXAMPLE: Plotting Points in a Coordinate Plane

Plot the ordered pairs. Connect the points to make a picture. Color the picture when you are done.

1$(4, 12)$	**2**$(9, 9)$	**3**$(12, 4)$	**4**$(12, -3)$	**5**$(10, -9)$
6$(9, -10)$	**7**$(7, -9)$	**8**$(2, -11)$	**9**$(-1, -11)$	**10**$(-3, -10)$
11$(-4, -8)$	**12**$(-11, -10)$	**13**$(-12, -9)$	**14**$(-11, -8)$	**15**$(-11, -6)$
16$(-12, -5)$	**17**$(-11, -4)$	**18**$(-4, -6)$	**19**$(-3, -3)$	**20**$(-4, 0)$
21$(-8, 2)$	**22**$(-8, 3)$	**23**$(-5, 8)$	**24**$(-1, 11)$	

Wildcats

Chiefs

Bulldogs

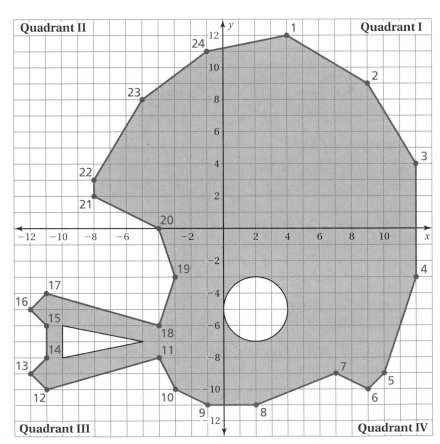

Work with a partner.

Plot the ordered pairs. Connect the points to make a picture.
Describe and color the picture when you are done.

1 (6, 9)	**2** (4, 11)	**3** (2, 12)	**4** (0, 11)	**5** (−2, 9)
6 (−6, 2)	**7** (−9, 1)	**8** (−11, −3)	**9** (−7, 0)	**10** (−5, −1)
11 (−5, −5)	**12** (−4, −8)	**13** (−6, −10)	**14** (−3, −9)	**15** (−3, −10)
16 (−4, −11)	**17** (−4, −12)	**18** (−3, −11)	**19** (−2, −12)	**20** (−2, −11)
21 (−1, −12)	**22** (−1, −11)	**23** (−2, −10)	**24** (−2, −9)	**25** (1, −9)
26 (2, −8)	**27** (2, −10)	**28** (1, −11)	**29** (1, −12)	**30** (2, −11)
31 (3, −12)	**32** (3, −11)	**33** (4, −12)	**34** (4, −11)	**35** (3, −10)
36 (3, −8)	**37** (4, −6)	**38** (6, 0)	**39** (9, −3)	**40** (9, −1)
41 (8, 1)	**42** (5, 3)	**43** (3, 6)	**44** (3, 7)	**45** (4, 8)

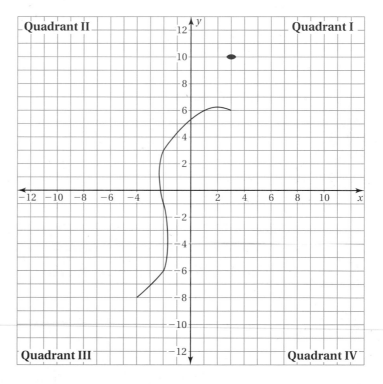

What Is Your Answer?

3. IN YOUR OWN WORDS How can you use ordered pairs to locate points in a coordinate plane?

4. Make up your own "dot-to-dot" picture. Use at least 20 points. Your picture should have at least two points in each quadrant.

Practice

Use what you learned about the coordinate plane to complete Exercises 15–18 on page 38.

Check It Out
Lesson Tutorials
BigIdeasMath ✓com

Key Idea

Key Vocabulary ◀))
coordinate plane, *p. 36*
origin, *p. 36*
quadrant, *p. 36*
x-axis, *p. 36*
y-axis, *p. 36*

The Coordinate Plane

A **coordinate plane** is formed by the intersection of a horizontal number line and a vertical number line. The number lines intersect at the **origin** and separate the coordinate plane into four regions called **quadrants.**

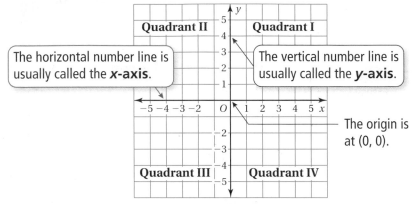

The horizontal number line is usually called the ***x*-axis**.

The vertical number line is usually called the ***y*-axis**.

The origin is at (0, 0).

An *ordered pair* is a pair of numbers that is used to locate a point in a coordinate plane.

ordered pair

$(4, -2)$

The *x-coordinate* corresponds to a number on the *x*-axis.

The *y-coordinate* corresponds to a number on the *y*-axis.

EXAMPLE **1** **Standardized Test Practice**

Which ordered pair corresponds to point *T*?

Ⓐ $(-3, -3)$ Ⓑ $(-3, 3)$

Ⓒ $(3, -3)$ Ⓓ $(3, 3)$

Point *T* is 3 units to the right of the origin and 3 units down. So, the *x*-coordinate is 3 and the *y*-coordinate is -3.

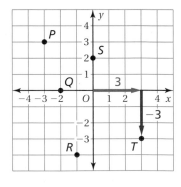

∴ The ordered pair $(3, -3)$ corresponds to point *T*. The correct answer is Ⓒ.

On Your Own

Now You're Ready
Exercises 5–14

Use the graph in Example 1 to write an ordered pair corresponding to the point.

1. Point *P*   **2.** Point *Q*   **3.** Point *R*   **4.** Point *S*

◀) Multi-Language Glossary at BigIdeasMath ✓com.

EXAMPLE 2 Plotting Ordered Pairs

Plot (a) $(-4, 2)$ and (b) $(0, -3)$ in a coordinate plane. Describe the location of each point.

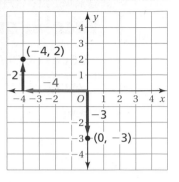

a. Start at the origin. Move 4 units left and 2 units up. Then plot the point.

⋮ The point is in Quadrant II.

b. Start at the origin. Move 3 units down. Then plot the point.

⋮ The point is on the *y*-axis.

On Your Own

Now You're Ready
Exercises 15–26

Plot the ordered pair in a coordinate plane. Describe the location of the point.

5. $A(2, 3)$

6. $B(-1, 0)$

7. $C(-5, -1)$

8. $D(3, -6)$

EXAMPLE 3 Real-Life Application

You and a friend have tickets to see a football game. You sit in the Hall of Fame Section and your friend sits at $(-4, -2)$.

a. Write an ordered pair for your location. In which quadrant are you seated?

b. In which quadrant is your friend seated?

c. A fan in Quadrant II is chosen to win a prize. Do you or your friend have a chance to win the prize?

a. The Hall of Fame Section is 6 units to the right of the origin and 1 unit down. So, your seat is located at $(6, -1)$. You are seated in Quadrant IV.

b. Move 4 units to the left of the origin and 2 units down. Your friend is seated in Quadrant III.

c. You are seated in Quadrant IV and your friend is seated in Quadrant III. So, you and your friend do not have a chance to win the prize.

On Your Own

9. **WHAT IF?** In Example 3, a fan sitting in the level closest to the playing field is chosen to win a prize. Do you or your friend have a chance to win the prize?

Vocabulary and Concept Check

1. **VOCABULARY** How many quadrants are in a coordinate plane?

2. **VOCABULARY** Is the point $(0, -7)$ on the x-axis or the y-axis?

3. **WRITING** How are the locations of the points $(2, -2)$ and $(-2, 2)$ different?

4. **WRITING** Describe the characteristics of ordered pairs in each of the four quadrants.

 Practice and Problem Solving

Write an ordered pair corresponding to the point.

 5. Point A 6. Point B

7. Point C 8. Point D

9. Point E 10. Point F

11. Point G 12. Point H

13. Point I 14. Point J

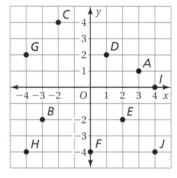

Plot the ordered pair in a coordinate plane. Describe the location of the point.

 15. $K(4, 3)$ 16. $L(-1, 2)$ 17. $M(0, -6)$ 18. $N(3, -2)$

19. $P(2, -4)$ 20. $Q(-2, 4)$ 21. $R(-4, 1)$ 22. $S(7, 0)$

23. $T(-4, -5)$ 24. $U(-2, 5)$ 25. $V(-3, 8)$ 26. $W(-5, -1)$

ERROR ANALYSIS Describe and correct the error in the solution.

27. ✗ To plot $(4, 5)$, start at $(0, 0)$ and move 5 units right and 4 units up.

28. ✗ To plot $(-6, 3)$, start at $(0, 0)$ and move 6 units right and 3 units down.

29. **REASONING** The coordinates of three vertices of a square are shown in the figure. What are the coordinates of the fourth vertex?

30. **GEOMETRY** The points $D(1, 1)$, $E(1, -2)$, $F(-2, -2)$, and $G(-2, 1)$ are vertices of a figure.

   a. Draw the figure in a coordinate plane.

   b. Find the perimeter of the figure.

   c. Find the area of the figure.

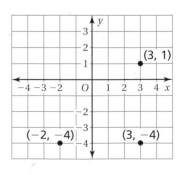

Tell whether the statement is *sometimes*, *always*, or *never* true. Explain your reasoning.

31. The *x*-coordinate of a point on the *x*-axis is zero.

32. The *y*-coordinate of points in Quadrant III are positive.

33. The *x*-coordinate of a point in Quadrant II has the same sign as the *y*-coordinate of a point in Quadrant IV.

ZOO **In Exercises 34–38, use the map of the zoo.**

34. Which exhibit is located at $(2, 1)$?

35. Name an attraction on the positive *y*-axis.

36. Is parking available in Quadrant II? If not, name a quadrant in which you can park.

37. Write two different ordered pairs that represent the location of the Rainforest.

38. Which exhibit is closest to $(-8, -3)$?

39. **NUMBER SENSE** Name the ordered pair that is 5 units right and 2 units down from $(-3, 4)$.

Plot the ordered pair in a coordinate plane. Describe the location of the point.

40. $A\left(3, -\dfrac{3}{2}\right)$ **41.** $B\left(-\dfrac{5}{2}, \dfrac{10}{3}\right)$ **42.** $C(-5.25, -3.5)$ **43.** $D(-4.75, 0)$

44. **Reasoning** Your school is located at $(2, -1)$, which is 2 blocks east and 1 block south of the center of town. To get from your house to the school, you walk 5 blocks west and 2 blocks north.

    a. What ordered pair corresponds to the location of your house?

    b. Is your house or your school closer to the center of town? Explain.

Fair Game Review What you learned in previous grades & lessons

Copy and complete the statement using <, >, or =. *(Section 1.5 and Skills Review Handbook)*

45. $\dfrac{-16}{2}$ ▭ $\dfrac{-12}{3}$ **46.** $2\dfrac{2}{5}$ ▭ $\dfrac{24}{10}$ **47.** 3.45 ▭ $3\dfrac{3}{8}$

48. **MULTIPLE CHOICE** What is $\dfrac{1}{3}$ of $3\dfrac{1}{2}$? *(Skills Review Handbook)*

    (A) $\dfrac{1}{2}$ **(B)** $1\dfrac{1}{6}$ **(C)** $1\dfrac{1}{2}$ **(D)** $10\dfrac{1}{2}$

Simplify the expression. *(Section 1.4 and Section 1.5)*

1. $-7(6)$

2. $-1(-9)$

3. $\dfrac{-72}{-9}$

4. $-24 \div 3$

Evaluate the expression when $a = 4$, $b = -6$, and $c = -12$.
(Section 1.4 and Section 1.5)

5. c^2

6. $\dfrac{|c - b|}{a}$

Write an ordered pair corresponding to the point.
(Section 1.6)

7. Point A

8. Point B

9. Point C

10. Point D

11. SPEECH In speech class, you lose 3 points for every 30 seconds you go over the time limit. Your speech is 90 seconds over the time limit. What integer represents the change in your points? *(Section 1.4)*

12. MOUNTAIN CLIMBING On a mountain, the temperature decreases by 18°F every 5000 feet. What integer represents the change in temperature at 20,000 feet? *(Section 1.4)*

13. GAMING You play a video game for 15 minutes. You lose 165 points. What integer represents the average change in points per minute? *(Section 1.5)*

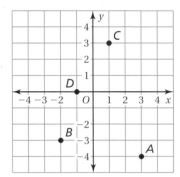

14. GEOMETRY The points $A(-4, 2)$, $B(1, -1)$, $C(1, 2)$, and $D(-4, -1)$ are the vertices of a figure. *(Section 1.6)*

   a. Draw the figure in a coordinate plane.

   b. Find the perimeter of the figure.

   c. Find the area of the figure.

1 Chapter Review

Check It Out
Vocabulary Help
BigIdeasMath ✓com

Review Key Vocabulary

integer, *p. 4*

absolute value, *p. 4*

opposites, *p. 10*

additive inverse, *p. 10*

coordinate plane, *p. 36*

origin, *p. 36*

quadrant, *p. 36*

x-axis, *p. 36*

y-axis, *p. 36*

Review Examples and Exercises

1.1 Integers and Absolute Value (pp. 2–7)

Find the absolute value of −2.

Graph −2 on a number line.

The distance between −2 and 0 is 2.

∴ So, $|-2| = 2$.

Exercises

Find the absolute value of the integer.

1. 3   **2.** −9   **3.** −17   **4.** 8

5. ELEVATION The elevation of Death Valley, CA is −282 feet. The Mississippi River in Illinois has an elevation of 279 feet. Which is closer to sea level?

1.2 Adding Integers (pp. 8–13)

Find 6 + (−14).

$$6 + (-14) = -8$$

$|6|$ is less than $|-14|$. So, subtract $|6|$ from $|-14|$.

Use the sign of −14.

∴ The sum is −8.

Exercises

Add.

6. −16 + (−11)   **7.** −15 + 5   **8.** 100 + (−75)   **9.** −32 + (−2)

1.3 Subtracting Integers *(pp. 14–19)*

Subtract.

a. $7 - 19 = 7 + (-19)$ Add the opposite of 19.

           $= -12$ Add.

   •• The difference is -12.

b. $-6 - (-10) = -6 + 10$ Add the opposite of -10.

                $= 4$ Add.

   •• The difference is 4.

Exercises

Subtract.

10. $8 - 18$ **11.** $-16 - (-5)$ **12.** $-18 - 7$ **13.** $-12 - (-27)$

14. GAME SHOW Your score on a game show is -300. You answer the final question incorrectly, so you lose 400 points. What is your final score?

1.4 Multiplying Integers *(pp. 22–27)*

a. Find $-7 \cdot (-9)$.

The integers have the same sign.

$$-7 \cdot (-9) = 63$$

The product is positive.

   •• The product is 63.

b. Find $-6(14)$.

The integers have different signs.

$$-6(14) = -84$$

The product is negative.

   •• The product is -84.

Exercises

Multiply.

15. $-8 \cdot 6$ **16.** $10(-7)$ **17.** $-3 \cdot (-6)$ **18.** $-12(5)$

1.5 Dividing Integers (pp. 28–33)

Find 30 ÷ (−10).

> The integers have different signs.

$$30 \div (-10) = -3$$

> The quotient is negative.

∴ The quotient is −3.

Exercises

Divide.

19. $-18 \div 9$

20. $\dfrac{-42}{-6}$

21. $\dfrac{-30}{6}$

22. $84 \div (-7)$

Find the mean of the integers.

23. $-3, -8, 12, -15, 9$

24. $-54, -32, -70, -25, -65, -42$

25. PROFITS The table shows the weekly profits of a fruit vendor. What is the mean profit for these weeks?

Week	1	2	3	4
Profit	−$125	−$86	$54	−$35

1.6 The Coordinate Plane (pp. 34–39)

Plot (a) $(-3, 0)$ and (b) $(4, -4)$ in a coordinate plane. Describe the location of each point.

a. Start at the origin. Move 3 units left. Then plot the point.

The point is on the x-axis.

b. Start at the origin. Move 4 units right and 4 units down. Then plot the point.

The point is in Quadrant IV.

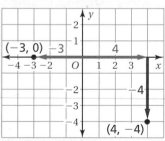

Exercises

Plot the ordered pair in a coordinate plane. Describe the location of the point.

26. $A(1, 3)$

27. $B(0, -3)$

28. $C(-4, -2)$

29. $D(-1, 2)$

30. GEOMETRY The points $A(-3, 5)$, $B(-3, -3)$, and $C(4, -3)$ are vertices of a figure. Draw the figure in a coordinate plane. Name three points that lie inside the figure.

Check It Out
Test Practice
BigIdeasMath ✓com

Find the absolute value of the integer.

1. -9

2. 64

3. -22

Copy and complete the statement using $<, >,$ **or** $=$.

4. $4 \boxed{} |-8|$

5. $-12 \boxed{} |-7|$

6. $-7 \boxed{} |3|$

Simplify the expression.

7. $-6 + (-11)$

8. $2 - (-9)$

9. $-9 \cdot 2$

10. $-72 \div (-3)$

11. $-5 + 17$

12. $-14(21)$

Plot the ordered pair in a coordinate plane. Describe the location of the point.

13. $K(1, 3)$

14. $L(-3, 0)$

15. $M(-4, 5)$

16. $N(2, -1)$

17. BANKING The balance of your checking account is \$86. You withdraw \$98. What is your new balance?

18. NASCAR A driver receives -25 points for each rule violation. What integer represents the change in points after four rule violations?

19. GOLF The table shows your scores, relative to *par*, for nine holes of golf. What is your total score for the nine holes?

Hole	1	2	3	4	5	6	7	8	9	Total
Score	+1	−2	−1	0	−1	+3	−1	−3	+1	?

20. VISITORS In a recent 10-year period, the change in the number of visitors to U.S. National Parks was about $-11{,}150{,}000$ visitors.

    a. What was the mean yearly change in the number of visitors?

    b. During the seventh year, the change in the number of visitors was about $10{,}800{,}000$. Explain how the change for the 10-year period can be negative.

Test-Taking Strategy

Solve Directly or Eliminate Choices

You ripped out $(-1)^2 + (-2)(-3)$ whiskers. How many did you rip out?

Ⓐ -5   Ⓑ 5   Ⓒ -7   Ⓓ 7

Yeow, why the biggest number?

"You can eliminate A and C. Then, solve directly to determine that the correct answer is D."

1. A football team gains 2 yards on the first play, loses 5 yards on the second play, loses 3 yards on the third play, and gains 4 yards on the fourth play. What is the team's overall gain or loss for all four plays?

   A. a gain of 14 yards   **C.** a loss of 2 yards

   B. a gain of 2 yards   **D.** a loss of 14 yards

2. Point P is plotted in the coordinate plane below.

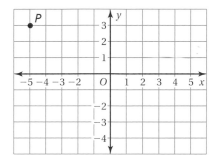

   What are the coordinates of point P?

   F. $(-5, -3)$ **H.** $(-3, -5)$

   G. $(-5, 3)$ **I.** $(3, -5)$

3. What is the value of the expression below?

   $$17 - (-8)$$

4. Sam was simplifying an expression in the box below.

   $$\left|-8 + 6 + (-3)\right| = \left|-8\right| + \left|6\right| + \left|-3\right|$$
   $$= 8 + 6 + 3$$
   $$= 17$$

   What should Sam do to correct the error that he made?

   A. Find the absolute value of the sum of 8, 6, and 3 and make that the final answer.

   B. Find the sum of -8, -6, and -3 and make that the final answer.

   C. Find the sum of -8, 6, and -3 and make that the final answer.

   D. Find the absolute value of the sum of -8, 6, and -3 and make that the final answer.

5. The expression below can be used to find the temperature in degrees Celsius when given F, the temperature in degrees Fahrenheit.

$$\frac{5}{9}(F - 32)$$

What is the temperature in degrees Celsius, to the nearest degree, when the temperature in degrees Fahrenheit is 27°?

F. −33°

G. −17°

H. −5°

I. −3°

6. What is the missing number in the sequence below?

$$39, 24, 9, \underline{\quad}, -21$$

7. Which equation is *not* true for all numbers n?

A. $-n + 0 = -n$

B. $n \cdot (-1) = -n$

C. $n - 0 = -n$

D. $-n \cdot 1 = -n$

8. What is the area of the semicircle below? (Use 3.14 for π.)

├─ 6 cm ─┤

F. 18.84 cm^2

G. 37.68 cm^2

H. 56.52 cm^2

I. 226.08 cm^2

9. The campers at a summer camp held a contest in which they had to run across a field carrying buckets of water that were full at the beginning. The team who lost the least water from its bucket was the winner.

- Team A *lost* 40% of the water from its bucket.
- Team B *lost* 0.3 of the water from its bucket.
- Team C *kept* $\frac{5}{8}$ of the water in its bucket.
- Team D *kept* 67% of the water in its bucket.

Which team was the winner?

A. Team A

B. Team B

C. Team C

D. Team D

10. Which integer is closest to the value of the expression below?

$$-5.04 \cdot (16.89 - 20.1)$$

F. -105 **H.** 15

G. -15 **I.** 105

11. Answer the following questions in the coordinate plane.

Part A Draw an *x*-axis and *y*-axis in the coordinate plane. Then plot and label the point $(2, -3)$.

Part B Plot and label *four* points that are 3 units away from $(2, -3)$.

12. What is the mean of the data set in the box below?

$$-8, -6, -2, 0, -6, -8, 4, -7, -8, 1$$

A. -8 **C.** -6

B. -7 **D.** -4

13. Jane and Manuel measured the lengths of their pet rats.

- Jane's pet rat
  - Body length: $10\frac{1}{2}$ inches
  - Tail length: $7\frac{3}{4}$ inches

- Manuel's pet rat
  - Body length: $9\frac{5}{8}$ inches
  - Tail length: $8\frac{1}{4}$ inches

The total length of each rat is determined by the sum of its body length and its tail length. Whose rat has the longer total length and by how much?

F. Jane's rat is longer by $\frac{3}{8}$ inch.   **H.** Manuel's rat is longer by $\frac{5}{8}$ inch.

G. Jane's rat is longer by $\frac{1}{6}$ inch.   **I.** Manuel's rat is longer by $\frac{1}{4}$ inch.

2 Rational Numbers and Equations

"I can't find my algebra tiles, so I am painting some of my dog biscuits."

"I hope the paint is edible."

"Now I will be able to solve the equation $2x + (-2) = 2$."

"Nice!"

"On the count of 5, I'm going to give you half of my dog biscuits."

"I knew this was too good to be true."

"1, 2, 3, 4, $4\frac{1}{2}$, $4\frac{3}{4}$, $4\frac{7}{8}$,…"

What You Learned Before

"Let's play a game. The goal is to say a positive rational number that is less than the other pet's number... You go first."

This feels like a setup.

● Writing Decimals and Fractions

Example 1 Write 0.37 as a fraction.

$$0.37 = \frac{37}{100}$$

Example 2 Write $\frac{2}{5}$ as a decimal.

$$\frac{2}{5} = \frac{2 \cdot 2}{5 \cdot 2} = \frac{4}{10} = 0.4$$

Try It Yourself
Write the decimal as a fraction or the fraction as a decimal.

1. 0.51
2. 0.731
3. $\frac{3}{5}$
4. $\frac{7}{8}$

● Adding and Subtracting Fractions

Example 3 Find $\frac{1}{3} + \frac{1}{5}$.

$$\frac{1}{3} + \frac{1}{5} = \frac{1 \cdot 5}{3 \cdot 5} + \frac{1 \cdot 3}{5 \cdot 3}$$

$$= \frac{5}{15} + \frac{3}{15}$$

$$= \frac{8}{15}$$

Example 4 Find $\frac{1}{4} - \frac{2}{9}$.

$$\frac{1}{4} - \frac{2}{9} = \frac{1 \cdot 9}{4 \cdot 9} - \frac{2 \cdot 4}{9 \cdot 4}$$

$$= \frac{9}{36} - \frac{8}{36}$$

$$= \frac{1}{36}$$

● Multiplying and Dividing Fractions

Example 5 Find $\frac{5}{6} \cdot \frac{3}{4}$.

$$\frac{5}{6} \cdot \frac{3}{4} = \frac{5 \cdot \overset{1}{\cancel{3}}}{\underset{2}{\cancel{6}} \cdot 4}$$

$$= \frac{5}{8}$$

Example 6 Find $\frac{2}{3} \div \frac{9}{10}$.

$$\frac{2}{3} \div \frac{9}{10} = \frac{2}{3} \cdot \frac{10}{9}$$

$$= \frac{2 \cdot 10}{3 \cdot 9}$$

$$= \frac{20}{27}$$

Multiply by the reciprocal of the divisor.

Try It Yourself
Evaluate the expression.

5. $\frac{1}{4} + \frac{13}{20}$
6. $\frac{14}{15} - \frac{1}{3}$
7. $\frac{3}{7} \cdot \frac{9}{10}$
8. $\frac{4}{5} \div \frac{16}{17}$

2.1 Rational Numbers

Essential Question How can you use a number line to order rational numbers?

The Meaning of a Word ● Rational

The word **rational** comes from the word *ratio*.

If you sleep for 8 hours in a day, then the *ratio* of your sleeping time to the total hours in a day can be written as

$$\frac{8\text{ h}}{24\text{ h}}.$$

A **rational number** is a number that can be written as the ratio of two integers.

$$2 = \frac{2}{1} \qquad -3 = \frac{-3}{1} \qquad -\frac{1}{2} = \frac{-1}{2} \qquad 0.25 = \frac{1}{4}$$

1 ACTIVITY: Ordering Rational Numbers

Work in groups of five. Order the numbers from least to greatest.

a. **Sample:** $-0.5,\ 1.25,\ -\dfrac{1}{3},\ 0.5,\ -\dfrac{5}{3}$

● Make a number line on the floor using masking tape and a marker.

● Write the numbers on pieces of paper. Then each person should choose one.

● Stand on the location of your number on the number line.

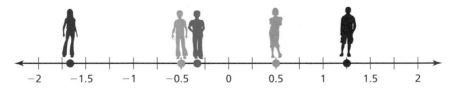

● Use your positions to order the numbers from least to greatest.

∴ So, the numbers from least to greatest are $-\dfrac{5}{3},\ -0.5,\ -\dfrac{1}{3},\ 0.5,$ and 1.25.

b. $-\dfrac{7}{4},\ 1.1,\ \dfrac{1}{2},\ -\dfrac{1}{10},\ -1.3$

c. $-\dfrac{1}{4},\ 2.5,\ \dfrac{3}{4},\ -1.7,\ -0.3$

d. $-1.4,\ -\dfrac{3}{5},\ \dfrac{9}{2},\ \dfrac{1}{4},\ 0.9$

e. $\dfrac{9}{4},\ 0.75,\ -\dfrac{5}{4},\ -0.8,\ -1.1$

ACTIVITY: The Game of Math Card War

Preparation:

- Cut index cards to make 40 playing cards.
- Write each number in the table on a card.

To Play:

- Play with a partner.
- Deal 20 cards to each player face-down.
- Each player turns one card face-up. The player with the greater number wins. The winner collects both cards and places them at the bottom of his or her cards.
- Suppose there is a tie. Each player lays three cards face-down, then a new card face-up. The player with the greater of these new cards wins. The winner collects all ten cards and places them at the bottom of his or her cards.
- Continue playing until one player has all the cards. This player wins the game.

$-\dfrac{3}{2}$	$\dfrac{3}{10}$	$-\dfrac{3}{4}$	-0.6	1.25	-0.15	$\dfrac{5}{4}$	$\dfrac{3}{5}$	-1.6	-0.3
$\dfrac{3}{20}$	$\dfrac{8}{5}$	-1.2	$\dfrac{19}{10}$	0.75	-1.5	$-\dfrac{6}{5}$	$-\dfrac{3}{5}$	1.2	0.3
1.5	1.9	-0.75	-0.4	$\dfrac{3}{4}$	$-\dfrac{5}{4}$	-1.9	$\dfrac{2}{5}$	$-\dfrac{3}{20}$	$-\dfrac{19}{10}$
$\dfrac{6}{5}$	$-\dfrac{3}{10}$	1.6	$-\dfrac{2}{5}$	0.6	0.15	$\dfrac{3}{2}$	-1.25	0.4	$-\dfrac{8}{5}$

What Is Your Answer?

3. **IN YOUR OWN WORDS** How can you use a number line to order rational numbers? Give an example.

The numbers are in order from least to greatest. Fill in the blank spaces with rational numbers.

4. $-\dfrac{1}{2}$, ____ , $\dfrac{1}{3}$, ____ , $\dfrac{7}{5}$, ____

5. $-\dfrac{5}{2}$, ____ , -1.9, ____ , $-\dfrac{2}{3}$,

6. $-\dfrac{1}{3}$, ____ , -0.1, ____ , $\dfrac{4}{5}$, ____

7. -3.4, ____ , -1.5, ____ , 2.2, ____

Practice

Use what you learned about ordering rational numbers to complete Exercises 28–30 on page 54.

2.1 Lesson

Check It Out
Lesson Tutorials
BigIdeasMath.com

Key Vocabulary
terminating decimal,
p. 52
repeating decimal,
p. 52
rational number,
p. 52

A **terminating decimal** is a decimal that ends.

1.5, −0.25, 10.625

A **repeating decimal** is a decimal that has a pattern that repeats.

$$-1.333\ldots = -1.\overline{3}$$
$$0.151515\ldots = 0.\overline{15}$$

> Use *bar notation* to show which of the digits repeat.

Terminating and repeating decimals are examples of *rational numbers*.

Key Idea

Rational Numbers

A **rational number** is a number that can be written as $\dfrac{a}{b}$ where a and b are integers and $b \neq 0$.

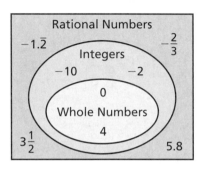

Rational Numbers

$-1.\overline{2}$ $-\dfrac{2}{3}$

Integers

-10 -2

0

Whole Numbers

4

$3\dfrac{1}{2}$ 5.8

EXAMPLE (1) **Writing Rational Numbers as Decimals**

a. Write $-2\dfrac{1}{4}$ as a decimal.

Notice that $-2\dfrac{1}{4} = -\dfrac{9}{4}$.

> Divide 9 by 4.

$$\begin{array}{r} 2.25 \\ 4\overline{)9.00} \\ -8 \\ \hline 1\,0 \\ -8 \\ \hline 20 \\ -20 \\ \hline 0 \end{array}$$

> The remainder is 0. So, it is a terminating decimal.

∴ So, $-2\dfrac{1}{4} = -2.25$.

b. Write $\dfrac{5}{11}$ as a decimal.

> Divide 5 by 11.

$$\begin{array}{r} 0.4545 \\ 11\overline{)5.0000} \\ -4\,4 \\ \hline 60 \\ -55 \\ \hline 50 \\ -44 \\ \hline 60 \\ -55 \\ \hline 5 \end{array}$$

> The remainder repeats. So, it is a repeating decimal.

∴ So, $\dfrac{5}{11} = 0.\overline{45}$.

On Your Own

Now You're Ready
Exercises 11–18

Write the rational number as a decimal.

1. $-\dfrac{6}{5}$ **2.** $-7\dfrac{3}{8}$ **3.** $-\dfrac{3}{11}$ **4.** $1\dfrac{5}{27}$

EXAMPLE 2   Writing a Decimal as a Fraction

Write -0.26 as a fraction in simplest form.

$$-0.26 = -\frac{26}{100}$$

> Write the digits after the decimal point in the numerator.

> The last digit is in the hundredths place. So, use 100 in the denominator.

$$= -\frac{13}{50}$$ Simplify.

On Your Own

Now You're Ready
Exercises 20–27

Write the decimal as a fraction or mixed number in simplest form.

5. -0.7 **6.** 0.125 **7.** -3.1 **8.** -10.25

EXAMPLE 3   Ordering Rational Numbers

Creature	Elevations (km)
Anglerfish	$-\dfrac{13}{10}$
Squid	$-2\dfrac{1}{5}$
Shark	$-\dfrac{2}{11}$
Whale	0.8

The table shows the elevations of four sea creatures relative to sea level. Which of the sea creatures are deeper than the whale? Explain.

Write each rational number as a decimal.

$$-\frac{13}{10} = -1.3$$

$$-2\frac{1}{5} = -2.2$$

$$-\frac{2}{11} = -0.\overline{18}$$

Then graph each decimal on a number line.

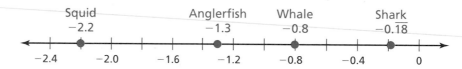

Squid -2.2 Anglerfish -1.3 Whale -0.8 Shark $-0.\overline{18}$

-2.4 -2.0 -1.6 -1.2 -0.8 -0.4 0

∴ Both -2.2 and -1.3 are less than -0.8. So, the squid and the anglerfish are deeper than the whale.

On Your Own

Now You're Ready
Exercises 28–33

9. WHAT IF? The elevation of a dolphin is $-\dfrac{1}{10}$ kilometer. Which of the sea creatures in Example 3 are deeper than the dolphin? Explain.

Vocabulary and Concept Check

1. **VOCABULARY** How can you tell that a number is rational?

2. **WRITING** You have to write 0.63 as a fraction. How do you choose the denominator?

Tell whether the number belongs to each of the following number sets: *rational numbers, integers, whole numbers.*

3. -5 4. $-2.1\overline{6}$ 5. 12 6. 0

Tell whether the decimal is *terminating* **or** *repeating.*

7. $-0.4848\ldots$ 8. -0.151 9. 72.72 10. $-5.2\overline{36}$

 Practice and Problem Solving

Write the rational number as a decimal.

1. 11. $\dfrac{7}{8}$ 12. $\dfrac{5}{11}$ 13. $-\dfrac{7}{9}$ 14. $-\dfrac{17}{40}$

15. $1\dfrac{5}{6}$ 16. $-2\dfrac{17}{18}$ 17. $-5\dfrac{7}{12}$ 18. $8\dfrac{15}{22}$

19. **ERROR ANALYSIS** Describe and correct the error in writing the rational number as a decimal.

$$\text{✗} \quad -\dfrac{7}{11} = -0.6\overline{3}$$

Write the decimal as a fraction or mixed number in simplest form.

2. 20. -0.9 21. 0.45 22. -0.258 23. -0.312

24. -2.32 25. -1.64 26. 6.012 27. -12.405

Order the numbers from least to greatest.

3. 28. $-\dfrac{3}{4}, 0.5, \dfrac{2}{3}, -\dfrac{7}{3}, 1.2$ 29. $\dfrac{9}{5}, -2.5, -1.1, -\dfrac{4}{5}, 0.8$ 30. $-1.4, -\dfrac{8}{5}, 0.6, -0.9, \dfrac{1}{4}$

31. $2.1, -\dfrac{6}{10}, -\dfrac{9}{4}, -0.75, \dfrac{5}{3}$ 32. $-\dfrac{7}{2}, -2.8, -\dfrac{5}{4}, \dfrac{4}{3}, 1.3$ 33. $-\dfrac{11}{5}, -2.4, 1.6, \dfrac{15}{10}, -2.25$

34. **COINS** You lose one quarter, two dimes and two nickels.

     a. Write the amount as a decimal.

     b. Write the amount as a fraction in simplest form.

35. **HIBERNATION** A box turtle hibernates in sand at $-1\dfrac{5}{8}$ feet. A spotted turtle hibernates at $-1\dfrac{16}{25}$ feet. Which turtle is deeper?

Copy and complete the statement using <, >, or =.

36. -2.2 ◻ -2.42

37. -1.82 ◻ -1.81

38. $\dfrac{15}{8}$ ◻ $1\dfrac{7}{8}$

39. $-4\dfrac{6}{10}$ ◻ -4.65

40. $-5\dfrac{3}{11}$ ◻ $-5.\overline{2}$

41. $-2\dfrac{13}{16}$ ◻ $-2\dfrac{11}{14}$

42. OPEN-ENDED Find one terminating decimal and one repeating decimal between $-\dfrac{1}{2}$ and $-\dfrac{1}{3}$.

Player	Hits	At Bats
Eva	42	90
Michelle	38	80

43. SOFTBALL In softball, a batting average is the number of hits divided by the number of times at bat. Does Eva or Michelle have the higher batting average?

44. QUIZ You miss 3 out of 10 questions on a science quiz and 4 out of 15 questions on a math quiz. Which quiz has a higher percent of correct answers?

45. SKATING Is the half pipe deeper than the skating pool? Explain.

46. ENVIRONMENT The table shows the changes from the average water level of a pond over several weeks. Order the numbers from least to greatest.

Week	1	2	3	4
Change (inches)	$-\dfrac{7}{5}$	$-1\dfrac{5}{11}$	-1.45	$-1\dfrac{91}{200}$

47. **Critical Thinking** Given: a and b are integers.

  a. When is $-\dfrac{1}{a}$ positive?

  b. When is $\dfrac{1}{ab}$ positive?

Fair Game Review What you learned in previous grades & lessons

Add or subtract. *(Skills Review Handbook)*

48. $\dfrac{3}{5} + \dfrac{2}{7}$

49. $\dfrac{9}{10} - \dfrac{2}{3}$

50. $8.79 - 4.07$

51. $11.81 + 9.34$

52. MULTIPLE CHOICE In one year, a company has a profit of $-\$2$ million. In the next year, the company has a profit of $\$7$ million. How much more money did the company make the second year? *(Section 1.3)*

Ⓐ $2 million   Ⓑ $5 million   Ⓒ $7 million   Ⓓ $9 million

2.2 Adding and Subtracting Rational Numbers

Essential Question How does adding and subtracting rational numbers compare with adding and subtracting integers?

1 ACTIVITY: Adding and Subtracting Rational Numbers

Work with a partner. Use a number line to find the sum or difference.

a. **Sample:** $2.7 + (-3.4)$

Start at 0. Move 2.7 units to the right.

Add −3.4.

2.7

Then move 3.4 units left to end at −0.7.

∴ So, $2.7 + (-3.4) = -0.7$.

b. $\dfrac{3}{10} + \left(-\dfrac{9}{10}\right)$ c. $-\dfrac{6}{10} - 1\dfrac{3}{10}$

d. $1.3 + (-3.4)$ e. $-1.9 - 0.8$

2 ACTIVITY: Adding and Subtracting Rational Numbers

Work with a partner. Write the numerical expression shown on the number line. Then find the sum or difference.

a.

Start at 0. Move 1.5 units to the right.

Add −2.3.

1.5

Then move 2.3 units left to end at −0.8.

b.

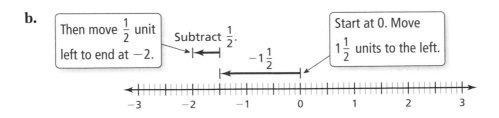

Then move $\dfrac{1}{2}$ unit left to end at −2.

Subtract $\dfrac{1}{2}$.

$-1\dfrac{1}{2}$

Start at 0. Move $1\dfrac{1}{2}$ units to the left.

ACTIVITY: Financial Literacy

Work with a partner. The table shows the balance in a checkbook.

- Black numbers are amounts added to the account.
- Red numbers are amounts taken from the account.

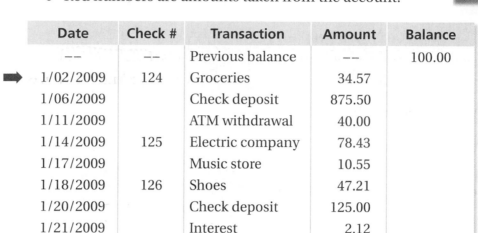

Date	Check #	Transaction	Amount	Balance
--	--	Previous balance	--	100.00
➡ 1/02/2009	124	Groceries	34.57	
1/06/2009		Check deposit	875.50	
1/11/2009		ATM withdrawal	40.00	
1/14/2009	125	Electric company	78.43	
1/17/2009		Music store	10.55	
1/18/2009	126	Shoes	47.21	
1/20/2009		Check deposit	125.00	
1/21/2009		Interest	2.12	
➡ 1/22/2009	127	Cell phone	59.99	

You can find the balance in the **second row** two different ways.

$$100.00 - 34.57 = 65.43 \qquad \text{Subtract 34.57 from 100.00.}$$
$$100.00 + (-34.57) = 65.43 \qquad \text{Add } -34.57 \text{ to 100.00.}$$

a. Copy the table. Then complete the balance column.

b. How did you find the balance in the **tenth row**?

c. Use a different way to find the balance in part (b).

What Is Your Answer?

4. IN YOUR OWN WORDS How does adding and subtracting rational numbers compare with adding and subtracting integers? Give an example.

PUZZLE Find a path through the table so that the numbers add up to the sum. You can move horizontally or vertically.

5. Sum: $\dfrac{3}{4}$

Start → $\dfrac{1}{2}$	$\dfrac{2}{3}$	$-\dfrac{5}{7}$
$-\dfrac{1}{8}$	$-\dfrac{3}{4}$	$\dfrac{1}{3}$ ← End

6. Sum: -0.07

Start → 2.43	1.75	-0.98
-1.09	3.47	-4.88 ← End

Practice ➤ Use what you learned about adding and subtracting rational numbers to complete Exercises 7–9 and 16–18 on page 60.

Key Idea

Adding and Subtracting Rational Numbers

Words To add or subtract rational numbers, use the same rules for signs as you used for integers.

Numbers $\dfrac{4}{5} - \dfrac{1}{5} = \dfrac{4-1}{5} = \dfrac{3}{5}$

$-\dfrac{1}{3} + \dfrac{1}{6} = \dfrac{-2}{6} + \dfrac{1}{6} = \dfrac{-2+1}{6} = \dfrac{-1}{6} = -\dfrac{1}{6}$

EXAMPLE ① **Adding Rational Numbers**

Find $-\dfrac{8}{3} + \dfrac{5}{6}$.   **Estimate** $-3 + 1 = -2$

Study Tip

In Example 1, notice how $-\dfrac{8}{3}$ is written as $-\dfrac{8}{3} = \dfrac{-8}{3} = \dfrac{-16}{6}$.

$-\dfrac{8}{3} + \dfrac{5}{6} = \dfrac{-16}{6} + \dfrac{5}{6}$ Rewrite using the LCD (least common denominator).

$\qquad = \dfrac{-16+5}{6}$ Write the sum of the numerators over the like denominator.

$\qquad = \dfrac{-11}{6}$, or $-1\dfrac{5}{6}$ Simplify.

∴ The sum is $-1\dfrac{5}{6}$.   **Reasonable?** $-1\dfrac{5}{6} \approx -2$ ✔

EXAMPLE ② **Adding Rational Numbers**

Find $-4.05 + 7.62$.

$-4.05 + 7.62 = 3.57$ $|7.62| > |-4.05|$. So, subtract $|-4.05|$ from $|7.62|$.

Use the sign of 7.62.

∴ The sum is 3.57.

On Your Own

Now You're Ready
Exercises 4–12

Add.

1. $-\dfrac{7}{8} + \dfrac{1}{4}$ 2. $-6\dfrac{1}{3} + \dfrac{20}{3}$ 3. $2 + \left(-\dfrac{7}{2}\right)$

4. $-12.5 + 15.3$ 5. $-8.15 + (-4.3)$ 6. $0.65 + (-2.75)$

EXAMPLE **3** **Subtracting Rational Numbers**

Find $-4\frac{1}{7} - \left(-\frac{6}{7}\right)$. **Estimate** $-4 - (-1) = -3$

$$-4\frac{1}{7} - \left(-\frac{6}{7}\right) = -4\frac{1}{7} + \frac{6}{7}$$ Add the opposite of $-\frac{6}{7}$.

$$= -\frac{29}{7} + \frac{6}{7}$$ Write the mixed number as an improper fraction.

$$= \frac{-23}{7}, \text{ or } -3\frac{2}{7}$$ Simplify.

∴ The difference is $-3\frac{2}{7}$. **Reasonable?** $-3\frac{2}{7} \approx -3$ ✓

● **On Your Own**

Subtract.

7. $\frac{1}{3} - \left(-\frac{1}{3}\right)$ **8.** $-3\frac{1}{3} - \frac{5}{6}$ **9.** $4\frac{1}{2} - 5\frac{1}{4}$

EXAMPLE **4** **Real-Life Application**

Clearance: 11 ft 8 in.

In the water, the bottom of a boat is 2.1 feet below the surface and the top of the boat is 8.7 feet above it. Towed on a trailer, the bottom of the boat is 1.3 feet above the ground. Can the boat and trailer pass under the bridge?

Step 1: Find the height h of the boat.

$h = 8.7 - (-2.1)$ Subtract the lowest point from the highest point.

$= 8.7 + 2.1$ Add the opposite of -2.1.

$= 10.8$ Add.

Step 2: Find the height t of the boat and trailer.

$t = 10.8 + 1.3$ Add the trailer height to the boat height.

$= 12.1$ Add.

∴ Because 12.1 feet is greater than 11 feet 8 inches, the boat and trailer cannot pass under the bridge.

● **On Your Own**

10. WHAT IF? In Example 4, the clearance is 12 feet 1 inch. Can the boat and trailer pass under the bridge?

✓ Vocabulary and Concept Check

1. **WRITING** Explain how to find the sum $-8.46 + 5.31$.

2. **OPEN-ENDED** Write an addition expression using fractions that equals $-\dfrac{1}{2}$.

3. **DIFFERENT WORDS, SAME QUESTION** Which is different? Find "both" answers.

| Add -4.8 and 3.9. | What is 3.9 less than -4.8? |
| What is -4.8 increased by 3.9? | Find the sum of -4.8 and 3.9. |

Practice and Problem Solving

Add. Write fractions in simplest form.

4. $\dfrac{11}{12} + \left(-\dfrac{7}{12}\right)$

5. $-\dfrac{9}{14} + \dfrac{2}{7}$

6. $\dfrac{15}{4} + \left(-4\dfrac{1}{3}\right)$

7. $2\dfrac{5}{6} + \left(-\dfrac{8}{15}\right)$

8. $4 + \left(-1\dfrac{2}{3}\right)$

9. $-4.2 + 3.3$

10. $-3.1 + (-0.35)$

11. $12.48 + (-10.636)$

12. $20.25 + (-15.711)$

Subtract. Write fractions in simplest form.

13. $\dfrac{5}{8} - \left(-\dfrac{7}{8}\right)$

14. $\dfrac{1}{4} - \dfrac{11}{16}$

15. $-\dfrac{1}{2} - \left(-\dfrac{5}{9}\right)$

16. $-5 - \dfrac{5}{3}$

17. $-8\dfrac{3}{8} - 10\dfrac{1}{6}$

18. $-1 - 2.5$

19. $5.5 - 8.1$

20. $-7.34 - (-5.51)$

21. $6.673 - (-8.29)$

22. **ERROR ANALYSIS** Describe and correct the error in finding the difference.

$$\cancel{\times}\quad \dfrac{3}{4} - \dfrac{9}{2} = \dfrac{3-9}{4-2} = \dfrac{-6}{2} = -3$$

23. **SPORTS DRINK** Your sports drink bottle is $\dfrac{5}{6}$ full. After practice the bottle is $\dfrac{3}{8}$ full. Write the difference of the amounts after practice and before practice.

24. **BANKING** Your bank account balance is $-\$20.85$. You deposit $\$15.50$. What is your new balance?

Evaluate.

25. $2\dfrac{1}{6} - \left(-\dfrac{8}{3}\right) + \left(-4\dfrac{7}{9}\right)$

26. $6.3 + (-7.8) - (-2.41)$

27. $-\dfrac{12}{5} + \left|-\dfrac{13}{6}\right| + \left(-3\dfrac{2}{3}\right)$

28. **REASONING** When is the difference of two decimals an integer? Explain.

29. **RECIPE** A cook has $2\frac{2}{3}$ cups of flour. A recipe calls for $2\frac{3}{4}$ cups of flour. Does the cook have enough flour? If not, how much more flour is needed?

30. **ROADWAY** A new road that connects Uniontown to Springville is $4\frac{1}{3}$ miles long. What is the change in distance when using the new road instead of the dirt roads?

RAINFALL In Exercises 31–33, the bar graph shows the differences in a city's rainfall from the historical average.

31. What is the difference in rainfall between the wettest and driest months?

32. Find the sum of the differences for the year.

33. What does the sum in Exercise 32 tell you about the rainfall for the year?

ALGEBRA Add or subtract. Write the answer in simplest form.

34. $-4x + 8x - 6x$

35. $-\dfrac{3n}{8} + \dfrac{2n}{8} - \dfrac{n}{8}$

36. $-4a - \dfrac{a}{3}$

37. $\dfrac{5b}{8} + \left(-\dfrac{2b}{3}\right)$

38. **Puzzle** Fill in the blanks to make the solution correct.

$$5.\ \rule{0.5cm}{0.4pt}4 - \left(\rule{0.5cm}{0.4pt}.8\rule{0.5cm}{0.4pt}\right) = -3.61$$

 Fair Game Review What you learned in previous grades & lessons

Evaluate. *(Skills Review Handbook)*

39. 5.2×6.9

40. $7.2 \div 2.4$

41. $2\frac{2}{3} \times 3\frac{1}{4}$

42. $9\frac{4}{5} \div 3\frac{1}{2}$

43. **MULTIPLE CHOICE** A sports store has 116 soccer balls. Over 6 months, it sells eight soccer balls per month. How many soccer balls are in inventory at the end of the 6 months? *(Section 1.3 and Section 1.4)*

Ⓐ -48 Ⓑ 48 Ⓒ 68 Ⓓ 108

Essential Question
How can you use operations with rational numbers in a story?

Share Your Work at... My.BigIdeasMath.com

1 EXAMPLE: Writing a Story

Write a story that uses addition, subtraction multiplication, or division of rational numbers. Draw pictures for your story.

There are many possible stories. Here is an example.

24 Lemons	-$11.75
5 cups sugar	-$1.50
30 plastic glasses	-$1.50
18 sales ($0.50 each)	$9.00
PROFIT	-$5.75

LEMONADE

All You Can Drink For 50¢!

Lauryn decides to earn some extra money. She sets up a lemonade stand. To get customers, she uses big plastic glasses and makes a sign saying "All you can drink for 50¢!"

Lauryn can see that her daily profit is negative. But, she decides to keep trying. After one week, she has the same profit each day.

Sunday	Monday	Tuesday	Wednesday	Thursday	Friday	Saturday
-$5.75	-$5.75	-$5.75	-$5.75	-$5.75	-$5.75	-$5.75

Lauryn is frustrated. Her profit for the first week is

$$7(-5.75) = (-5.75) + (-5.75) + (-5.75) + (-5.75) + (-5.75) + (-5.75) + (-5.75)$$
$$= -40.25.$$

She realizes that she has too many customers who are drinking a second and even a third glass of lemonade. So, she decides to try a new strategy. Soon, she has a customer. He buys a glass of lemonade and drinks it.

He hands the empty glass to Lauryn and says *"That was great. I'll have another glass."* Today, Lauryn says *"That will be 50¢ more, please."* The man says *"But, you only gave me one glass and the sign says 'All you can drink for 50¢!'"* Lauryn replies, *"One glass IS all you can drink for 50¢."*

With her new sales strategy, Lauryn starts making a profit of $8.25 per day. Her profit for the second week is

$$7(8.25) = (8.25) + (8.25) + (8.25) + (8.25) + (8.25) + (8.25) + (8.25) = 57.75.$$

Her profit for the two weeks is $-40.25 + 57.75 = \$17.50$. So, Lauryn has made some money. She decides that she is on the right track.

Work with a partner. Write a story that uses addition, subtraction, multiplication, or division of rational numbers.

- At least one of the numbers in the story has to be negative and *not* an integer.
- Draw pictures to help illustrate what is happening in the story.
- Include the solution of the problem in the story.

If you are having trouble thinking of a story, here are some common uses of negative numbers.

- A profit of −$15 is a loss of $15.
- An elevation of −100 feet is a depth of 100 feet below sea level.
- A gain of −5 yards in football is a loss of 5 yards.
- A score of −4 in golf is 4 strokes under par.
- A balance of −$25 in your checking account means the account is overdrawn by $25.

What Is Your Answer?

3. **IN YOUR OWN WORDS** How can you use operations with rational numbers in a story? You already used rational numbers in your story. Describe another use of a negative rational number in a story.

PUZZLE Read the cartoon. Fill in the blanks using 4s or 8s to make the equation true.

"Dear Mom, I'm in a hurry. To save time I won't be typing any 4's or 8's."

4. $\left(-\dfrac{1}{\Box}\right) + \left(-\dfrac{1}{\Box}\right) = -\dfrac{1}{\Box}$

5. $\left(-\dfrac{1}{\Box}\right) \times \left(-\dfrac{1}{\Box}\right) = \dfrac{1}{6\Box}$

6. $1.\Box \times \left(-0.\Box\right) = -1.\Box\Box$

7. $\left(-\dfrac{3}{\Box}\right) \div \left(\dfrac{3}{\Box}\right) = -\dfrac{1}{2}$

8. $-4.\Box \div 2 = -2.\Box$

2.3 Lesson

Remember

The *reciprocal* of $\frac{a}{b}$ is $\frac{b}{a}$.

Key Idea

Multiplying and Dividing Rational Numbers

Words To multiply or divide rational numbers, use the same rules for signs as you used for integers.

Numbers
$$-\frac{2}{7} \cdot \frac{1}{3} = \frac{-2 \cdot 1}{7 \cdot 3} = \frac{-2}{21} = -\frac{2}{21}$$

$$-\frac{1}{2} \div \frac{4}{9} = \frac{-1}{2} \cdot \frac{9}{4} = \frac{-1 \cdot 9}{2 \cdot 4} = \frac{-9}{8} = -\frac{9}{8}$$

EXAMPLE 1 Dividing Rational Numbers

Find $-5\frac{1}{5} \div 2\frac{1}{3}$. **Estimate** $-5 \div 2 = -2\frac{1}{2}$

$$-5\frac{1}{5} \div 2\frac{1}{3} = -\frac{26}{5} \div \frac{7}{3}$$ Write mixed numbers as improper fractions.

$$= \frac{-26}{5} \cdot \frac{3}{7}$$ Multiply by the reciprocal of $\frac{7}{3}$.

$$= \frac{-26 \cdot 3}{5 \cdot 7}$$ Multiply the numerators and the denominators.

$$= \frac{-78}{35}, \text{ or } -2\frac{8}{35}$$ Simplify.

The quotient is $-2\frac{8}{35}$. **Reasonable?** $-2\frac{8}{35} \approx -2\frac{1}{2}$ ✓

EXAMPLE 2 Multiplying Rational Numbers

Find $-2.5 \cdot 3.6$.

$$\begin{array}{r} -2.5 \\ \times\ 3.6 \\ \hline 1\ 5\ 0 \\ 7\ 5\ 0 \\ \hline -9.0\ 0 \end{array}$$

The decimals have different signs.

The product is negative.

The product is -9.

EXAMPLE 3 **Standardized Test Practice**

Which number, when multiplied by $-\dfrac{5}{3}$, gives a product between 5 and 6?

(A) -6 (B) $-3\dfrac{1}{4}$ (C) $-\dfrac{1}{4}$ (D) 3

Use the guess, check, and revise method.

Guess 1: Because the product is positive and the known factor is negative, choose a number that is negative. Try Choice (C).

$$-\dfrac{1}{4}\left(-\dfrac{5}{3}\right) = \dfrac{-1 \cdot (-5)}{4 \cdot 3} = \dfrac{5}{12}$$

Guess 2: The result of Choice (C) is not between 5 and 6. So, choose another number that is negative. Try Choice (B).

$$-3\dfrac{1}{4}\left(-\dfrac{5}{3}\right) = -\dfrac{13}{4}\left(-\dfrac{5}{3}\right) = \dfrac{-13 \cdot (-5)}{4 \cdot 3} = \dfrac{65}{12} = 5\dfrac{5}{12}$$

∴ $5\dfrac{5}{12}$ is between 5 and 6. So, the correct answer is (B).

On Your Own

Now You're Ready
Exercises 10–33

Multiply or divide.

1. $-\dfrac{6}{5} \div \left(-\dfrac{1}{2}\right)$

2. $\dfrac{1}{3} \div \left(-2\dfrac{2}{3}\right)$

3. $\left(-\dfrac{1}{2}\right)^3$

4. $1.8(-5.1)$

5. $-6.3(-0.6)$

6. $(-1.3)^2$

EXAMPLE 4 **Real-Life Application**

Account Positions ⟳			
Stock	Original Value	Current Value	Change
A	600.54	420.15	-180.39
B	391.10	518.38	127.28
C	380.22	99.70	-280.52

An investor owns stocks A, B, and C. What is the mean change in value of the stocks?

$$\text{mean} = \dfrac{-180.39 + 127.28 + (-280.52)}{3} = \dfrac{-333.63}{3} = -111.21$$

∴ The mean change in value of the stocks is $-\$111.21$.

On Your Own

7. In Example 4, the change in value of stock D is $568.23. What is the mean change in value of the four stocks?

Vocabulary and Concept Check

1. WRITING How is multiplying and dividing rational numbers similar to multiplying and dividing integers?

Find the reciprocal.

2. $-\dfrac{2}{5}$ **3.** -3 **4.** $\dfrac{16}{9}$ **5.** $-2\dfrac{1}{3}$

Tell whether the expression is *positive* or *negative* without evaluating.

6. $-\dfrac{3}{10} \times \left(-\dfrac{8}{15}\right)$ **7.** $1\dfrac{1}{2} \div \left(-\dfrac{1}{4}\right)$ **8.** -6.2×8.18 **9.** $\dfrac{-8.16}{-2.72}$

 ## Practice and Problem Solving

Divide. Write fractions in simplest form.

① 10. $-\dfrac{7}{10} \div \dfrac{2}{5}$ **11.** $\dfrac{1}{4} \div \left(-\dfrac{3}{8}\right)$ **12.** $-\dfrac{8}{9} \div \left(-\dfrac{8}{9}\right)$ **13.** $-\dfrac{1}{5} \div 20$

14. $-2\dfrac{4}{5} \div (-7)$ **15.** $-10\dfrac{2}{7} \div \left(-4\dfrac{4}{11}\right)$ **16.** $-9 \div 7.2$ **17.** $8 \div 2.2$

18. $-3.45 \div (-15)$ **19.** $-0.18 \div 0.03$ **20.** $8.722 \div (-3.56)$ **21.** $12.42 \div (-4.8)$

Multiply. Write fractions in simplest form.

② ③ 22. $-\dfrac{2}{3} \times \dfrac{2}{9}$ **23.** $-\dfrac{1}{4} \times \left(-\dfrac{4}{3}\right)$ **24.** $\dfrac{5}{6}\left(-\dfrac{8}{15}\right)$ **25.** $-2\left(-1\dfrac{1}{4}\right)$

26. $-3\dfrac{1}{3} \cdot \left(-2\dfrac{7}{10}\right)$ **27.** $\left(-1\dfrac{2}{3}\right)^3$ **28.** $0.4 \times (-0.03)$ **29.** $-0.05 \times (-0.5)$

30. $-8(0.09)$ **31.** $-9.3 \cdot (-5.1)$ **32.** $-95.2 \cdot (-0.12)$ **33.** $(-0.4)^3$

ERROR ANALYSIS Describe and correct the error.

34.

$-2.2 \times 3.7 = 8.14$

35.

$-\dfrac{1}{4} \div \dfrac{3}{2} = -\dfrac{4}{1} \times \dfrac{3}{2} = -\dfrac{12}{2} = -6$

36. HOUR HAND The hour hand of a clock moves $-30°$ every hour. How many degrees does it move in $2\dfrac{1}{5}$ hours?

37. SUNFLOWER SEEDS How many 0.75-pound packages can be made with 6 pounds of sunflower seeds?

Evaluate.

38. $-4.2 + 8.1 \times (-1.9)$

39. $2.85 - 6.2 \div 2^2$

40. $-3.64 \cdot |-5.3| - 1.5^3$

41. $1\frac{5}{9} \div \left(-\frac{2}{3}\right) + \left(-2\frac{3}{5}\right)$

42. $-3\frac{3}{4} \times \frac{5}{6} - 2\frac{1}{3}$

43. $\left(-\frac{2}{3}\right)^2 - \frac{3}{4}\left(2\frac{1}{3}\right)$

44. OPEN-ENDED Write two fractions whose product is $-\frac{3}{5}$.

$30\frac{2}{9}$ yd

$50\frac{5}{8}$ yd

45. FENCING A farmer needs to enclose two adjacent rectangular pastures. How much fencing does the farmer need?

46. GASOLINE A 14.5-gallon gasoline tank is $\frac{3}{4}$ full. How many gallons will it take to fill the tank?

47. BOARDWALK A section of a boardwalk is made using 15 boards. Each board is $9\frac{1}{4}$ inches wide. The total width of the section is 144 inches. The spacing between each board is equal. What is the width of the spacing between each board?

48. RUNNING The table shows the changes in the times (in seconds) of four teammates. What is the mean change?

Teammate	Change
1	−2.43
2	−1.85
3	0.61
4	−1.45

49. 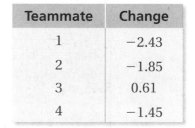 **Critical Thinking** Consider $(-2)^1$, $(-2)^2$, $(-2)^3$, $(-2)^4$, $(-2)^5$, and $(-2)^6$.

a. Evaluate each expression.

b. What pattern do you notice?

c. What is the sign of $(-2)^{49}$?

Fair Game Review What you learned in previous grades & lessons

Add or subtract. *(Section 2.2)*

50. $-6.2 + 4.7$

51. $-8.1 - (-2.7)$

52. $\frac{9}{5} - \left(-2\frac{7}{10}\right)$

53. $-4\frac{5}{6} + \left(-3\frac{4}{9}\right)$

54. MULTIPLE CHOICE What are the coordinates of the point in quadrant IV? *(Section 1.6)*

Ⓐ $(-4, 1)$

Ⓑ $(-3, -3)$

Ⓒ $(0, -2)$

Ⓓ $(3, -3)$

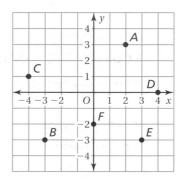

Check It Out
Graphic Organizer
BigIdeasMath com

You can use a **process diagram** to show the steps involved in a procedure. Here is an example of a process diagram for adding rational numbers.

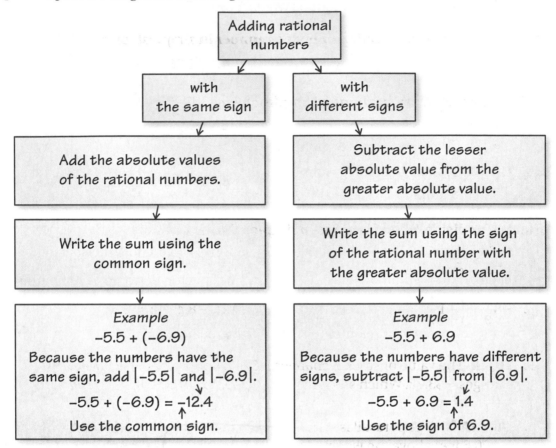

Adding rational numbers

with the same sign

Add the absolute values of the rational numbers.

Write the sum using the common sign.

Example
–5.5 + (–6.9)
Because the numbers have the same sign, add |–5.5| and |–6.9|.
–5.5 + (–6.9) = –12.4
Use the common sign.

with different signs

Subtract the lesser absolute value from the greater absolute value.

Write the sum using the sign of the rational number with the greater absolute value.

Example
–5.5 + 6.9
Because the numbers have different signs, subtract |–5.5| from |6.9|.
–5.5 + 6.9 = 1.4
Use the sign of 6.9.

On Your Own

Make a process diagram with examples to help you study these topics. Your process diagram can have one or more branches.

1. writing rational numbers as decimals

2. subtracting rational numbers

3. dividing rational numbers

After you complete this chapter, make process diagrams with examples for the following topics.

4. solving equations using addition or subtraction

5. solving equations using multiplication or division

6. solving two-step equations

Pounce onto sofa.

Extend claws.

Claw fabric.

I'm pleading the 5th amendment!

"Does this process diagram accurately show how a cat claws furniture?"

Write the rational number as a decimal. *(Section 2.1)*

1. $-\dfrac{3}{20}$

2. $-\dfrac{11}{6}$

Write the decimal as a fraction or mixed number in simplest form. *(Section 2.1)*

3. -0.325

4. -1.28

Add or subtract. Write fractions in simplest form. *(Section 2.2)*

5. $-\dfrac{4}{5} + \left(-\dfrac{3}{8}\right)$

6. $-5.8 + 2.6$

7. $\dfrac{12}{7} - \left(-\dfrac{2}{9}\right)$

8. $9.1 - 12.9$

Multiply or divide. Write fractions in simplest form. *(Section 2.3)*

9. $-2\dfrac{3}{8} \times \dfrac{8}{5}$

10. $-9.4 \times (-4.7)$

11. $-8\dfrac{5}{9} \div \left(-1\dfrac{4}{7}\right)$

12. $-8.4 \div 2.1$

13. **STOCK** The value of stock A changes $-\$3.68$ and the value of stock B changes $-\$3.72$. Which stock has the greater loss? Explain. *(Section 2.1)*

14. **PARASAILING** A parasail is at 200.6 feet above the water. After five minutes, the parasail is at 120.8 feet above the water. What is the change in height of the parasail? *(Section 2.2)*

15. **FOOTBALL** The table shows the statistics of a running back in a football game. How many total yards did he gain? *(Section 2.2)*

Quarter	1	2	3	4	Total
Yards	$-8\dfrac{1}{2}$	23	$42\dfrac{1}{2}$	$-2\dfrac{1}{4}$	?

16. **LATE FEES** You were overcharged $4.52 on your cell phone bill three months in a row. The cell phone company will add $-\$4.52$ to your next bill for each month you were overcharged. How much will be added to your next bill? *(Section 2.3)*

Essential Question How can you use inverse operations to solve an equation?

Key:	$+$ = Variable	$+$ = 1	$-$ = -1	$+$ $-$ = Zero Pair

1 EXAMPLE: Using Addition to Solve an Equation

Use algebra tiles to model and solve $x - 3 = -4$.

Model the equation $x - 3 = -4$.

To get the green tile by itself, remove the red tiles on the left side by adding three yellow tiles to each side.

Remove the three "zero pairs" from each side.

The remaining tile shows the value of x.

So, $x = -1$.

2 EXAMPLE: Using Addition to Solve an Equation

Use algebra tiles to model and solve $-5 = n + 2$.

Model the equation $-5 = n + 2$.

Remove the yellow tiles on the right side by adding two red tiles to each side.

Remove the two "zero pairs" from the right side.

The remaining tiles show the value of n.

So, $-7 = n$ or $n = -7$.

3 ACTIVITY: Solving Equations Using Algebra Tiles

Work with a partner. Use algebra tiles to model and solve the equation.

a. $y + 10 = -5$ **b.** $p - 7 = -3$

c. $-15 = t - 5$ **d.** $8 = 12 + z$

4 ACTIVITY: Writing and Solving Equations

Work with a partner. Write an equation shown by the algebra tiles. Then solve.

a. ◼◼ / ◼◼ = [+] [+]

b. [+] ◼◼ / ◼ = [+][+] / [+]

c. [+] ◼◼◼ / ◼◼ = ◼◼ / ◼◼

d. [+][+][+] / [+][+] = [+] ◼ / ◼

What Is Your Answer?

5. Decide whether the statement is *true* or *false*. Explain your reasoning.

   a. In an equation, any letter can be used as a variable.

   b. The goal in solving an equation is to get the variable by itself.

   c. In the solution, the variable always has to be on the left side of the equal sign.

   d. If you add a number to one side, you should add it to the other side.

6. IN YOUR OWN WORDS How can you use inverse operations to solve an equation without algebra tiles? Give two examples.

7. What makes the cartoon funny?

8. The word *variable* comes from the word *vary*. For example, the temperature in Maine varies a lot from winter to summer.

Write two other English sentences that use the word *vary*.

"**Dear Sir: Yesterday you said** $x = 2$. **Today you are saying** $x = 3$. **Please make up your mind.**"

Practice ▶ Use what you learned about solving equations using inverse operations to complete Exercises 5–8 on page 74.

Check It Out
Lesson Tutorials
BigIdeasMath ✓com

Key Vocabulary 🔊
equivalent equations,
p. 72

 Key Ideas

Addition Property of Equality

Words   Two equations are **equivalent equations** if they have the same solutions. Adding the same number to each side of an equation produces an equivalent equation.

Algebra   If $a = b$, then $a + c = b + c$.

Subtraction Property of Equality

Words   Subtracting the same number from each side of an equation produces an equivalent equation.

Algebra   If $a = b$, then $a - c = b - c$.

EXAMPLE ① **Solving Equations**

a. Solve $x - 5 = -1$.

$x - 5 = -1$	Write the equation.
$\underline{+5 \quad +5}$	Add 5 to each side.
$x = 4$	Simplify.

⁝• So, the solution is $x = 4$.

Check

$x - 5 = -1$

$4 - 5 \stackrel{?}{=} -1$

$-1 = -1$ ✔

Remember

To solve equations, use *inverse operations* that "undo" each other. For example, use addition to solve an equation with subtraction.

b. Solve $z + \dfrac{3}{2} = \dfrac{1}{2}$.

$z + \dfrac{3}{2} = \dfrac{1}{2}$	Write the equation.
$\underline{-\dfrac{3}{2} \quad -\dfrac{3}{2}}$	Subtract $\dfrac{3}{2}$ from each side.
$z = -1$	Simplify.

⁝• So, the solution is $z = -1$.

⬤ **On Your Own**

Now You're Ready
Exercises 5–20

Solve the equation. Check your solution.

1. $p - 5 = -2$ **2.** $w + 13.2 = 10.4$ **3.** $x - \dfrac{5}{6} = -\dfrac{1}{6}$

EXAMPLE 2

Standardized Test Practice

A company has a profit of $750 this week. This profit is $900 more than the profit P last week. Which equation can be used to find P?

(A) $750 = 900 - P$ (B) $750 = P + 900$

(C) $900 = P - 750$ (D) $900 = P + 750$

Words   The profit this week is $900 more than the profit last week.

Equation   750   = P +   900

The equation is $750 = P + 900$. The correct answer is (B).

On Your Own

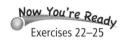
Now You're Ready
Exercises 22–25

4. A company has a profit of $120.50 today. This profit is $145.25 less than the profit P yesterday. Write an equation that can be used to find P.

EXAMPLE 3

Real-Life Application

The line graph shows the scoring while you and your friend played a video game. Write and solve an equation to find your score after Level 4.

You can determine the following from the graph.

Video Game Scoring

Score (points) vs Level

You · Your Friend

33 points

$(4, -8)$

Words   Your friend's score is 33 points less than your score.

Variable Let s be your score after Level 4.

Equation -8 = s $-$ 33

$-8 = s - 33$ Write equation.

$\underline{+\ 33\quad +\ 33}$ Add 33 to each side.

$25 = s$ Simplify.

Your score after Level 4 is 25 points.

Reasonable? From the graph, your score after Level 4 is between 20 points and 30 points. So, 25 points is a reasonable answer.

On Your Own

5. **WHAT IF?** In Example 3, you have -12 points after Level 1. Your score is 27 points less than your friend's score. What is your friend's score?

Check It Out
Help with Homework
BigIdeasMath ✓com

 Vocabulary and Concept Check

1. **VOCABULARY** What property would you use to solve $m + 6 = -4$?

2. **VOCABULARY** Name two inverse operations.

3. **WRITING** Are the equations $m + 3 = -5$ and $m = -2$ equivalent? Explain.

4. **WHICH ONE DOESN'T BELONG?** Which equation does *not* belong with the other three? Explain your reasoning.

$x + 3 = -1$	$x + 1 = -5$	$x - 2 = -6$	$x - 9 = -13$

 Practice and Problem Solving

Solve the equation. Check your solution.

① 5. $a - 6 = 13$ 6. $-3 = z - 8$ 7. $-14 = k + 6$ 8. $x + 4 = -14$

9. $c - 7.6 = -4$ 10. $-10.1 = w + 5.3$ 11. $\frac{1}{2} = q + \frac{2}{3}$ 12. $p - 3\frac{1}{6} = -2\frac{1}{2}$

13. $g - 9 = -19$ 14. $-9.3 = d - 3.4$ 15. $4.58 + y = 2.5$ 16. $x - 5.2 = -18.73$

17. $q + \frac{5}{9} = \frac{1}{6}$ 18. $-2\frac{1}{4} = r - \frac{4}{5}$ 19. $w + 3\frac{3}{8} = 1\frac{5}{6}$ 20. $4\frac{2}{5} + k = -3\frac{2}{11}$

21. **ERROR ANALYSIS** Describe and correct the error in finding the solution.

$$\begin{array}{rcl} x + 8 &=& 10 \\ + 8 & & + 8 \\ \hline x &=& 18 \end{array}$$

Write the verbal sentence as an equation. Then solve.

② 22. 4 less than a number n is -15.   23. 10 more than a number c is 3.

24. The sum of a number y and -3 is -8.

25. The difference between a number p and 6 is -14.

In Exercises 26–28, write an equation. Then solve.

26. **DRY ICE** The temperature of dry ice is $-109.3°F$. This is $184.9°F$ less than the outside temperature. What is the outside temperature?

27. **PROFIT** A company makes a profit of $1.38 million. This is $2.54 million more than last year. What was the profit last year?

28. **PIER** The difference between the lengths of a paddle boat and a pier is $-7\frac{3}{4}$ feet. The pier is $18\frac{1}{2}$ feet long. How long is the paddle boat?

GEOMETRY Write and solve an equation to find the unknown side length.

29. Perimeter = 12 cm

? 3 cm
5 cm

30. Perimeter = 24.2 in.

8.3 in.
? 3.8 in.
8.3 in.

31. Perimeter = 34.6 ft

?
5.2 ft 6.4 ft
11.1 ft

In Exercises 32–36, write an equation. Then solve.

305 ft

32. STATUE OF LIBERTY The total height of the Statue of Liberty and its pedestal is 153 feet more than the height of the statue. What is the height of the statue?

33. BUNGEE JUMPING Your first jump is $50\frac{1}{6}$ feet higher than your second jump. Your first jump reaches $-200\frac{2}{5}$ feet. What is the height of your second jump?

34. TRAVEL Boatesville is $65\frac{3}{5}$ kilometers from Stanton. A bus traveling from Stanton is $24\frac{1}{3}$ kilometers from Boatesville. How far has the bus traveled?

35. GEOMETRY The sum of the measures of the angles of a triangle equals 180°. What is the measure of the missing angle?

$m°$
30.3° 40.8°

36. SKATEBOARDING The table shows your scores in a skateboarding competition. The leader has 311.62 points. What score do you need in the fourth round to win?

Round	1	2	3	4
Points	63.43	87.15	81.96	?

37. CRITICAL THINKING Find the value of $2x - 1$ when $x + 6 = 2$.

 Find the values of x.

38. $|x| = 2$

39. $|x| - 2 = 4$

40. $|x| + 5 = 18$

 Fair Game Review What you learned in previous grades & lessons

Multiply or divide. (*Section 1.4 and Section 1.5*)

41. -7×8

42. $6 \times (-12)$

43. $18 \div (-2)$

44. $-26 \div 4$

45. MULTIPLE CHOICE A class of 144 students voted for a class president. Three-fourths of the students voted for you. Of the students who voted for you, $\frac{5}{9}$ are female. How many female students voted for you? (*Section 2.3*)

Ⓐ 50 Ⓑ 60 Ⓒ 80 Ⓓ 108

2.5 Solving Equations Using Multiplication or Division

Essential Question How can you use multiplication or division to solve an equation?

1 ACTIVITY: Using Division to Solve an Equation

Work with a partner. Use algebra tiles to model and solve the equation.

a. **Sample:** $3x = -12$

Model the equation $3x = -12$.

Your goal is to get one green tile by itself. Because there are three green tiles, divide the red tiles into three equal groups.

Keep one of the groups. This shows the value of x.

∴ So, $x = -4$.

b. $2k = -8$

c. $-15 = 3t$

d. $-20 = 5m$

e. $4h = -16$

2 ACTIVITY: Writing and Solving Equations

Work with a partner. Write an equation shown by the algebra tiles. Then solve.

a.

b.

c.

d.

Preparation:

- Cut index cards to make 40 playing cards.
- Write each equation in the table on a card.

To Play:

- Play with a partner. Deal 20 cards to each player face-down.
- Each player turns one card face-up. The player with the greater solution wins. The winner collects both cards and places them at the bottom of his or her cards.
- Suppose there is a tie. Each player lays three cards face-down, then a new card face-up. The player with the greater solution of these new cards wins. The winner collects all ten cards, and places them at the bottom of his or her cards.
- Continue playing until one player has all the cards. This player wins the game.

$-4x = -12$	$x - 1 = 1$	$x - 3 = 1$	$2x = -10$	$-9 = 9x$
$3 + x = -2$	$x = -2$	$-3x = -3$	$\dfrac{x}{-2} = -2$	$x = -6$
$6x = -36$	$-3x = -9$	$-7x = -14$	$x - 2 = 1$	$-1 = x + 5$
$x = -1$	$9x = -27$	$\dfrac{x}{3} = -1$	$-8 = -2x$	$x = 3$
$-7 = -1 + x$	$x = -5$	$-10 = 10x$	$x = -4$	$-2 = -3 + x$
$-20 = 10x$	$x + 9 = 8$	$-16 = 8x$	$x = 2$	$x + 13 = 11$
$x = -3$	$-8 = 2x$	$x = 1$	$\dfrac{x}{2} = -2$	$-4 + x = -2$
$\dfrac{x}{5} = -1$	$-6 = x - 3$	$x = 4$	$x + 6 = 2$	$x - 5 = -4$

What Is Your Answer?

4. **IN YOUR OWN WORDS** How can you use multiplication or division to solve an equation without using algebra tiles? Give two examples.

Use what you learned about solving equations to complete Exercises 7–10 on page 80.

Key Ideas

Multiplication Property of Equality

Words Multiplying each side of an equation by the same number produces an equivalent equation.

Algebra If $a = b$, then $a \cdot c = b \cdot c$.

Division Property of Equality

Words Dividing each side of an equation by the same number produces an equivalent equation.

Algebra If $a = b$, then $a \div c = b \div c, c \neq 0$.

EXAMPLE 1 **Solving Equations**

a. **Solve $\dfrac{x}{3} = -6$.**

$$\frac{x}{3} = -6 \qquad \text{Write the equation.}$$

$$3 \cdot \frac{x}{3} = 3 \cdot (-6) \qquad \text{Multiply each side by 3.}$$

$$x = -18 \qquad \text{Simplify.}$$

∴ So, the solution is $x = -18$.

b. **Solve $18 = -4y$.**

$$18 = -4y \qquad \text{Write the equation.}$$

$$\frac{18}{-4} = \frac{-4y}{-4} \qquad \text{Divide each side by } -4.$$

$$-4.5 = y \qquad \text{Simplify.}$$

∴ So, the solution is $y = -4.5$.

Check

$18 = -4y$

$18 \overset{?}{=} -4(-4.5)$

$18 = 18$ ✔

On Your Own

Now You're Ready
Exercises 7–18

Solve the equation. Check your solution.

1. $\dfrac{x}{5} = -2$
2. $-a = -24$
3. $3 = -1.5n$

EXAMPLE **2** **Solving an Equation Using a Reciprocal**

Solve $-\dfrac{4}{5}x = -8$.

$$-\dfrac{4}{5}x = -8 \qquad \text{Write the equation.}$$

$$-\dfrac{5}{4} \cdot \left(-\dfrac{4}{5}x\right) = -\dfrac{5}{4} \cdot (-8) \qquad \text{Multiply each side by } -\dfrac{5}{4}, \text{ the reciprocal of } -\dfrac{4}{5}.$$

$$x = 10 \qquad \text{Simplify.}$$

∴ So, the solution is $x = 10$.

On Your Own

Now You're Ready
Exercises 19–22

Solve the equation. Check your solution.

4. $-14 = \dfrac{2}{3}x$ 　　　**5.** $-\dfrac{8}{5}b = 5$ 　　　**6.** $\dfrac{3}{8}h = -9$

EXAMPLE **3** **Real-Life Application**

Record low temperature in Arizona

The record low temperature in Arizona is 1.6 times the record low temperature in Rhode Island. What is the record low temperature in Rhode Island?

Words　　The record low in Arizona is 1.6 times the record low in Rhode Island.

Variable　Let t be the record low in Rhode Island.

Equation　　　　　-40 　　$= 1.6$ 　$\times$ 　　　t

$$-40 = 1.6t \qquad \text{Write equation.}$$

$$-\dfrac{40}{1.6} = \dfrac{1.6t}{1.6} \qquad \text{Divide each side by 1.6.}$$

$$-25 = t \qquad \text{Simplify.}$$

∴ The record low temperature in Rhode Island is $-25°F$.

On Your Own

7. The record low temperature in Hawaii is –0.15 times the record low temperature in Alaska. The record low temperature in Hawaii is 12°F. What is the record low temperature in Alaska?

Vocabulary and Concept Check

1. **WRITING** Explain why multiplication can be used to solve equations involving division.

2. **OPEN-ENDED** Turning a light on and then turning the light off are considered to be inverse operations. Describe two other real-life situations that can be thought of as inverse operations.

Describe the inverse operation that will undo the given operation.

3. Multiplying by 5   4. Subtracting 12   5. Dividing by -8 6. Adding -6

Practice and Problem Solving

Solve the equation. Check your solution.

① 7. $3h = 15$

8. $-5t = -45$

9. $\dfrac{n}{2} = -7$

10. $\dfrac{k}{-3} = 9$

11. $5m = -10$

12. $8t = -32$

13. $-0.2x = 1.6$

14. $-10 = -\dfrac{b}{4}$

15. $-6p = 48$

16. $-72 = 8d$

17. $\dfrac{n}{1.6} = 5$

18. $-14.4 = -0.6p$

② 19. $\dfrac{3}{4}g = -12$

20. $8 = -\dfrac{2}{5}c$

21. $-\dfrac{4}{9}f = -3$

22. $26 = -\dfrac{8}{5}y$

23. **ERROR ANALYSIS** Describe and correct the error in finding the solution.

$$
\begin{array}{c}
-4.2x = 21 \\[4pt]
\dfrac{-4.2x}{4.2} = \dfrac{21}{4.2} \\[4pt]
x = 5
\end{array}
$$

Write the verbal sentence as an equation. Then solve.

24. A number divided by -9 is -16.

25. A number multiplied by $\dfrac{2}{5}$ is $\dfrac{3}{20}$.

26. The product of 15 and a number is -75.

27. The quotient of a number and -1.5 is 21.

In Exercises 28 and 29, write an equation. Then solve.

28. **NEWSPAPERS** You make $0.75 for every newspaper you sell. How many newspapers do you have to sell to buy the soccer cleats?

29. **ROCK CLIMBING** A rock climber averages $12\dfrac{3}{5}$ feet per minute.

How many feet does the rock climber climb in 30 minutes?

Soccer Cleats 36^{00}

OPEN-ENDED (a) Write a multiplication equation that has the given solution.
(b) Write a division equation that has the same solution.

30. -3 **31.** -2.2 **32.** $-\dfrac{1}{2}$ **33.** $-1\dfrac{1}{4}$

34. REASONING Which of the methods can you use to solve $-\dfrac{2}{3}c = 16$?

Multiply each side by $-\dfrac{2}{3}$.	Multiply each side by $-\dfrac{3}{2}$.
Divide each side by $-\dfrac{2}{3}$.	Multiply each side by 3, then divide each side by -2.

35. STOCK A stock has a return of $-\$1.26$ per day. Write and solve an equation to find the number of days until the total return is $-\$10.08$.

36. ELECTION In a school election, $\dfrac{3}{4}$ of the students vote. There are 1464 ballots. Write and solve an equation to find the number of students.

37. OCEANOGRAPHY Aquarius is an underwater ocean laboratory located in the Florida Keys National Marine Sanctuary. Solve the equation $\dfrac{31}{25}x = -62$ to find the value of x.

38. SHOPPING The price of a bike at store A is $\dfrac{5}{6}$ the price at store B. The price at store A is $\$150.60$. Write and solve an equation to find how much you save by buying the bike at store A.

39. CRITICAL THINKING Solve $-2|m| = -10$.

40. In four days, your family drives $\dfrac{5}{7}$ of a trip. Your rate of travel is the same throughout the trip. The total trip is 1250 miles. How many more days until you reach your destination?

Fair Game Review *What you learned in previous grades & lessons*

Subtract. *(Section 1.3)*

41. $5 - 12$ **42.** $-7 - 2$ **43.** $4 - (-8)$ **44.** $-14 - (-5)$

45. MULTIPLE CHOICE Of the 120 apartments in a building, 75 have been scheduled to receive new carpet. What fraction of the apartments have not been scheduled to receive new carpet? *(Section 2.1)*

     Ⓐ $\dfrac{1}{4}$ Ⓑ $\dfrac{3}{8}$ Ⓒ $\dfrac{5}{8}$ Ⓓ $\dfrac{3}{4}$

2.6 Solving Two-Step Equations

Essential Question In a two-step equation, which step should you do first?

1 EXAMPLE: Solving a Two-Step Equation

Use algebra tiles to model and solve $2x - 3 = -5$.

Model the equation $2x - 3 = -5$.

Remove the three red tiles on the left side by adding three yellow tiles to each side.

Remove the three "zero pairs" from each side.

Because there are two green tiles, divide the red tiles into two equal groups.

Keep one of the groups. This shows the value of x.

So, $x = -1$.

2 EXAMPLE: The Math Behind the Tiles

Solve $2x - 3 = -5$ without using algebra tiles. Describe each step. Which step is first, adding 3 to each side or dividing each side by 2?

Use the steps in Example 1 as a guide.

$2x - 3 = -5$	Write the equation.
$2x - 3 + 3 = -5 + 3$	Add 3 to each side.
$2x = -2$	Simplify.
$\dfrac{2x}{2} = \dfrac{-2}{2}$	Divide each side by 2.
$x = -1$	Simplify.

So, $x = -1$. Adding 3 to each side is the first step.

3 ACTIVITY: Solving Equations Using Algebra Tiles

Work with a partner.

- Write an equation shown by the algebra tiles.
- Use algebra tiles to model and solve the equation.
- Check your answer by solving the equation without using algebra tiles.

a.

b.

4 ACTIVITY: Working Backwards

Work with a partner.

a. **Sample:** Your friend pauses a video game to get a drink. You continue the game. You double the score by saving a princess. Then you lose 75 points because you do not collect the treasure. You finish the game with −25 points. How many points did you start with?

One way to solve the problem is to work backwards. To do this, start with the end result and retrace the events.

You have −25 points at the end of the game.	**−25**
You lost 75 points for not collecting the treasure, so add 75 to −25.	**−25 + 75 = 50**
You doubled your score for saving the princess, so find half of 50.	**50 ÷ 2 = 25**

∴ So, you started the game with 25 points.

b. You triple your account balance by making a deposit. Then you withdraw $127.32 to buy groceries. Your account is now overdrawn by $10.56. By working backwards, find your account balance before you made the deposit.

What Is Your Answer?

5. **IN YOUR OWN WORDS** In a two-step equation, which step should you do first? Give four examples.

6. Solve the equation $2x - 75 = -25$. How do your steps compare with the strategy of working backwards in Activity 4?

Practice Use what you learned about solving two-step equations to complete Exercises 6–11 on page 86.

2.6 Lesson

EXAMPLE 1   Solving a Two-Step Equation

Solve $-3x + 5 = 2$. Check your solution.

$-3x + 5 = 2$	Write the equation.	
$\underline{ -5 \quad -5}$	Subtract 5 from each side.	
$-3x = -3$	Simplify.	
$\dfrac{-3x}{-3} = \dfrac{-3}{-3}$	Divide each side by -3.	
$x = 1$	Simplify.	

Check

$-3x + 5 = 2$

$-3(1) + 5 \overset{?}{=} 2$

$-3 + 5 \overset{?}{=} 2$

$2 = 2$ ✓

∴ So, the solution is $x = 1$.

On Your Own

Now You're Ready
Exercises 6–17

Solve the equation. Check your solution.

1. $2x + 12 = 4$ 2. $-5c + 9 = -16$ 3. $3(x - 4) = 9$

EXAMPLE 2   Solving a Two-Step Equation

Solve $\dfrac{x}{8} - \dfrac{1}{2} = -\dfrac{7}{2}$.

Study Tip

You can simplify the equation in Example 2 before solving. Multiply each side by the LCD of the fractions, 8.

$\dfrac{x}{8} - \dfrac{1}{2} = -\dfrac{7}{2}$

$x - 4 = -28$

$x = -24$

$\dfrac{x}{8} - \dfrac{1}{2} = -\dfrac{7}{2}$	Write the equation.	
$\underline{\phantom{\dfrac{x}{8}} +\dfrac{1}{2} \quad +\dfrac{1}{2}}$	Add $\dfrac{1}{2}$ to each side.	
$\dfrac{x}{8} = -3$	Simplify.	
$8 \cdot \dfrac{x}{8} = 8 \cdot (-3)$	Multiply each side by 8.	
$x = -24$	Simplify.	

∴ So, the solution is $x = -24$.

On Your Own

Now You're Ready
Exercises 20–25

Solve the equation. Check your solution.

4. $\dfrac{m}{2} + 6 = 10$ 5. $-\dfrac{z}{3} + 5 = 9$ 6. $\dfrac{2}{5} + 4a = -\dfrac{6}{5}$

EXAMPLE 3 **Combining Like Terms Before Solving**

Solve $3y - 8y = 25$.

$3y - 8y = 25$	Write the equation.
$-5y = 25$	Combine like terms.
$y = -5$	Divide each side by -5.

⋰ So, the solution is $y = -5$.

EXAMPLE 4 **Real-Life Application**

The height at the top of a roller coaster hill is 10 times the height h of the starting point. The height decreases 100 feet from the top to the bottom of the hill. The height at the bottom of the hill is -10 feet. Find h.

Location	Verbal Description	Expression
Start	The height at the start is h.	h
Top of hill	The height at the top of the hill is 10 times the starting height h.	$10h$
Bottom of hill	Height decreases by 100 feet. So, subtract 100.	$10h - 100$

The height at the bottom of the hill is -10 feet. Solve $10h - 100 = -10$ to find h.

$10h - 100 = -10$	Write equation.
$10h = 90$	Add 100 to each side.
$h = 9$	Divide each side by 10.

⋰ The height at the start is 9 feet.

On Your Own

Now You're Ready
Exercises 29–34

Solve the equation. Check your solution.

7. $4 - 2y + 3 = -9$ 8. $7x - 10x = 15$ 9. $-8 = 1.3m - 2.1m$

10. **WHAT IF?** In Example 4, the height at the bottom of the hill is -5 feet. Find the height h.

Vocabulary and Concept Check

1. **WRITING** How do you solve two-step equations?

Match the equation with the first step to solve it.

2. $4 + 4n = -12$ 3. $4n = -12$ 4. $\dfrac{n}{4} = -12$ 5. $\dfrac{n}{4} - 4 = -12$

  A. Add 4.   B. Subtract 4.   C. Multiply by 4.   D. Divide by 4.

 Practice and Problem Solving

Solve the equation. Check your solution.

6. $2v + 7 = 3$ 7. $4b + 3 = -9$ 8. $17 = 5k - 2$

9. $-6t - 7 = 17$ 10. $8n + 16.2 = 1.6$ 11. $-5g + 2.3 = -18.8$

12. $2t - 5 = -10$ 13. $-4p + 9 = -5$ 14. $11 = -5x - 2$

15. $4 + 2.2h = -3.7$ 16. $-4.8f + 6.4 = -8.48$ 17. $7.3y - 5.18 = -51.9$

ERROR ANALYSIS Describe and correct the error in finding the solution.

18.

$$-6 + 2x = -10$$
$$-6 + \frac{2x}{2} = -\frac{10}{2}$$
$$-6 + x = -5$$
$$x = 1$$

19.
$$-3x + 2 = -7$$
$$-3x = -9$$
$$-\frac{3x}{3} = \frac{-9}{3}$$
$$x = -3$$

Solve the equation. Check your solution.

20. $\dfrac{3}{5}g - \dfrac{1}{3} = -\dfrac{10}{3}$ 21. $\dfrac{a}{4} - \dfrac{5}{6} = -\dfrac{1}{2}$ 22. $-\dfrac{1}{3} + 2z = -\dfrac{5}{6}$

23. $2 - \dfrac{b}{3} = -\dfrac{5}{2}$ 24. $-\dfrac{2}{3}x + \dfrac{3}{7} = \dfrac{1}{2}$ 25. $-\dfrac{9}{4}v + \dfrac{4}{5} = \dfrac{7}{8}$

In Exercises 26–28, write an equation. Then solve.

26. **WEATHER** Starting at 1:00 P.M., the temperature changes -4 degrees per hour. How long will it take to reach $-1°$?

27. **BOWLING** It costs $2.50 to rent bowling shoes. Each game costs $2.25. You have $9.25. How many games can you bowl?

28. **CELL PHONES** A cell phone company charges a monthly fee plus $0.25 for each text message. The monthly fee is $30.00 and you owe $59.50. How many text messages did you have?

Temperature
at 1:00 P.M.

35°F

Solve the equation. Check your solution.

29. $3v - 9v = 30$

30. $12t - 8t = -52$

31. $-8d - 5d + 7d = 72$

32. $6(x - 2) = -18$

33. $-4(m + 3) = 24$

34. $-8(y + 9) = -40$

35. WRITING Write a real-world problem that can be modeled by $\frac{1}{2}x - 2 = 8$. Then solve the equation.

36. GEOMETRY The perimeter of the parallelogram is 102 feet. Find m.

REASONING Exercises 37 and 38 are missing information. Tell what information is needed to solve the problem.

37. TAXI A taxi service charges an initial fee plus $1.80 per mile. How far can you travel for $12?

38. EARTH The coldest surface temperature on the moon is 57 degrees colder than twice the coldest surface temperature on Earth. What is the coldest surface temperature on Earth?

39. SCIENCE On Saturday, you catch insects for your science class. Five of the insects escape. The remaining insects are divided into three groups to share in class. Each group has nine insects. How many insects did you catch on Saturday?

    a. Solve the problem by working backwards.

    b. Solve the equation $\frac{x - 5}{3} = 9$. How does the answer compare with the answer to part (a)?

40. UNDERWATER HOTEL You must scuba dive to the entrance of your room at Jule's Undersea Lodge in Key Largo, Florida. The diver is 1 foot deeper than $\frac{2}{3}$ of the elevation of the entrance. What is the elevation of the entrance?

41. **Geometry** How much should you change the length of the rectangle so that the perimeter is 54 centimeters? Write an equation that shows how you found your answer.

Fair Game Review What you learned in previous grades & lessons

Multiply or divide. *(Section 2.3)*

42. -6.2×5.6

43. $\frac{8}{3} \times \left(-2\frac{1}{2}\right)$

44. $\frac{5}{2} \div \left(-\frac{4}{5}\right)$

45. $-18.6 \div (-3)$

46. MULTIPLE CHOICE Which fraction is *not* equivalent to 0.75? *(Skills Review Handbook)*

    Ⓐ $\frac{15}{20}$ Ⓑ $\frac{9}{12}$ Ⓒ $\frac{6}{9}$ Ⓓ $\frac{3}{4}$

Solve the equation. Check your solution. *(Section 2.4 and Section 2.5)*

1. $-6.5 + x = -4.12$

2. $4\frac{1}{2} + p = -5\frac{3}{4}$

3. $-\dfrac{b}{7} = 4$

4. $2h = -57$

Write the verbal sentence as an equation. Then solve. *(Section 2.4 and Section 2.5)*

5. The difference between a number b and 7.4 is -6.8.

6. $5\frac{2}{5}$ more than a number a is $7\frac{1}{2}$.

7. A number x multiplied by $\dfrac{3}{8}$ is $-\dfrac{15}{32}$.

8. The quotient of two times a number k and -2.6 is 12.

Write and solve an equation to find the value of *x*. *(Section 2.4 and Section 2.6)*

9. Perimeter = 26

10. Perimeter = 23.59

11. Perimeter = 33

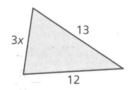

12. **BANKING** You withdraw $29.79 from your bank account. Now, your balance is $-\$20.51$. Write and solve an equation to find the amount of money in your bank account before you withdrew the money. *(Section 2.4)*

13. **WATER LEVEL** During a drought, the water level of a lake changes $-3\frac{1}{5}$ feet per day. Write and solve an equation to find how long it takes for the water level to change -16 feet. *(Section 2.5)*

14. **BASKETBALL** A basketball game has four quarters. The length of a game is 32 minutes. You play the entire game except $4\frac{1}{2}$ minutes. Write and solve an equation to find the mean time you play per quarter. *(Section 2.6)*

15. **SCRAPBOOKING** The mat needs to be cut to have a 0.5-inch border on all four sides. *(Section 2.6)*

    a. How much should you cut from the left and right sides?

    b. How much should you cut from the top and bottom?

2 Chapter Review

Check It Out
Vocabulary Help
BigIdeasMath ✓com

Review Key Vocabulary

terminating decimal, *p. 52*   rational number, *p. 52*

repeating decimal, *p. 52*   equivalent equations, *p. 72*

Review Examples and Exercises

2.1 Rational Numbers *(pp. 50–55)*

Write −0.14 as a fraction in simplest form.

$$-0.14 = -\frac{14}{100}$$ ← Write the digits after the decimal point in the numerator.

The last digit is in the hundredths place. So, use 100 in the denominator.

$$= -\frac{7}{50}$$ Simplify.

Exercises

Write the rational number as a decimal.

1. $-\frac{8}{15}$ 2. $\frac{5}{8}$ 3. $-\frac{13}{6}$ 4. $1\frac{7}{16}$

Write the decimal as a fraction or mixed number in simplest form.

5. -0.6 6. -0.35 7. -5.8 8. 24.23

2.2 Adding and Subtracting Rational Numbers *(pp. 56–61)*

Find −8.18 + 3.64.

$$-8.18 + 3.64 = -4.54$$ $|-8.18| > |3.64|$. So, subtract $|3.64|$ from $|-8.18|$.

Use the sign of -8.18.

Exercises

Add or subtract. Write fractions in simplest form.

9. $-4\frac{5}{9} + \frac{8}{9}$ 10. $-\frac{5}{12} - \frac{3}{10}$ 11. $-2.53 + 4.75$ 12. $3.8 - (-7.45)$

13. **TURTLES** A turtle is $20\frac{5}{6}$ inches below the surface of a pond. It dives to a depth of $32\frac{1}{4}$ inches. How far did it dive?

Multiplying and Dividing Rational Numbers (pp. 62–67)

Find $-4\frac{1}{6} \div 1\frac{1}{3}$.

$$-4\frac{1}{6} \div 1\frac{1}{3} = -\frac{25}{6} \div \frac{4}{3} \qquad \text{Write mixed numbers as improper fractions.}$$

$$= \frac{-25}{6} \cdot \frac{3}{4} \qquad \text{Multiply by the reciprocal of } \frac{4}{3}.$$

$$= \frac{-25 \cdot 3}{6 \cdot 4} \qquad \text{Multiply the numerators and the denominators.}$$

$$= \frac{-25}{8}, \text{ or } -3\frac{1}{8} \qquad \text{Simplify.}$$

Exercises

Multiply or divide. Write fractions in simplest form.

14. $-\frac{4}{9}\left(-\frac{7}{9}\right)$ **15.** $\frac{9}{10} \div \left(-\frac{6}{5}\right)$ **16.** $\frac{8}{15}\left(-\frac{2}{3}\right)$ **17.** $-\frac{4}{11} \div \frac{2}{7}$

18. $-5.9(-9.7)$ **19.** $6.4 \div (-3.2)$ **20.** $4.5(-5.26)$ **21.** $-15.4 \div (-2.5)$

22. SUNKEN SHIP The elevation of a sunken ship is -120 feet. Your elevation is $\frac{5}{8}$ of the ship's elevation. What is your elevation?

Solving Equations Using Addition or Subtraction (pp. 70–75)

Solve $x - 9 = -6$.

$$x - 9 = -6 \qquad \text{Write the equation.}$$

$$\underline{+ 9 \quad + 9} \qquad \text{Add 9 to each side.}$$

$$x = 3 \qquad \text{Simplify.}$$

Exercises

Solve the equation. Check your solution.

23. $p - 3 = -4$ **24.** $6 + q = 1$ **25.** $-2 + j = -22$ **26.** $b - 19 = -11$

27. $n + \frac{3}{4} = \frac{1}{4}$ **28.** $v - \frac{5}{6} = -\frac{7}{8}$ **29.** $t - 3.7 = 1.2$ **30.** $\ell + 15.2 = -4.5$

31. GIFT CARD A shirt costs $24.99. After using a gift card as a partial payment, you still owe $9.99. What is the value of the gift card?

Solving Equations Using Multiplication or Division *(pp. 76–81)*

Solve $\dfrac{x}{5} = -7$.

$\dfrac{x}{5} = -7$	Write the equation.
$5 \cdot \dfrac{x}{5} = 5 \cdot (-7)$	Multiply each side by 5.
$x = -35$	Simplify.

Exercises

Solve the equation. Check your solution.

32. $\dfrac{x}{3} = -8$ **33.** $-7 = \dfrac{y}{7}$ **34.** $-\dfrac{z}{4} = -\dfrac{3}{4}$ **35.** $-\dfrac{w}{20} = -2.5$

36. $4x = -8$ **37.** $-10 = 2y$ **38.** $-5.4z = -32.4$ **39.** $-6.8w = 3.4$

40. TEMPERATURE The mean temperature change is $-3.2°F$ per day for five days. What is the total change over the five-day period?

Solving Two-Step Equations *(pp. 82–87)*

Solve $\dfrac{x}{5} + \dfrac{7}{10} = -\dfrac{3}{10}$.

$\dfrac{x}{5} + \dfrac{7}{10} = -\dfrac{3}{10}$	Write the equation.
$\dfrac{x}{5} = -1$	Subtract $\dfrac{7}{10}$ from each side.
$x = -5$	Multiply each side by 5.

Exercises

Solve the equation. Check your solution.

41. $-2c + 6 = -8$ **42.** $3(3w - 4) = -20$

43. $\dfrac{w}{6} + \dfrac{5}{8} = -1\dfrac{3}{8}$ **44.** $-3x - 4.6 = 5.9$

45. EROSION The floor of a canyon has an elevation of -14.5 feet. Erosion causes the elevation to change by -1.5 feet per year. How many years will it take for the canyon floor to have an elevation of -31 feet?

Check It Out
Test Practice
BigIdeasMath ✓.com

Write the rational number as a decimal.

1. $\dfrac{7}{40}$ **2.** $-\dfrac{1}{9}$ **3.** $-\dfrac{21}{16}$ **4.** $\dfrac{36}{5}$

Write the decimal as a fraction or mixed number in simplest form.

5. -0.122 **6.** 0.33 **7.** -4.45 **8.** -7.09

Add or subtract. Write fractions in simplest form.

9. $-\dfrac{4}{9} + \left(-\dfrac{23}{18}\right)$ **10.** $\dfrac{17}{12} - \left(-\dfrac{1}{8}\right)$ **11.** $9.2 + (-2.8)$ **12.** $2.86 - 12.1$

Multiply or divide. Write fractions in simplest form.

13. $3\dfrac{9}{10} \times \left(-\dfrac{8}{3}\right)$ **14.** $-1\dfrac{5}{6} \div 4\dfrac{1}{6}$ **15.** $-4.4 \times (-6.02)$ **16.** $-5 \div 1.5$

Solve the equation. Check your solution.

17. $7x = -3$ **18.** $2(x + 1) = -2$ **19.** $\dfrac{2}{9}g = -8$

20. $z + 14.5 = 5.4$ **21.** $-14 = 6c$ **22.** $\dfrac{2}{7}k - \dfrac{3}{8} = -\dfrac{19}{8}$

23. MARATHON A marathon is a 26.2-mile race. You run three marathons in one year. How many miles do you run?

24. RECORD A runner is compared with the world record holder during a race. A negative number means the runner is ahead of the time of the world record holder, and a positive number means that the runner is behind the time of the world record holder. The table shows the time difference between the runner and the world record holder for each lap. What time difference does the runner need for the fourth lap to match the world record?

Lap	Time Difference
1	-1.23
2	0.45
3	0.18
4	?

25. GYMNASTICS You lose 0.3 point for stepping out of bounds during a floor routine. Your final score is 9.124. Write and solve an equation to find your score before the penalty.

26. PERIMETER The perimeter of the triangle is 45. Find the value of x.

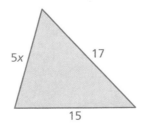

1. When José and Sean were each 5 years old, José was $1\frac{1}{2}$ inches taller than Sean. José grew at an average rate of $2\frac{3}{4}$ inches per year from the time that he was 5 years old until the time he was 13 years old. José was 63 inches tall when he was 13 years old. How tall was Sean when he was 5 years old?

   A. $39\frac{1}{2}$ in.

   B. $42\frac{1}{2}$ in.

   C. $44\frac{3}{4}$ in.

   D. $47\frac{3}{4}$ in.

Test-Taking Strategy
Estimate the Answer

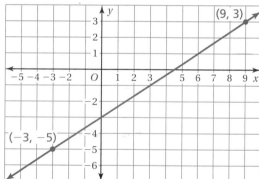

One-fourth of the 36 cats in our town are tabbies. How many are not tabbies?

Ⓐ 9 Ⓑ 18 Ⓒ 27 Ⓓ 36

IC.

"Using estimation you can see that there are about 10 tabbies. So about 30 are not tabbies."

2. A line is graphed in the coordinate plane below.

   Which point is *not* on the line?

   F. $(-3, 0)$

   G. $(0, -3)$

   H. $(3, -1)$

   I. $(6, 1)$

3. What is the missing number in the sequence below?

$$\frac{9}{16}, \ -\frac{9}{8}, \ \frac{9}{4}, \ -\frac{9}{2}, \ 9, \ \underline{\hspace{1cm}}$$

4. What is the value of the expression below?

$$\left| -2 - (-2.5) \right|$$

   A. -4.5

   B. -0.5

   C. 0.5

   D. 4.5

5. Which equation is equivalent to the equation shown below?

$$-\frac{3}{4}x + \frac{1}{8} = -\frac{3}{8}$$

F. $-\frac{3}{4}x = -\frac{3}{8} - \frac{1}{8}$

G. $-\frac{3}{4}x = -\frac{3}{8} + \frac{1}{8}$

H. $x + \frac{1}{8} = -\frac{3}{8} \cdot \left(-\frac{4}{3}\right)$

I. $x + \frac{1}{8} = -\frac{3}{8} \cdot \left(-\frac{3}{4}\right)$

6. What is the value of the expression below?

$$-5 \div 20$$

7. Karina was solving the equation in the box below.

$$-96 = -6(15 - 2x)$$
$$-96 = -90 - 12x$$
$$-96 + 90 = -90 + 90 - 12x$$
$$-6 = -12x$$
$$\frac{-6}{-12} = \frac{-12x}{-12}$$
$$\frac{1}{2} = x$$

What should Karina do to correct the error that she made?

A. First add 6 to both sides of the equation.

B. First add $2x$ to both sides of the equation.

C. Distribute the -6 to get $90 - 12x$.

D. Distribute the -6 to get $-90 + 12x$.

8. Current, voltage, and resistance are related according to the formula below, where I represents the current, in amperes, V represents the voltage, in volts, and R represents the resistance, in ohms.

$$I = \frac{V}{R}$$

What is the voltage when the current is 0.5 ampere and the resistance is 0.8 ohm?

F. 4.0 volts

G. 1.3 volts

H. 0.4 volt

I. 0.3 volt

9. What is the area of a triangle with a base length of $2\frac{1}{2}$ inches and a height of 3 inches?

A. $2\frac{3}{4}$ in.^{2}

B. $3\frac{3}{4}$ in.^{2}

C. $5\frac{1}{2}$ in.^{2}

D. $7\frac{1}{2}$ in.^{2}

10. What is the circumference of the circle below? (Use 3.14 for π.)

10.2 cm

F. 64.056 cm

H. 32.028 cm

G. 60.028 cm

I. 30.028 cm

11. Four points are graphed on the number line below.

Part A   Choose the two points whose values have the greatest sum. Approximate this sum. Explain your reasoning.

Part B   Choose the two points whose values have the greatest difference. Approximate this difference. Explain your reasoning.

Part C   Choose the two points whose values have the greatest product. Approximate this product. Explain your reasoning.

Part D   Choose the two points whose values have the greatest quotient. Approximate this quotient. Explain your reasoning.

12. What number belongs in the box to make the equation true?

$$\frac{-0.4}{\boxed{}} + 0.8 = -1.2$$

A. 1

B. 0.2

C. -0.2

D. -1

3 Proportions and Variation

"I am doing an experiment with slope. I want you to run up and down the board 10 times."

"Now with 2 more dog biscuits, do it again and we'll compare your rates."

"Dear Sir: I counted the number of bacon, cheese, and chicken dog biscuits in the box I bought."

"There were 16 bacon, 12 cheese, and only 8 chicken. That's a ratio of 4:3:2. Please go back to the original ratio of 1:1:1."

What You Learned Before

"I wonder if our rate is proportional to the slope of the hill."

...or possibly proportional to our stupidity!

● Simplifying Fractions

Example 1 Simplify $\dfrac{4}{8}$.

$$\dfrac{4 \div 4}{8 \div 4} = \dfrac{1}{2}$$

> Simplify fractions by using the Greatest Common Factor.

Example 2 Simplify $\dfrac{10}{15}$.

$$\dfrac{10 \div 5}{15 \div 5} = \dfrac{2}{3}$$

Try It Yourself
Simplify.

1. $\dfrac{75}{100}$
2. $\dfrac{16}{24}$
3. $\dfrac{12}{144}$
4. $\dfrac{15}{45}$

● Comparing Equivalent Fractions

Example 3 Is $\dfrac{1}{4}$ equivalent to $\dfrac{13}{52}$?

$$\dfrac{13 \div 13}{52 \div 13} = \dfrac{1}{4}$$

∴ $\dfrac{1}{4}$ is equivalent to $\dfrac{13}{52}$.

Example 4 Is $\dfrac{30}{64}$ equivalent to $\dfrac{5}{8}$?

$$\dfrac{30 \div 2}{64 \div 2} = \dfrac{15}{32}$$

∴ $\dfrac{30}{64}$ is *not* equivalent to $\dfrac{5}{8}$.

Try It Yourself
Are the fractions equivalent? Explain.

5. $\dfrac{15}{60} \overset{?}{=} \dfrac{3}{4}$
6. $\dfrac{2}{5} \overset{?}{=} \dfrac{24}{144}$
7. $\dfrac{15}{20} \overset{?}{=} \dfrac{3}{5}$
8. $\dfrac{2}{8} \overset{?}{=} \dfrac{16}{64}$

● Converting Measures

Example 5 A person must be at least 56 inches tall to drive a race car at an amusement park. Gina is 4 feet 11 inches tall. Is she tall enough to drive?

$$4 \text{ feet} \times \dfrac{12 \text{ inches}}{1 \text{ foot}} + 11 \text{ inches} = 48 \text{ inches} + 11 \text{ inches} = 59 \text{ inches}$$

∴ Because 59 inches is greater than 56 inches, Gina is tall enough to drive.

Try It Yourself
Convert.

9. 15 feet = ▢ yards
10. 5 quarts = ▢ pints
11. 6000 pounds = ▢ tons

Essential Question How do rates help you describe real-life problems?

The Meaning of a Word ● Rate

When you rent snorkel gear at the beach, you should pay attention to the rental **rate**. The rental rate is in dollars per hour.

Snorkel Rentals
$8.75 per hour

Snorkel Rentals
$7.25 per hour

1 ACTIVITY: Finding Reasonable Rates

Work with a partner.

a. Match each description with a verbal rate.

b. Match each verbal rate with a numerical rate.

c. Give a reasonable numerical rate for each description. Then give an unreasonable rate.

Description	*Verbal Rate*	*Numerical Rate*
Your pay rate for washing cars	inches per month	$\dfrac{\text{m}}{\text{sec}}$
The average rainfall rate in a rain forest	pounds per acre	$\dfrac{\text{people}}{\text{yr}}$
Your average driving rate along an interstate	meters per second	$\dfrac{\text{lb}}{\text{acre}}$
The growth rate for the length of a baby alligator	people per year	$\dfrac{\text{mi}}{\text{h}}$
Your running rate in a 100-meter dash	dollars per hour	$\dfrac{\text{in.}}{\text{yr}}$
The population growth rate of a large city	dollars per year	$\dfrac{\text{in.}}{\text{mo}}$
The average pay rate for a professional athlete	miles per hour	$\dfrac{\$}{\text{h}}$
The fertilization rate for an apple orchard	inches per year	$\dfrac{\$}{\text{yr}}$

2 ACTIVITY: Unit Analysis

Work with a partner. Some real-life problems involve the product of an amount and a rate. Find each product. List the units.

a. **Sample:** $6 \text{ h} \times \dfrac{\$12}{\text{h}} = 6 \cancel{\text{h}} \times \dfrac{\$12}{\cancel{\text{h}}}$ Divide out "hours."

$= \$72$ Multiply. Answer is in dollars.

b. $6 \text{ mo} \times \dfrac{\$700}{\text{mo}}$ **c.** $10 \text{ gal} \times \dfrac{22 \text{ mi}}{\text{gal}}$

d. $9 \text{ lb} \times \dfrac{\$3}{\text{lb}}$ **e.** $13 \text{ min} \times \dfrac{60 \text{ sec}}{\text{min}}$

3 ACTIVITY: Writing a Story

Work with a partner.

- **Think of a story that compares two different rates.**
- **Write the story.**
- **Draw pictures for the story.**

What Is Your Answer?

4. RESEARCH Use newspapers, the Internet, or magazines to find examples of salaries. Try to find examples of each of the following ways to write salaries.

   a. dollars per hour   **b.** dollars per month   **c.** dollars per year

5. IN YOUR OWN WORDS How do rates help you describe real-life problems? Give two examples.

6. To estimate the annual salary for a given hourly pay rate, multiply by 2 and insert "000" at the end.

Sample: $10 per hour is about $20,000 per year.

   a. Explain why this works. Assume the person is working 40 hours a week.
   b. Estimate the annual salary for an hourly pay rate of $8 per hour.
   c. You earn $1 million per month. What is your annual salary?
   d. Why is the cartoon funny?

"We had someone apply for the job. He says he would like $1 million a month, but will settle for $8 an hour."

Practice   Use what you discovered about ratios and rates to complete Exercises 7–10 on page 102.

Check It Out
Lesson Tutorials
BigIdeasMath ✓com

Key Vocabulary
ratio, p. 100
rate, p. 100
unit rate, p. 100

A **ratio** is a comparison of two quantities using division.

$$\frac{3}{4}, 3 \text{ to } 4, 3:4$$

A **rate** is a ratio of two quantities with different units.

$$\frac{60 \text{ miles}}{2 \text{ hours}}$$

A rate with a denominator of 1 is called a **unit rate**.

$$\frac{30 \text{ miles}}{1 \text{ hour}}$$

EXAMPLE ① **Finding Ratios and Rates**

There are 45 males and 60 females in a subway car. The subway car travels 2.5 miles in 5 minutes.

a. Find the ratio of males to females.

b. Find the speed of the subway car.

a. $\dfrac{\text{males}}{\text{females}} = \dfrac{45}{60} = \dfrac{3}{4}$

⋮∙ The ratio of males to females is $\dfrac{3}{4}$.

b. 2.5 miles in 5 minutes $= \dfrac{2.5 \text{ mi}}{5 \text{ min}} = \dfrac{2.5 \text{ mi} \div 5}{5 \text{ min} \div 5} = \dfrac{0.5 \text{ mi}}{1 \text{ min}}$

⋮∙ The speed is 0.5 mile per minute.

EXAMPLE ② **Finding a Rate from a Table**

The table shows the amount of money you can raise by walking for a charity. Find your unit rate in dollars per mile.

Distance (miles)	2	4	6	8
Money (dollars)	24	48	72	96

Use the table to find the unit rate.

$\dfrac{\text{change in money}}{\text{change in distance}} = \dfrac{\$24}{2 \text{ mi}}$ The money raised increases by \$24 every 2 miles.

$= \dfrac{\$12}{1 \text{ mi}}$ Simplify.

⋮∙ Your unit rate is \$12 per mile.

◀) Multi-Language Glossary at BigIdeasMath✓com.

On Your Own

Now You're Ready
Exercises 11–26

1. In Example 1, find the ratio of females to males.

2. In Example 1, find the ratio of females to total passengers.

3. The table shows the distance that the International Space Station travels while orbiting Earth. Find the speed in miles per second.

Time (seconds)	3	6	9	12
Distance (miles)	14.4	28.8	43.2	57.6

EXAMPLE 3 **Finding a Rate from a Line Graph**

The graph shows the distance that sound travels through water. Find the speed of sound in kilometers per second.

Sound through Water

Step 1: Choose a point on the line.

The point (2, 3) shows you that sound travels 3 kilometers in 2 seconds.

Step 2: Find the speed.

$$\frac{\text{distance traveled}}{\text{elapsed time}} = \frac{3}{2} \quad \begin{array}{l} \leftarrow \text{kilometers} \\ \leftarrow \text{seconds} \end{array}$$

$$= \frac{1.5 \text{ km}}{1 \text{ sec}} \qquad \text{Simplify.}$$

∴ The speed is 1.5 kilometers per second.

On Your Own

4. **WHAT IF?** In Example 3, you use the point (4, 6) to find the speed. Does your answer change? Why or why not?

5. The graph shows the distance that sound travels through air. Find the speed of sound in kilometers per second.

6. Does sound travel faster in water or in air? Explain.

Sound through Air

Check It Out
Help with Homework
BigIdeasMath.com

Vocabulary and Concept Check

1. **VOCABULARY** How can you tell when a rate is a unit rate?

2. **WRITING** Why do you think rates are usually written as unit rates?

3. **OPEN-ENDED** Write a real-life rate that applies to you.

Estimate the unit rate.

4. $74.75   Gloss White PAINT 5 gal

5. $1.19   GRAPE JUICE 12 fl oz

6. $2.35   12 Grade AA Eggs

Practice and Problem Solving

Find the product. List the units.

7. $8 \text{ h} \times \dfrac{\$9}{\text{h}}$

8. $8 \text{ lb} \times \dfrac{\$3.50}{\text{lb}}$

9. $14 \text{ sec} \times \dfrac{60 \text{ MB}}{\text{sec}}$

10. $6 \text{ h} \times \dfrac{19 \text{ mi}}{\text{h}}$

Write the ratio as a fraction in simplest form.

11. 25 to 45

12. 63 : 28

13. 35 girls : 15 boys

14. 2 feet : 8 feet

15. 16 dogs to 12 cats

16. 51 correct : 9 incorrect

Find the unit rate.

17. 180 miles in 3 hours

18. 256 miles per 8 gallons

19. $9.60 for 4 pounds

20. $4.80 for 6 cans

21. 297 words in 5.5 minutes

22. 54 meters in 2.5 hours

Use the table to find the rate.

23.
Servings	0	1	2	3
Calories	0	90	180	270

24.
Days	0	1	2	3
Liters	0	1.6	3.2	4.8

25.
Packages	3	6	9	12
Servings	13.5	27	40.5	54

26.
Years	2	6	10	14
Feet	7.2	21.6	36	50.4

27. **DOWNLOAD** At 1 P.M., you have 24 megabytes of a movie. At 1:15 P.M., you have 96 megabytes. What is the download rate in megabytes per minute?

28. **POPULATION** In 2000, the U.S. population was 281 million people. In 2008, it was 305 million. What was the rate of population change per year?

29. **TICKETS** The graph shows the cost of buying tickets to a concert.

   a. What does the point (4, 122) represent?
   b. What is the unit rate?
   c. What is the cost of buying 10 tickets?

30. **CRITICAL THINKING** Are the two statements equivalent? Explain your reasoning.

   • The ratio of boys to girls is 2 to 3.

   • The ratio of girls to boys is 3 to 2.

31. **TENNIS** A sports store sells three different packs of tennis balls. Which pack is the best buy? Explain.

Beverage	Serving Size	Calories	Sodium
Whole milk	1 cup	146	98 mg
Orange juice	1 pt	210	10 mg
Apple juice	24 fl oz	351	21 mg

32. **NUTRITION** The table shows nutritional information for three beverages.

   a. Which has the most calories per fluid ounce?
   b. Which has the least sodium per fluid ounce?

33. **Open-Ended** Fire hydrants are painted four different colors to indicate the rate at which water comes from the hydrant.

   a. **RESEARCH** Use the Internet to find the ranges of the rates for each color.

   b. Research why a firefighter needs to know the rate at which water comes out of the hydrant.

 Fair Game Review What you learned in previous grades & lessons

Plot the ordered pair in a coordinate plane. *(Section 1.6)*

34. $A(-5, -2)$ 35. $B(-3, 0)$ 36. $C(-1, 2)$ 37. $D(1, 4)$

38. **MULTIPLE CHOICE** Which fraction is greater than $-\frac{2}{3}$ and less than $-\frac{1}{2}$? *(Section 2.1)*

   Ⓐ $-\frac{3}{4}$ Ⓑ $-\frac{7}{12}$ Ⓒ $-\frac{5}{12}$ Ⓓ $-\frac{3}{8}$

3.2 Slope

Essential Question How can you compare two rates graphically?

1 ACTIVITY: Comparing Unit Rates

Work with a partner. The table shows the maximum speeds of several animals.

a. Find the missing speeds. Round your answers to the nearest tenth.

b. Which animal is fastest? Which animal is slowest?

c. Explain how you convert between the two units of speed.

Animal	Speed (miles per hour)	Speed (feet per second)
Antelope	61.0	
Black Mamba Snake		29.3
Cheetah		102.6
Chicken		13.2
Coyote	43.0	
Domestic Pig		16.0
Elephant		36.6
Elk		66.0
Giant Tortoise	0.2	
Giraffe	32.0	
Gray Fox		61.6
Greyhound	39.4	
Grizzly Bear		44.0
Human		41.0
Hyena	40.0	
Jackal	35.0	
Lion		73.3
Peregrine Falcon	200.0	
Quarter Horse	47.5	
Spider		1.76
Squirrel	12.0	
Thomson's Gazelle	50.0	
Three-Toed Sloth		0.2
Tuna	47.0	

ACTIVITY: Comparing Two Rates Graphically

Work with a partner. A cheetah and a Thomson's gazelle are running at constant speeds.

a. Find the missing distances.

Time (seconds)	Cheetah Distance (feet)	Gazelle Distance (feet)
0	0	0
1	102.6	
2		
3		
4		
5		
6		
7		

b. Use the table to complete the line graph for each animal.

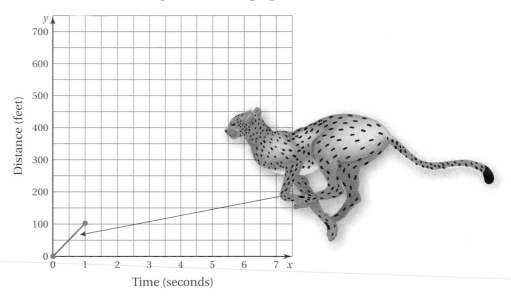

c. Which graph is steeper? The speed of which animal is greater?

What Is Your Answer?

3. **IN YOUR OWN WORDS** How can you compare two rates graphically? Explain your reasoning. Give some examples with your answer.

4. Choose 10 animals from Activity 1.

    a. Make a table for each animal similar to the table in Activity 2.
    b. Sketch a graph of the distances for each animal.
    c. Compare the steepness of the 10 graphs. What can you conclude?

Check It Out
Lesson Tutorials
BigIdeasMath ✓com

Key Vocabulary ◀))
slope, p. 106

 Key Idea

Slope

Slope is the rate of change between any two points on a line. It is a measure of the *steepness* of a line.

To find the slope of a line, find the ratio of the change in *y* (vertical change) to the change in *x* (horizontal change).

$$\text{slope} = \frac{\text{change in } y}{\text{change in } x}$$

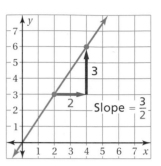

EXAMPLE **1**   **Finding Slopes**

Find the slope of each line.

a.
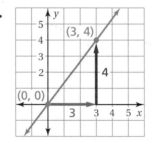

$$\text{slope} = \frac{\text{change in } y}{\text{change in } x}$$

$$= \frac{4}{3}$$

∵· The slope of the line is $\frac{4}{3}$.

b.
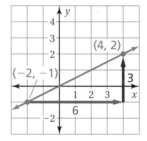

$$\text{slope} = \frac{\text{change in } y}{\text{change in } x}$$

$$= \frac{3}{6} = \frac{1}{2}$$

∵· The slope of the line is $\frac{1}{2}$.

 On Your Own

Now You're Ready
Exercises 4–9

Find the slope of the line.

1.

2.

◀)) Multi-Language Glossary at BigIdeasMath✓com.

EXAMPLE **2** **Finding a Slope**

The table shows your earnings for babysitting.

a. Graph the data.

b. Find and interpret the slope of the line through the points.

Hours, x	0	2	4	6	8	10
Earnings, y (dollars)	0	10	20	30	40	50

a. Graph the data. Draw a line through the points.

b. Choose any two points to find the slope of the line.

$$\text{slope} = \frac{\text{change in } y}{\text{change in } x}$$

$$= \frac{20 \leftarrow \boxed{\text{dollars}}}{4 \leftarrow \boxed{\text{hours}}}$$

$$= 5$$

∴ The slope of the line is 5. So, you earn $5 per hour babysitting.

On Your Own

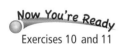
Now You're Ready
Exercises 10 and 11

3. In Example 2, use two other points to find the slope. Does the slope change?

4. The graph shows the earnings of you and your friend for babysitting.

a. Compare the steepness of the lines. What does this mean in the context of the problem?

b. Find and interpret the slope of the blue line.

Vocabulary and Concept Check

1. **VOCABULARY** Is there a connection between rate and slope? Explain.

2. **REASONING** Which line has the greatest slope?

3. **REASONING** Is it more difficult to run up a ramp with a slope of $\frac{1}{5}$ or a ramp with a slope of 5? Explain.

Practice and Problem Solving

Find the slope of the line.

① 4.

5.

6.

7.

8.

9.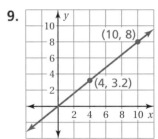

Graph the data. Then find the slope of the line through the points.

② 10.

Minutes, x	3	5	7	9
Words, y	135	225	315	405

11.

Gallons, x	5	10	15	20
Miles, y	162.5	325	487.5	650

Graph the line that passes through the two points. Then find the slope of the line.

12. $(0, 0), (5, 8)$

13. $(-2, -2), (2, 2)$

14. $(10, 4), (-5, -2)$

15. ERROR ANALYSIS Describe and correct the error in finding the slope of the line passing through $(0, 0)$ and $(4, 5)$.

$$slope = \frac{4}{5}$$

16. **CAMPING** The graph shows the amount of money you and a friend are saving for a camping trip.

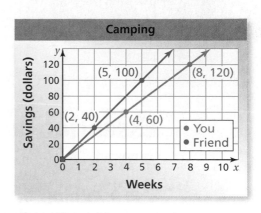

Camping

a. Compare the steepness of the lines. What does this mean in the context of the problem?

b. Find the slope of each line.

c. How much more money does your friend save each week than you?

d. The camping trip costs $165. How long will it take you to save enough money?

17. **MAPS** The table shows data from a key to a map of Ohio.

Distance on Map (mm), x	10	20	30	40
Actual Distance (mi), y	25	50	75	100

a. Graph the data.

b. Find the slope of the line. What does this mean in the context of the problem?

c. The map distance between Toledo and Columbus is 48 millimeters. What is the actual distance?

d. Cincinnati is about 225 miles from Cleveland. What is the distance between these cities on the map?

18. **CRITICAL THINKING** What is the slope of a line that passes through the points (2, 0) and (5, 0)? Explain.

19. **Number Sense** A line has a slope of 2. It passes through the points (1, 2) and (3, y). What is the value of y?

Fair Game Review What you learned in previous grades & lessons

Copy and complete the statement using <, >, or =. *(Section 2.1)*

20. $\dfrac{9}{2}$ ☐ $\dfrac{8}{3}$

21. $-\dfrac{8}{15}$ ☐ $\dfrac{10}{18}$

22. $\dfrac{-6}{24}$ ☐ $\dfrac{-2}{8}$

Multiply. *(Section 2.3)*

23. $-\dfrac{3}{5} \times \dfrac{8}{6}$

24. $1\dfrac{1}{2} \times \left(-\dfrac{6}{15}\right)$

25. $-2\dfrac{1}{4} \times -1\dfrac{1}{3}$

26. **MULTIPLE CHOICE** You have 18 stamps from Mexico in your stamp collection. These stamps are $\dfrac{3}{8}$ of your collection. The rest of the stamps are from the United States. How many stamps are from the United States? *(Section 2.5)*

Ⓐ 12 Ⓑ 24 Ⓒ 30 Ⓓ 48

Essential Question How can proportions help you decide when things are "fair?"

The Meaning of a Word ● Proportional

When you work toward a goal, your success is usually **proportional** to the amount of work you put in.

An equation stating that two ratios are equal is a **proportion**.

1 ACTIVITY: Determining Proportions

Work with a partner. Tell whether the two ratios are equivalent. If they are not equivalent, change the second day to make the ratios equivalent. Explain your reasoning.

a. On the first day, you pay $5 for 2 boxes of popcorn. The next day, you pay $7.50 for 3 boxes.

First Day

$$\dfrac{\$5.00}{\$7.50} \overset{?}{=} \dfrac{2 \text{ boxes}}{3 \text{ boxes}}$$

Next Day

b. On the first day, it takes you 3 hours to drive 135 miles. The next day, it takes you 5 hours to drive 200 miles.

First Day

$$\dfrac{3 \text{ h}}{5 \text{ h}} \overset{?}{=} \dfrac{135 \text{ mi}}{200 \text{ mi}}$$

Next Day

c. On the first day, you walk 4 miles and burn 300 calories. The next day, you walk 3 miles and burn 225 calories.

First Day

$$\dfrac{4 \text{ mi}}{3 \text{ mi}} \overset{?}{=} \dfrac{300 \text{ cal}}{225 \text{ cal}}$$

Next Day

d. On the first day, you download 5 songs and pay $2.25. The next day, you download 4 songs and pay $2.00.

First Day

$$\dfrac{5 \text{ songs}}{4 \text{ songs}} \overset{?}{=} \dfrac{\$2.25}{\$2.00}$$

Next Day

2 ACTIVITY: Checking a Proportion

Work with a partner.

a. It is said that "one year in a dog's life is equivalent to seven years in a human's life." Explain why Newton thinks he has a score of 105 points. Did he solve the proportion correctly?

$$\frac{1 \text{ year}}{7 \text{ years}} \stackrel{?}{=} \frac{15 \text{ points}}{105 \text{ points}}$$

b. If Newton thinks his score is 98 points, how many points does he actually have? Explain your reasoning.

"I got 15 on my online test. That's 105 in dog points! Isn't that an A+?"

3 ACTIVITY: Determining Fairness

Work with a partner. Write a ratio for each sentence. If they are equal, then the answer is "It is fair." If they are not equal, then the answer is "It is not fair." Explain your reasoning.

a. You pay $184 for 2 tickets to a concert. & I pay $266 for 3 tickets to the same concert. → Is this fair?

b. You get 75 points for answering 15 questions correctly. & I get 70 points for answering 14 questions correctly. → Is this fair?

c. You trade 24 football cards for 15 baseball cards. & I trade 20 football cards for 32 baseball cards. → Is this fair?

What Is Your Answer?

4. Find a recipe for something you like to eat. Then show how two of the ingredient amounts are proportional when you double or triple the recipe.

5. **IN YOUR OWN WORDS** How can proportions help you decide when things are "fair?" Give an example.

Practice → Use what you discovered about proportions to complete Exercises 17–22 on page 114.

Key Idea

Key Vocabulary
proportion, *p. 112*
proportional, *p. 112*
cross products, *p. 113*

Proportions

Words A **proportion** is an equation stating that two ratios are equivalent. Two quantities that form a proportion are **proportional**.

Numbers $\dfrac{2}{3} = \dfrac{4}{6}$ The proportion is read "2 is to 3 as 4 is to 6."

EXAMPLE 1 **Determining Whether Ratios Form a Proportion**

Tell whether the ratios form a proportion.

a. $\dfrac{4}{10}$ and $\dfrac{10}{25}$

Compare the ratios in simplest form.

$$\frac{4}{10} = \frac{4 \div 2}{10 \div 2} = \frac{2}{5}$$

$$\frac{10}{25} = \frac{10 \div 5}{25 \div 5} = \frac{2}{5}$$

The ratios are equivalent.

So, $\dfrac{4}{10}$ and $\dfrac{10}{25}$ form a proportion.

b. $\dfrac{6}{4}$ and $\dfrac{8}{12}$

Compare the ratios in simplest form.

$$\frac{6}{4} = \frac{6 \div 2}{4 \div 2} = \frac{3}{2}$$

$$\frac{8}{12} = \frac{8 \div 4}{12 \div 4} = \frac{2}{3}$$

The ratios are not equivalent.

So, $\dfrac{6}{4}$ and $\dfrac{8}{12}$ do not form a proportion.

On Your Own

Now You're Ready
Exercises 5–16

Tell whether the ratios form a proportion.

1. $\dfrac{1}{2}, \dfrac{5}{10}$

2. $\dfrac{4}{6}, \dfrac{18}{24}$

3. $\dfrac{10}{3}, \dfrac{5}{6}$

4. $\dfrac{25}{20}, \dfrac{15}{12}$

Multi-Language Glossary at BigIdeasMath.com.

Key Ideas

Cross Products

In the proportion $\frac{a}{b} = \frac{c}{d}$, the products $a \cdot d$ and $b \cdot c$ are called **cross products**.

Cross Products Property

Words The cross products of a proportion are equal.

Numbers

$$2 \cdot 6 = 3 \cdot 4$$

Algebra

$$\frac{a}{b} = \frac{c}{d}$$

$$ad = bc,$$
where $b \neq 0$ and $d \neq 0$

EXAMPLE 2 | **Identifying Proportional Relationships**

1 length   1 lap

You swim your first 4 laps in 2.4 minutes. You complete 16 laps in 12 minutes. Is the number of laps proportional to your time?

Method 1: Compare unit rates.

$$\frac{2.4 \text{ min}}{4 \text{ laps}} = \frac{0.6 \text{ min}}{1 \text{ lap}} \qquad \frac{12 \text{ min}}{16 \text{ laps}} = \frac{0.75 \text{ min}}{1 \text{ lap}}$$

÷ 4 ... ÷ 4   ÷ 16 ... ÷ 16

The unit rates are not equivalent.

⋮ So, the number of laps is not proportional to the time.

Method 2: Use the Cross Products Property.

$$\frac{2.4 \text{ min}}{4 \text{ laps}} \stackrel{?}{=} \frac{12 \text{ min}}{16 \text{ laps}}$$ 	Test to see if the rates are equivalent.

$$2.4 \cdot 16 \stackrel{?}{=} 4 \cdot 12$$ 	Find the cross products.

$$38.4 \neq 48$$ 	The cross products are not equal.

⋮ So, the number of laps is not proportional to the time.

On Your Own

Exercises 17–22

5. You read the first 20 pages of a book in 25 minutes. You read 36 pages in 45 minutes. Is the number of pages read proportional to your time?

Vocabulary and Concept Check

1. **VOCABULARY** What does it mean for two ratios to form a proportion?

2. **VOCABULARY** What are two ways you can tell that two ratios form a proportion?

3. **OPEN-ENDED** Write two ratios that are equivalent to $\frac{3}{5}$.

4. **WHICH ONE DOESN'T BELONG?** Which ratio does *not* belong with the other three? Explain your reasoning.

$$\frac{4}{10} \qquad \frac{2}{5} \qquad \frac{3}{5} \qquad \frac{6}{15}$$

 Practice and Problem Solving

Tell whether the ratios form a proportion.

① 5. $\frac{1}{3}, \frac{7}{21}$ 6. $\frac{1}{5}, \frac{6}{30}$ 7. $\frac{3}{4}, \frac{24}{18}$

8. $\frac{2}{5}, \frac{40}{16}$ 9. $\frac{48}{9}, \frac{16}{3}$ 10. $\frac{18}{27}, \frac{33}{44}$

11. $\frac{7}{2}, \frac{16}{6}$ 12. $\frac{12}{10}, \frac{14}{12}$ 13. $\frac{27}{15}, \frac{18}{10}$

14. $\frac{4}{15}, \frac{15}{42}$ 15. $\frac{76}{36}, \frac{19}{9}$ 16. $\frac{49}{77}, \frac{38}{57}$

Tell whether the two rates form a proportion.

② 17. 7 inches in 9 hours; 42 inches in 54 hours

18. 12 players from 21 teams; 15 players from 24 teams

19. 440 calories in 4 servings; 300 calories in 3 servings

20. 120 units made in 5 days; 88 units made in 4 days

21. 66 wins in 82 games; 99 wins in 123 games

22. 68 hits in 172 at bats; 43 hits in 123 at bats

23. **FITNESS** You can do 90 sit-ups in 2 minutes. Your friend can do 135 sit-ups in 3 minutes. Are these rates proportional? Explain.

24. **HEARTBEAT** Find the heartbeat rates of you and your friend. Do these rates form a proportion? Explain.

	Heartbeats	Seconds
You	22	20
Friend	18	15

Tell whether the ratios form a proportion.

25. $\dfrac{3}{8}, \dfrac{31.5}{84}$

26. $\dfrac{14}{30}, \dfrac{75.6}{180}$

27. $\dfrac{2.5}{4}, \dfrac{7}{11.2}$

28. **PAY RATE** You earn $56 walking your neighbor's dog for 8 hours. Your friend earns $36 painting your neighbor's fence for 4 hours.

   a. What is your pay rate?

   b. What is your friend's pay rate?

   c. Are the pay rates equivalent? Explain.

29. **GEOMETRY** Are the ratios of h to b in the two triangles proportional? Explain.

30. **MUSIC** You can buy 3 CDs for $52.20 or 5 CDs for $62.45. Are the rates proportional? Explain.

31. **BASEBALL** The table shows pitching statistics for four pitchers during the 2008 season.

   a. Which pitcher has the highest ratio of strikeouts to walks?

   b. Which of the pitchers have equivalent strikeout to walk ratios?

2008 Season		
Pitcher	**Strikeouts**	**Walks**
Pitcher 1	6	8
Pitcher 2	8	4
Pitcher 3	10	1
Pitcher 4	10	5

32. **NAIL POLISH** A specific shade of red nail polish requires 7 parts red to 2 parts yellow. A mixture contains 35 quarts of red and 8 quarts of yellow. How can you fix the mixture to make the correct shade of red?

33. **COIN COLLECTION** The ratio of quarters to dimes in a coin collection is 5 : 3. The same number of new quarters and dimes are added to the collection.

   a. Is the ratio of quarters to dimes still 5 : 3?

   b. If so, illustrate your answer with an example. If not, show why with a "counterexample."

34. **Critical Thinking** Ratio A is equivalent to ratio B. Ratio B is equivalent to ratio C. Is ratio A equivalent to ratio C? Explain.

Fair Game Review What you learned in previous grades & lessons

Add or subtract. *(Sections 1.2 and 1.3)*

35. $-28 + 15$

36. $-6 + (-11)$

37. $-10 - 8$

38. $-17 - (-14)$

39. **MULTIPLE CHOICE** Which fraction is not equivalent to $\dfrac{2}{6}$? *(Skills Review Handbook)*

   Ⓐ $\dfrac{1}{3}$
   Ⓑ $\dfrac{12}{36}$
   Ⓒ $\dfrac{4}{12}$
   Ⓓ $\dfrac{6}{9}$

Essential Question How can you write a proportion that solves a problem in real life?

1 ACTIVITY: Writing Proportions

Work with a partner. A rough rule for finding the correct bat length is "The bat length should be half of the batter's height." So, a 62-inch-tall batter uses a bat that is 31 inches long. Write a proportion to find the bat length for each given batter height.

a. 58 inches

b. 60 inches

c. 64 inches

2x

x

2 ACTIVITY: Bat Lengths

Work with a partner. Here is a more accurate table for determining the bat length for a batter. Find all of the batter heights for which the rough rule in Activity 1 is exact.

	Height of Batter (inches)							
Weight of Batter (pounds)	45–48	49–52	53–56	57–60	61–64	65–68	69–72	Over 72
Under 61	28	29	29					
61–70	28	29	30	30				
71–80	28	29	30	30	31			
81–90	29	29	30	30	31	32		
91–100	29	30	30	31	31	32		
101–110	29	30	30	31	31	32		
111–120	29	30	30	31	31	32		
121–130	29	30	30	31	32	33	33	
131–140	30	30	31	31	32	33	33	
141–150	30	30	31	31	32	33	33	
151–160	30	31	31	32	32	33	33	33
161–170		31	31	32	32	33	33	34
171–180				32	33	33	34	34
Over 180					33	33	34	34

Bat length

Work with a partner. The batting average of a baseball player is the number of "hits" divided by the number of "at bats."

$$\text{Batting average} = \frac{\text{Hits } (H)}{\text{At bats } (A)}$$

A player whose batting average is 0.250 is said to be "batting 250."

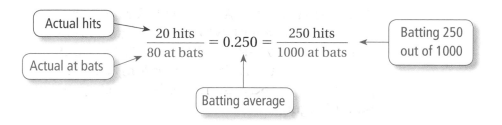

Write a proportion to find how many hits H a player needs to achieve the given batting average. Then solve the proportion.

a. 50 times at bat; batting average is 0.200.

b. 84 times at bat; batting average is 0.250.

c. 80 times at bat; batting average is 0.350.

d. 1 time at bat; batting average is 1.000.

What Is Your Answer?

4. **IN YOUR OWN WORDS** How can you write a proportion that solves a problem in real life?

5. Two players have the same batting average.

	At Bats	Hits	Batting Average
Player 1	132	45	
Player 2	132	45	

Player 1 gets four hits in the next five at bats. Player 2 gets three hits in the next three at bats.

a. Who has the higher batting average?

b. Does this seem fair? Explain your reasoning.

Practice

Use what you discovered about proportions to complete Exercises 4–7 on page 120.

One way to write a proportion is to use a table.

	Last Month	This Month
Purchase	2 ringtones	3 ringtones
Total Cost	6 dollars	x dollars

Use the columns or the rows to write a proportion.

Use columns:

$$\frac{2 \text{ ringtones}}{6 \text{ dollars}} = \frac{3 \text{ ringtones}}{x \text{ dollars}}$$

← Numerators have the same units.

← Denominators have the same units.

Use rows:

$$\frac{2 \text{ ringtones}}{3 \text{ ringtones}} = \frac{6 \text{ dollars}}{x \text{ dollars}}$$

The units are the same on each side of the proportion.

EXAMPLE 1 Writing a Proportion

Black Bean Soup

1.5 cups black beans
0.5 cup salsa
2 cups water
1 tomato
2 teaspoons seasoning

A chef increases the amounts of ingredients in a recipe to make a proportional recipe. The new recipe has 6 cups of black beans. Write a proportion that gives the number x of tomatoes in the new recipe.

Organize the information in a table.

	Original Recipe	New Recipe
Black Beans	1.5 cups	6 cups
Tomatoes	1 tomato	x tomatoes

∴ One proportion is $\dfrac{1.5 \text{ cups beans}}{1 \text{ tomato}} = \dfrac{6 \text{ cups beans}}{x \text{ tomatoes}}$.

On Your Own

Now You're Ready
Exercises 8–11

1. In Example 1, write a different proportion that gives the number x of tomatoes in the new recipe.

2. In Example 1, write a proportion that gives the amount y of water in the new recipe.

EXAMPLE 2 **Solving Proportions Using Mental Math**

Solve $\dfrac{3}{2} = \dfrac{x}{8}$.

Step 1: Think: The product of 2 and what number is 8?

$$\dfrac{3}{2} = \dfrac{x}{8}$$

$2 \times ? = 8$

Step 2: Because the product of 2 and 4 is 8, multiply the numerator by 4 to find x.

$3 \times 4 = 12$

$$\dfrac{3}{2} = \dfrac{x}{8}$$

$2 \times 4 = 8$

∴ The solution is $x = 12$.

EXAMPLE 3 **Solving Proportions Using Mental Math**

In Example 1, how many tomatoes are in the new recipe?

Solve the proportion $\dfrac{1.5}{1} = \dfrac{6}{x}$. ← cups black beans
← tomatoes

Step 1: Think: The product of 1.5 and what number is 6?

$1.5 \times ? = 6$

$$\dfrac{1.5}{1} = \dfrac{6}{x}$$

Step 2: Because the product of 1.5 and 4 is 6, multiply the denominator by 4 to find x.

$1.5 \times 4 = 6$

$$\dfrac{1.5}{1} = \dfrac{6}{x}$$

$1 \times 4 = 4$

∴ So, there are 4 tomatoes in the new recipe.

● **On Your Own**

Now You're Ready
Exercises 16–21

Solve the proportion.

3. $\dfrac{5}{8} = \dfrac{20}{d}$

4. $\dfrac{7}{z} = \dfrac{14}{10}$

5. $\dfrac{21}{24} = \dfrac{x}{8}$

6. A school has 950 students. The ratio of female students to all students is $\dfrac{48}{95}$. Write and solve a proportion to find the number f of students that are female.

Vocabulary and Concept Check

1. **WRITING** Describe two ways you can use a table to write a proportion.

2. **WRITING** What is your first step when solving $\frac{x}{15} = \frac{3}{5}$? Explain.

3. **OPEN-ENDED** Write a proportion using an unknown value x and the ratio $5:6$. Then solve it.

 Practice and Problem Solving

Write a proportion to find how many points a student needs to score on the test to get the given score.

4. Test worth 50 points; test score of 40%

5. Test worth 50 points; test score of 78%

6. Test worth 80 points; test score of 80%

7. Test worth 150 points; test score of 96%

Use the table to write a proportion.

8.

	Game 1	Game 2
Points	12	18
Shots	14	w

9.

	May	June
Winners	n	34
Entries	85	170

10.

	Today	Yesterday
Miles	15	m
Hours	2.5	4

11.

	Race 1	Race 2
Meters	100	200
Seconds	x	22.4

12. **ERROR ANALYSIS** Describe and correct the error in writing the proportion.

	Monday	Tuesday
Dollars	2.08	d
Ounces	8	16

$$\frac{2.08}{16} = \frac{d}{8}$$

13. **T-SHIRTS** You can buy three T-shirts for $24. Write a proportion that gives the cost c of buying seven T-shirts.

14. **COMPUTERS** A school requires two computers for every five students. Write a proportion that gives the number c of computers needed for 145 students.

15. **SWIM TEAM** The school team has 80 swimmers. The ratio of 6th grade swimmers to all swimmers is $5:16$. Write a proportion that gives the number s of 6th grade swimmers.

Solve the proportion.

 16. $\dfrac{1}{4} = \dfrac{z}{20}$

17. $\dfrac{3}{4} = \dfrac{12}{y}$

18. $\dfrac{35}{k} = \dfrac{7}{3}$

19. $\dfrac{15}{8} = \dfrac{45}{c}$

20. $\dfrac{b}{36} = \dfrac{5}{9}$

21. $\dfrac{1.4}{2.5} = \dfrac{g}{25}$

22. ORCHESTRA In an orchestra, the ratio of trombones to violas is 1 to 3.

    a. There are nine violas. Write a proportion that gives the number t of trombones in the orchestra.

    b. How many trombones are in the orchestra?

23. ATLANTIS Your science teacher has a $1:200$ scale model of the Space Shuttle Atlantis. Which of the proportions can be used to find the actual length x of Atlantis? Explain.

$$\dfrac{1}{200} = \dfrac{19.5}{x} \qquad \dfrac{1}{200} = \dfrac{x}{19.5} \qquad \dfrac{200}{19.5} = \dfrac{x}{1} \qquad \dfrac{x}{200} = \dfrac{1}{19.5}$$

19.5 cm

24. YOU BE THE TEACHER Your friend says "$48x = 6 \cdot 12$." Is your friend right? Explain.

> Solve $\dfrac{6}{x} = \dfrac{12}{48}$.

25. **Reasoning** There are 180 white lockers in the school. There are 3 white lockers for every 5 blue lockers. How many lockers are in the school?

 Fair Game Review What you learned in previous grades & lessons

Solve the equation. *(Section 2.5)*

26. $\dfrac{x}{6} = 25$

27. $8x = 72$

28. $150 = 2x$

29. $35 = \dfrac{x}{4}$

30. MULTIPLE CHOICE Which is the slope of a line? *(Section 3.2)*

    Ⓐ $\dfrac{\text{change in } y}{1}$ Ⓑ $\dfrac{\text{change in } x}{1}$ Ⓒ $\dfrac{\text{change in } x}{\text{change in } y}$ Ⓓ $\dfrac{\text{change in } y}{\text{change in } x}$

3.5 Solving Proportions

Essential Question
How can you use ratio tables and cross products to solve proportions in science?

1 ACTIVITY: Solving a Proportion in Science

SCIENCE Scientists use *ratio tables* to determine the amount of a compound (like salt) that is dissolved in a solution. Work with a partner to show how scientists use cross products to determine the unknown quantity in a ratio.

a. Sample: Salt Water

Salt Water	1 L	3 L
Salt	250 g	x g

1 liter   3 liter

$$\frac{3\,\cancel{L}}{1\,\cancel{L}} = \frac{x\,\cancel{g}}{250\,\cancel{g}} \qquad \text{Write proportion.}$$

$$3 \cdot 250 = 1 \cdot x \qquad \text{Set cross products equal.}$$

$$750 = x \qquad \text{Simplify.}$$

So, there are 750 grams of salt in the 3-liter solution.

b. White Glue Solution

Water	½ cup	1 cup
White Glue	½ cup	x cups

c. Borax Solution

Borax	1 tsp	2 tsp
Water	1 cup	x cups

d. Slime (see recipe)

Borax Solution	½ cup	1 cup
White Glue Solution	y cups	x cups

Recipe for SLIME

1. Add ½ cup of water and ½ cup white glue. Mix thoroughly. This is your white glue solution.

2. Add a couple drops of food coloring to the glue solution. Mix thoroughly.

3. Add 1 teaspoon of borax to 1 cup of water. Mix thoroughly. This is your borax solution (about 1 cup).

4. Pour the borax solution and the glue solution into a separate bowl.

5. Place the slime that forms in a plastic bag and squeeze the mixture repeatedly to mix it up.

ACTIVITY: The Game of Criss Cross

CRISS CROSS

Preparation:

- Cut index cards to make 48 playing cards.

- Write each number on a card.

  1, 1, 1, 2, 2, 2, 3, 3, 3, 4, 4, 4, 5, 5, 5, 6, 6, 6, 7, 7,

  7, 8, 8, 8, 9, 9, 9, 10, 10, 10, 12, 12, 12, 13, 13,

  13, 14, 14, 14, 15, 15, 15, 16, 16, 16, 18, 20, 25

- Make a copy of the game board.

To Play:

- Play with a partner.

- Deal 8 cards to each player.

- Begin by drawing a card from the remaining cards. Use four of your cards to try to form a proportion.

- Lay the four cards on the game board. If you form a proportion, say "Criss Cross" and you earn 4 points. Place the four cards in a discard pile. Now it is your partner's turn.

- If you cannot form a proportion, then it is your partner's turn.

- When the original pile of cards is empty, shuffle the cards in the discard pile and start again.

- The first player to reach 20 points wins.

What Is Your Answer?

3. **IN YOUR OWN WORDS** How can you use ratio tables and cross products to solve proportions in science? Give an example.

4. **PUZZLE** Use each number once to form three proportions.

1	2	10	4	12	20

15	5	16	6	8	3

Practice ➤ Use what you discovered about solving proportions to complete Exercises 10–13 on page 126.

Check It Out
Lesson Tutorials
BigIdeasMath $\checkmark$com

 Key Idea

Solving Proportions

Method 1 Use mental math. *(Section 3.4)*

Method 2 Use the Multiplication Property of Equality. *(Section 3.5)*

Method 3 Use the Cross Products Property. *(Section 3.5)*

EXAMPLE 1 **Solving Proportions Using Multiplication**

Solve $\dfrac{5}{7} = \dfrac{x}{21}$.

$\dfrac{5}{7} = \dfrac{x}{21}$ Write the proportion.

$21 \cdot \dfrac{5}{7} = 21 \cdot \dfrac{x}{21}$ Multiply each side by 21.

$15 = x$ Simplify.

∴ The solution is 15.

On Your Own

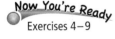
Now You're Ready
Exercises 4−9

Solve the proportion using multiplication.

1. $\dfrac{w}{6} = \dfrac{6}{9}$ 2. $\dfrac{12}{10} = \dfrac{a}{15}$ 3. $\dfrac{y}{6} = \dfrac{2}{4}$

EXAMPLE 2 **Solving Proportions Using the Cross Products Property**

Solve each proportion.

a. $\dfrac{x}{8} = \dfrac{7}{10}$ b. $\dfrac{9}{y} = \dfrac{3}{17}$

$x \cdot 10 = 8 \cdot 7$ Use the Cross Products Property. $9 \cdot 17 = y \cdot 3$

$10x = 56$ Multiply. $153 = 3y$

$x = 5.6$ Divide. $51 = y$

∴ The solution is 5.6.   ∴ The solution is 51.

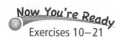
Now You're Ready
Exercises 10–21

On Your Own

Solve the proportion using the Cross Products Property.

4. $\dfrac{2}{7} = \dfrac{x}{28}$

5. $\dfrac{12}{5} = \dfrac{6}{y}$

6. $\dfrac{40}{z+1} = \dfrac{15}{6}$

EXAMPLE 3 **Real-Life Application**

The toll due on a turnpike is proportional to the number of miles driven. How much does it cost to drive 150 miles?

> **TOLL PLAZA**
> **$^1/_2$ MILE**
> **REDUCE SPEED**

Turnpike

Method 1: Interpret the slope as a unit rate.

$$\text{slope} = \frac{\text{change in } y}{\text{change in } x}$$

$$= \frac{7.5}{100} \qquad \text{Substitute.}$$

$$= 0.075 \qquad \text{Divide.}$$

The unit rate is $0.075 per mile. Multiply to find the total cost.

$$150 \text{ mi} \cdot \frac{\$0.075}{1 \text{ mi}} = \$11.25$$

∴ It costs $11.25 to drive 150 miles on the turnpike.

Method 2: Write and solve a proportion.

$$\frac{7.5}{100} = \frac{x}{150} \quad \leftarrow \text{dollars} \atop \leftarrow \text{miles} \qquad \text{Use (100, 7.5) to write a proportion.}$$

$$150 \cdot \frac{7.5}{100} = 150 \cdot \frac{x}{150} \qquad \text{Multiply each side by 150.}$$

$$11.25 = x \qquad \text{Simplify.}$$

∴ It costs $11.25 to drive 150 miles on the turnpike.

On Your Own

7. **WHAT IF?** In Example 3, how much does it cost to drive 75 miles on the turnpike?

Vocabulary and Concept Check

1. **WRITING** What are three ways you can solve a proportion?

2. **OPEN-ENDED** Which way would you choose to solve $\dfrac{3}{x} = \dfrac{6}{14}$? Explain your reasoning.

3. **NUMBER SENSE** Does $\dfrac{x}{4} = \dfrac{15}{3}$ have the same solution as $\dfrac{x}{15} = \dfrac{4}{3}$? Use the Cross Products Property to explain your answer.

Practice and Problem Solving

Solve the proportion using multiplication.

4. $\dfrac{9}{5} = \dfrac{z}{20}$

5. $\dfrac{h}{15} = \dfrac{16}{3}$

6. $\dfrac{w}{4} = \dfrac{42}{24}$

7. $\dfrac{35}{28} = \dfrac{n}{12}$

8. $\dfrac{7}{16} = \dfrac{x}{4}$

9. $\dfrac{y}{9} = \dfrac{44}{54}$

Solve the proportion using the Cross Products Property.

10. $\dfrac{a}{6} = \dfrac{15}{2}$

11. $\dfrac{10}{7} = \dfrac{8}{k}$

12. $\dfrac{3}{4} = \dfrac{v}{14}$

13. $\dfrac{5}{n} = \dfrac{16}{32}$

14. $\dfrac{36}{42} = \dfrac{24}{r}$

15. $\dfrac{9}{10} = \dfrac{d}{6.4}$

16. $\dfrac{x}{8} = \dfrac{3}{12}$

17. $\dfrac{8}{m} = \dfrac{6}{15}$

18. $\dfrac{4}{24} = \dfrac{c}{36}$

19. $\dfrac{20}{16} = \dfrac{d}{12}$

20. $\dfrac{30}{20} = \dfrac{w}{14}$

21. $\dfrac{2.4}{1.8} = \dfrac{7.2}{k}$

22. **ERROR ANALYSIS** Describe and correct the error in solving the proportion $\dfrac{m}{8} = \dfrac{15}{24}$.

$$\times \quad \dfrac{m}{8} = \dfrac{15}{24}$$
$$8 \cdot m = 24 \cdot 15$$
$$m = 45$$

23. **PENS** Forty-eight pens are packaged in four boxes. How many pens are packaged in nine boxes?

24. **PIZZA PARTY** How much does it cost to buy 10 medium pizzas?

3 Medium Pizzas for $10.50

Solve the proportion.

25. $\dfrac{2x}{5} = \dfrac{9}{15}$

26. $\dfrac{5}{2} = \dfrac{d-2}{4}$

27. $\dfrac{4}{k+3} = \dfrac{8}{14}$

28. TRUE OR FALSE? Tell whether the statement is *true* or *false*. Explain.

If $\dfrac{a}{b} = \dfrac{2}{3}$, then $\dfrac{3}{2} = \dfrac{b}{a}$.

29. CLASS TRIP It costs $95 for 20 students to visit an aquarium. How much does it cost for 162 students?

30. GRAVITY A person who weighs 120 pounds on Earth weighs 20 pounds on the moon. How much does a 93-pound person weigh on the moon?

31. HAIR The length of human hair is proportional to the number of months it has grown.

    a. How long does it take hair to grow 8 inches?

    b. Use a different method than the one in part (a) to find how long it takes hair to grow 20 inches.

32. CHEETAH Cheetahs are the fastest mammals in the world. They can reach speeds of 70 miles per hour.

    a. At this speed, how long would it take a cheetah to run 17 miles?

    b. **RESEARCH** Use the Internet or library to find how long a cheetah can maintain a speed of 70 miles per hour.

33. AUDIENCE There are 144 people in an audience. The ratio of adults to children is 5 to 3. How many are adults?

34. LAWN SEED Three pounds of lawn seed covers 1800 square feet. How many bags are needed to cover 8400 square feet?

35. **Critical Thinking** Consider the proportions $m = \dfrac{1}{2}$ and $k = \dfrac{1}{4}$.

What is the ratio $\dfrac{m}{k}$? Explain your reasoning.

Fair Game Review What you learned in previous grades & lessons

Copy and complete. *(Skills Review Handbook)*

36. $530 \text{ cm} = \underline{} \text{ m}$

37. $6.4 \text{ kg} = \underline{} \text{ g}$

38. $56 \text{ oz} = \underline{} \text{ lb}$

39. $1\dfrac{1}{2} \text{ mi} = \underline{} \text{ ft}$

40. MULTIPLE CHOICE How many cups of milk are shown? *(Skills Review Handbook)*

  A $\dfrac{7}{10}$ c   **B** $\dfrac{7}{8}$ c

  C $1\dfrac{3}{4}$ c   **D** 14 c

You can use an **information wheel** to organize information about a concept. Here is an example of an information wheel for slope.

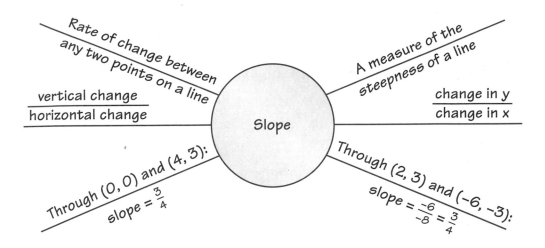

On Your Own

Make an information wheel to help you study these topics.

1. ratio
2. rate
3. unit rate
4. proportion
5. cross products
6. solving proportions

After you complete this chapter, make information wheels for the following topics.

7. U.S. customary system
8. metric system
9. converting units
10. direct variation
11. inverse variation

"My information wheel summarizes how cats act when they get baths."

Write the ratio as a fraction in simplest form. *(Section 3.1)*

1. 18 red buttons : 12 blue buttons

2. 30 inches to 3 inches

Find the unit rate. *(Section 3.1)*

3. 108 feet per 3 seconds

4. 360 miles per 12 gallons

Find the slope of the line. *(Section 3.2)*

5.

6.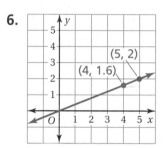

Tell whether the ratios form a proportion. *(Section 3.3)*

7. $\dfrac{1}{8}, \dfrac{4}{32}$

8. $\dfrac{2}{3}, \dfrac{10}{30}$

Use the table to write a proportion. *(Section 3.4)*

9.

	Monday	Tuesday
Dollars	42	56
Hours	6	h

10.

	Series 1	Series 2
Games	g	6
Wins	4	3

Solve the proportion. *(Section 3.5)*

11. $\dfrac{x}{2} = \dfrac{40}{16}$

12. $\dfrac{3}{11} = \dfrac{27}{z}$

13. **MUSIC DOWNLOAD** The amount of time needed to download music is shown in the table. Find the rate in megabytes per second. *(Section 3.1)*

Megabytes	Seconds
2	6
4	12
6	18
8	24

14. **GAMING** You advance 3 levels in 15 minutes. Your friend advances 5 levels in 20 minutes. Are these rates proportional? Explain. *(Section 3.3)*

15. **CLASS TIME** You spend 150 minutes in three classes. Write and solve a proportion to find how many minutes you spend in five classes. *(Section 3.4)*

16. **CONCERT** A benefit concert with three performers lasts 8 hours. At this rate, how many hours is a concert with four performers? *(Section 3.5)*

Essential Question How can you compare lengths between the customary and metric systems?

1 yard

6 feet

---

1 ACTIVITY: Customary Measure History

Work with a partner.

a. Match the measure of length with its historical beginning.

Length	Historical Beginning
Inch	The length of a human foot.
Foot	The width of a human thumb.
Yard	The distance a human can walk in 1000 paces (two steps).
Mile	The distance from a human nose to the end of an outstretched human arm.

b. Use a ruler to measure your thumb, arm, and foot. How do your measurements compare to your answers from part (a)? Are they close to the historical measures?

You know how to convert measures within the customary and metric systems.

Equivalent Customary Lengths

1 ft = 12 in.   1 yd = 3 ft   1 mi = 5280 ft

Equivalent Metric Lengths

1 m = 1000 mm   1 m = 100 cm   1 km = 1000 m

You will learn how to convert between the two systems.

Converting Between Systems

1 in. ≈ 2.54 cm

1 mi ≈ 1.6 km

2.54 cm

1 cm   2   3

1 in.

1 in.

Work with a partner. Answer each question. Explain your answer. Use a diagram in your explanation.

		Metric	*Customary*
a.	**Car Speed:** Which is faster?	80 km/h	60 mi/h
b.	**Trip Distance:** Which is farther?	200 km	200 mi
c.	**Human Height:** Who is taller?	180 cm	5 ft 8 in.
d.	**Wrench Width:** Which is wider?	8 mm	5/16 in.
e.	**Swimming Pool Depth:** Which is deeper?	1.4 m	4 ft
f.	**Mountain Elevation:** Which is higher?	2000 m	7000 ft
g.	**Room Width:** Which is wider?	3.5 m	12 ft

What Is Your Answer?

3. **IN YOUR OWN WORDS** How can you compare lengths between the customary and metric systems? Give examples with your description.

4. **HISTORY** The meter and the metric system originated in France. In 1791, the French Academy of Sciences was instructed to create a new system of measurement. This new system would be based on powers of 10.

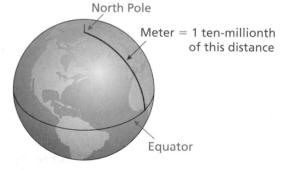

North Pole

Meter = 1 ten-millionth of this distance

Equator

The fundamental units of this system would be based on natural values that were unchanging. The French Academy of Sciences decided to find the length of an imaginary arc that began at the North Pole and ended at the equator.

They would then divide this arc into exactly ten million identical pieces. The length of one of these pieces would be the base unit of length for the new system of measurement.

a. Find the distance around Earth in meters.

b. Find the distance around Earth in kilometers.

5. Find the distance around Earth in miles.

Practice

Use what you learned about converting measures between systems to complete Exercises 4–9 on page 134.

Key Vocabulary ◄))
U.S. customary
system, *p. 132*
metric system, *p. 132*

The **U.S. customary system** is a system of measurement that contains units for length, capacity, and weight. The **metric system** is a decimal system of measurement, based on powers of 10, that contains units for length, capacity, and mass.

Use the relationships below to convert units *between* systems.

Length	Capacity	Weight and Mass
1 in. ≈ 2.54 cm	1 qt ≈ 0.95 L	1 lb ≈ 0.45 kg
1 mi ≈ 1.6 km		

EXAMPLE **1** **Converting Units**

Convert 5 liters to quarts.

Method 1: Convert using a ratio.

1 qt ≈ 0.95 L

$$5\,L \times \frac{1\text{ qt}}{0.95\,L} \approx 5.26\text{ qt}$$

∴ So, 5 liters is about 5.26 quarts.

Method 2: Convert using a proportion.

Let x be the number of quarts equivalent to 5 liters.

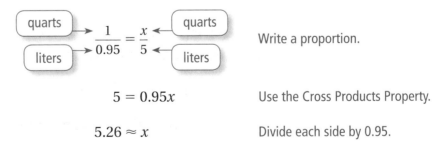

quarts → $\dfrac{1}{0.95} = \dfrac{x}{5}$ ← quarts
liters → ← liters   Write a proportion.

$5 = 0.95x$ Use the Cross Products Property.

$5.26 \approx x$ Divide each side by 0.95.

∴ So, 5 liters is about 5.26 quarts.

● **On Your Own**

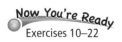
Now You're Ready
Exercises 10–22

Copy and complete the statement. Round to the nearest hundredth, if necessary.

1. 7 mi ≈ ▢ km

2. 12 qt ≈ ▢ L

3. 25 kg ≈ ▢ lb

4. 8 cm ≈ ▢ in.

EXAMPLE 2 Comparing Units

Copy and complete the statement using < or >: 25 oz ___ 2 kg.

Convert 25 ounces to kilograms.

| 1 lb = 16 oz | | 1 lb ≈ 0.45 kg |

$$25 \text{ oz} \times \frac{1 \text{ lb}}{16 \text{ oz}} \times \frac{0.45 \text{ kg}}{1 \text{ lb}} = \frac{25 \cdot 1 \cdot 0.45 \text{ kg}}{16 \cdot 1} \approx 0.70 \text{ kg}$$

∴ Because 0.70 kilogram is less than 2 kilograms, 25 oz < 2 kg.

On Your Own

Now You're Ready
Exercises 25–30

Copy and complete the statement using < or >.

5. 7 cm ___ 3 in. **6.** 8 c ___ 2 L **7.** 3 oz ___ 70 g

EXAMPLE 3 Converting a Rate

Which of the two remote controlled planes is faster?

Convert 50 miles per hour to kilometers per hour.

$$\frac{50 \text{ mi}}{1 \text{ h}} \times \frac{1.6 \text{ km}}{1 \text{ mi}} = \frac{80 \text{ km}}{1 \text{ h}}$$

Biplane
70 kilometers per hour

Monoplane
50 miles per hour

The speed of the monoplane is 80 kilometers per hour. The speed of the biplane is 70 kilometers per hour.

∴ So, the monoplane is faster.

Check Convert 70 kilometers per hour to miles per hour.

$$\frac{70 \text{ km}}{1 \text{ h}} \times \frac{1 \text{ mi}}{1.6 \text{ km}} = \frac{44 \text{ mi}}{1 \text{ h}}$$

| *Monoplane* | | *Biplane* |
| $\frac{50 \text{ mi}}{1 \text{ h}}$ | > | $\frac{44 \text{ mi}}{1 \text{ h}}$ ✓ |

On Your Own

Now You're Ready
Exercises 31–34

8. The speed of a remote controlled car is 0.2 kilometer per minute. Order the speeds of the car and the two planes in Example 3 from least to greatest.

Vocabulary and Concept Check

1. **WRITING** Describe two methods you can use to convert measurements.

2. **OPEN-ENDED** Which method would you use to convert 10 miles to kilometers? Explain your reasoning.

3. **DIFFERENT WORDS, SAME QUESTION** Which is different? Find "both" answers.

Convert 5 inches to centimeters.	Find the number of inches in 5 centimeters.
How many centimeters are in 5 inches?	Five inches equals how many centimeters?

Practice and Problem Solving

Copy and complete the statement using < or >.

4. 1 ft ⬚ 1 cm

5. 450 yd ⬚ 450 cm

6. 30 in. ⬚ 30 mm

7. 125 in. ⬚ 125 cm

8. 100 ft/h ⬚ 100 km/h

9. 10 L ⬚ 10 gal

Copy and complete the statement using a ratio. Round to the nearest hundredth, if necessary.

10. 3 mi ≈ ⬚ km

11. 10 qt ≈ ⬚ L

12. 68 kg ≈ ⬚ lb

13. 8.3 in. ≈ ⬚ cm

14. 25.5 lb ≈ ⬚ kg

15. 5 km ≈ ⬚ mi

16. **ERROR ANALYSIS** Describe and correct the error in using a ratio to convert 12 kilometers to miles.

$$\cancel{12 \ km} \times \frac{1.6 \ mi}{1 \ \cancel{km}} \approx 19.2 \ mi$$

Copy and complete the statement using a proportion. Round to the nearest hundredth, if necessary.

17. 48 in. ≈ ⬚ cm

18. 2 km ≈ ⬚ mi

19. 165 cm ≈ ⬚ in.

20. 85 lb ≈ ⬚ kg

21. 2.5 qt ≈ ⬚ L

22. 14.2 L ≈ ⬚ qt

23. **CAVES** Mammoth Cave is the longest cave system in the world. So far, 365 miles of the cave have been explored. What is this distance in kilometers?

24. **IGUANA** How long is the iguana in inches?

Length: 24.7 cm

Copy and complete the statement using < or >.

② **25.** 8 kg ▨ 30 oz

26. 6 ft ▨ 300 cm

27. 3 gal ▨ 6 L

28. 10 in. ▨ 200 mm

29. 1200 g ▨ 5 lb

30. 1500 m ▨ 3000 ft

Copy and complete the statement. Round to the nearest hundredth, if necessary.

③ **31.** 45 mi/h ≈ ▨ km/h

32. 5 gal/min ≈ ▨ L/min

33. 120 mm/sec ≈ ▨ in./sec

34. 900 g/day ≈ ▨ lb/day

35. **BRACHIOSAURUS** One of the largest dinosaurs was the brachiosaurus. How much did it weigh in kilograms?

36. **BOTTLE** Can you pour the water from a full 2-liter bottle into a 2-quart pitcher without spilling any? Explain.

Weight: 172,000 lb

37. **AUTOBAHN** Germany suggests a speed limit of 130 kilometers per hour on highways.

   a. Is the speed shown greater than the suggested limit?

   b. Suppose the speed drops 30 miles per hour. Is the new speed below the suggested limit?

38. **SOCCER** The size of a soccer field is 50 yards wide by 80 yards long. What is the size in meters?

39. **PAINT** One liter of paint covers 100 square feet. How many gallons does it take to cover 1400 square feet?

40. **Critical Thinking** The speed of light is about 300,000 kilometers per second. Convert the speed to miles per hour.

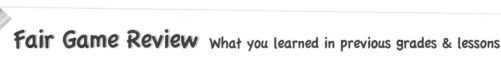

Fair Game Review *What you learned in previous grades & lessons*

Graph the data. Then find the slope of the line through the points. *(Section 3.2)*

41.

Months, x	Height, y
2	3
4	6
6	9

42.

Hours, x	Units, y
4	60
8	120
12	180

43. **MULTIPLE CHOICE** Which equation has a solution of 4? *(Section 2.6)*

   Ⓐ $2x + 7 = -1$ **Ⓑ** $-3 + 2x = -11$ **Ⓒ** $2x - 11 = -3$ **Ⓓ** $11 + 2x = 3$

Essential Question How can you use a graph to show the relationship between two variables that vary directly? How can you use an equation?

1 ACTIVITY: Math in Literature

Gulliver's Travels was written by Jonathan Swift and published in 1725. Gulliver was shipwrecked on the island Lilliput, where the people were only 6 inches tall. When the Lilliputians decided to make a shirt for Gulliver, a Lilliputian tailor stated that he could determine Gulliver's measurements by simply measuring the distance around Gulliver's thumb. He said "Twice around the thumb equals once around the wrist. Twice around the wrist is once around the neck. Twice around the neck is once around the waist."

Work with a partner. Use the tailor's statement to complete the table.

Thumb, t	Wrist, w	Neck, n	Waist, x
0 in.	0 in.		
1 in.	2 in.		
2 in.	4 in.		
3 in.	6 in.		
4 in.	8 in.		
5 in.	10 in.		

2 EXAMPLE: Drawing a Graph

Use the information from Activity 1 to draw a graph of the relationship between the distance around the thumb *t* and the distance around the wrist *w*.

Use the table to write ordered pairs. Then plot the ordered pairs.

$(0, 0), (1, 2), (2, 4), (3, 6), (4, 8), (5, 10)$

Notice the following about the graph:

1. All the points lie on a line.

2. The line passes through the origin.

This type of relationship is called **direct variation**. You can write an equation to describe the relationship between *t* and *w*.

$w = 2t$ Wrist is twice thumb.

3 ACTIVITY: Drawing a Graph

Work with a partner. Use the information from Activity 1 to draw a graph of the relationship. Write an equation that describes the relationship between the two variables.

a. Thumb *t* and neck *n* $(n = \boxed{} \; t)$

b. Wrist *w* and waist *x* $(x = \boxed{} \; w)$

c. Wrist *w* and thumb *t* $(t = \boxed{} \; w)$

d. Waist *x* and wrist *w* $(w = \boxed{} \; x)$

What Is Your Answer?

4. **IN YOUR OWN WORDS** How can you use a graph to show the relationship between two variables that vary directly? How can you use an equation?

5. Give a real-life example of two variables that vary directly.

6. Work with a partner. Use string to find the distance around your thumb, wrist, and neck. Do your measurements agree with those of the tailor in *Gulliver's Travels*? Explain your reasoning.

Practice

Use what you learned about direct variation to complete Exercises 4–7 on page 140.

Check It Out
Lesson Tutorials
BigIdeasMath.com

Key Vocabulary))
direct variation,
   p. 138

 Key Idea

Direct Variation

Words Two quantities x and y show
direct variation when $y = kx$,
where k is a number and $k \neq 0$.

Graph The graph of $y = kx$ is a line that
passes through the origin.

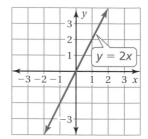

$y = 2x$

EXAMPLE **1** **Identifying Direct Variation**

Tell whether x and y show direct variation. Explain your reasoning.

a.

x	1	2	3	4
y	−2	0	2	4

Plot the points. Draw a line
through the points.

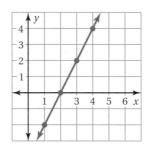

b.

x	0	2	4	6
y	0	2	4	6

Plot the points. Draw a line
through the points.

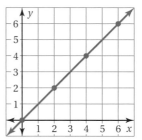

Study Tip

Other ways to say that
x and y show direct
variation are "y varies
directly with x" and
"x and y are directly
proportional."

∴ The line does not pass
through the origin. So, x and y
do *not* show direct variation.

∴ The line passes through
the origin. So, x and y show
direct variation.

EXAMPLE **2** **Identifying Direct Variation**

Tell whether x and y show direct variation. Explain your reasoning.

a. $y + 1 = 2x$

$y = 2x - 1$ Solve for y.

∴ The equation *cannot* be
written as $y = kx$. So, x and y
do *not* show direct variation.

b. $\dfrac{1}{2}y = x$

$y = 2x$ Solve for y.

∴ The equation can be
written as $y = kx$. So, x and
y show direct variation.

)) Multi-Language Glossary at BigIdeasMath.com.

● On Your Own

Tell whether *x* and *y* show direct variation. Explain your reasoning.

1.

x	y
0	−2
1	1
2	4
3	7

2.

x	y
1	4
2	8
3	12
4	16

3.

x	y
−2	4
−1	2
0	0
1	2

4. $xy = 3$

5. $x = \dfrac{1}{3}y$

6. $y + 1 = x$

EXAMPLE 3 Using a Direct Variation Model

The height *y* of a television screen varies directly with its width *x*.

$y = \dfrac{9}{16}x$

a. **Find the height when the width is 48 inches.**

b. **Sketch the graph of the equation.**

a. Use the equation to find the height when $x = 48$ inches.

$$y = \frac{9}{16}(48) \qquad \text{Substitute 48 for } x.$$

$$= 27 \qquad \text{Simplify.}$$

⋮• So, when the width is 48 inches, the height is 27 inches.

b. To sketch a graph, plot the point (48, 27). Then draw the line that passes through this point and the origin.

● On Your Own

7. Your earnings *y* (in dollars) vary directly with the number *x* of lawns you mow. Use the equation $y = 7.5x$ to find how much you earn when you mow 5 lawns.

Vocabulary and Concept Check

1. **VOCABULARY** What does it mean for x and y to vary directly?

2. **WRITING** What point is on the graph of every direct variation equation?

3. **WHICH ONE DOESN'T BELONG?** Which graph does *not* belong with the other three? Explain your reasoning.

Practice and Problem Solving

Tell whether x and y show direct variation. Explain your reasoning.

4. $(-1, -1), (0, 0), (1, 1), (2, 2)$

5. $(-4, -2), (-2, 0), (0, 2), (2, 4)$

6. $(1, 2), (1, 4), (1, 6), (1, 8)$

7. $(2, 1), (6, 3), (10, 5) (14, 7)$

8.

x	1	2	3	4
y	2	4	6	8

9.

x	-2	-1	0	1
y	0	2	4	6

10.

x	-1	0	1	2
y	-2	-1	0	1

11.

x	4	8	12	16
y	1	2	3	4

12.

x	-1	0	1	2
y	1	0	1	2

13.

x	3	6	9	12
y	2	4	6	8

14. $y - x = 4$

15. $x = \dfrac{2}{5}y$

16. $y + 3 = x + 6$

17. $y - 5 = 2x$

18. $x - y = 0$

19. $\dfrac{x}{y} = 2$

20. $8 = xy$

21. $x^2 = y$

22. **ERROR ANALYSIS** Describe and correct the error in telling whether x and y show direct variation.

The graph is a line, so it shows direct variation.

23. **RECYCLING** The table shows the profit y for recycling x pounds of aluminum. Tell whether x and y show direct variation.

Aluminum, x	10	20	30	40
Profit, y	$4.50	$9.00	$13.50	$18.00

The variables x and y vary directly. Use the values to write an equation that relates x and y.

③ 24. $y = 4; x = 2$

25. $y = 25; x = 5$

26. $y = 60; x = 15$

27. $y = 72; x = 3$

28. $y = 20; x = 12$

29. $y = 45; x = 40$

2.54 cm
1 in.

30. MEASUREMENT Write a direct variation equation that relates x inches to y centimeters.

31. JET SKI RAMP Design a jet ski ramp. Show how you can use direct variation to plan the heights of the vertical supports.

Vertical supports

32. JUPITER The weight of an object in our solar system varies directly with the weight of the object on Earth.

   a. Copy and complete the table.

   b. RESEARCH Why does weight vary throughout our solar system?

Location	Earth	Jupiter	Moon
Weight (lb)	100	214	
Weight (lb)	120		20

Minutes, x	500	700	900	1200
Cost, y	$40	$50	$60	$75

33. CELL PHONE PLANS Tell whether x and y show direct variation. If so, write an equation of direct variation.

34. CHLORINE The amount of chlorine in a swimming pool varies directly with the volume of water. The pool has 2.5 milligrams of chlorine per liter of water. How much chlorine is in the pool?

8000 gallons

35. **Critical Thinking** Is the graph of every direct variation equation a line? Does the graph of every line represent a direct variation equation? Explain your reasoning.

Fair Game Review What you learned in previous grades & lessons

Solve the equation. *(Section 2.5)*

36. $-4x = 36$

37. $\dfrac{y}{6} = -10$

38. $-\dfrac{3}{4}m = 24$

39. $-17 = \dfrac{2}{7}d$

40. MULTIPLE CHOICE Which rate is *not* equivalent to 180 feet per 8 seconds? *(Section 3.1)*

(A) $\dfrac{225 \text{ ft}}{10 \text{ sec}}$

(B) $\dfrac{45 \text{ ft}}{2 \text{ sec}}$

(C) $\dfrac{135 \text{ ft}}{6 \text{ sec}}$

(D) $\dfrac{180 \text{ ft}}{1 \text{ sec}}$

Essential Question How can you recognize when two variables are inversely proportional?

1 ACTIVITY: Comparing the Height and the Base

Work with a partner.

a. There are nine ways to arrange 36 square blocks to form a rectangle. Here are two ways. Find the other seven ways.

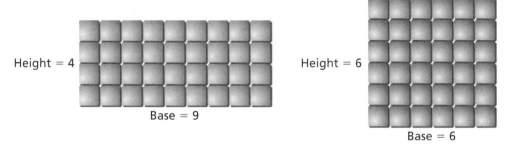

Height = 4   Base = 9

Height = 6   Base = 6

b. Order the nine ways according to height. Record your results in a table.

Height, *h*	Base, *b*	Area, *A*
4	9	$A = 9 \cdot 4 = 36$
6	6	$A = 6 \cdot 6 = 36$

c. Look at the first and second columns. Complete each sentence.

- When the height increases, the base [   ].

- When the height decreases, the base [   ].

In Activity 1, the relationship between the height and the base is an example of **inverse variation**. You can describe the relationship with an equation.

$$h = \frac{36}{b}$$ *h* and *b* are inversely proportional.

Work with a partner. Discuss each description. Tell whether the two variables are examples of *direct variation* or *inverse variation*. Use a table to explain your reasoning. Write an equation that relates the variables.

a. You bring 200 cookies to a party. Let n represent the number of people at the party and c represent the number of cookies each person receives.

b. You work at a restaurant for 20 hours. Let r represent your hourly pay rate and p represent the total amount you earn.

c. You are going on a 240-mile trip. Let t represent the number of hours driving and s represent the speed of the car.

What Is Your Answer?

3. **IN YOUR OWN WORDS** How can you recognize when two variables are inversely proportional? Explain how a table can help you recognize inverse variation.

4. **SCIENCE** The *wing beat frequency* of a bird is the number of times per second the bird flaps its wings.

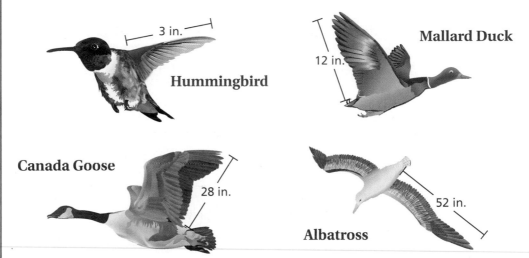

Which of the following seems true? Explain your reasoning.

- Wing length and wing beat frequency are directly proportional.
- Wing length and wing beat frequency are inversely proportional.
- Wing length and wing beat frequency are unrelated.

5. **SCIENCE** Think of an example in science where two variables are inversely proportional.

Practice

Use what you learned about inverse variation to complete Exercises 4–7 on page 146.

Check It Out
Lesson Tutorials
BigIdeasMath.com

Key Vocabulary 🔊
inverse variation, p. 144

 Key Idea

Inverse Variation

Words

Two quantities x and y show **inverse variation** when $y = \dfrac{k}{x}$, where k is a number and $k \neq 0$.

Graph

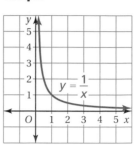

$y = \dfrac{1}{x}$

EXAMPLE 1 Identifying Direct and Inverse Variation

Tell whether x and y show *direct variation, inverse variation,* or *neither.* Explain your reasoning.

Study Tip

Other ways to say that x and y show inverse variation are "y varies inversely with x" and "x and y are inversely proportional."

a. $5y = x$

$y = \dfrac{1}{5}x$ Solve for y.

∴ The equation can be written as $y = kx$. So, x and y show direct variation.

b. $\dfrac{1}{3}y = \dfrac{1}{x}$

$y = \dfrac{3}{x}$ Solve for y.

∴ The equation can be written as $y = \dfrac{k}{x}$. So, x and y show inverse variation.

c. $-x = y + 7$

$-x - 7 = y$ Solve for y.

∴ The equation cannot be written as $y = kx$ *or* $y = \dfrac{k}{x}$. So, x and y do *not* show direct or inverse variation.

On Your Own

Now You're Ready
Exercises 4–15

Tell whether x and y show *direct variation, inverse variation,* or *neither.* Explain your reasoning.

1. $y - 1 = 2x$ **2.** $\dfrac{1}{5}y = x$ **3.** $2y = \dfrac{1}{x}$

🔊 Multi-Language Glossary at BigIdeasMath.com.

EXAMPLE **2**   **Standardized Test Practice**

In the graph, *x* and *y* show inverse variation. Which equation relates *x* and *y*?

(A) $y = -\dfrac{2}{x}$

(B) $y = \dfrac{2}{x}$

(C) $y = -2x$

(D) $y = 2x$

The graph passes through (2, 1). Substitute to find *k*.

$$y = \dfrac{k}{x}$$ Write inverse variation equation.

$$1 = \dfrac{k}{2}$$ Substitute 2 for *x* and 1 for *y*.

$$2 = k$$ Solve for *k*.

∴ So, the equation $y = \dfrac{2}{x}$ relates *x* and *y*. The correct answer is (B).

EXAMPLE **3**   **Real-Life Application**

Painting

Time (hours)

Workers

$y = \dfrac{8}{x}$

The graph shows the number of hours *y* it takes *x* workers to paint a room. (a) How does *y* change as *x* increases? (b) Do *x* and *y* show direct or inverse variation? (c) How many hours does it take five workers to paint the room?

a. From the graph, you can see that *y* decreases as *x* increases. So, as the number of workers increases, the time to paint the room decreases.

b. The equation is written as $y = \dfrac{k}{x}$. So, *x* and *y* show inverse variation.

c. Use the equation to find *y* when *x* = 5.

$$y = \dfrac{8}{x}$$ Write equation.

$$= \dfrac{8}{5} = 1.6$$ Substitute. Then simplify.

∴ It takes 1.6 hours for five workers to paint the room.

On Your Own

Now You're Ready
Exercises 23 and 24

4. Suppose *y* varies inversely with *x* and *y* = 3 when *x* = 1. Write an equation that relates *x* and *y*.

5. **WHAT IF?** In Example 3, how many hours does it take three workers to paint the room?

Vocabulary and Concept Check

1. **WRITING** What does it mean for x and y to vary inversely?

2. **NUMBER SENSE** When x increases from 1 to 10, does $\frac{1}{x}$ increase or decrease?

3. **OPEN-ENDED** Describe a real-life situation that shows inverse variation.

Practice and Problem Solving

Tell whether x and y show *direct variation*, *inverse variation*, or *neither*. Explain your reasoning.

 4. $y = \dfrac{1}{x}$

5. $xy = 8$

6. $y - x = 0$

7. $\dfrac{1}{2}y = 2x$

8. $\dfrac{y}{3} = \dfrac{2}{x}$

9. $y - 2 = \dfrac{7}{x}$

10. $x = y + 9$

11. $x = 4y$

12. $y = \dfrac{5}{2x}$

13. $2y = \dfrac{6}{x}$

14. $\dfrac{5x}{3} = \dfrac{y}{4}$

15. $x = \dfrac{7 + y}{2}$

16. **ERROR ANALYSIS** Describe and correct the error in telling whether x and y show inverse variation.

> ✗ $\dfrac{y}{2} = \dfrac{8}{x}$
>
> The equation does not show inverse variation because it is not of the form $y = \dfrac{k}{x}$.

Graph the data. Tell whether x and y show *direct variation* or *inverse variation*.

17.

x	−2	2	4	6
y	−1	1	2	3

18.

x	0.5	1	3	6
y	6	3	1	0.5

19.

x	2	5	8	20
y	10	4	2.5	1

20.

x	2	4	8	11
y	1.5	3	6	8.25

Tell whether x and y show *direct variation* or *inverse variation*. Explain.

21. **STADIUM** The time y it takes to empty a stadium and the number x of open exits are related by the equation $y = \dfrac{0.8}{x}$.

22. **TRAVEL** The number y of miles driven and the number x of gallons of gas used are related by the equation $y = 28.5x$.

The variables x and y vary inversely. Write an equation relating x and y.

② 23.

24.

25. BICYCLING The table shows the times it takes to bicycle 12 miles at various speeds.

Speed (mi/h)	12	6	3	2
Time (h)	1	2	4	6

    a. Does the time t vary inversely with the speed s? If so, write an equation relating t and s.

    b. What time corresponds to a speed of 4 miles per hour?

3 ft

26. MARTIAL ARTS It takes 3.6 pounds of force to break a 5-foot board.

    a. You remember from science that force and board length vary directly or inversely, but you've forgotten which. How can you use reason to remember?

    b. How much force does it take to break the board shown?

27. SALARY A salesperson has a fixed weekly salary. The person works twice as many hours this week as last week. What happens to the person's hourly rate?

28. Reasoning The price per person to rent a limousine varies inversely with the number of passengers. It costs $90 each for five people. How many people are renting the limousine when the cost per person is $56.25?

Fair Game Review *What you learned in previous grades & lessons*

Find the percent of the number. *(Skills Review Handbook)*

29. 40% of 220   **30.** 32% of 275   **31.** 84% of 75   **32.** 21% of 300

Tell whether the ratios form a proportion. *(Section 3.3)*

33. $\dfrac{9}{15}, \dfrac{18}{30}$ **34.** $\dfrac{21}{9}, \dfrac{18}{8}$ **35.** $\dfrac{42}{91}, \dfrac{24}{52}$ **36.** $\dfrac{24}{38}, \dfrac{36}{57}$

37. MULTIPLE CHOICE A gumball machine contains 1000 gumballs. The ratio of red gumballs to the total number of gumballs is $1 : 4$. How many red gumballs are in the machine? *(Section 3.5)*

    Ⓐ 150   **Ⓑ** 250   **Ⓒ** 400   **Ⓓ** 750

Check It Out
Progress Check
BigIdeasMath ✓com

Copy and complete the statement. Round to the nearest hundredth, if necessary.
(Section 3.6)

1. $10 \text{ mi} \approx$ ☐ km

2. $3 \text{ qt} \approx$ ☐ L

3. $29 \text{ kg} \approx$ ☐ lb

4. $6.8 \text{ in.} \approx$ ☐ cm

Tell whether x and y show direct variation. Explain your reasoning. *(Section 3.7)*

5.

x	y
−3	0
−1	1
1	2
3	3

6.

x	y
−1	−2
0	0
1	2
2	4

7. $y - 9 = 6 + x$

8. $x = \dfrac{5}{8}y$

Tell whether x and y show *direct variation*, *inverse variation*, or *neither*. Explain your reasoning. *(Section 3.8)*

9. $y = \dfrac{12}{x}$

10. $y - x = 9$

11.

x	y
−3	−2
−1	0
1	0
3	2

12.

x	y
1	2
2	1
4	0.5
8	0.25

13. HEIGHT The tallest player in Euroleague Basketball is 229 centimeters. The tallest player in the National Basketball Association is 90 inches. Which league has the tallest player? *(Section 3.6)*

14. PIE SALE The table shows the profit of a pie sale. Tell whether there is direct variation between the two data sets. If so, write the equation of direct variation. *(Section 3.7)*

Pies Sold	10	12	14	16
Profit	$79.50	$95.40	$111.30	$127.20

15. JEWELRY The number of beads on a bracelet varies inversely with the length of the beads. You use 8-millimeter beads to make a bracelet with 25 beads. How many 10-millimeter beads would you need to make a bracelet? *(Section 3.8)*

Check It Out
Vocabulary Help
BigIdeasMath ✓com

Review Key Vocabulary

ratio, *p. 100*
rate, *p. 100*
unit rate, *p. 100*
slope, *p. 106*

proportion, *p. 112*
proportional, *p. 112*
cross products, *p. 113*
U.S. customary system, *p. 132*

metric system, *p. 132*
direct variation, *p. 138*
inverse variation, *p. 144*

Review Examples and Exercises

 Ratios and Rates   *(pp. 98–103)*

Find the unit rate of calories per serving.

Servings	2	4	6	8
Calories	240	480	720	960

The calories increase by 240 for every 2 servings.

$$\frac{\text{change in calories}}{\text{change in servings}} = \frac{240}{2} = \frac{120}{1}$$

⋰ The rate is 120 calories per serving.

Exercises

Find the unit rate.

1. 289 miles on 10 gallons

2. 975 revolutions in 3 minutes

 Slope   *(pp. 104–109)*

Find the slope of the line.

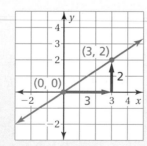

$$\text{slope} = \frac{\text{change in } y}{\text{change in } x}$$

$$= \frac{2}{3}$$

⋰ The slope of the line is $\frac{2}{3}$.

Exercises

Graph the line that passes through the two points. Then find the slope of the line.

3. $(-3, -3), (1, 1)$

4. $(-3, -2), (3, 2)$

5. $(3, 9), (-2, -6)$

Tell whether the ratios $\dfrac{9}{12}$ and $\dfrac{6}{8}$ form a proportion.

$$\frac{9}{12} = \frac{9 \div 3}{12 \div 3} = \frac{3}{4} \qquad \frac{6}{8} = \frac{6 \div 2}{8 \div 2} = \frac{3}{4}$$

∴ The ratios are equivalent. So, the ratios form a proportion.

Exercises

Tell whether the ratios form a proportion.

6. $\dfrac{4}{9}, \dfrac{2}{3}$

7. $\dfrac{12}{22}, \dfrac{18}{33}$

8. $\dfrac{8}{50}, \dfrac{4}{10}$

9. $\dfrac{32}{40}, \dfrac{12}{15}$

3.4 **Writing Proportions** *(pp. 116–121)*

Write a proportion that gives the number r of returns on Saturday.

	Friday	Saturday
Sales	40	85
Returns	32	r

$$\frac{40 \text{ sales}}{32 \text{ returns}} = \frac{85 \text{ sales}}{r \text{ returns}}$$

Exercises

Use the table to write a proportion.

10.

	Game 1	Game 2
Penalties	6	8
Minutes	16	m

11.

	Concert 1	Concert 2
Songs	15	18
Hours	2.5	h

3.5 **Solving Proportions** *(pp. 122–127)*

Solve $\dfrac{x}{9} = \dfrac{4}{5}$.

$x \cdot 5 = 9 \cdot 4$ Use the Cross Products Property.

$5x = 36$ Multiply.

$x = 7.2$ Divide.

Exercises

Solve the proportion.

12. $\dfrac{x}{4} = \dfrac{2}{5}$

13. $\dfrac{5}{12} = \dfrac{y}{15}$

14. $\dfrac{z}{7} = \dfrac{3}{16}$

15. $\dfrac{8}{20} = \dfrac{6}{w}$

Converting Measures Between Systems *(pp. 130–135)*

Convert 8 kilometers to miles.

$$8 \text{ km} \times \frac{1 \text{ mi}}{1.6 \text{ km}} \approx 5 \text{ mi} \qquad 1 \text{ mi} \approx 1.6 \text{ km, so use the ratio } \frac{1 \text{ mi}}{1.6 \text{ km}}.$$

Exercises

Copy and complete the statement. Round to the nearest hundredth, if necessary.

16. $3 \text{ L} \approx \boxed{} \text{ qt}$ 　　　　**17.** $9 \text{ in.} \approx \boxed{} \text{ cm}$ 　　　　**18.** $15 \text{ lb} \approx \boxed{} \text{ kg}$

Direct Variation *(pp. 136–141)*

Tell whether x and y show direct variation. Explain your reasoning.

a. $x + y - 1 = 3$

$y = 4 - x$ 　　Solve for y.

⋮ The equation *cannot* be written as $y = kx$. So, x and y do *not* show direct variation.

b. $x = 8y$

$\frac{1}{8}x = y$ 　　Solve for y.

⋮ The equation can be written as $y = kx$. So, x and y show direct variation.

Exercises

Tell whether x and y show direct variation. Explain your reasoning.

19. $x + y = 6$ 　　　**20.** $y - x = 0$ 　　　**21.** $\frac{x}{y} = 20$ 　　　**22.** $x = y + 2$

Inverse Variation *(pp. 142–147)*

Tell whether x and y show inverse variation. Explain your reasoning.

$xy = 5$

$y = \frac{5}{x}$ 　　Solve for y.

⋮ The equation can be written as $y = \frac{k}{x}$. So, x and y show inverse variation.

Exercises

Tell whether x and y show *direct variation*, *inverse variation*, or *neither*. Explain your reasoning.

23. $\frac{x}{y} = 6$ 　　　**24.** $3x + y = 7$ 　　　**25.** $8y = 4x$ 　　　**26.** $xy = 12$

3 Chapter Test

Check It Out
Test Practice
BigIdeasMath.com

Write the ratio as a fraction in simplest form.

1. 34 cars : 26 trucks

2. 3 feet to 9 feet

Find the unit rate.

3. 84 miles in 12 days

4. $3.20 for 8 ounces

Graph the line that passes through the two points. Then find the slope of the line.

5. $(15, 9), (-5, -3)$

6. $(2, 9), (4, 18)$

Tell whether the ratios form a proportion.

7. $\dfrac{1}{9}, \dfrac{6}{54}$

8. $\dfrac{9}{12}, \dfrac{8}{72}$

Use the table to write a proportion.

9.

	Monday	Tuesday
Gallons	6	8
Miles	180	m

10.

	Thursday	Friday
Classes	6	c
Hours	8	4

Solve the proportion.

11. $\dfrac{x}{8} = \dfrac{9}{4}$

12. $\dfrac{17}{3} = \dfrac{y}{6}$

Copy and complete the statement. Round to the nearest hundredth, if necessary.

13. $5 \text{ L} \approx$ ☐ qt

14. $56 \text{ lb} \approx$ ☐ kg

Tell whether x and y show *direct variation*, *inverse variation*, or *neither*. Explain your reasoning.

15. $xy - 11 = 5$

16. $x = \dfrac{3}{y}$

17. $\dfrac{y}{x} = 8$

18. **MOVIE TICKETS** Five movie tickets cost $36.25. What is the cost of eight movie tickets?

19. **VOLLEYBALL COURT** Find the dimensions of the volleyball court in feet.

9 m
18 m

20. **GLAZE** A specific shade of green glaze requires 5 parts blue to 3 parts yellow. A glaze mixture contains 25 quarts of blue and 9 quarts of yellow. How can you fix the mixture to make the specific shade of green glaze?

1. The school store sells 4 pencils for $0.50. At that rate, what would be the cost of 10 pencils?

   A. $1.10   **C.** $2.00

   B. $1.25   **D.** $5.00

2. Which expressions do *not* have a value of 3?

   I. $|3|$ II. $|-3|$

   III. $-|3|$ IV. $-|-3|$

   F. I and II   **H.** II and IV

   G. I and III   **I.** III and IV

3. What is the value of y in the equation below when $x = 12$ and $k = 3$?

   $$xy = k$$

4. Use the coordinate plane to answer the question below.

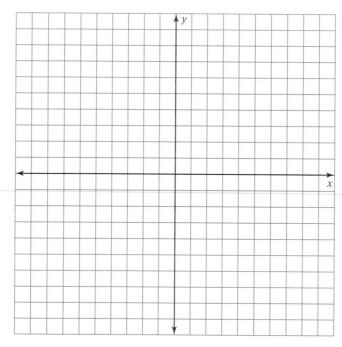

   A line contains both the point $(0, 5)$ and the point $(5, 0)$. Which of the following points is also on this line?

   A. $(0, -5)$ **C.** $(5, 5)$

   B. $(3, 3)$ **D.** $(7, -2)$

5. The scores from a diving competition are shown in the line plot below.

What is the median score?

F. 7

H. 5

G. 6

I. 4

6. Meli was solving the equation in the box below.

$$-\frac{1}{2}(4x - 10) = -16$$

$$-2x - 5 = -16$$

$$-2x - 5 + 5 = -16 + 5$$

$$-2x = -11$$

$$\frac{-2x}{-2} = \frac{-11}{-2}$$

$$x = \frac{11}{2}$$

What should Meli do to correct the error that she made?

A. Distribute the $-\frac{1}{2}$ to get $-2x + 5$.

B. Distribute the $-\frac{1}{2}$ to get $2x - 5$.

C. Divide -11 by -2 to get $-\frac{11}{2}$.

D. Add 2 to -11 to get -9.

7. What is the value of the expression below when $n = -8$ and $p = -4$?

$$-9n - p$$

F. 76

H. -68

G. 68

I. -76

8. How many millimeters are equivalent to 20 inches?
(Use 1 millimeter ≈ 0.04 inch.)

9. If 5 dogs share equally a bag of dog treats, each dog gets 24 treats. Suppose 8 dogs share equally the bag of treats. How many treats does each dog get?

A. 3

C. 21

B. 15

D. 38

10. The figure below consists of a rectangle and a right triangle.

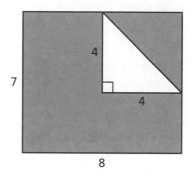

What is the area of the shaded region?

F. 23 units²

H. 48 units²

G. 40 units²

I. 60 units²

11. You can mow 800 square feet of lawn in 15 minutes. At this rate, how many minutes will you take to mow a lawn that measures 6000 square feet?

Think
Solve
Explain

Part A Write a proportion to represent the problem. Use m to represent the number of minutes. Explain your reasoning.

Part B Solve the proportion you wrote in Part A and use it to answer the problem. Show your work.

12. What number belongs in the box to make the equation true?

$$5\frac{7}{8} = \boxed{} \cdot \left(-\frac{1}{4}\right)$$

A. $-23\frac{1}{2}$

C. $6\frac{1}{8}$

B. $-1\frac{15}{32}$

D. $23\frac{1}{2}$

4 Percents

"Here's my sales strategy. I buy each dog bone for $0.05."

"Then I mark each one up to $1. Then, I have a 75% off sale. Cool, huh?"

"Dear Vet: I have this strange feeling that I am wagging my tail 15% fewer times than I used to wag it."

"Oh look. He already answered me."

"Dear Newton, I only practice general vet work. I need to refer you to a dog tail specialist."

What You Learned Before

"The fact that these two percents do not total 100 is a sad commentary on humans."

Writing Percents Using Models

What percent of the model is shaded?

Example 1

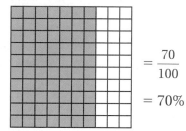

$$= \frac{70}{100}$$

$$= 70\%$$

Example 2

$$= \frac{45}{100}$$

$$= 45\%$$

Try It Yourself
What percent of the model is shaded?

1.

2.

3.

Writing Decimals, Percents, and Fractions

Example 3   Write $\frac{3}{5}$ as a decimal.

$$\frac{3}{5} = \frac{3 \cdot 2}{5 \cdot 2} = \frac{6}{10} = 0.6$$

Example 4   Write $\frac{3}{5}$ as a percent.

$$\frac{3}{5} = \frac{3 \cdot 20}{5 \cdot 20} = \frac{60}{100} = 60\%$$

Multiply to make the denominator 100.

Try It Yourself
Copy and complete the table.

	Percent	Decimal	Fraction
4.	35%		
5.		0.6	
6.			$\frac{13}{25}$

	Percent	Decimal	Fraction
7.	10%		
8.		0.85	
9.			$\frac{1}{5}$

4.1 The Percent Equation

Essential Question How can you use models to estimate percent questions?

1 ACTIVITY: Estimating a Percent

Work with a partner. Estimate the locations of 50%, 75%, 40%, 6%, and 65% on the model. 50% is done for you.

0%   50%   100%

2 ACTIVITY: Estimating a Part of a Number

The statement "25% of 12 is 3" has three numbers. In real-life problems, any one of these numbers can be unknown.

Part ⟶ $\dfrac{3}{12} = 0.25 = 25\%$ ⟵ Percent
Whole ⟶

Which number is missing?	Question	Type of Question
3	What is 25% of 12?	Find a part of a number.
25%	3 is what percent of 12?	Find a percent.
12	3 is 25% of what?	Find the whole.

Work with a partner. Estimate the answer to each question using a model.

a. **Sample:** What number is 50% of 30?

0%   50%   100%
0   15   30

So, from the model, 15 is 50% of 30.

b. What number is 75% of 30?   c. What number is 40% of 30?

d. What number is 6% of 30?   e. What number is 65% of 30?

3 ACTIVITY: Estimating a Percent

Work with a partner. Estimate the answer to the question using a model.

a. **Sample:** 15 is what percent of 75?

∴ So, 15 is 20% of 75.

b. 5 is what percent of 20?   c. 18 is what percent of 40?

d. 50 is what percent of 80?   e. 75 is what percent of 50?

4 ACTIVITY: Estimating a Whole

Work with a partner. Estimate the answer to the question using a model.

a. **Sample:** 24 is $33\frac{1}{3}$% of what number?

∴ So, 24 is $33\frac{1}{3}$% of 72.

b. 13 is 25% of what number?   c. 110 is 20% of what number?

d. 75 is 75% of what number?   e. 81 is 45% of what number?

What Is Your Answer?

5. **IN YOUR OWN WORDS** How can you use models to estimate percent questions? Give examples to support your answer.

Practice

Use what you learned about estimating percent questions to complete Exercises 4–9 on page 162.

Check It Out
Lesson Tutorials
BigIdeasMath com

Key Vocabulary
percent, p. 160

A **percent** is a ratio whose denominator is 100. Here are two examples.

$$4\% = \frac{4}{100} = 0.04 \qquad\qquad 25\% = \frac{25}{100} = 0.25$$

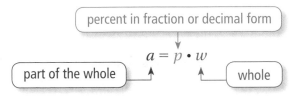 **Key Idea**

The Percent Equation

Words To represent "a is p percent of w," use an equation.

percent in fraction or decimal form

$$a = p \cdot w$$

part of the whole   whole

Numbers $\qquad\qquad 15 = 0.5 \cdot 30$

EXAMPLE **1** **Finding a Part of a Number**

What number is 24% of 50? **Estimate**

0%   25%   100%
0   12.5   50

Common Error

Remember to convert a percent to a fraction or decimal before using the percent equation. For Example 1, write 24% as $\frac{24}{100}$.

$a = p \cdot w$ Write percent equation.

$= \dfrac{24}{100} \cdot 50$ Substitute $\dfrac{24}{100}$ for p and 50 for w.

$= 12$ Multiply.

∴ So, 12 is 24% of 50. **Reasonable?** $12 \approx 12.5$ ✓

EXAMPLE **2** **Finding a Percent**

9.5 is what percent of 25? **Estimate**

0%   40%   100%
0   10   25

$a = p \cdot w$ Write percent equation.

$9.5 = p \cdot 25$ Substitute 9.5 for a and 25 for w.

$0.38 = p$ Divide each side by 25.

∴ Because 0.38 equals 38%, 9.5 is 38% of 25. **Reasonable?** $38\% \approx 40\%$ ✓

 Multi-Language Glossary at BigIdeasMath com.

EXAMPLE 3 Finding a Whole

39 is 52% of what number?   **Estimate**

$$a = p \bullet w \qquad \text{Write percent equation.}$$

$$39 = 0.52 \bullet w \qquad \text{Substitute 39 for } a \text{ and 0.52 for } p.$$

$$75 = w \qquad \text{Divide each side by 0.52.}$$

So, 39 is 52% of 75.   **Reasonable?** $75 \approx 78$ ✔

On Your Own

Now You're Ready
Exercises 10–17

Write and solve an equation to answer the question.

1. What number is 10% of 20?   **2.** What number is 150% of 40?

3. 3 is what percent of 600?   **4.** 18 is what percent of 20?

5. 8 is 80% of what number?   **6.** 90 is 18% of what number?

EXAMPLE 4 Real-Life Application

8th Street Cafe

DATE: MAY04'10 05:45PM
TABLE: 29
SERVER: CHARITY

Food Total	27.50
Tax	1.65
Subtotal	**29.15**

TIP: _____

TOTAL: _____

Thank You

a. Find the percent of sales tax on the food total.

b. Find the amount of a 16% tip on the food total.

a. Answer the question: $1.65 is what percent of $27.50?

$$a = p \bullet w \qquad \text{Write percent equation.}$$

$$1.65 = p \bullet 27.50 \qquad \text{Substitute 1.65 for } a \text{ and 27.50 for } w.$$

$$0.06 = p \qquad \text{Divide each side by 27.50.}$$

Because 0.06 equals 6%, the percent of sales tax is 6%.

b. Answer the question: What tip amount is 16% of $27.50?

$$a = p \bullet w \qquad \text{Write percent equation.}$$

$$= 0.16 \bullet 27.50 \qquad \text{Substitute 0.16 for } p \text{ and 27.50 for } w.$$

$$= 4.40 \qquad \text{Multiply.}$$

So, the amount of the tip is $4.40.

On Your Own

7. **WHAT IF?** In Example 4, find the amount of a 20% tip on the food total.

Vocabulary and Concept Check

1. **VOCABULARY** Write the percent equation in words.

2. **REASONING** A number n is 150% of number m. Is n *greater than*, *less than*, or *equal to m*? Explain your reasoning.

3. **DIFFERENT WORDS, SAME QUESTION** Which is different? Find "both" answers.

What number is 20% of 55?	55 is 20% of what number?

20% of 55 is what number?	0.2 • 55 is what number?

Practice and Problem Solving

Estimate the answer to the question using a model.

4. What number is 24% of 80?

5. 15 is what percent of 40?

6. 15 is 30% of what number?

7. What number is 120% of 70?

8. 20 is what percent of 52?

9. 48 is 75% of what number?

Write and solve an equation to answer the question.

 10. 20% of 150 is what number?

11. 45 is what percent of 60?

 12. 35% of what number is 35?

13. 32% of 25 is what number?

 14. 29 is what percent of 20?

15. 0.5% of what number is 12?

16. What percent of 300 is 51?

17. 120% of what number is 102?

ERROR ANALYSIS Describe and correct the error in using the percent equation.

18. What number is 35% of 20?

19. 30 is 60% of what number?

$$\times \quad \begin{aligned} a &= p \cdot w \\ &= 35 \cdot 20 \\ &= 700 \end{aligned}$$

$$\times \quad \begin{aligned} a &= p \cdot w \\ &= 0.6 \cdot 30 \\ &= 18 \end{aligned}$$

20. **BASEBALL** A pitcher throws 75 pitches. Of these, 72% were strikes. How many strikes did the pitcher throw?

21. **FUNDRAISING** Your school raised 125% of its fundraising goal. The school raised $6750. What was the goal?

22. **SURFBOARD** The sales tax on a surfboard is $12. What is the percent of sales tax?

SALE
$240

PUZZLE There were *w* signers of the Declaration of Independence. The youngest was Edward Rutledge, who was *x* years old. The oldest was Benjamin Franklin, who was *y* years old.

23. *x* is 25% of 104. What was Rutledge's age?

24. 7 is 10% of *y*. What was Franklin's age?

25. *w* is 80% of *y*. How many signers were there?

26. *y* is what percent of $(w + y - x)$?

Favorite Sport

Other

40.0%

37.5%

27. **REASONING** How can you tell whether the percent of a number will be *greater than*, *less than*, or *equal to* the number?

28. **SURVEY** In a survey, a group of students were asked their favorite sport. "Other" sports were chosen by 18 people.

    a. How many students participated?

    b. How many chose football?

29. **WATER TANK** Water tank *A* has a capacity of 550 gallons and is 66% full. Water tank *B* is 53% full. The ratio of the capacity of tank *A* to tank *B* is 11 : 15.

    a. How much water is in tank *A*?

    b. What is the capacity of tank *B*?

    c. How much water is in tank *B*?

30. **TRUE OR FALSE?** Tell whether the statement is *true* or *false*. Explain your reasoning.

    If *W* is 25% of *Z*, then *Z* : *W* is 75 : 25.

31. **Reasoning** The table shows your test results for math class. What test score is needed on the last exam to earn 90% of the total points?

Test Score	Point Value
83%	100
91.6%	250
88%	150
?	300

 Fair Game Review *What you learned in previous grades & lessons*

Simplify. Write as a decimal. *(Skills Review Handbook)*

32. $\dfrac{10 - 4}{10}$

33. $\dfrac{25 - 3}{25}$

34. $\dfrac{105 - 84}{84}$

35. $\dfrac{170 - 125}{125}$

36. **MULTIPLE CHOICE** There are 160 people in a grade. The ratio of boys to girls is 3 to 5. Which proportion can you use to find the number *x* of boys? *(Section 3.4)*

    (A) $\dfrac{3}{8} = \dfrac{x}{160}$
    (B) $\dfrac{3}{5} = \dfrac{x}{160}$
    (C) $\dfrac{5}{8} = \dfrac{x}{160}$
    (D) $\dfrac{3}{5} = \dfrac{160}{x}$

Essential Question

What is a percent of decrease? What is a percent of increase?

1 ACTIVITY: Percent of Decrease

Each year in the Columbia River Basin, adult salmon swim up river to streams to lay eggs and hatch their young.

To go up the river, the adult salmon use fish ladders. But, to go down the river, the young salmon must pass through several dams.

There are electric turbines at each of the eight dams on the main stem of the Columbia and Snake Rivers. About 88% of the young salmon pass through these turbines unharmed.

Copy and complete the table and the bar graph to show the number of young salmon that make it through the dams.

Dam	0	1	2	3	4	5	6	7	8
Salmon	1000	880	774						

88% of 1000 = 0.88 • 1000   88% of 880 = 0.88 • 880

        = 880   = 774.4 ≈ 774

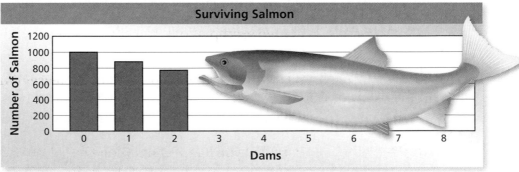

Surviving Salmon

From 2000 to 2006, the population of Florida increased about 2% each year. Copy and complete the table and the bar graph using this pattern. Predict the population in 2015.

For 2007:

$$2\% \text{ of } 18{,}000{,}000 = 0.02 \cdot 18{,}000{,}000$$
$$= 360{,}000$$

$$\underbrace{18{,}000{,}000}_{\substack{\text{2006} \\ \text{Population}}} + \underbrace{360{,}000}_{\text{Increase}} = \underbrace{18{,}360{,}000}_{\substack{\text{2007} \\ \text{Population}}}$$

2006 Population 18,000,000

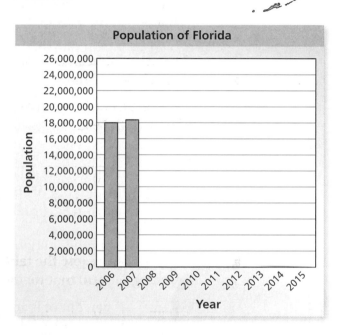

Year	Population
2006	18,000,000
2007	18,360,000
2008	
2009	
2010	
2011	
2012	
2013	
2014	
2015	

What Is Your Answer?

3. In Activity 1, by what percent does the number of young salmon decrease with each dam?

4. Describe real-life examples of a percent of decrease and a percent of increase.

5. **IN YOUR OWN WORDS** What is a percent of decrease? What is a percent of increase?

Practice

Use what you learned about percent of increase and percent of decrease to complete Exercises 13–18 on page 168.

Check It Out
Lesson Tutorials
BigIdeasMath com

Key Vocabulary
percent of change,
  p. 166
percent of increase,
  p. 166
percent of decrease,
  p. 166

A **percent of change** is the percent that a quantity changes from the original amount.

$$\text{percent of change} = \frac{\text{amount of change}}{\text{original amount}}$$

Key Idea

Percents of Increase and Decrease

When the original amount increases, the percent of change is called a **percent of increase**.

$$\text{percent of increase} = \frac{\text{new amount} - \text{original amount}}{\text{original amount}}$$

When the original amount decreases, the percent of change is called a **percent of decrease**.

$$\text{percent of decrease} = \frac{\text{original amount} - \text{new amount}}{\text{original amount}}$$

EXAMPLE 1 **Finding a Percent of Increase**

The table shows the number of hours you spent online last weekend. What is the percent of change in your online time from Saturday to Sunday?

Day	Hours Online
Saturday	2
Sunday	4.5

The number of hours on Sunday is greater than the number of hours on Saturday. So, the percent of change is a percent of increase.

$$\text{percent of increase} = \frac{\text{new amount} - \text{original amount}}{\text{original amount}}$$

$$= \frac{4.5 - 2}{2} \qquad \text{Substitute.}$$

$$= \frac{2.5}{2} \qquad \text{Subtract.}$$

$$= 1.25, \text{ or } 125\% \qquad \text{Write as a percent.}$$

∴ Your online time increased 125% from Saturday to Sunday.

On Your Own

Find the percent of change. Round to the nearest tenth of a percent, if necessary.

1. 10 inches to 25 inches

2. 57 people to 65 people

Multi-Language Glossary at BigIdeasMath.com.

EXAMPLE 2 **Finding a Percent of Decrease**

The bar graph shows a softball player's home run totals. What was the percent of change from 2007 to 2008?

Softball

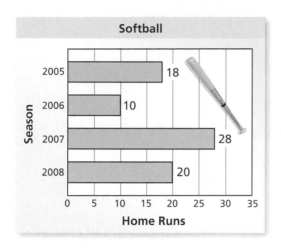

The number of home runs decreased from 2007 to 2008. So, the percent of change is a percent of decrease.

$$\text{percent of decrease} = \frac{\text{original amount} - \text{new amount}}{\text{original amount}}$$

$$= \frac{28 - 20}{28} \qquad \text{Substitute.}$$

$$= \frac{8}{28} \qquad \text{Subtract.}$$

$$\approx 0.286, \text{ or } 28.6\% \qquad \text{Write as a percent.}$$

∴ The number of home runs decreased about 28.6%.

On Your Own

Now You're Ready
Exercises 4–11

3. What was the percent of change from 2005 to 2006?

EXAMPLE 3 **Standardized Test Practice**

You have 250 songs on your MP3 player. You delete 20% of the songs. How many songs are left?

   A 50   **B** 150   **C** 200   **D** 300

Find the amount of decrease.

$$20\% \text{ of } 250 = 0.2 \cdot 250 \qquad \text{Write as multiplication.}$$

$$= 50 \qquad \text{Multiply.}$$

The decrease is 50 songs. So, there are $250 - 50 = 200$ songs left.

∴ The correct answer is **C**.

On Your Own

Now You're Ready
Exercises 13–22

4. WHAT IF? After deleting the 50 songs in Example 3, you add 10% more songs. How many songs are on the MP3 player?

Check It Out
Help with Homework
BigIdeasMath.com

✓ Vocabulary and Concept Check

1. **VOCABULARY** How do you know whether a percent of change is a *percent of increase* or a *percent of decrease*?

2. **NUMBER SENSE** Without calculating, which has a greater percent of increase?
   - 5 bonus points on a 50-point exam
   - 5 bonus points on a 100-point exam

3. **WRITING** What does it mean to have a 100% decrease?

Practice and Problem Solving

Identify the percent of change as an *increase* or *decrease*. Then find the percent of change. Round to the nearest tenth of a percent, if necessary.

4. 12 inches to 36 inches

5. 75 people to 25 people

6. 50 pounds to 35 pounds

7. 24 songs to 78 songs

8. 10 gallons to 24 gallons

9. 72 paper clips to 63 paper clips

10. 16 centimeters to 44.2 centimeters

11. 68 miles to 42.5 miles

12. **ERROR ANALYSIS** Describe and correct the error in finding the percent increase from 18 to 26.

$$\times \quad \frac{26 - 18}{26} \approx 0.31 = 31\%$$

Find the new amount.

13. 8 meters increased by 25%

14. 15 liters increased by 60%

15. 50 points decreased by 26%

16. 25 penalties decreased by 32%

17. 68 students increased by 125%

18. 1000 grams decreased by 94%

19. 62 kilograms decreased by 32%

20. 124 ounces decreased by 67%

21. **ERROR ANALYSIS** Describe and correct the error in using the percent of change to find a new amount.

> ✗ 25 is decreased by 40%.
> 40% of 25 = 0.4 • 25
> = 10
> So, 25 + 10 = 35.

22. **VIDEO GAME** Last week, you finished Level 2 of a video game in 32 minutes. Today, you finish Level 2 in 28 minutes. What is your percent of change?

Identify the percent of change as an *increase* or *decrease*. Then find the percent of change. Round to the nearest tenth of a percent, if necessary.

23. $\frac{1}{4}$ to $\frac{1}{2}$

24. $\frac{4}{5}$ to $\frac{3}{5}$

25. $\frac{3}{8}$ to $\frac{7}{8}$

26. $\frac{5}{4}$ to $\frac{3}{8}$

27. CRITICAL THINKING Explain why a change from 20 to 40 is a 100% increase, but a change from 40 to 20 is a 50% decrease.

28. POPULATION The table shows population data for a community.

Year	Population
2000	118,000
2006	138,000

   a. What is the percent of change from 2000 to 2006?

   b. Use this percent of change to predict the population in 2012.

29. GEOMETRY Suppose the length and width of the sandbox are doubled.

6 ft

10 ft

   a. Find the percent of change in the perimeter.

   b. Find the percent of change in the area.

7:45 June
5:51 September

30. RUNNING Find the percent of change in the time to run a mile from June to September.

31. CRITICAL THINKING A number increases by 10% and then decreases by 10%. Will the result be *greater than*, *less than*, or *equal to* the original number? Explain.

32. DONATIONS Donations to an annual fundraiser are 15% greater this year than last year. Last year, donations were 10% greater than the year before. The amount raised this year is $10,120. How much was raised 2 years ago?

33. Reasoning Forty students are in the science club. Of those, 45% are girls. This percent increases to 56% after new girls join the club. How many new girls join?

Fair Game Review What you learned in previous grades & lessons

Write and solve an equation to answer the question. *(Section 4.1)*

34. What number is 25% of 64?

35. 39.2 is what percent of 112?

36. 5 is 5% of what number?

37. 18 is 32% of what number?

38. MULTIPLE CHOICE Which equation shows direct variation? *(Section 3.7)*

   Ⓐ $y - x = 1$

   Ⓑ $\frac{y}{x} = 10$

   Ⓒ $y = \frac{4}{x}$

   Ⓓ $xy = 5$

You can use a **summary triangle** to explain a concept. Here is an example of a summary triangle for finding a percent of a number.

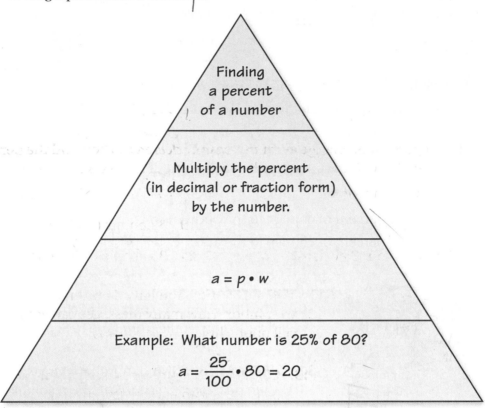

Finding
a percent
of a number

Multiply the percent
(in decimal or fraction form)
by the number.

$$a = p \cdot w$$

Example: What number is 25% of 80?

$$a = \frac{25}{100} \cdot 80 = 20$$

On Your Own

Make a summary triangle to help you study these topics.

1. finding the percent given a number and a part of the number

2. finding the number given a part of the number and a percent

3. percent of increase

4. percent of decrease

After you complete this chapter, make summary triangles for the following topics.

5. discount

6. markup

7. simple interest

"I hope my owner sees my summary triangle. I just can't seem to learn 'roll over'."

Write and solve an equation to answer the question.   *(Section 4.1)*

1. What number is 28% of 75?

2. 42 is 21% of what number?

3. 36 is what percent of 45?

4. What number is 68% of 12?

5. 66 is what percent of 55?

Identify the percent of change as an *increase* or *decrease*. Then find the percent of change. Round to the nearest tenth of a percent, if necessary.   *(Section 4.2)*

6. 8 inches to 24 inches

7. 300 miles to 210 miles

8. $42.00 to $16.00

9. 32 points to 46 points

10. 185 pounds to 153 pounds

11. 35 people to 70 people

12. **TEXT MESSAGES** You have 44 text messages in your inbox. How many messages can your cell phone hold?   *(Section 4.1)*

13. **COMPLETIONS** A quarterback completed 68% of his passes in a game. He threw 25 passes. How many passes did the quarterback complete?   *(Section 4.1)*

14. **QUIZ** You answered 14 questions correctly on a 15-question quiz. What percent did you receive on the quiz? Round to the nearest hundredth.   *(Section 4.1)*

15. **FRUIT JUICE** The graph shows the amount of fruit juice available per person in the United States during a six-year period.   *(Section 4.2)*

    a. What is the percent of change from 2002 to 2005?

    b. What is the percent of change from 2002 to 2003?

16. **CAR** A car loses 15% of its original value each year. After one year, a car has a value of $13,600. What is the original value of the car?   *(Section 4.2)*

Essential Question How can you find discounts and markups efficiently?

1 ACTIVITY: Comparing Discounts

Work with a partner. The same pair of sneakers is on sale at three stores. Which one is the best buy?

a. Regular Price: $45   **b.** Regular Price: $49   **c.** Regular Price: $39

40% off

50% off

up to **70% off**

a.

$0 $9 $18 $27 $36 $45

b.

$0 $9.80 $19.60 $29.40 $39.20 $49

c.

$0 $7.80 $15.60 $23.40 $31.20 $39

2 ACTIVITY: Finding the Original Price

Work with a partner. You buy a shirt that is on sale for 30% off. You pay $22.40. Your friend wants to know the original price of the shirt. How can your friend find the original price?

clearance
30% off
ORIGINAL PRICE

$0 $22.40   Original Price

You own a small jewelry store. You increase the price of the jewelry by 125%.

Work with a partner. Use a model to estimate the selling price of the jewelry. Then use a calculator to find the selling price.

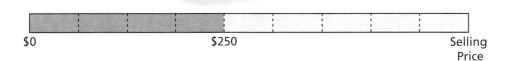

a. Your cost is $250.

$0 $250   Selling Price

b. Your cost is $50.

$0 $50   Selling Price

c. Your cost is $20.

$0 $20   Selling Price

What Is Your Answer?

4. IN YOUR OWN WORDS How can you find discounts and markups efficiently? Give examples of each.

Practice

Use what you learned about discounts and markups to complete Exercises 4, 9, 14, and 18–20 on pages 176 and 177.

Check It Out
Lesson Tutorials
BigIdeasMath.com

Key Vocabulary
discount, *p. 174*
markup, *p. 174*

Key Ideas

Discounts

A **discount** is a decrease in the original price of an item.

Markups

To make a profit, stores charge more than what they pay. The increase from what the store pays to the selling price is called a **markup**.

EXAMPLE 1 **Finding a Sale Price**

The original price of the shorts is $35. What is the sale price?

Method 1: First, find the discount. The discount is 25% of $35.

$$a = p \cdot w \qquad \text{Write percent equation.}$$
$$= 0.25 \cdot 35 \qquad \text{Substitute 0.25 for } p \text{ and 35 for } w.$$
$$= 8.75 \qquad \text{Multiply.}$$

Next, find the sale price.

sale price	=	original price	−	discount
	=	35	−	8.75
	=	26.25		

∴ The sale price is $26.25.

Method 2: First, find the percent of the original price.

$$100\% - 25\% = 75\%$$

Next, find the sale price.

$$\text{sale price} = 75\% \text{ of } \$35$$
$$= 0.75 \cdot 35$$
$$= 26.25$$

Study Tip

A 25% discount is the same as paying 75% of the original price.

∴ The sale price is $26.25. **Check**

On Your Own

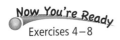
Now You're Ready
Exercises 4–8

1. The original price of a skateboard is $50. The sale price includes a 20% discount. What is the sale price?

🔊 Multi-Language Glossary at BigIdeasMath.com.

EXAMPLE 2 **Finding an Original Price**

What is the original price of the shoes?

The sale price is
100% − 40% = 60%
of the original price.

Answer the question: 33 is 60% of what number?

$a = p \cdot w$	Write percent equation.
$33 = 0.6 \cdot w$	Substitute 33 for a and 0.6 for p.
$55 = w$	Divide each side by 0.6.

∴ The original price of the shoes is $55.

Check

60%   100%

33   55   ✓

EXAMPLE 3 **Finding a Selling Price**

A store pays $70 for a bicycle. The percent of markup is 20%. What is the selling price?

First, find the markup. The markup is 20% of $70.

$a = p \cdot w$	Write percent equation.
$= 0.20 \cdot 70$	Substitute 0.20 for p and 70 for w.
$= 14$	Multiply.

Next, find the selling price.

selling price	=	cost to store	+	markup
	=	70	+	14
	= 84			

∴ The selling price is $84.

● **On Your Own**

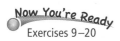
Now You're Ready
Exercises 9–20

2. The discount on a DVD is 50%. It is on sale for $10. What is the original price of the DVD?

3. A store pays $75 for an aquarium. The markup is 20%. What is the selling price?

4. Solve Example 3 using a different method.

Vocabulary and Concept Check

1. **WRITING** Describe how to find the sale price of an item that has been discounted 25%.

2. **WRITING** Describe how to find the selling price of an item that has been marked up 110%.

3. **REASONING** Which would you rather pay? Explain your reasoning.

   a. | 6% tax on a discounted price | or | 6% tax on the original price |

   b. | 30% markup on a $30 shirt | or | $30 markup on a $30 shirt |

Practice and Problem Solving

Copy and complete the table.

		Original Price	Percent of Discount	Sale Price
①	4.	$80	20%	
	5.	$42	15%	
	6.	$120	80%	
	7.	$112	32%	
	8.	$69.80	60%	
②	9.		25%	$40
	10.		5%	$57
	11.		80%	$90
	12.		64%	$72
	13.		15%	$146.54
	14.	$60		$45
	15.	$82		$65.60
	16.	$95		$61.75

17. **YOU BE THE TEACHER** The cost to a store for an MP3 player is $60. The selling price is $105. A classmate says that the markup is 175% because $\frac{\$105}{\$60} = 1.75$. Is your classmate correct? If not, explain how to find the correct percent of markup.

Find the cost to store, percent of markup, or selling price.

③ 18. Cost to store: $70
Markup: 10%
Selling price: ▩

19. Cost to store: ▩
Markup: 75%
Selling price: $63

20. Cost to store: $75
Markup: ▩
Selling price: $180

21. SCOOTER The scooter is on sale for 90% off the original price. Which of the methods can you use to find the sale price? Which method do you prefer? Explain.

Multiply $45.85 by 0.9.

Multiply $45.85 by 0.1.

Multiply $45.85 by 0.9, then add to $45.85.

Multiply $45.85 by 0.9, then subtract from $45.85.

22. GAMING You are shopping for a video game system.

a. At which store should you buy the system?

b. Store A has a weekend sale. How can this change your decision in part (a)?

Store	Cost to Store	Markup
A	$162	40%
B	$155	30%
C	$160	25%

23. STEREO A $129.50 stereo is discounted 40%. The next month, the sale price is discounted 60%. Is the stereo now "free"? If not, what is the sale price?

24. CLOTHING You buy a pair of jeans at a department store.

a. What is the percent of discount to the nearest percent?

b. What is the percent of sales tax to the nearest tenth of a percent?

c. The price of the jeans includes a 60% markup. After the discount, what is the percent of markup to the nearest percent?

Department Store

Jeans	39.99
Discount	-10.00
Subtotal	29.99
Sales Tax	1.95
Total	31.94

Thank You

25. You buy a bicycle helmet for $22.26, which includes 6% sales tax. The helmet is discounted 30% off the selling price. What is the original price?

Fair Game Review *What you learned in previous grades & lessons*

Evaluate. *(Skills Review Handbook)*

26. 2000(0.085)

27. 1500(0.04)(3)

28. 3200(0.045)(8)

29. MULTIPLE CHOICE Which measurement is greater than 1 meter? *(Section 3.6)*

Ⓐ 38 inches Ⓑ 1 yard Ⓒ 3.4 feet Ⓓ 98 centimeters

4.4 Simple Interest

Essential Question
How can you find the amount of simple interest earned on a savings account? How can you find the amount of interest owed on a loan?

Share Your Work at... My.BigIdeasMath.com

Simple interest is money earned on a savings account or an investment. It can also be money you pay for borrowing money.

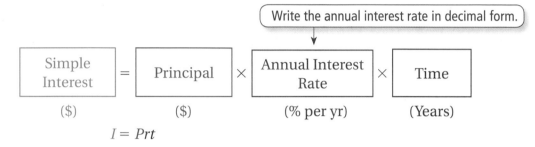

Write the annual interest rate in decimal form.

Simple Interest	=	Principal	×	Annual Interest Rate	×	Time
($)		($)		(% per yr)		(Years)

$$I = Prt$$

1 ACTIVITY: Finding Simple Interest

Work with a partner. You put $100 in a savings account. The account earns 6% simple interest per year. (a) Find the interest earned and the balance at the end of 6 months. (b) Copy and complete the table. Then make a bar graph that shows how the balance grows in 6 months.

a.

$I = Prt$	Write simple interest formula
$= 100(0.06)\left(\dfrac{6}{12}\right)$	Substitute values.
$= 3$	Multiply.

∴ At the end of 6 months, you earn $3 in interest. So, your balance is $100 + $3 = $103.

b.

Time	Interest	Balance
0 month	$0	$100
1 month		
2 months		
3 months		
4 months		
5 months		
6 months	$3	$103

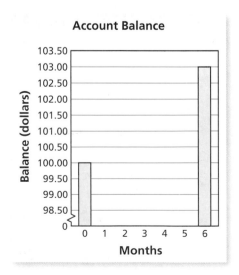

Account Balance

2 ACTIVITY: Financial Literacy

Work with a partner. Use the following information to write a report about credit cards. In the report, describe how a credit card works. Include examples that show the amount of interest paid each month on a credit card.

U.S. Credit Card Data

- A typical family in the United States owes about $5000 in credit card debt.

- A typical credit card interest rate is 18% to 20% per year. This is called the annual percentage rate.

3 ACTIVITY: The National Debt

Work with a partner. In 2010, the United States owed about $10 trillion in debt. The interest rate on the national debt is about 3% per year.

a. Write $10 trillion in decimal form. How many zeros does this number have?

b. How much interest does the United States pay each year on its national debt?

c. How much interest does the United States pay each day on its national debt?

d. The United States has a population of about 300 million people. Estimate the amount of interest that each person pays per year toward interest on the national debt.

What Is Your Answer?

4. IN YOUR OWN WORDS How can you find the amount of simple interest earned on a savings account? How can you find the amount of interest owed on a loan? Give examples with your answer.

Use what you learned about simple interest to complete Exercises 4–7 on page 182.

4.4 Lesson

Check It Out
Lesson Tutorials
BigIdeasMath V.com

Key Vocabulary
interest, *p. 180*
principal, *p. 180*
simple interest,
    p. 180

Interest is money paid or earned for the use of money. The **principal** is the amount of money borrowed or deposited.

Key Idea

Simple Interest

Words **Simple interest** is money paid or earned only on the principal.

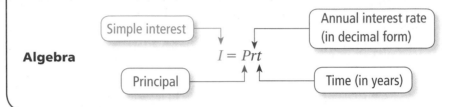

Algebra $I = Prt$

EXAMPLE 1 **Finding Interest Earned**

You put $500 in a savings account. The account earns 3% simple interest per year. (a) What is the interest earned after 3 years? (b) What is the balance after 3 years?

a. $I = Prt$ Write simple interest formula.

$\quad = 500(0.03)(3)$ Substitute 500 for *P*, 0.03 for *r*, and 3 for *t*.

$\quad = 45$ Multiply.

∴ The interest earned is $45 after 3 years.

b. To find the balance, add the interest to the principal.

∴ So, the balance is $500 + $45 = $545 after 3 years.

EXAMPLE 2 **Finding an Annual Interest Rate**

You put $1000 in an account. The account earns $100 simple interest in 4 years. What is the annual interest rate?

$I = Prt$ Write simple interest formula.

$100 = 1000(r)(4)$ Substitute 100 for *I*, 1000 for *P*, and 4 for *t*.

$100 = 4000r$ Simplify.

$0.025 = r$ Divide each side by 4000.

∴ The annual interest rate of the account is 0.025, or 2.5%.

Multi-Language Glossary at BigIdeasMath✓.com.

Now You're Ready
Exercises 4–16

1. In Example 1, what is the balance of the account after 9 months?

2. You put $350 in an account. The account earns $17.50 simple interest in 2.5 years. What is the annual interest rate?

EXAMPLE **3** **Finding an Amount of Time**

A bank offers three savings accounts. The simple interest rate is determined by the principal. How long does it take an account with a principal of $800 to earn $100 interest?

1.5%
Less than $500

2.0%
$500-$5000

3.0%
More than $5000

The pictogram shows that the interest rate for a principal of $800 is 2%.

$I = Prt$	Write simple interest formula.
$100 = 800(0.02)(t)$	Substitute 100 for I, 800 for P, and 0.02 for r.
$100 = 16t$	Simplify.
$6.25 = t$	Divide each side by 16.

:∴: The account earns $100 in interest in 6.25 years.

EXAMPLE **4** **Finding Amount Paid on a Loan**

You borrow $600 to buy a violin. The simple interest rate is 15%. You pay off the loan after 5 years. How much do you pay for the loan?

$I = Prt$	Write simple interest formula.
$= 600(0.15)(5)$	Substitute 600 for P, 0.15 for r, and 5 for t.
$= 450$	Multiply.

To find the amount you pay, add the interest to the loan amount.

:∴: So, you pay $600 + $450 = $1050 for the loan.

On Your Own

Now You're Ready
Exercises 17–27

3. In Example 3, how long does it take an account with a principal of $10,000 to earn $750 interest?

4. **WHAT IF?** In Example 4, you pay off the loan after 2 years. How much money do you save?

✓ Vocabulary and Concept Check

1. **VOCABULARY** Define each variable in $I = Prt$.

2. **WRITING** In each situation, tell whether you would want a *higher* or *lower* interest rate. Explain your reasoning.

   a. You borrow money

   b. You open a savings account

3. **REASONING** An account earns 6% simple interest. You want to find the interest earned on $200 after 8 months. What conversions do you need to make before you can use the formula $I = Prt$?

Practice and Problem Solving

An account earns simple interest. (a) Find the interest earned. (b) Find the balance of the account.

4. $600 at 5% for 2 years

5. $1500 at 4% for 5 years

6. $350 at 3% for 10 years

7. $1800 at 6.5% for 30 months

8. $700 at 8% for 6 years

9. $1675 at 4.6% for 4 years

10. $925 at 2% for 2.4 years

11. $5200 at 7.36% for 54 months

12. **ERROR ANALYSIS** Describe and correct the error in finding the simple interest earned on $500 at 6% for 18 months.

   ✗ $I = (500)(0.06)(18)$
   $= \$540$

Find the annual simple interest rate.

13. $I = \$24$, $P = \$400$, $t = 2$ years

14. $I = \$562.50$, $P = \$1500$, $t = 5$ years

15. $I = \$54$, $P = \$900$, $t = 18$ months

16. $I = \$160.67$, $P = \$2000$, $t = 8$ months

Find the amount of time.

17. $I = \$30$, $P = \$500$, $r = 3\%$

18. $I = \$720$, $P = \$1000$, $r = 9\%$

19. $I = \$54$, $P = \$800$, $r = 4.5\%$

20. $I = \$450$, $P = \$2400$, $r = 7.5\%$

21. **BANKING** A savings account earns 5% annual simple interest. The principal is $1200. What is the balance after 4 years?

22. **SAVINGS** You put $400 in an account. The account earns $18 simple interest in 9 months. What is the annual interest rate?

23. **CD** You put $3000 in a CD (certificate of deposit) at the promotional rate. How long will it take to earn $336 in interest?

Promotional Rate 5.6% Simple Interest

Find the amount paid for the loan.

④ 24. $1500 at 9% for 2 years

25. $2000 at 12% for 3 years

26. $2400 at 10.5% for 5 years

27. $4800 at 9.9% for 4 years

Copy and complete the table.

	Principal	Interest Rate	Time	Simple Interest
28.	$12,000	4.25%	5 years	
29.		6.5%	18 months	$828.75
30.	$15,500	8.75%		$5425.00
31.	$18,000		54 months	$4252.50

32. ZOO A family charges a trip to the zoo on a credit card. The simple interest rate is 12%. The charges are paid after 3 months. What is the total amount paid for the trip?

Zoo Trip

Tickets	67.70
Food	62.34
Gas	45.50
Total Cost	?

33. MONEY MARKET You deposit $5000 in an account earning 7.5% simple interest. How long will it take for the balance of the account to be $6500?

34. LOANS A music company offers a loan to buy a drum set for $1500. What is the monthly payment?

11.8% Simple Interest
Equal monthly
payments for 2 years.

35. REASONING How many years will it take for $2000 to double at a simple interest rate of 8%? Explain how you found your answer.

36. LOANS You have two loans, for 2 years each. The total interest for the two loans is $138. On the first loan, you pay 7.5% simple interest on a principal of $800. On the second loan, you pay 3% simple interest. What is the principal for the second loan?

37. *Critical Thinking* You put $500 in an account that earns 4% annual interest. The interest earned each year is added to the principal to create a new principal. Find the total amount in your account after each year for 3 years.

 Fair Game Review *What you learned in previous grades & lessons*

Solve the proportion. *(Section 3.5)*

38. $\dfrac{4}{9} = \dfrac{12}{x}$

39. $\dfrac{15}{36} = \dfrac{n}{12}$

40. $\dfrac{m}{6.5} = \dfrac{14}{26}$

41. $\dfrac{2.4}{z} = \dfrac{3}{11.25}$

42. MULTIPLE CHOICE What is the solution of $4x + 5 = -11$? *(Section 2.6)*

Ⓐ -4　　　Ⓑ -1.5　　　Ⓒ 1.5　　　Ⓓ 4

Find the price, discount, markup, or cost to store. *(Section 4.3)*

1. Original price: $30
Discount: 10%
Sale price: ?

2. Original price: $55
Discount: ?
Sale price: $46.75

3. Original price: ?
Discount: 75%
Sale price: $74.75

4. Cost to store: $152
Markup: 50%
Selling price: ?

5. Cost to store: $20
Markup: ?
Selling price: $32

6. Cost to store: ?
Markup: 80%
Selling price: $21.60

An account earns simple interest. Find the interest earned, principal, interest rate, or time. *(Section 4.4)*

7. Interest earned: ?
Principal: $1200
Interest rate: 2%
Time: 5 years

8. Interest earned: $25
Principal: $500
Interest rate: 5%
Time: ?

9. Interest earned: $76
Principal: $800
Interest rate: ?
Time: 2 years

10. Interest earned: $119.88
Principal: ?
Interest rate: 3.6%
Time: 3 years

11. DIGITAL CAMERA A digital camera costs $229. The camera is on sale for 30% off and you have a coupon for an additional 15% off the original price. What is the final price? *(Section 4.3)*

12. WATER SKIS The original price of the water skis was $200. What is the percent of discount? *(Section 4.3)*

SALE $150

2 Ways to Own:

1. $75 cash back with 3.5% simple interest

2. No interest for 2 years

13. SAXOPHONE A saxophone costs $1200. A store offers two loan options. Which option saves more money if you pay the loan in 2 years? *(Section 4.4)*

14. LOAN You borrow $200. The simple interest rate is 12%. You pay off the loan after 2 years. How much do you pay for the loan? *(Section 4.4)*

Check It Out
Vocabulary Help
BigIdeasMath ✓.com

Review Key Vocabulary

percent, *p. 160*
percent of change, *p. 166*
percent of increase, *p. 166*

percent of decrease, *p. 166*
discount, *p. 174*
markup, *p. 174*

interest, *p. 180*
principal, *p. 180*
simple interest, *p. 180*

Review Examples and Exercises

4.1 The Percent Equation *(pp. 158–163)*

What number is 72% of 25?

$a = p \cdot w$	Write percent equation.
$= 0.72 \cdot 25$	Substitute 0.72 for p and 25 for w.
$= 18$	Multiply.

∴ So, 72% of 25 is 18.

28 is what percent of 70?

$a = p \cdot w$	Write percent equation.
$28 = p \cdot 70$	Substitute 28 for a and 70 for w.
$0.4 = p$	Divide each side by 70.

∴ Because $0.4 = 40\%$, 28 is 40% of 70.

22.1 is 26% of what number?

$a = p \cdot w$	Write percent equation.
$22.1 = 0.26 \cdot w$	Substitute 22.1 for a and 0.26 for p.
$85 = w$	Divide each side by 0.26.

∴ So, 22.1 is 26% of 85.

Exercises

Write and solve an equation to answer the question.

1. What number is 24% of 25?

2. 9 is what percent of 20?

3. 85% of what number is 10.2?

4. 83% of 20 is what number?

5. PARKING 15% of the school parking spaces are handicap spaces. The school has 18 handicap spaces. How many parking spaces are there?

4.2 Percents of Increase and Decrease *(pp. 164–169)*

The table shows the number of skim boarders at a beach on Saturday and Sunday. What was the percent of change in boarders from Saturday to Sunday?

The number of skim boarders on Sunday is less than the number of skim boarders on Saturday. So, the percent of change is a percent of decrease.

Day	Number of Skim Boarders
Saturday	12
Sunday	9

$$\text{percent of decrease} = \frac{\text{original amount} - \text{new amount}}{\text{original amount}}$$

$$= \frac{12 - 9}{12} \qquad \text{Substitute.}$$

$$= \frac{3}{12} \qquad \text{Subtract.}$$

$$= 0.25 = 25\% \qquad \text{Write as a percent.}$$

∴ The number of skim boarders decreased by 25% from Saturday to Sunday.

Exercises

Identify the percent of change as an *increase* or *decrease*. Then find the percent of change. Round to the nearest tenth of a percent, if necessary.

6. 6 yards to 36 yards

7. 6 hits to 3 hits

8. 120 meals to 52 meals

9. 35 words to 115 words

4.3 Discounts and Markups *(pp. 172–177)*

What is the original price of the tennis racquet?

The sale price is 100% − 30% = 70% of the original price.

Answer the question: 21 is 70% of what number?

$$a = p \cdot w \qquad \text{Write percent equation.}$$

$$21 = 0.7 \cdot w \qquad \text{Substitute 21 for } a \text{ and 0.7 for } p.$$

$$30 = w \qquad \text{Divide each side by 0.7.}$$

∴ The original price of the tennis racquet is $30.

Exercises

Find the price.

10. Original price: $50
Discount: 15%
Sale price: ?

11. Original price: ?
Discount: 20%
Sale price: $75

Simple Interest *(pp. 178–183)*

You put $200 in a savings account. The account earns 2% simple interest per year.

a. What is the interest after 4 years?

b. What is the balance after 4 years?

a. $\quad I = Prt$ Write simple interest formula.

       $= 200(0.02)(4)$ Substitute 200 for P, 0.02 for r, and 4 for t.

       $= 16$ Multiply.

     ∴ The interest earned is $16 after 4 years.

b. The balance is the principal plus the interest.

     ∴ So, the balance is $200 + $16 = $216 after 4 years.

You put $500 in an account. The account earns $55 simple interest in 5 years. What is the annual interest rate?

          $I = Prt$ Write simple interest formula.

       $55 = 500(r)(5)$ Substitute 55 for I, 500 for P, and 5 for t.

       $55 = 2500r$ Simplify.

    $0.022 = r$ Divide each side by 2500.

∴ The annual interest rate of the account is 0.022, or 2.2%.

Exercises

An account earns simple interest.

a. Find the interest earned.

b. Find the balance of the account.

12. $300 at 4% for 3 years

13. $2000 at 3.5% for 4 years

Find the annual simple interest rate.

14. $I = \$17$, $P = \$500$, $t = 2$ years

15. $I = \$426$, $P = \$1200$, $t = 5$ years

Find the amount of time.

16. $I = \$60$, $P = \$400$, $r = 5\%$

17. $I = \$237.90$, $P = \$1525$, $r = 2.6\%$

18. SAVINGS You put $100 in an account. The account earns $2 simple interest in 6 months. What is the annual interest rate?

Write and solve an equation to answer the question.

1. 16% of 150 is what number?

2. 10 is 40% of what number?

3. 27 is what percent of 75?

4. What number is 35% of 56?

Identify the percent of change as an *increase* or *decrease*. Then find the percent of change. Round to the nearest tenth of a percent, if necessary.

5. 4 strikeouts to 10 strikeouts

6. $24.00 to $18.00

Find the price, discount, or markup.

7. Original price: $15
   Discount: 5%
   Sale price: ?

8. Original price: $189
   Discount: ?
   Sale price: $75.60

9. Cost to store: $15
   Markup: ?
   Selling price: $24.75

10. Cost to store: $5.50
    Markup: 75%
    Selling price: ?

An account earns simple interest. Find the interest earned, principal, interest rate, or time.

11. Interest earned: ?
    Principal: $450
    Interest rate: 6%
    Time: 8 years

12. Interest earned: $27
    Principal: ?
    Interest rate: 1.5%
    Time: 2 years

13. Interest earned: $116.25
    Principal: $1550
    Interest rate: ?
    Time: 9 months

14. Interest earned: $45.60
    Principal: $2400
    Interest rate: 3.8%
    Time: ?

15. **MOVIE PREVIEWS** There are eight previews before a movie. Seventy-five percent of the previews are for comedies. How many previews are for comedies?

16. **BOOK** What was the original price of the book?

17. **TEXT MESSAGES** The cost of a text message increases from $0.10 per message to $0.25 per message. What is the percent increase in the cost of sending a text message?

The WORLD around us
20% off
A pictu
Only $7.00

18. **INVESTMENT** You put $800 in an account that earns 4% simple interest. Find the total amount in your account after each year for 3 years.

1. A movie theatre offers 30% off the price of a movie ticket to students from your school. The regular price of a movie ticket is $8.50. What is the discounted price that you would pay for a ticket?

   A. $2.55   **C.** $5.95

   B. $5.50   **D.** $8.20

2. You are comparing the prices of four boxes of cereal. Two of the boxes contain free extra cereal.

   - Box F costs $3.59 and contains 16 ounces.

   - Box G costs $3.79 and contains 16 ounces, plus an additional 10% for free.

   - Box H costs $4.00 and contains 500 grams.

   - Box I costs $4.69 and contains 500 grams, plus an additional 20% for free.

   Which box has the least unit cost? (1 ounce = 28.35 grams)

   F. Box F   **H.** Box H

   G. Box G   **I.** Box I

3. James is getting ready for wrestling season. As part of his preparation, he plans to lose 5% of his body weight. James currently weighs 160 pounds. How much will he weigh, in pounds, after he loses 5% of his weight?

4. Which proportion represents the problem below?

   "17% of a number is 43. What is the number?"

   A. $\dfrac{17}{43} = \dfrac{n}{100}$ **C.** $\dfrac{n}{43} = \dfrac{17}{100}$

   B. $\dfrac{n}{17} = \dfrac{43}{100}$ **D.** $\dfrac{43}{n} = \dfrac{17}{100}$

5. Betty was simplifying the expression in the box below.

$$-|8 + (-13)| = -(|8| + |-13|)$$
$$= -|8 + 13|$$
$$= -|21|$$
$$= -21$$

What should Betty do to correct the error that she made?

F. Simplify $-|8 + (-13)|$ to get $-|-5|$.

G. Find the opposite of $|21|$, which is 21.

H. Find the absolute value of 8, which is -8.

I. Distribute the negative sign to get $|-8 + (-13)|$.

6. The students from the Math Club participated in a long-distance walk as a fundraiser. The number of hours each club member took to complete the walk is shown in the bar graph below.

What is the mean number of hours the club members took to complete the walk?

A. 3.5 h

B. 4 h

C. 5 h

D. 7.5 h

7. A lighting store is holding a clearance sale. The store is offering discounts on all the lamps it sells. As the sale progresses, the store will increase the percent of discount it is offering.

You want to buy a lamp that has an original price of $40. You will buy the lamp when its price is marked down to $10. What percent discount will you have received?

8. A student scored 600 the first time she took the mathematics portion of her college entrance exam. The next time she took the exam, she scored 660. Her second score represents what percent increase over her first score?

F. 9.1%

G. 10%

H. 39.6%

I. 60%

9. Which inequality is represented by the graph on the number line below?

A. $x < -4$

B. $x \leq -4$

C. $x > -4$

D. $x \geq -4$

10. You are planning to deposit $4000 into an account that earns 5% simple interest per year. You will not make any other deposits or withdrawals.

Part A How long would it take for your account to contain $4500? Show your work and explain your reasoning.

Part B You would like the account to contain $5100 after 4 years. Would your initial $4000 deposit be large enough? Show your work and explain your reasoning.

11. Brad was solving the equation in the box shown.

What should Brad do to correct the error that he made?

F. Distribute -3 to get $6 - 15w$.

G. Distribute -3 to get $-6 - 15w$.

H. Add 6 to both sides to get $15w = -51$.

I. Add 6 to both sides to get $15w = -39$.

$$-3(2 - 5w) = -45$$
$$-6 + 15w = -45$$
$$9w = -45$$
$$\frac{9w}{9} = \frac{-45}{9}$$
$$w = -5$$

12. Which integer is closest to the value of the expression below?

$$-7\frac{1}{4} \cdot \left(-9\frac{7}{8}\right)$$

A. -70

B. -63

C. 63

D. 70

5 Similarity and Transformations

"Just 2 more minutes. I'm almost done with my 'cat tessellation' painting."

"If you hold perfectly still..."

"...each frame becomes a horizontal..."

"...translation of the previous frame..."

What You Learned Before

"These clouds are making me hungry."

Finding Perimeter

Example 1 Find the perimeter.

15 ft
6 ft
20 ft
6 ft

$P = 15 + 6 + 9 + 14 + 6 + 20$
$= 70 \text{ ft}$

Example 2 Find the circumference.

10 cm

$C = 2\pi r$
$= 2 \cdot 3.14 \cdot 5$ ← $r = \dfrac{d}{2} = \dfrac{10}{2} = 5$
$= 31.4 \text{ cm}$

Try It Yourself
Find the perimeter.

1.

4 mm
5 mm   5 mm
7 mm   7 mm
12 mm

2.
4 in.
4 in.   5 in.
7 in.

3.
13 cm

Solving Proportions

Example 3 Solve the proportion.

a. $\dfrac{x}{32} = \dfrac{3}{4}$

$\dfrac{x}{32} = \dfrac{3}{4}$ Write the proportion.

$4x = 96$ Use the Cross Products Property.

$x = 24$ Solve for x.

b. $\dfrac{3x}{20} = \dfrac{3}{5}$

$\dfrac{3x}{20} = \dfrac{3}{5}$

$15x = 60$

$x = 4$

Try It Yourself
Solve the proportion.

4. $\dfrac{2}{7} = \dfrac{x}{21}$ **5.** $\dfrac{3}{4} = \dfrac{3y}{8}$ **6.** $\dfrac{3}{14} = \dfrac{9}{y}$ **7.** $\dfrac{8}{9x} = \dfrac{2}{9}$

5.1 Identifying Similar Figures

Essential Question How can you use proportions to help make decisions in art, design, and magazine layouts?

Original Photograph

In a computer art program, when you click and drag on a side of a photograph, you distort it.

But when you click and drag on a corner of the photograph, it remains proportional to the original.

Distorted

Distorted

Proportional

1 ACTIVITY: Reducing Photographs

Work with a partner. You are trying to reduce the photograph to the indicated size for a nature magazine. Can you reduce the photograph to the indicated size without distorting or cropping? Explain your reasoning.

a.

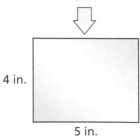

5 in.

6 in.

4 in.

5 in.

b.

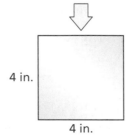

5 in.

5 in.

4 in.

4 in.

c.

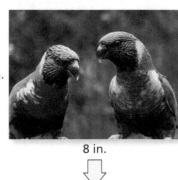

6 in.

8 in.

3 in.

4 in.

Work with a partner.

a. Tell whether the new designs are proportional to the original design. Explain your reasoning.

Original

8   8

7

Design 1

7   7

6

Design 2

$6\frac{6}{7}$ $6\frac{6}{7}$

6

b. Draw two designs that are proportional to the given design. Make one bigger and one smaller. Label the sides of the designs with their lengths.

5

4

8   10

6

6

10   8   10

6

What Is Your Answer?

3. IN YOUR OWN WORDS How can you use proportions to help make decisions in art, design, and magazine layouts? Give two examples.

4. a. Use a computer art program to draw two rectangles that are proportional to each other.

> You've got to hand it to him. He's right.

"I love this statue. It seems similar to a big statue I saw in New York."

b. Print the two rectangles on the same piece of paper.

c. Use a centimeter ruler to measure the length and width of each rectangle.

d. Find the following ratios. What can you conclude?

$$\frac{\text{Length of Larger}}{\text{Length of Smaller}} \qquad \frac{\text{Width of Larger}}{\text{Width of Smaller}}$$

Practice

Use what you learned about similar figures to complete Exercises 9 and 10 on page 198.

Check It Out
Lesson Tutorials
BigIdeasMath ✓com

 Key Idea

Key Vocabulary 🔊
similar figures, *p. 196*
corresponding angles,
    p. 196
corresponding sides,
    p. 196

Similar Figures

Figures that have the same shape but not necessarily the same size are called **similar figures**. The triangles below are similar.

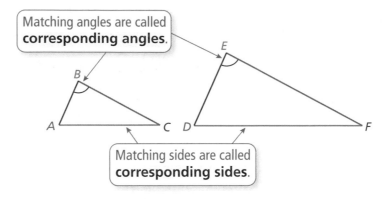

Matching angles are called **corresponding angles**.

Matching sides are called **corresponding sides**.

EXAMPLE 1 **Naming Corresponding Parts**

The trapezoids are similar. (a) Name the corresponding angles.
(b) Name the corresponding sides.

Reading

∠A is read as "angle A."

a. **Corresponding angles:**

∠A and ∠P

∠B and ∠Q

∠C and ∠R

∠D and ∠S

b. **Corresponding sides:**

Side AB and Side PQ

Side BC and Side QR

Side CD and Side RS

Side AD and Side PS

⬤ **On Your Own**

Now You're Ready
Exercises 5 and 6

1. The figures are similar.

   a. Name the corresponding angles.

   b. Name the corresponding sides.

Key Idea

Identifying Similar Figures

Triangle ABC is similar to triangle DEF: $\triangle ABC \sim \triangle DEF$

Words Two figures are similar if

- corresponding side lengths are proportional, and
- corresponding angles have the same measure.

Symbols

Side Lengths

$$\frac{AB}{DE} = \frac{BC}{EF} = \frac{AC}{DF}$$

Angles

$\angle A$ has the same measure as $\angle D$.

$\angle B$ has the same measure as $\angle E$.

$\angle C$ has the same measure as $\angle F$.

EXAMPLE ② **Identifying Similar Figures**

Which rectangle is similar to Rectangle A?

Rectangle A   Rectangle B   Rectangle C

3   6   2   4   2

6

Each figure is a rectangle. So, corresponding angles have the same measure. Check to see if corresponding side lengths are proportional.

Rectangle A and Rectangle B

$$\frac{\text{Length of A}}{\text{Length of B}} = \frac{6}{6} = 1 \qquad \frac{\text{Width of A}}{\text{Width of B}} = \frac{3}{2} \qquad \text{Not proportional}$$

Rectangle A and Rectangle C

$$\frac{\text{Length of A}}{\text{Length of C}} = \frac{6}{4} = \frac{3}{2} \qquad \frac{\text{Width of A}}{\text{Width of C}} = \frac{3}{2} \qquad \text{Proportional}$$

∴ So, Rectangle C is similar to Rectangle A.

On Your Own

Now You're Ready
Exercises 7–12

2. Rectangle D is 3 units long and 1 unit wide. Which rectangle in Example 2 is similar to Rectangle D?

Vocabulary and Concept Check

1. **VOCABULARY** How are corresponding angles of two similar figures related?

2. **VOCABULARY** How are corresponding side lengths of two similar figures related?

3. **OPEN-ENDED** Give examples of two real-world objects whose shapes are similar.

4. **CRITICAL THINKING** Are two figures that have the same size and shape similar? Explain.

 Practice and Problem Solving

Name the corresponding angles and the corresponding sides of the similar figures.

① 5.

6.

In a coordinate plane, draw the figures with the given vertices. Which figures are similar? Explain your reasoning.

② 7. Triangle A: (0, 0), (3, 0), (0, 3)
Triangle B: (0, 0), (5, 0), (0, 5)
Triangle C: (0, 0), (3, 0), (0, 6)

8. Rectangle A: (0, 0), (4, 0), (4, 2), (0, 2)
Rectangle B: (0, 0), (−6, 0), (−6, 3), (0, 3)
Rectangle C: (0, 0), (4, 0), (4, 2), (0, 2)

Tell whether the two figures are similar. Explain your reasoning.

9.

10.

11. **MEXICO** A Mexican flag is 63 inches long and 36 inches high. Is the drawing at the right similar to the Mexican flag?

12. **DESKS** A student's rectangular desk is 30 inches long and 18 inches wide. The teacher's rectangular desk is 60 inches long and 36 inches wide. Are the desks similar?

The two triangles are similar. Find the measure of the angle.

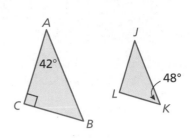

13. ∠B   **14.** ∠L   **15.** ∠J

16. REASONING Given △FGH ~ △QRT, name the corresponding angles and the corresponding sides.

17. PHOTOS You want to buy only photos that are similar rectangles. Which of the photo sizes should you buy?

18. CRITICAL THINKING Are the following figures *always, sometimes,* or *never* similar? Explain.

   a. Two triangles   **b.** Two squares

   c. Two rectangles   **d.** A square and a triangle

Photo Size
4 in. × 5 in.
5 in. × 7 in.
8 in. × 12 in.
11 in. × 14 in.
18 in. × 27 in.

19. CRITICAL THINKING Can you draw two quadrilaterals each having two 130° angles and two 50° angles that are *not* similar? Justify your answer.

20. SIGN All of the angle measures in the sign are 90°.

   a. Each side length is increased by 20%. Is the new sign similar to the original?

   b. Each side length is increased by 6 inches. Is the new sign similar to the original?

21. GEOMETRY Use a ruler to draw two different isosceles triangles similar to the one shown. Measure the heights of each triangle to the nearest centimeter.

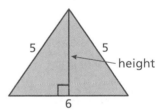

   a. Is the ratio of the corresponding heights proportional to the ratio of the corresponding side lengths?

   b. Do you think this is true for all similar triangles? Explain.

22. **Critical Thinking** Given △ABC ~ △DEF and △DEF ~ △JKL, is △ABC ~ △JKL? Give an example or non-example.

Fair Game Review *What you learned in previous grades & lessons*

Simplify. *(Skills Review Handbook)*

23. $\left(\dfrac{4}{9}\right)^2$ **24.** $\left(\dfrac{3}{8}\right)^2$ **25.** $\left(\dfrac{7}{4}\right)^2$ **26.** $\left(\dfrac{6.5}{2}\right)^2$

27. MULTIPLE CHOICE Which equation shows inverse variation? *(Section 3.8)*

   Ⓐ $3y = 8x$ Ⓑ $y = \dfrac{8}{3x}$ Ⓒ $\dfrac{y}{3} = \dfrac{x}{8}$ Ⓓ $y = 8x - 3$

Essential Question How do changes in dimensions of similar geometric figures affect the perimeters and areas of the figures?

1 ACTIVITY: Comparing Perimeters and Areas

Work with a partner. Use pattern blocks to make a figure whose dimensions are 2, 3, and 4 times greater than those of the original figure. Find the perimeter P and area A of each larger figure.

a. **Sample:** Square

$P = 4$	$P = 8$	$P = 12$	$P = 16$
$A = 1$	$A = 4$	$A = 9$	$A = 16$

b. Triangle

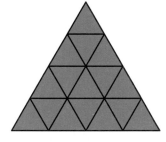

$P = 3$	$P = 6$	$P = $	$P = $
$A = B$	$A = 4B$	$A = $	$A = $

c. Rectangle

$P = 6$

$A = 2$

d. Parallelogram

$P = 4$

$A = C$

Work with a partner. Copy and complete the table for the perimeters of the figures in Activity 1. Describe the pattern.

Perimeters	Figure	Original Side Lengths	Double Side Lengths	Triple Side Lengths	Quadruple Side Lengths
	◻	$P = 4$	$P = 8$	$P = 12$	$P = 16$
	△	$P = 3$	$P = 6$		
	▭	$P = 6$			
	▱	$P = 4$			

Work with a partner. Copy and complete the table for the areas of the figures in Activity 1. Describe the pattern.

Areas	Figure	Original Side Lengths	Double Side Lengths	Triple Side Lengths	Quadruple Side Lengths
	◻	$A = 1$	$A = 4$	$A = 9$	$A = 16$
	△	$A = B$	$A = 4B$		
	▭	$A = 2$			
	▱	$A = C$			

What Is Your Answer?

4. **IN YOUR OWN WORDS** How do changes in dimensions of similar geometric figures affect the perimeters and areas of the figures?

Practice

Use what you learned about perimeters and areas of similar figures to complete Exercises 8–11 on page 204.

Check It Out
Lesson Tutorials
BigIdeasMath.com

Key Idea

Perimeters of Similar Figures

If two figures are similar, then the ratio of their perimeters is equal to the ratio of their corresponding side lengths.

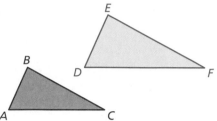

$$\frac{\text{Perimeter of } \triangle ABC}{\text{Perimeter of } \triangle DEF} = \frac{AB}{DE} = \frac{BC}{EF} = \frac{AC}{DF}$$

EXAMPLE 1 Finding Ratios of Perimeters

Find the ratio (red to blue) of the perimeters of the similar rectangles.

$$\frac{\text{Perimeter of red rectangle}}{\text{Perimeter of blue rectangle}} = \frac{4}{6} = \frac{2}{3}$$

∴ The ratio of the perimeters is $\frac{2}{3}$.

On Your Own

1. The height of Figure A is 9 feet. The height of a similar Figure B is 15 feet. What is the ratio of the perimeter of A to the perimeter of B?

Key Idea

Areas of Similar Figures

If two figures are similar, then the ratio of their areas is equal to the *square* of the ratio of their corresponding side lengths.

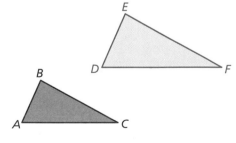

$$\frac{\text{Area of } \triangle ABC}{\text{Area of } \triangle DEF} = \left(\frac{AB}{DE}\right)^2 = \left(\frac{BC}{EF}\right)^2 = \left(\frac{AC}{DF}\right)^2$$

EXAMPLE 2 | **Finding Ratios of Areas**

Find the ratio (red to blue) of the areas
of the similar triangles.

$$\frac{\text{Area of red triangle}}{\text{Area of blue triangle}} = \left(\frac{6}{10}\right)^2$$

$$= \left(\frac{3}{5}\right)^2 = \frac{9}{25}$$

⋮• The ratio of the areas is $\frac{9}{25}$.

EXAMPLE 3 | **Real-Life Application**

├——— 6 in. ———┤
├———— 8 in. ————┤

You place a picture on a page of a photo album. The page and the
picture are similar rectangles.

a. How many times greater is the area of the page than the area
of the picture?

b. The area of the picture is 45 square inches. What is the area
of the page?

a. Find the ratio of the area of the page to the area of the picture.

$$\frac{\text{Area of page}}{\text{Area of picture}} = \left(\frac{\text{length of page}}{\text{length of picture}}\right)^2$$

$$= \left(\frac{8}{6}\right)^2 = \left(\frac{4}{3}\right)^2 = \frac{16}{9}$$

⋮• The area of the page is $\frac{16}{9}$ times greater than the area
of the picture.

b. Multiply the area of the picture by $\frac{16}{9}$.

$$45 \cdot \frac{16}{9} = 80$$

⋮• The area of the page is 80 square inches.

On Your Own

Now You're Ready
Exercises 4–13

2. The base of Triangle P is 8 meters. The base of a similar
Triangle Q is 7 meters. What is the ratio of the area of P
to the area of Q?

3. In Example 3, the perimeter of the picture is 27 inches.
What is the perimeter of the page?

✓ Vocabulary and Concept Check

1. **WRITING** How are the perimeters of two similar figures related?

2. **WRITING** How are the areas of two similar figures related?

3. **VOCABULARY** Rectangle *ABCD* is similar to Rectangle *WXYZ*. The area of *ABCD* is 30 square inches. What is the area of *WXYZ*? Explain.

$$\frac{AD}{WZ} = \frac{1}{2} \qquad \frac{AB}{WX} = \frac{1}{2}$$

Practice and Problem Solving

The two figures are similar. Find the ratios (red to blue) of the perimeters and of the areas.

 4.

11   6

5.

5   8

6.

7   4

7.

9   14

8. How does doubling the side lengths of a triangle affect its perimeter?

9. How does tripling the side lengths of a triangle affect its perimeter?

10. How does doubling the side lengths of a rectangle affect its area?

11. How does quadrupling the side lengths of a rectangle affect its area?

12. **FOOSBALL** The playing surfaces of two foosball tables are similar. The ratio of the corresponding side lengths is 10 : 7. What is the ratio of the areas?

13. **LAPTOP** The ratio of the corresponding side lengths of two similar computer screens is 13 : 15. The perimeter of the smaller screen is 39 inches. What is the perimeter of the larger screen?

Triangle *ABC* is similar to Triangle *DEF*. Tell whether the statement is *true* or *false*. Explain your reasoning.

14. $\dfrac{\text{Perimeter of } \triangle ABC}{\text{Perimeter of } \triangle DEF} = \dfrac{AB}{DE}$

15. $\dfrac{\text{Area of } \triangle ABC}{\text{Area of } \triangle DEF} = \dfrac{AB}{DE}$

21 in.

9 in.

16. FABRIC The cost of the fabric is $1.31. What would you expect to pay for a similar piece of fabric that is 18 inches by 42 inches?

15 in.

17. AMUSEMENT PARK A model of a merry-go-round has a base area of about 77 square inches. What is the percent of increase of the base area from the model to the actual merry-go-round? Explain.

Model 77 sq in.

10 ft

18. CRITICAL THINKING The circumference of Circle K is π. The circumference of Circle L is 4π.

   a. What is the ratio of their circumferences? of their radii? of their areas?

   b. What do you notice?

Circle K

Circle L

19. GEOMETRY Rhombus A is similar to Rhombus B. What is the ratio (A to B) of the corresponding side lengths?

A

B

Area = 36 cm²

Area = 64 cm²

20. **Geometry** A triangle with an area of 10 square meters has a base of 4 meters. A similar triangle has an area of 90 square meters. What is the *height* of the larger triangle?

Fair Game Review What you learned in previous grades & lessons

Find the percent of change. Round to the nearest tenth of a percent, if necessary. *(Section 4.2)*

21. 24 feet to 30 feet   **22.** 90 miles to 63 miles   **23.** 150 liters to 86 liters

24. MULTIPLE CHOICE A runner completes an 800-meter race in 2 minutes 40 seconds. What is the runner's speed? *(Section 3.1)*

   Ⓐ $\dfrac{3 \text{ sec}}{10 \text{ m}}$ Ⓑ $\dfrac{160 \text{ sec}}{1 \text{ m}}$ Ⓒ $\dfrac{5 \text{ m}}{1 \text{ sec}}$ Ⓓ $\dfrac{10 \text{ m}}{3 \text{ sec}}$

Essential Question What information do you need to know to find the dimensions of a figure that is similar to another figure?

> **1** **ACTIVITY: Drawing and Labeling Similar Figures**

Work with a partner. You are given the red rectangle. Find a blue rectangle that is similar and has one side from $(-1, -6)$ to $(5, -6)$. Label the vertices.

a. **Sample:**

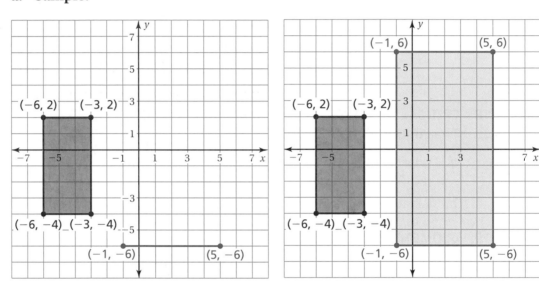

You can see that the two rectangles are similar by showing that ratios of corresponding sides are equal.

$$\frac{\text{Red Length}}{\text{Blue Length}} \overset{?}{=} \frac{\text{Red Width}}{\text{Blue Width}}$$

$$\frac{\text{change in } y}{\text{change in } y} \overset{?}{=} \frac{\text{change in } x}{\text{change in } x}$$

$$\frac{6}{12} \overset{?}{=} \frac{3}{6}$$

$$\frac{1}{2} = \frac{1}{2}$$

∴ The ratios are equal. So, the rectangles are similar.

b. There are three other blue rectangles that are similar to the red rectangle and have the given side.

- Draw each one. Label the vertices of each.

- Show that each is similar to the original red rectangle.

Work with a partner.

a. The red and blue rectangles are similar. Find the length of the blue rectangle. Explain your reasoning.

b. The distance marked by the vertical red line on the map is 1 mile. Find the distance marked by the horizontal red line. Explain your reasoning.

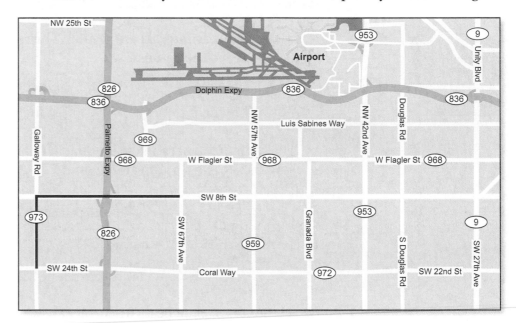

What Is Your Answer?

3. **IN YOUR OWN WORDS** What information do you need to know to find the dimensions of a figure that is similar to another figure? Give some examples using two rectangles.

4. When you know the length and width of one rectangle and the length of a similar rectangle, can you always find the missing width? Why or why not?

Practice

Use what you learned about finding unknown measures in similar figures to complete Exercises 3 and 4 on page 210.

EXAMPLE 1 Finding an Unknown Measure

Key Vocabulary
indirect measurement,
p. 209

The two triangles are similar. Find the value of x.

Corresponding side lengths are proportional. So, use a proportion to find x.

$$\frac{6}{9} = \frac{8}{x} \qquad \text{Write a proportion.}$$

$$6x = 72 \qquad \text{Use Cross Products Property.}$$

$$x = 12 \qquad \text{Divide each side by 6.}$$

So, x is 12 meters.

EXAMPLE 2 Standardized Test Practice

15 in.

x

The two quadrilaterals are similar. The ratio of their perimeters is $12:5$. Find the value of x.

  (A) 2.4 inches   **(B)** 4 inches

  (C) 6.25 inches   **(D)** 36 inches

The ratio of the perimeters is equal to the ratio of corresponding side lengths. So, use a proportion to find x.

$$\frac{12}{5} = \frac{15}{x} \qquad \text{Write a proportion.}$$

$$12x = 75 \qquad \text{Use Cross Products Property.}$$

$$x = 6.25 \qquad \text{Divide each side by 12.}$$

So, x is 6.25 inches. The correct answer is **(C)**.

On Your Own

Now You're Ready
Exercises 3–8

1. The two quadrilaterals are similar. The ratio of the perimeters is $3:4$. Find the value of x.

12 ft

x

Indirect measurement uses similar figures to find a missing measure that is difficult to find directly.

EXAMPLE ③ **Using Indirect Measurement**

h ft

6 ft

15 ft   3 ft

A person that is 6 feet tall casts a 3-foot-long shadow. A nearby palm tree casts a 15-foot-long shadow. What is the height *h* of the palm tree? Assume the triangles are similar.

Corresponding side lengths are proportional.

$$\frac{h}{6} = \frac{15}{3}$$ Write a proportion.

$$6 \cdot \frac{h}{6} = \frac{15}{3} \cdot 6$$ Multiply each side by 6.

$$h = 30$$ Simplify.

⋮• The palm tree is 30 feet tall.

On Your Own

Now You're Ready
Exercise 9

2. **WHAT IF?** Later in the day, the palm tree in Example 3 casts a 25-foot-long shadow. How long is the shadow of the person?

EXAMPLE ④ **Using Proportions to Find Area**

A swimming pool is similar in shape to a volleyball court. What is the area *A* of the pool?

$$\frac{\text{Area of court}}{\text{Area of pool}} = \left(\frac{\text{width of court}}{\text{width of pool}}\right)^2$$

$$\frac{200}{A} = \left(\frac{10}{18}\right)^2$$ Substitute.

$$\frac{200}{A} = \frac{100}{324}$$ Simplify.

$$A = 648$$ Solve the proportion.

18 yd

10 yd

Area = 200 yd²

⋮• The area of the pool is 648 square yards.

On Your Own

3. The length of the volleyball court in Example 4 is 20 yards. What is the perimeter of the pool?

5.3   **Exercises**

Vocabulary and Concept Check

1. **REASONING** How can you use corresponding side lengths to find unknown measures in similar figures?

2. **CRITICAL THINKING** In which of the situations would you likely use indirect measurement? Explain your reasoning.

Finding the height of a statue

Finding the width of a doorway

Finding the width of a river

Finding the length of a lake

Practice and Problem Solving

The polygons are similar. Find the value of x.

1 2 3.

4.

5.

6.

7. The ratio of the perimeters is 7 : 10.

8. The ratio of the perimeters is 8 : 5.
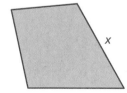

3 9. FLAGPOLE What is the height x of the flagpole? Assume the triangles are similar.

10. **CHEERLEADING** A rectangular school banner has a length of 44 inches and a perimeter of 156 inches. The cheerleaders make signs similar to the banner. The length of a sign is 11 inches. What is its perimeter?

11. **SQUARE** The ratio of the side length of Square A to the side length of Square B is 4 : 9. The side length of Square A is 12 yards. What is the perimeter of Square B?

12. **RIVER** Is the distance QP across the river greater than 100 meters? Explain.

$\triangle PQR \sim \triangle STR$

13. **STREET LIGHT** A person standing 20 feet from a street light casts a shadow as shown. How many times taller is the street light than the person? Assume the triangles are similar.

14. **AREA** A school playground is similar in shape to the community park. You can mow 250 square yards of grass in 15 minutes. How long would it take you to mow the grass on the playground?

15. **Critical Thinking** Two bottles of fertilizer are needed to treat the flower garden shown. How many bottles are needed to treat a similar garden with a perimeter of 105 feet?

Fair Game Review What you learned in previous grades & lessons

Copy and complete the statement using a ratio. Round to the nearest hundredth, if necessary. *(Section 3.6)*

16. 4 mi ≈ ____ km

17. 12.5 in. ≈ ____ cm

18. 110 kg ≈ ____ lb

19. 6.2 km ≈ ____ mi

20. 10 cm ≈ ____ in.

21. 92.5 lb ≈ ____ kg

22. **MULTIPLE CHOICE** A recipe that makes 8 pints of salsa uses 22 tomatoes. Which proportion can you use to find the number n of tomatoes needed to make 12 pints of salsa? *(Section 3.4)*

Ⓐ $\dfrac{n}{8} = \dfrac{22}{12}$

Ⓑ $\dfrac{8}{22} = \dfrac{12}{n}$

Ⓒ $\dfrac{22}{n} = \dfrac{12}{8}$

Ⓓ $\dfrac{8}{22} = \dfrac{n}{12}$

Essential Question
How can you use a scale drawing to estimate the cost of painting a room?

1 ACTIVITY: Making Scale Drawings

Work with a partner. You have decided that your classroom needs to be painted. Start by making a scale drawing of each of the four walls.

- Measure each of the walls.
- Measure the locations and dimensions of parts that will *not* be painted.
- Decide on a scale for your drawings.
- Make a scale drawing of each of the walls.

Sample: Wall #1

Blue region needs to be painted.

Scale: 1 cm : 1 ft

Chalk Board

Wall

9 ft

26 ft

- For each wall, find the area of the part that needs to be painted.

	Dimensions	Area
Dimensions of the wall	9 ft by 26 ft	9 × 26 = 234 sq ft
Dimensions of the part that will *not* be painted	5 ft by 17 ft	5 × 17 = 85 sq ft
Area of painted part		149 sq ft

Work with a partner.

You are using a paint that covers 200 square feet per gallon. Each wall will need two coats of paint.

a. Find the total area of the walls from Activity 1 that needs to be painted.

b. Find the amount of paint you need to buy.

c. Estimate the total cost of painting your classroom.

| Interior latex paint | $40 per gallon |
| Roller, pan, and brush set | $12 |

What Is Your Answer?

3. IN YOUR OWN WORDS How can you use a scale drawing to estimate the cost of painting a room?

4. Use a scale drawing to estimate the cost of painting another room, such as your bedroom or another room in your house.

5. Look at some maps in your school library or on the Internet. Make a list of the different scales used on the maps.

0   1   2   3   4

Miles

6. When you view a map on the Internet, how does the scale change when you zoom out? How does the scale change when you zoom in?

Oh brother!

"I don't get it. According to this map, we only have to drive $8\frac{1}{2}$ inches."

Practice

Use what you learned about scale drawings to complete Exercises 4–7 on page 216.

Check It Out
Lesson Tutorials
BigIdeasMath✓com

Key Vocabulary
scale drawing, *p. 214*
scale model, *p. 214*
scale, *p. 214*
scale factor, *p. 215*

Key Ideas

Scale Drawings and Models

A **scale drawing** is a proportional two-dimensional drawing of an object. A **scale model** is a proportional three-dimensional model of an object.

Scale

Measurements in scale drawings and models are proportional to the measurements of the actual object. The **scale** gives the ratio that compares the measurements of the drawing or model with the actual measurements.

$$\frac{1 \text{ in.}}{10 \text{ mi}} \leftarrow \text{drawing distance}$$
$$\leftarrow \text{actual distance}$$

1 in. : 10 mi
↑ drawing ↑ actual

Study Tip

Scales are written so that the drawing distance comes first in the ratio.

EXAMPLE ① **Finding an Actual Distance**

What is the actual distance *d* between Cadillac and Detroit?

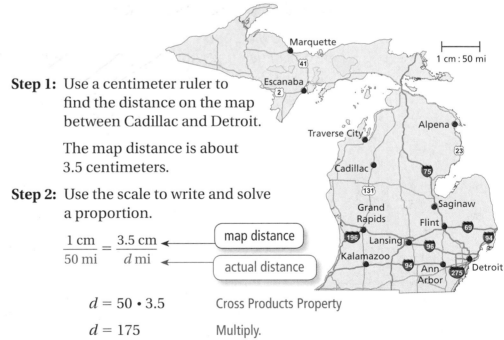

Step 1: Use a centimeter ruler to find the distance on the map between Cadillac and Detroit.

The map distance is about 3.5 centimeters.

Step 2: Use the scale to write and solve a proportion.

$$\frac{1 \text{ cm}}{50 \text{ mi}} = \frac{3.5 \text{ cm}}{d \text{ mi}} \leftarrow \text{map distance}$$
$$\leftarrow \text{actual distance}$$

$$d = 50 \cdot 3.5 \qquad \text{Cross Products Property}$$
$$d = 175 \qquad \text{Multiply.}$$

∴ The distance between Cadillac and Detroit is about 175 miles.

On Your Own

Now You're Ready
Exercises 8–11

1. What is the actual distance between Traverse City and Marquette?

◀) Multi-Language Glossary at BigIdeasMath✓com.

EXAMPLE 2

Standardized Test Practice

The liquid outer core of Earth is 2300 kilometers thick. A scale model of the layers of Earth has a scale of 1 in. : 500 km. How thick is the liquid outer core of the model?

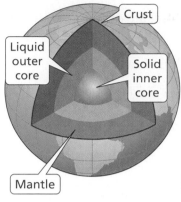

Ⓐ 0.2 in.　　Ⓑ 4.6 in.　　Ⓒ 0.2 km　　Ⓓ 4.6 km

$$\frac{1 \text{ in.}}{500 \text{ km}} = \frac{x \text{ in.}}{2300 \text{ km}}$$ ← model thickness
← actual thickness

$$\frac{1 \text{ in.}}{500 \text{ km}} \cdot 2300 \text{ km} = \frac{x \text{ in.}}{2300 \text{ km}} \cdot 2300 \text{ km}$$　　Multiply each side by 2300 km.

$$4.6 = x$$　　Simplify.

∴ The liquid outer core of the model is 4.6 inches thick. The correct answer is Ⓑ.

On Your Own

2. The mantle of Earth is 2900 kilometers thick. How thick is the mantle of the model?

A scale can be written without units when the units are the same. A scale without units is called a **scale factor**.

EXAMPLE 3

Finding a Scale Factor

A scale drawing of a spider is 5 centimeters long. The actual spider is 10 millimeters long. (a) What is the scale of the drawing? (b) What is the scale factor of the drawing?

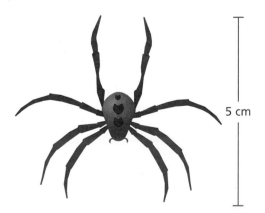

5 cm

a. $$\frac{\text{drawing length}}{\text{actual length}} = \frac{5 \text{ cm}}{10 \text{ mm}} = \frac{1 \text{ cm}}{2 \text{ mm}}$$

∴ The scale is 1 cm : 2 mm.

b. Write the scale with the same units. Use the fact that 1 cm = 10 mm.

$$\text{scale factor} = \frac{1 \text{ cm}}{2 \text{ mm}} = \frac{10 \text{ mm}}{2 \text{ mm}} = \frac{5}{1}$$

∴ The scale factor is 5 : 1.

On Your Own

Now You're Ready
Exercises 12–16

3. A model has a scale of 1 mm : 20 cm. What is the scale factor of the model?

Vocabulary and Concept Check

1. **VOCABULARY** Compare and contrast the terms *scale* and *scale factor*.

2. **CRITICAL THINKING** The scale of a drawing is 2 cm : 1 mm. Is the scale drawing *larger* or *smaller* than the actual object? Explain.

3. **REASONING** How would you find a scale factor of a drawing that shows a length of 4 inches when the actual object is 8 feet long?

 Practice and Problem Solving

Use the drawing and a centimeter ruler.

4. What is the actual length of the flower garden?

5. What are the actual dimensions of the rose bed?

6. What are the actual perimeters of the perennial beds?

7. The area of the tulip bed is what percent of the area of the rose bed?

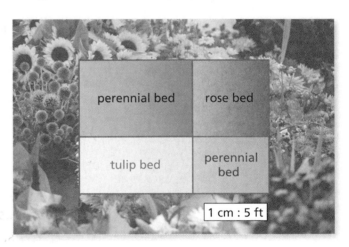

Use the map in Example 1 to find the actual distance between the cities.

① 8. Kalamazoo and Ann Arbor

9. Lansing and Flint

10. Grand Rapids and Escabana

11. Saginaw and Alpena

Find the missing dimension. Use the scale factor 1 : 12.

	Item	Model	Actual
② ③ 12.	Mattress	Length: 6.25 in.	Length: ____ in.
13.	Corvette	Length: ____ in.	Length: 15 ft
14.	Water Tower	Depth: 32 cm	Depth: ____ m
15.	Wingspan	Width: 5.4 ft	Width: ____ yd
16.	Football Helmet	Diameter: ____ mm	Diameter: 21 cm

17. **ERROR ANALYSIS** A scale is 1 cm : 20 m. Describe and correct the error in finding the actual distance that corresponds to 5 cm.

$$\frac{1\ cm}{20\ m} = \frac{x\ m}{5\ cm}$$

$$x = 0.25\ m$$

Use a centimeter ruler to measure the segment shown. Find the scale of the drawing.

18. |————— 120 m —————|

19.

Iris
Cornea
Pupil
Vitreous humor
Lens
24 mm

20. REASONING You know the length and width of a scale model. What additional information do you need to know to find the scale of the model?

21. OPEN-ENDED You are in charge of creating a billboard advertisement with the dimensions shown.

    a. Choose a product. Then design the billboard using words and a picture.

    b. What is the scale factor of your design?

16 ft

8 ft

YOUR AD HERE

Reduced drawing of blueprint

Bedroom
Living room
Bathroom
1 in. : 16 ft

22. BLUEPRINT In a blueprint, each square has a side length of $\frac{1}{4}$ inch.

    a. Ceramic tile costs $5 per square foot. How much would it cost to tile the bathroom?

    b. Carpet costs $18 per square yard. How much would it cost to carpet the bedroom and living room?

    c. Which has a higher unit cost, the tile or the carpet? Explain.

23. REASONING You are making a scale model of the solar system. The radius of Earth is 6378 kilometers. The radius of the Sun is 695,500 kilometers. Is it reasonable to choose a baseball as a model of Earth? Explain your reasoning.

24. *Critical Thinking* A map on the Internet has a scale of 1 in. : 10 mi. You zoom out one level. The map has been reduced so that 2.5 inches on the old map appears as 1 inch on the new map. What is the scale of the new map?

Fair Game Review What you learned in previous grades & lessons

Plot and label the ordered pair in a coordinate plane. *(Section 1.6)*

25. $A(-4, 3)$ **26.** $B(2, -6)$ **27.** $C(5, 1)$ **28.** $D(-3, -7)$

29. MULTIPLE CHOICE A backpack is on sale for 15% off the original price. The original price is $68. What is the sale price? *(Section 4.3)*

    A $10.20   **B** $53   **C** $57.80   **D** $78.20

You can use an **example and non-example chart** to list examples and non-examples of a vocabulary word or term. Here is an example and non-example chart for similar figures.

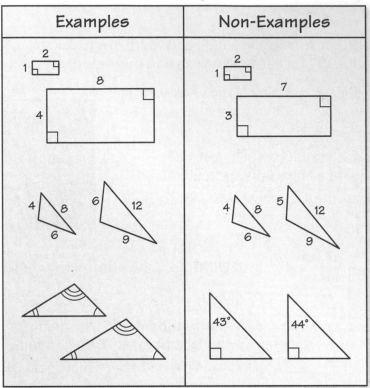

On Your Own

Make an example and non-example chart to help you study these topics.

1. corresponding angles

2. corresponding sides

3. perimeters of similar figures

4. areas of similar figures

5. indirect measurements

6. scale drawings

After you complete this chapter, make example and non-example charts for the following topics.

7. transformations

   a. translations   **b.** reflections   **c.** rotations

"I'm using an example and non-example chart for a talk on cat hygiene."

1. Tell whether the two rectangles are similar. Explain your reasoning. *(Section 5.1)*

4 m
8 m

10 m
20 m

The two figures are similar. Find the ratios (red to blue) of the perimeters and of the areas. *(Section 5.2)*

2.

12
8

3.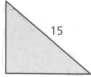

4
15

The polygons are similar. Find the value of x. *(Section 5.3)*

4.

8
6
14
x

5.

x
22

3
4

Find the missing dimension. Use the scale factor 1 : 20. *(Section 5.4)*

	Item	Model	Actual
6.	Basketball Player	Height: in.	Height: 90 in.
7.	Dinosaur	Length: 3.75 ft	Length: ft

8. POSTERS The ratio of the corresponding side lengths of two similar posters is 7 in. : 20 in. What is the ratio of the perimeters? *(Section 5.2)*

9. DOLPHIN A dolphin in an aquarium is 12 feet long. A scale model of the dolphin is $3\frac{1}{2}$ inches long. What is the scale factor of the model? *(Section 5.4)*

10. TENNIS COURT The tennis courts for singles and doubles matches are different sizes. Are the courts similar? Explain. *(Section 5.1)*

Singles

27 ft
78 ft

Doubles
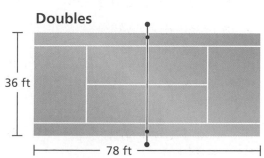
36 ft
78 ft

5.5 Translations

Share Your Work at...
My.BigIdeasMath.com

Essential Question How can you use translations to make a tessellation?

When you slide a tile it is called a **translation**. When tiles can be used to cover a floor with no empty spaces, the collection of tiles is called a *tessellation*.

1 ACTIVITY: Describing Tessellations

Work with a partner. Can you make the pattern by using a translation of single tiles that are all of the same shape and design? If so, show how.

a. Sample:

Tile Pattern   Single Tiles

b.

c.

d.

e.

2 ACTIVITY: Tessellations and Basic Shapes

Work with a partner.

a. Which pattern blocks can you use to make a tessellation?

b. For each one that works, draw the tessellation.

c. Can you make the tessellation using only translation, or do you have to rotate or flip the pattern blocks?

3 ACTIVITY: Designing Tessellations

Work with a partner. Design your own tessellation. Use one of the basic shapes from Activity 2.

Sample:

Start with a square.

Cut a design out of one side.

Tape it to the other side to make your pattern.

Use the pattern and translations to make your tessellation.

Color the tessellation.

What Is Your Answer?

4. IN YOUR OWN WORDS How can you use translations to make a tessellation? Give an example.

5. Draw any parallelogram. Does it tessellate? Is it true that any parallelogram can be translated to make a tessellation? Explain why.

Practice

Use what you learned about translations to complete Exercises 4–6 on page 224.

Check It Out
Lesson Tutorials
BigIdeasMath⟍com

A **transformation** changes a figure into another figure. The new figure is called the **image**.

Key Vocabulary ◀))
transformation, *p. 222*
image, *p. 222*
translation, *p. 222*

 Key Idea

Translations

A **translation** is a transformation in which a figure *slides* but does not turn. Every point of the figure moves the same distance and in the same direction.

Slide

Slide

The original figure and its image have the same size and shape.

EXAMPLE ① **Identifying a Translation**

Tell whether the blue figure is a translation of the red figure.

a.

b. **3 ⌣**

The red figure *slides* to form the blue figure.

∴ So, the blue figure is a translation of the red figure.

The red figure *turns* to form the blue figure.

∴ So, the blue figure is *not* a translation of the red figure.

● On Your Own

Tell whether the blue figure is a translation of the red figure. Explain.

Now You're Ready
Exercises 4–9

1.

2.

3. **5**
   5

4. **G G**

EXAMPLE 2   **Translating a Figure**

Translate the red triangle 3 units right and 3 units down. What are the coordinates of the image?

Reading

A' is read "A prime." Use *prime* symbols when naming an image.

$A \longrightarrow A'$

$B \longrightarrow B'$

$C \longrightarrow C'$

Move each vertex 3 units right and 3 units down.

Connect the vertices. Label as A', B', and C'.

∴ The coordinates of the image are $A'(1, -2)$, $B'(5, 2)$, and $C'(4, -1)$.

On Your Own

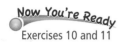

Now You're Ready
Exercises 10 and 11

5. The red triangle is translated 4 units left and 2 units up. What are the coordinates of the image?

EXAMPLE 3   **Translating a Figure**

The vertices of a square are $A(1, -2)$, $B(3, -2)$, $C(3, -4)$, and $D(1, -4)$. Draw the figure and its image after a translation 4 units left and 6 units up.

Subtract 4 from each x-coordinate.

Add 6 to each y-coordinate.

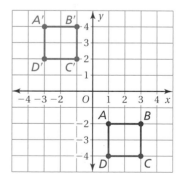

Vertices of $ABCD$	$(x - 4, y + 6)$	Vertices of $A'B'C'D'$
$A(1, -2)$	$(1 - 4, -2 + 6)$	$A'(-3, 4)$
$B(3, -2)$	$(3 - 4, -2 + 6)$	$B'(-1, 4)$
$C(3, -4)$	$(3 - 4, -4 + 6)$	$C'(-1, 2)$
$D(1, -4)$	$(1 - 4, -4 + 6)$	$D'(-3, 2)$

∴ The figure and its image are shown at the right.

On Your Own

Now You're Ready
Exercises 12–15

6. The vertices of a triangle are $A(-2, -2)$, $B(0, 2)$, and $C(3, 0)$. Draw the figure and its image after a translation 1 unit left and 2 units up.

Vocabulary and Concept Check

1. **VOCABULARY** Which figure is the image?

2. **VOCABULARY** How do you translate a figure in a coordinate plane?

3. **CRITICAL THINKING** Can you translate the letters in the word TOKYO to form the word KYOTO? Explain.

Slide

A   B

Practice and Problem Solving

Tell whether the blue figure is a translation of the red figure.

① 4. 5. 6.

7. 8. 9.

② 10. Translate the triangle 4 units right and 3 units down. What are the coordinates of the image?

11. Translate the figure 2 units left and 4 units down. What are the coordinates of the image?

The vertices of a triangle are $L(0, 1)$, $M(1, -2)$, and $N(-2, 1)$. Draw the figure and its image after the translation.

③ 12. 1 unit left and 6 units up

13. 5 units right

14. 2 units right and 3 units up

15. 3 units left and 4 units down

16. **ICONS** You can click and drag an icon on a computer screen. Is this an example of a translation? Explain.

HURRY!

Describe the translation of the point to its image.

17. $(3, -2) \rightarrow (1, 0)$

18. $(-8, -4) \rightarrow (-3, 5)$

Describe the translation from the red figure to the blue figure.

19.

20.

21. FISHING A school of fish translates from point F to point D.

    a. Describe the translation of the school of fish.

    b. Can the fishing boat make a similar translation? Explain.

    c. Describe a translation the fishing boat could make to get to point D.

22. REASONING A triangle is translated 5 units right and 2 units up. Then the image is translated 3 units left and 8 units down. Write a translation of the original triangle to the ending position.

23. **Critical Thinking** In chess, a knight can move only in an L-shape pattern:

- *two* vertical squares then *one* horizontal square;
- *two* horizontal squares then *one* vertical square;
- *one* vertical square then *two* horizontal squares; or
- *one* horizontal square then *two* vertical squares.

Write a series of translations to move the knight from g8 to g5.

Tell whether each figure can be folded in half so that one side matches the other. *(Skills Review Handbook)*

24.

25.

26.

27.

28. MULTIPLE CHOICE You put $550 in an account that earns 4.4% simple interest per year. How much interest do you earn in 6 months? *(Section 4.4)*

    A $1.21

    B $12.10

    C $121.00

    D $145.20

5.6 Reflections

Essential Question
How can you use reflections to classify a frieze pattern?

The Meaning of a Word ● Reflection

When you look at a mountain by a lake, you can see the **reflection**, or mirror image, of the mountain in the lake.

If you fold the photo on its axis, the mountain and its reflection will align.

Actual mountain

Axis

Reflection of mountain

Frieze

A *frieze* is a horizontal band that runs at the top of a building. A frieze is often decorated with a design that repeats.

- All frieze patterns are translations of themselves.
- Some frieze patterns are reflections of themselves.

---

1 EXAMPLE: Frieze Patterns

Is the frieze pattern a reflection of itself when folded horizontally? vertically?

- Fold (reflect) on horizontal axis. The pattern coincides.

- Fold (reflect) on vertical axis. The pattern coincides.

∴ This frieze pattern is a reflection of itself when folded horizontally *and* vertically.

Work with a partner. Is the frieze pattern a reflection of itself when folded *horizontally*, *vertically*, or *neither*?

a.

b.

c.

d.

e.

f.

What Is Your Answer?

3. Draw a frieze pattern that is a reflection of itself when folded horizontally.

4. Draw a frieze pattern that is a reflection of itself when folded vertically.

5. Draw a frieze pattern that is not a reflection of itself when folded horizontally or vertically.

6. **IN YOUR OWN WORDS** How can you use reflections to classify a frieze pattern?

Practice

Use what you learned about reflections to complete Exercises 4–6 on page 230.

Check It Out
Lesson Tutorials
BigIdeasMath com

Key Vocabulary
reflection, *p. 228*
line of reflection,
    p. 228

 Key Idea

Reflections

A **reflection**, or flip, is a transformation in which a figure is reflected in a line called the **line of reflection**. A reflection creates a mirror image of the original figure.

The original figure and its image have the same size and shape.

EXAMPLE **1** **Identifying a Reflection**

Tell whether the blue figure is a reflection of the red figure.

a.

The red figure can be *flipped* to form the blue figure.

⁛ So, the blue figure is a reflection of the red figure.

b.

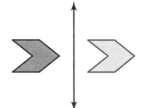

If the red figure were *flipped*, it would point to the left.

⁛ So, the blue figure is *not* a reflection of the red figure.

On Your Own

Now You're Ready
Exercises 4–9

Tell whether the blue figure is a reflection of the red figure. Explain.

1.

2.

3.

EXAMPLE **2** **Reflecting a Figure in the x-axis**

The vertices of a triangle are $A(-1, 1)$, $B(2, 3)$, and $C(6, 3)$. Draw this triangle and its reflection in the x-axis. What are the coordinates of the image?

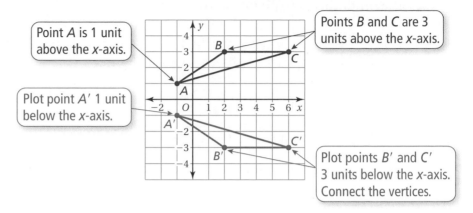

Point A is 1 unit above the x-axis.

Points B and C are 3 units above the x-axis.

Plot point A′ 1 unit below the x-axis.

Plot points B′ and C′ 3 units below the x-axis. Connect the vertices.

⋮• The coordinates of the image are $A'(-1, -1)$, $B'(2, -3)$, and $C'(6, -3)$.

EXAMPLE **3** **Reflecting a Figure in the y-axis**

The vertices of a quadrilateral are $P(-2, 5)$, $Q(-1, -1)$, $R(-4, 2)$, and $S(-4, 4)$. Draw this quadrilateral and its reflection in the y-axis. What are the coordinates of the image?

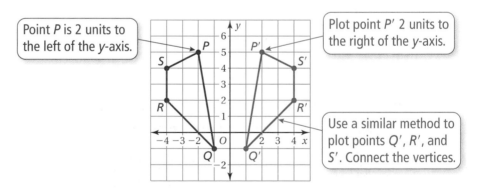

Point P is 2 units to the left of the y-axis.

Plot point P′ 2 units to the right of the y-axis.

Use a similar method to plot points Q′, R′, and S′. Connect the vertices.

⋮• The coordinates of the image are $P'(2, 5)$, $Q'(1, -1)$, $R'(4, 2)$, and $S'(4, 4)$.

On Your Own

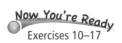
Now You're Ready
Exercises 10–17

4. The vertices of a rectangle are $A(-4, -3)$, $B(-4, -1)$, $C(-1, -1)$, and $D(-1, -3)$.

   a. Draw the rectangle and its reflection in the x-axis.

   b. Draw the rectangle and its reflection in the y-axis.

   c. Are the images in parts (a) and (b) the same size and shape? Explain.

Section 5.6   Reflections   **229**

Check It Out
Help with Homework
BigIdeasMath √com

Vocabulary and Concept Check

1. **WHICH ONE DOESN'T BELONG?** Which transformation does *not* belong with the other three? Explain your reasoning.

2. **WRITING** How can you tell when one figure is a reflection of another figure?

3. **REASONING** A figure lies entirely in Quadrant I. The figure is reflected in the *x*-axis. In which quadrant is the image?

Practice and Problem Solving

Tell whether the blue figure is a reflection of the red figure.

4.

5.

6.

7.

8.

9.

Find the coordinates of the figure after reflecting in the *x*-axis.

10. $A(3, 2)$, $B(4, 4)$, $C(1, 3)$

11. $M(-2, 1)$, $N(0, 3)$, $P(2, 2)$

12. $H(2, -2)$, $J(4, -1)$, $K(6, -3)$, $L(5, -4)$

13. $D(-2, -1)$, $E(0, -2)$, $F(1, -5)$, $G(-1, -4)$

Find the coordinates of the figure after reflecting in the *y*-axis.

14. $Q(-4, 2)$, $R(-2, 4)$, $S(-1, 1)$

15. $T(1, -1)$, $U(4, 2)$, $V(6, -2)$

16. $W(2, -1)$, $X(5, -2)$, $Y(5, -5)$, $Z(2, -4)$

17. $J(2, 2)$, $K(7, 4)$, $L(9, -2)$, $M(3, -1)$

18. **ALPHABET** Which letters look the same when reflected in the line ?

A B C D E F G H I J K L M N O P Q R S T U V W X Y Z

The coordinates of a point and its image are given. Is the reflection in the x-axis or y-axis?

19. $(2, -2) \longrightarrow (2, 2)$

20. $(-4, 1) \longrightarrow (4, 1)$

21. $(-2, -5) \longrightarrow (2, -5)$

22. $(-3, -4) \longrightarrow (-3, 4)$

23. Translate the triangle 1 unit right and 5 units down. Then reflect the image in the y-axis.

24. PROJECT Use a computer drawing program to create photographs of people by copying one side of the person's face and reflecting it in a vertical line. Does the person look normal or very different?

25. MIRROR IMAGE One of the faces shown is an exact reflection of itself. Which one is it? How can you tell?

26. EMERGENCY VEHICLE Hold a mirror to the left side of the photo of the vehicle.

   a. What word do you see in the mirror?

   b. Why do you think it is written that way on the front of the vehicle?

27. *Critical Thinking* Reflect the triangle in the line $y = x$. How are the x- and y-coordinates of the image related to the x- and y-coordinates of the original triangle?

 Fair Game Review *What you learned in previous grades & lessons*

Classify the angle as *acute*, *right*, *obtuse*, or *straight*. *(Skills Review Handbook)*

28.

29.

30.

31.

32. MULTIPLE CHOICE 36 is 75% of what number? *(Section 4.1)*

   A 27   **B** 48   **C** 54   **D** 63

Essential Question What are the three basic ways to move an object in a plane?

The Meaning of a Word ● Rotate

A bicycle wheel

can **rotate** clockwise

or counterclockwise.

① **ACTIVITY: Three Basic Ways to Move Things**

There are three basic ways to move objects on a flat surface.

1. Translate the object.

2. Reflect the object.

3. Rotate the object.

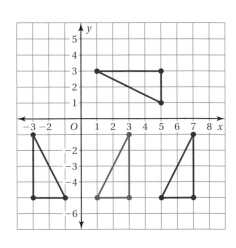

Work with a partner.

- Cut out a paper triangle that is the same size as the blue triangle shown.
- Decide how you can move the blue triangle to make each red triangle.
- Is each move a *translation*, a *reflection*, or a *rotation*?
- Draw four other red triangles in a coordinate plane. Describe how you can move the blue triangle to make each red triangle.

2 ACTIVITY: Tessellating a Plane

Work with a partner.

a. Describe how the figure labeled 1 in each diagram can be moved to make the other figures.

Triangles

Quadrilaterals

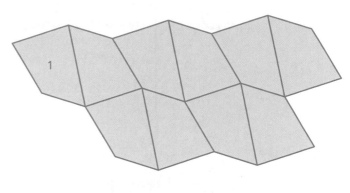

b. **EXPERIMENT** Will *any* triangle tessellate? Conduct an experiment to gather information to help form your conclusion. Draw a triangle. Cut it out. Then use it to trace other triangles so that you cover the plane with triangles that are all the same shape.

c. **EXPERIMENT** Will *any* quadrilateral tessellate? Conduct an experiment to gather information to help form your conclusion. Draw a quadrilateral. Cut it out. Then use it to trace other quadrilaterals so that you cover the plane with quadrilaterals that are all the same shape.

What Is Your Answer?

3. **IN YOUR OWN WORDS** What are the three basic ways to move an object in a plane? Draw an example of each.

"Dear Sub Shop: Why do you put the cheese on the subs so some parts have double coverage and some have none?"

"My suggestion is that you use the tessellation property of triangles for even cheese coverage."

Practice Use what you learned about rotations to complete Exercises 7–9 on page 236.

Check It Out
Lesson Tutorials
BigIdeasMath .com

Key Vocabulary 🔊
rotation, *p. 234*
center of rotation, *p. 234*
angle of rotation, *p. 234*

🔑 Key Idea

Rotations

A **rotation**, or *turn*, is a transformation in which a figure is rotated about a point called the **center of rotation**. The number of degrees a figure rotates is the **angle of rotation**.

The original figure and its image have the same size and shape.

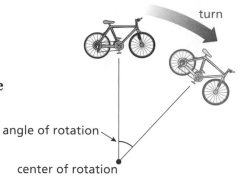

turn

angle of rotation

center of rotation

EXAMPLE 1 **Standardized Test Practice**

You must rotate the puzzle piece 270° clockwise about point *P* to fit it into a puzzle. Which piece fits in the puzzle as shown?

• *P*

Ⓐ Ⓑ Ⓒ Ⓓ

Rotate the puzzle piece 270° clockwise about point *P*.

Study Tip

When rotating figures, it may help to sketch the rotation in several steps, as shown in Example 1.

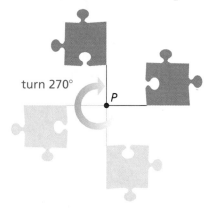

turn 270°

P

∴ The correct answer is Ⓒ.

On Your Own

Now You're Ready
Exercises 7–12

1. Which piece is a 90° counterclockwise rotation about point *P*?

2. Is choice D a rotation of the original puzzle piece? If not, what kind of transformation does the image show?

EXAMPLE 2 **Rotating a Figure**

The vertices of a trapezoid are $W(-4, 2)$, $X(-3, 4)$, $Y(-1, 4)$, and $Z(-1, 2)$. Rotate the trapezoid 180° clockwise about the origin. What are the coordinates of the image?

Draw *WXYZ*.

turn 180°

Plot Z', W', X', and Y'. Connect the vertices.

∴ The coordinates of the image are $W'(4, -2)$, $X'(3, -4)$, $Y'(1, -4)$, and $Z'(1, -2)$.

EXAMPLE 3 **Rotating a Figure**

The vertices of a triangle are $J(1, 2)$, $K(4, 2)$, and $L(1, -3)$. Rotate the triangle 90° counterclockwise about vertex L. What are the coordinates of the image?

Common Error

Be sure to pay attention to whether a rotation is clockwise or counterclockwise.

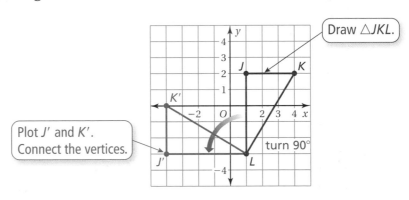

Draw △*JKL*.

Plot J' and K'. Connect the vertices.

turn 90°

∴ The coordinates of the image are $J'(-4, -3)$, $K'(-4, 0)$, and $L'(1, -3)$.

● **On Your Own**

Exercises 13–16

3. A triangle has vertices $Q(4, 5)$, $R(4, 0)$, and $S(1, 0)$.

   a. Rotate the triangle 90° counterclockwise about the origin.

   b. Rotate the triangle 180° about vertex S.

   c. Are the images in parts (a) and (b) the same size and shape? Explain.

✓ Vocabulary and Concept Check

1. VOCABULARY Identify the transformation shown.

a.

b.

c.

2. VOCABULARY What are the coordinates of the center of rotation in Example 2? Example 3?

MENTAL MATH A figure lies entirely in Quadrant II. In which quadrant will the figure lie after the given clockwise rotation about the origin?

3. 90°   **4.** 180°   **5.** 270°   **6.** 360°

Practice and Problem Solving

Tell whether the blue figure is a rotation of the red figure about the origin. If so, give the angle and direction of rotation.

7.

8.

9.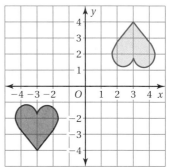

A figure has *rotational symmetry* if a rotation of 180° or less produces an image that fits exactly on the original figure. Explain why the figure has rotational symmetry.

10.

11.

12.

The vertices of a parallelogram are $A(-4, 1)$, $B(-3, 4)$, $C(-1, 4)$, **and** $D(-2, 1)$. **Rotate the parallelogram as described. Find the coordinates of the image.**

2 **3** **13.** 90° counterclockwise about the origin

14. 270° clockwise about the origin

15. 180° clockwise about vertex D

16. 90° counterclockwise about vertex B

17. WRITING Why is it *not* necessary to use the words *clockwise* and *counterclockwise* when describing a rotation of 180°?

18. DILATIONS A *dilation* is a transformation in which a figure is enlarged or reduced.

a. Dilate Rectangle *JKLM* by multiplying the *x*- and *y*-coordinates of each vertex by 2. Compare the original figure and its image.

b. Are the rectangles identical? Are they similar? Explain.

c. How do dilations differ from translations, reflections, and rotations?

19. TREASURE MAP You want to find the treasure located on the map at ✕. You are located at ●. The following transformations will lead you to the treasure, but they are not in the correct order. Find the correct order. Use each transformation exactly once.

- Rotate 180° about the origin.
- Reflect in the *y*-axis.
- Rotate 90° counterclockwise about the origin.
- Translate 1 unit right and 1 unit up.

20. **Reasoning** A triangle is rotated 90° counterclockwise about the origin. Its image is translated 1 unit left and 2 units down. The vertices of the final triangle are $(-5, 0)$, $(-2, 2)$, and $(-2, -1)$. What are the vertices of the original triangle?

 Fair Game Review What you learned in previous grades & lessons

Identify the solid. *(Skills Review Handbook)*

21.

22.

23. MULTIPLE CHOICE What is the value of $x - y$ when $x = -5$ and $y = -8$? *(Section 1.3)*

Ⓐ −13   Ⓑ −3   Ⓒ 3   Ⓓ 13

Check It Out
Progress Check
BigIdeasMath ✓com

1. Translate the triangle 2 units right and 3 units down. What are the coordinates of the image? *(Section 5.5)*

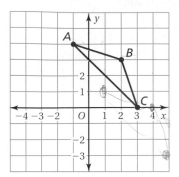

2. Translate the figure 2 units left and 4 units down. What are the coordinates of the image? *(Section 5.5)*

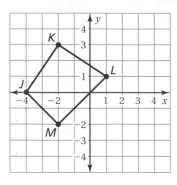

Find the coordinates of the figure after reflecting in the (a) x-axis and (b) y-axis. *(Section 5.6)*

3. $A(2, 0)$, $B(1, 5)$, $C(4, 3)$

4. $D(-2, -5)$, $E(-2, -2)$, $F(1, -2)$, $G(2, -5)$

Tell whether the blue figure is a rotation of the red figure about the origin. If so, give the angle and direction of rotation. *(Section 5.7)*

5.

6.

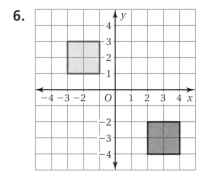

7. AIRPLANE Describe a translation of the airplane from point A to point B. *(Section 5.5)*

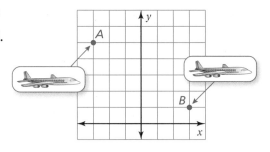

8. MINI GOLF You plan to hit the golf ball along the red path so that its image will be a reflection in the y-axis. Does the golf ball land in the hole? Explain. *(Section 5.6)*

9. GEOMETRY The pivot point of a compass is at the origin. A circle is drawn starting at (3, 6). What point is the compass pencil on when the compass has rotated 270° counterclockwise? *(Section 5.7)*

Check It Out
Vocabulary Help
BigIdeasMath ✓ com

Review Key Vocabulary

similar figures, *p. 196*
corresponding angles, *p. 196*
corresponding sides, *p. 196*
indirect measurement, *p. 209*
scale drawing, *p. 214*
scale model, *p. 214*
scale, *p. 214*
scale factor, *p. 215*

transformation, *p. 222*
image, *p. 222*
translation, *p. 222*
reflection, *p. 228*
line of reflection, *p. 228*
rotation, *p. 234*
center of rotation, *p. 234*
angle of rotation, *p. 234*

Review Examples and Exercises

5.1 Identifying Similar Figures *(pp. 194–199)*

Is Rectangle A similar to Rectangle B?

Each figure is a rectangle. So, corresponding angles have the same measure. Check to see if corresponding side lengths are proportional.

Rectangle A

Rectangle B

$$\frac{\text{Length of A}}{\text{Length of B}} = \frac{10}{5} = 2 \qquad \frac{\text{Width of A}}{\text{Width of B}} = \frac{4}{2} = 2$$

Proportional

∴ So, Rectangle A is similar to Rectangle B.

Exercises

Tell whether the two figures are similar. Explain your reasoning.

1.

2.

3.

4.

Perimeters and Areas of Similar Figures *(pp. 200–205)*

Find the ratio (red to blue) of the perimeters of the similar parallelograms.

$$\frac{\text{Perimeter of red parallelogram}}{\text{Perimeter of blue parallelogram}} = \frac{15}{9}$$

$$= \frac{5}{3}$$

∴ The ratio of the perimeters is $\frac{5}{3}$.

Find the ratio (red to blue) of the areas of the similar figures.

$$\frac{\text{Area of red figure}}{\text{Area of blue figure}} = \left(\frac{3}{4}\right)^2$$

$$= \frac{9}{16}$$

∴ The ratio of the areas is $\frac{9}{16}$.

Exercises

The two figures are similar. Find the ratios (red to blue) of the perimeters and of the areas.

5.

3 m
6 m
8 m

6.

16 m
28 m

7. PHOTOS Two photos are similar. The ratio of the corresponding side lengths is 3 : 4. What is the ratio of their areas?

Finding Unknown Measures in Similar Figures *(pp. 206–211)*

The two rectangles are similar. Find the value of x.

Corresponding side lengths of similar figures are proportional. So, use a proportion to find x.

$$\frac{10}{24} = \frac{4}{x}$$ Write a proportion.

$10x = 96$ Use Cross Products Property.

$x = 9.6$ Divide each side by 10.

10 m
4 m
24 m
x

∴ So, x is 9.6 meters.

Exercises

The polygons are similar. Find the value of x.

8.

 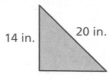

14 in.   20 in.   7 in.   x

9.

6 cm   x   4 cm   6 cm

10.

20   10   12   x

11.

26   8   25   x

5.4 **Scale Drawings** *(pp. 212–217)*

A lighthouse is 160 feet tall. A scale model of the lighthouse has a scale of 1 in. : 8 ft. How tall is the model of the lighthouse?

$$\frac{1 \text{ in.}}{8 \text{ ft}} = \frac{x \text{ in.}}{160 \text{ ft}}$$

model height ←
actual height ←

$$\frac{1 \text{ in.}}{8 \text{ ft}} \cdot 160 \text{ ft} = \frac{x \text{ in.}}{160 \text{ ft}} \cdot 160 \text{ ft} \quad \text{Multiply each side by 160 ft.}$$

$$20 = x \qquad \text{Simplify.}$$

∴ The model of the lighthouse is 20 inches tall.

Exercises

Use a centimeter ruler to measure the segment shown. Find the scale of the drawing.

12.

192 ft

13.

30 in.

Translations *(pp. 220–225)*

Translate the red triangle 4 units left and 1 unit down. What are the coordinates of the image?

Move each vertex 4 units left and 1 unit down.

Connect the vertices. Label as *A'*, *B'*, and *C'*.

⋰ The coordinates of the image are $A'(-1, 4)$, $B'(2, 2)$, and $C'(0, 0)$.

Exercises

Translate the figure as described. What are the coordinates of the image?

14. 3 units left and 2 units down

15. 5 units right and 4 units up

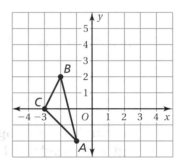

Reflections *(pp. 226–231)*

Tell whether the blue figure is a reflection of the red figure.

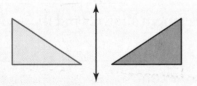

The red figure can be *flipped* to form the blue figure.

⋰ So, the blue figure is a reflection of the red figure.

Exercises

Tell whether the blue figure is a reflection of the red figure.

16.

17.

5.7 Rotations (pp. 232–237)

Tell whether the blue figure is a rotation of the red figure about a vertex. If so, give the angle and direction of rotation.

The red figure can be turned 90° clockwise about (0, 1) to form the blue figure.

∴ So, the blue figure is a 90° clockwise rotation of the red figure.

Rotate the red triangle 90° counterclockwise about the origin. What are the coordinates of the image?

Plot A', B', and C'. Connect the vertices.

∴ The coordinates of the image are $A'(-1, 1)$, $B'(-2, 3)$, and $C'(-4, 2)$.

Exercises

Tell whether the blue figure is a rotation of the red figure about the origin. If so, give the angle and direction of rotation.

18.

19.

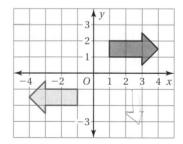

Rotate the figure as described. What are the coordinates of the image?

20. 270° counterclockwise about the origin

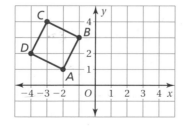

21. 180° clockwise about vertex M.

Check It Out
Test Practice
BigIdeasMath ✓.com

1. Tell whether the parallelograms are similar. Explain your reasoning.

The two figures are similar. Find the ratios (red to blue) of the perimeters and of the areas.

2.

3.

4. Use a centimeter ruler to measure the fish. Find the scale factor of the drawing.

├── 15 mm ──┤

5. The vertices of a triangle are $A(2, 4)$, $B(2, 1)$, and $C(5, 1)$. Draw the triangle and its image after a translation of 1 unit left and 3 units down.

6. Find the coordinates of the triangle whose vertices are $A(2, 5)$, $B(1, 2)$, and $C(3, 1)$ after reflecting in (a) the x-axis and (b) the y-axis.

The vertices of a triangle are $D(-2, -2)$, $E(-1, 1)$, and $F(1, -1)$. Rotate the triangle as described. Find the coordinates of the image.

7. 180° counterclockwise about the origin

8. 90° clockwise about the vertex D

9. **SCREENS** A wide screen television measures 36 inches by 54 inches. A movie theater screen measures 42 feet by 63 feet. Are the screens similar? Explain.

10. **HOCKEY** An air hockey table and an ice hockey rink are similar. The ratio of their corresponding side lengths is 1 inch : 2 feet. What is the ratio of their areas?

11. **HEIGHT** You are five feet tall and cast a seven-foot eight-inch shadow. At the same time, a basketball hoop casts a 19-foot shadow. How tall is the basketball hoop? Assume the triangles are similar.

1. A set of data is shown below. Two of the data are missing.

   8, 2, 10, 4, 8, 4, 8, 8, _____ , _____

   The mean of the complete set of data is 6, and the median is 7. What are the two missing data?

   A. 1 and 7   **C.** 4 and 4

   B. 2 and 6   **D.** 6 and 6

2. What is the area of the shaded region in the figure below? (Use 3.14 for π.)

   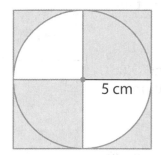

   5 cm

   F. 21.5 cm^2 **H.** 80.375 cm^2

   G. 60.75 cm^2 **I.** 84.3 cm^2

3. A clockwise rotation of 90° is equivalent to a counterclockwise rotation of how many degrees?

4. You are building a scale model of a park that is planned for a city. The model uses the scale below.

   1 centimeter = 2 meters

   The park will have a rectangular reflecting pool with a length of 20 meters and a width of 12 meters. In your scale model, what will be the area of the reflecting pool?

   A. 60 cm^2 **C.** 480 cm^2

   B. 120 cm^2 **D.** 960 cm^2

Test-Taking Strategy
Solve Problem Before Looking at Choices

Your paw has an area of 2 in.^{2}. A hyena's paw is twice as long. What is its area?
Ⓐ 4 in.^{2} Ⓑ 6 in.^{2} Ⓒ 8 in.^{2} Ⓓ 10 in.^{2}

4 times more area! Help!

CAT   HYENA

"Solve the problem before looking at the choices. You know area increases as the square of the scale. So, it's 8 in.^{2}."

5. In the figure, $\triangle EFG \sim \triangle HIJ$.

Which proportion is *not* necessarily correct for $\triangle EFG$ and $\triangle HIJ$?

F. $\dfrac{EF}{FG} = \dfrac{HI}{IJ}$

G. $\dfrac{EG}{HI} = \dfrac{FG}{IJ}$

H. $\dfrac{GE}{EF} = \dfrac{JH}{HI}$

I. $\dfrac{EF}{HI} = \dfrac{GE}{JH}$

6. Brett was solving the equation in the box below.

$$\frac{c}{5} - (-15) = -35$$

$$\frac{c}{5} + 15 = -35$$

$$\frac{c}{5} + 15 - 15 = -35 - 15$$

$$\frac{c}{5} = -50$$

$$\frac{c}{5} = \frac{-50}{5}$$

$$c = -10$$

What should Brett do to correct the error that he made?

A. Subtract 15 from -35 to get -20.

B. Rewrite $\dfrac{c}{5} - (-15)$ as $\dfrac{c}{5} - 15$.

C. Multiply both sides of the equation by 5 to get $c = -250$.

D. Multiply both sides of the equation by -5 to get $c = 250$.

7. In the figure below, $\triangle ABC \sim \triangle DEF$.

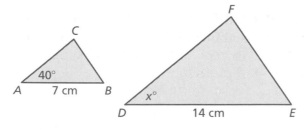

What is the value of x?

8. In the figure below, rectangle *EFGH* ~ rectangle *IJKL*.

What is the value of *x*?

F. 14 in.

G. 15 in.

H. 16 in.

I. 17 in.

9. Two cubes are shown below.

How many of the smaller cubes can be stacked to completely fill the larger cube?

A. 3

B. 9

C. 27

D. 54

10. A map of Donna's state has the following scale:

$$\frac{1}{2} \text{ inch} = 10 \text{ miles}$$

Part A Donna measured the distances between her town and the state capitol on the map. Her measurement was $4\frac{1}{2}$ inches. Based on Donna's measurement, what is the actual distance, in miles, between her town and the state capitol? Show your work and explain your reasoning.

Part B Donna wants to mark her favorite campsite on the map. She knows that the campsite is 65 miles north of her town. What distance, in inches, on the map represents an actual distance of 65 miles? Show your work and explain your reasoning.

6 Surface Areas of Solids

"I want to paint my dog house. To make sure I buy the correct amount of paint, I want to calculate the lateral surface area."

"Then, because I want to paint the inside and the outside, I will multiply by 2. Does this seem right to you?"

"Dear Sir: Why do you sell dog food in tall cans and sell cat food in short cans?"

"Neither of these shapes is the optimal use of surface area when compared to volume."

What You Learned Before

"Name these shapes."

Polly Prism, Prissy Pyramid, Cici Cylinder, and Connie Cone

- ## Finding the Area of a Composite Figure

Example 1 Find the area.

3 in.

10 in.

10 in.

Area = Area of square + Area of triangle

$$A = s^2 + \frac{1}{2}bh$$

$$= 10^2 + \left(\frac{1}{2} \cdot 10 \cdot 3\right)$$

$$= 100 + 15$$

$$= 115 \text{ in.}^2$$

Try It Yourself
Find the area.

1.

8 m

15 m

2.

9 cm

4 cm

14 cm

5 cm

- ## Finding the Area of Circles

Example 2 Find the area.

7 mm

$$A = \pi r^2$$

$$\approx 3.14(7)^2$$

$$= 3.14 \cdot 49$$

$$= 153.86 \text{ mm}^2$$

Example 3 Find the area.

24 yd

$$A = \pi r^2$$

$$\approx 3.14(12)^2$$

$$= 3.14 \cdot 144$$

$$= 452.16 \text{ yd}^2$$

Try It Yourself
Find the area.

3.

5 ft

4.

26 in.

5.

7 cm

Essential Question How can you draw three-dimensional figures?

Dot paper can help you draw three-dimensional figures, or solids. Shading parallel sides the same color helps create a three-dimensional illusion.

Square Dot Paper   **Isometric Dot Paper**

    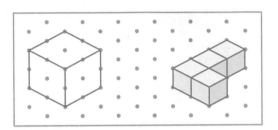

Face-On View   **Corner View**

1 ACTIVITY: Finding Surface Areas and Volumes

Work with a partner.

Draw the front, side, and top views of each stack of cubes. Then find the surface area and volume. Each small cube has side lengths of 1 unit.

a. Sample:

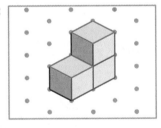

Volume: 3 cubic units

Surface Area: 14 square units

b.

c.

d.

e.

f.

g.

Work with a partner.

a. Draw all the different solids you can make by joining four cubes. (Two have been drawn.) Cubes must be joined on faces, not on edges only. Translations, reflections, and rotations do not count as different solids.

Same solid reflected

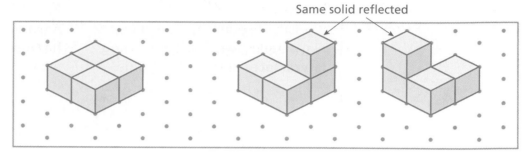

b. Do all the solids have the same surface area? Do all the solids have the same volume? Explain your reasoning.

What Is Your Answer?

3. **IN YOUR OWN WORDS** How can you draw three-dimensional figures? Draw and shade two prisms that have the same volume but different surface areas.

4. Maurits Escher (1898–1972) was a popular artist who drew optical illusions.

   a. What is the illusion in Escher's drawing?

   b. Why is the cartoon funny? What is the illusion in the cartoon?

©2008 M.C. Escher's "Ascending and Descending"

Practice

Use what you learned about three-dimensional figures to complete Exercises 7–9 on page 254.

Check It Out
Lesson Tutorials
BigIdeasMath⬐com

A **three-dimensional figure**, or *solid*, has length, width, and depth.
A **polyhedron** is a three-dimensional figure whose faces are all polygons.

🔑 Key Ideas

Prisms

A prism is a polyhedron that has two parallel, identical bases. The **lateral faces** are parallelograms.

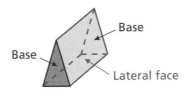

Base
Base
Lateral face

Triangular Prism

Pyramids

A pyramid is a polyhedron that has one base. The lateral faces are triangles.

Lateral face
Base

Rectangular Pyramid

The shape of the base tells the name of the prism or the pyramid.

Cylinders

A cylinder is a solid that has two parallel, identical circular bases.

Lateral surface
Bases

Cones

A cone is a solid that has one circular base and one vertex.

Vertex
Lateral surface
Base

EXAMPLE ① Drawing a Prism

Draw a rectangular prism.

Step 1

Draw identical rectangular bases.

Step 2

Connect corresponding vertices.

Step 3

Change any *hidden* lines to dashed lines.

2 **Drawing a Pyramid**

Draw a triangular pyramid.

Step 1

Draw a triangular base and a point.

Step 2

Connect the vertices of the triangle to the point.

Step 3

Change any *hidden* lines to dashed lines.

On Your Own

Draw the solid.

1. Square prism

2. Pentagonal pyramid

EXAMPLE **3** **Drawing Views of a Solid**

Draw the front, side, and top views of the paper cup.

The front view is a triangle.

The side view is a triangle.

The top view is a circle.

On Your Own

Draw the front, side, and top views of the solid.

3.

4.

5.

Check It Out
Help with Homework
BigIdeasMath.com

 Vocabulary and Concept Check

1. **VOCABULARY** Compare and contrast prisms and cylinders.

2. **VOCABULARY** Compare and contrast pyramids and cones.

3. **WRITING** Give examples of prisms, pyramids, cylinders, and cones in real life.

Identify the shape of the base. Then name the solid.

4.

5.

6.

 Practice and Problem Solving

Draw the front, side, and top views of the stack of cubes. Then find the surface area and volume.

7.

8.

9.

Draw the solid.

① ② 10. Triangular prism   11. Pentagonal prism   12. Rectangular pyramid

13. Hexagonal pyramid   14. Cone   15. Cylinder

Draw the front, side, and top views of the solid.

③ 16.

17.

18.

19.

20.

21.

22. **PYRAMID ARENA** The Pyramid of Caius Cestius in Rome is in the shape of a square pyramid. Draw a sketch of the pyramid.

23. **RESEARCH** Use the Internet to find a picture of the Washington Monument. Describe its shape.

Draw a solid with the following front, side, and top views.

24.

front   side   top

25.

front   side   top

26. **PROJECT** Design and draw a house. Name the different solids that can be used to make a model of the house.

27. **REASONING** Two of the three views of a solid are shown.

  a. What is the greatest number of unit cubes in the solid?

  b. What is the least number of unit cubes in the solid?

  c. Draw the front views of both solids in parts (a) and (b).

top

side

28. **Reasoning** Draw two different solids with five faces.

  a. Write the number of vertices and edges for each solid.

  b. Explain how knowing the numbers of edges and vertices helps you draw a three-dimensional figure.

 Fair Game Review *What you learned in previous grades & lessons*

Find the area. *(Skills Review Handbook)*

29.

4 m

7 m

30.

3 cm

8 cm

31.

6 ft

3 ft

4 ft

32. **MULTIPLE CHOICE** You borrow $200 and agree to repay $240 at the end of 2 years. What is the simple interest rate per year? *(Section 4.4)*

  Ⓐ 5%   Ⓑ 10%   Ⓒ 15%   Ⓓ 20%

6.2 Surface Areas of Prisms

Essential Question How can you use a net to find the surface area of a prism?

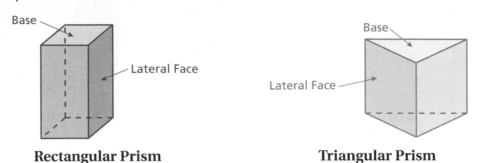

Rectangular Prism   **Triangular Prism**

The **surface area** of a prism is the sum of the areas of all its faces.
A two-dimensional representation of a solid is called a **net**.

1 ACTIVITY: Surface Area of a Right Rectangular Prism

Work with a partner.

a. Use the net for the rectangular prism to find its surface area.

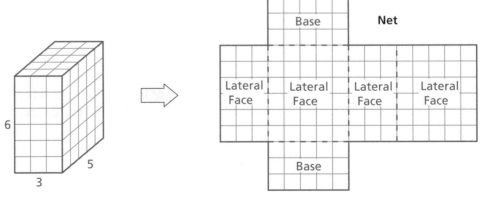

b. Copy the net for a rectangular prism. Label each side as h, w, or ℓ. Then use your drawing to write a formula for the surface area of a rectangular prism.

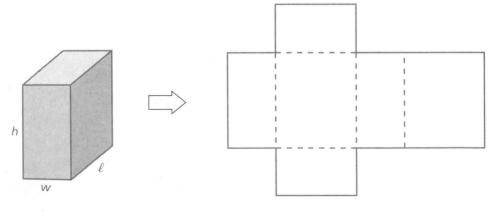

Work with a partner. Find the surface area of the solid shown by the net. Copy the net, cut it out, and fold it to form a solid. Identify the solid.

What Is Your Answer?

3. **IN YOUR OWN WORDS** How can you use a net to find the surface area of a prism? Draw a net, cut it out, and fold it to form a prism.

4. The greater the surface area of an ice block, the faster it will melt. Which will melt faster, the bigger block or the three smaller blocks? Explain your reasoning.

Practice Use what you learned about the surface area of a prism to complete Exercises 6–8 on page 260.

Check It Out
Lesson Tutorials
BigIdeasMath com

Key Vocabulary
surface area, *p. 256*
net, *p. 256*

Key Idea

Surface Area of a Rectangular Prism

Words The surface area *S* of a rectangular prism is the sum of the areas of the bases and the lateral faces.

Algebra $S = 2\ell w + 2\ell h + 2wh$

Area of bases   Area of lateral faces

EXAMPLE 1 **Finding the Surface Area of a Rectangular Prism**

Find the surface area of the prism.

Draw a net.

$$S = 2\ell w + 2\ell h + 2wh$$

$$= 2(3)(5) + 2(3)(6) + 2(5)(6)$$

$$= 30 + 36 + 60$$

$$= 126$$

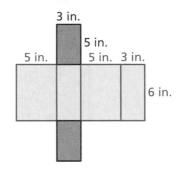

∴ The surface area is 126 square inches.

On Your Own

Now You're Ready
Exercises 9–11

Find the surface area of the prism.

1.

2.

Key Idea

Surface Area of a Prism

The surface area S of a prism is the sum of the areas of the bases and the lateral faces.

$$S = \text{areas of bases} + \text{areas of lateral faces}$$

EXAMPLE **2** **Finding the Surface Area of a Triangular Prism**

Find the surface area of the prism.

Draw a net.

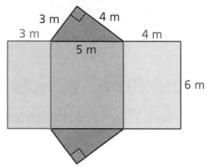

Remember

The area A of a triangle with base b and height h is $A = \frac{1}{2}bh$.

Area of a base

Red base: $\frac{1}{2} \cdot 3 \cdot 4 = 6$

Areas of lateral faces

Green lateral face: $3 \cdot 6 = 18$

Purple lateral face: $5 \cdot 6 = 30$

Blue lateral face: $4 \cdot 6 = 24$

Add the areas of the bases and the lateral faces.

$S = \text{areas of bases} + \text{areas of lateral faces}$

$= \underbrace{6 + 6} + 18 + 30 + 24$

There are two identical bases. Count the area twice.

$= 84$

∴ The surface area is 84 square meters.

On Your Own

Find the surface area of the prism.

 Now You're Ready
Exercises 12–14

3.

4.

✓ Vocabulary and Concept Check

1. **OPEN-ENDED** Describe a real-world situation in which you would want to find the surface area of a prism.

Find the indicated area for the rectangular prism.

2. Area of Face *A*

3. Area of Face *B*

4. Area of Face *C*

5. Surface area of the prism

✏️ Practice and Problem Solving

Draw a net for the prism. Then find the surface area.

6.

7.

8.

Find the surface area of the prism.

① 9.

10.

11.

② 12.

13.

14.

15. **GIFT BOX** What is the least amount of wrapping paper needed to wrap a gift box that measures 8 inches by 8 inches by 10 inches? Explain.

16. **TENT** What is the least amount of fabric needed to make the tent?

Find the surface area of the prism.

17.

12 in. 4 in.
3 in.
5 in. 5 in.
6 in.

18.

2 m
2.5 m
4 m
4 m

19. AQUARIUM A public library has an aquarium in the shape of a rectangular prism. The base is 6 feet by 2.5 feet. The height is 4 feet. How many square feet of glass were used to build the aquarium? (The top of the aquarium is open.)

20. STORAGE BOX The material used to make a storage box costs $1.25 per square foot. The boxes have the same volume. How much does a company save by choosing to make 50 of Box 2 instead of 50 of Box 1?

	Length	Width	Height
Box 1	20 in.	6 in.	4 in.
Box 2	15 in.	4 in.	8 in.

$25\frac{1}{12}$ ft

5 ft

25 in.

25 ft

21. RAMP A quart of stain covers 100 square feet. How many quarts should you buy to stain the wheelchair ramp? (Assume you do not have to stain the bottom of the ramp.)

22. LABEL A label that wraps around a box of golf balls covers 75% of its lateral surface area. What is the value of x?

23. **Critical Thinking** Write a formula for the surface area of a rectangular prism using the height h, the perimeter P of a base, and the area B of a base.

3 in.
SUPER
Golf Balls
SUPER
2 in.
Golf Balls
because YOU are a super golfer
2 in.
x

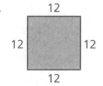 **Fair Game Review** *What you learned in previous grades & lessons*

Find the perimeter. *(Skills Review Handbook)*

24.

7 8
10

25.

12
12 12
12

26.

11 11
9 9
14

27. MULTIPLE CHOICE The class size increased 25% to 40 students. What was the original class size? *(Section 4.2)*

    (A) 10   (B) 30   (C) 32   (D) 50

Essential Question How can you find the surface area of a cylinder?

1 ACTIVITY: Finding Area

Work with a partner. Use a cardboard cylinder.

- Talk about how you can find the area of the outside of the roll.

- Use a ruler to estimate the area of the outside of the roll.

- Cut the roll and press it out flat. Then find the area of the flattened cardboard. How close is your estimate to the actual area?

Cut

Base
Lateral surface
Base
r
h

The surface area of a cylinder is the sum of the areas of the bases and the lateral surface.

2 ACTIVITY: Finding Surface Area

Work with a partner.

- Trace the top and bottom of a can on paper. Cut out the two shapes.

- Cut out a long paper rectangle. Make the width the same as the height of the can. Wrap the rectangle around the can. Cut off the excess paper so the edges just meet.

- Make a net for the can. Name the shapes in the net.

- How are the dimensions of the rectangle related to the dimensions of the can?

- Explain how to use the net to find the surface area of the can.

Work with a partner. From memory, estimate the dimensions of the real-life item in inches. Then use the dimensions to estimate the surface area of the item in square inches.

a.

b.

c.

d.

What Is Your Answer?

4. **IN YOUR OWN WORDS** How can you find the surface area of a cylinder? Give an example with your description. Include a drawing of the cylinder.

5. To eight decimal places, $\pi \approx 3.14159265$. Which of the following is closest to π?

   a. 3.14　　　　b. $\dfrac{22}{7}$　　　　c. $\dfrac{355}{113}$

"To approximate the irrational number $\pi \approx 3.141593$, I simply remember 1, 1, 3, 3, 5, 5."

"Then I compute the rational number $\dfrac{355}{113} \approx 3.141593$."

Practice ▶ Use what you learned about the surface area of a cylinder to complete Exercises 5–7 on page 266.

The diagram reviews some important facts for circles.

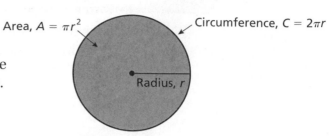

Area, $A = \pi r^2$ Circumference, $C = 2\pi r$ Radius, r

🔑 Key Idea

Surface Area of a Cylinder

Words   The surface area S of a cylinder is the sum of the areas of the bases and the lateral surface.

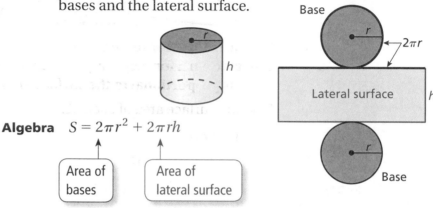

Base
r
$2\pi r$
Lateral surface h
r
Base

Algebra $S = 2\pi r^2 + 2\pi rh$

Area of bases

Area of lateral surface

Remember

$\pi = \dfrac{\text{circumference}}{\text{diameter}}$

Pi can be approximated as 3.14 or $\dfrac{22}{7}$.

EXAMPLE **1**   **Finding the Surface Area of a Cylinder**

4 mm
3 mm

Find the surface area of the cylinder. Round your answer to the nearest tenth.

Draw a net.

$S = 2\pi r^2 + 2\pi rh$

$ = 2\pi(4)^2 + 2\pi(4)(3)$

$ = 32\pi + 24\pi$

$ = 56\pi \approx 175.8$

∴ The surface area is about 175.8 square millimeters.

4 mm

3 mm

4 mm

⬤ On Your Own

Now You're Ready
Exercises 8–10

1. A cylinder has a radius of 2 meters and a height of 5 meters. Find the surface area of the cylinder. Round your answer to the nearest tenth.

EXAMPLE **2** **Finding Surface Area**

How much paper is used for the label on the can of peas?

Find the *lateral* surface area of the cylinder.

1 in.

2 in.

$S = 2\pi rh$ ← Do not include the area of the bases in the formula.

$= 2\pi(1)(2)$ Substitute.

$= 4\pi \approx 12.56$ Multiply.

⋮• About 12.56 square inches of paper is used for the label.

EXAMPLE **3** **Real-Life Application**

You earn $0.01 for recycling the can in Example 2. How much can you expect to earn for recycling the tomato can? Assume that the recycle value is proportional to the surface area.

Find the surface area of each can.

2 in.

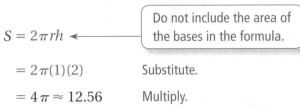

5.5 in.

Tomatoes	*Peas*
$S = 2\pi r^2 + 2\pi rh$	$S = 2\pi r^2 + 2\pi rh$
$= 2\pi(2)^2 + 2\pi(2)(5.5)$	$= 2\pi(1)^2 + 2\pi(1)(2)$
$= 8\pi + 22\pi$	$= 2\pi + 4\pi$
$= 30\pi$	$= 6\pi$

Use a proportion to find the recycle value x of the tomato can.

$$\frac{30\pi \text{ in.}^2}{x} = \frac{6\pi \text{ in.}^2}{\$0.01}$$ ← surface area
← recycle value

$30\pi \cdot 0.01 = x \cdot 6\pi$ Use Cross Products Property.

$5 \cdot 0.01 = x$ Divide each side by 6π.

$0.05 = x$ Simplify.

⋮• You can expect to earn $0.05 for recycling the tomato can.

On Your Own

Now You're Ready
Exercises 11–13

2. **WHAT IF?** In Example 3, the height of the can of peas is doubled.

   a. Does the amount of paper used in the label double?

   b. Does the recycle value double? Explain.

✓ Vocabulary and Concept Check

1. **CRITICAL THINKING** Which part of the formula $S = 2\pi r^2 + 2\pi rh$ represents the lateral surface area of a cylinder?

2. **CRITICAL THINKING** Given the height and the circumference of the base of a cylinder, describe how to find the surface area of the entire cylinder.

Find the indicated area of the cylinder.

3. Area of a base

4. Surface area

6 cm
3 cm

 Practice and Problem Solving

Make a net for the cylinder. Then find the surface area of the cylinder. Round your answer to the nearest tenth.

5.
3 ft
2 ft

6.
4 m
1 m

7.
7 ft
5 ft

Find the surface area of the cylinder. Round your answer to the nearest tenth.

1 8.
5 mm
2 mm

9.
6 ft
7 ft

10.
12 cm
6 cm

Find the lateral surface area of the cylinder. Round your answer to the nearest tenth.

2 11.
10 ft
6 ft

12.
9 in.
4 in.

13.
14 m
2 m

14. **TANKER** The truck's tank is a stainless steel cylinder. Find the surface area of the tank.

50 ft

radius = 4 ft

15. ERROR ANALYSIS Describe and correct the error in finding the surface area of the cylinder.

6 ft

11 ft

$$S = 2\pi rh$$
$$\approx 2\pi(6)(11)$$
$$= 132\pi \text{ ft}^2$$

├─ 16 in. ─┤

6 in.

8 in.

16. OTTOMAN What percent of the surface area of the ottoman is green (not including the bottom)?

17. REASONING You make two cylinders using 8.5-inch by 11-inch pieces of paper. One has a height of 8.5 inches and the other has a height of 11 inches. Without calculating, compare the surface areas of the cylinders.

18. INSTRUMENT A ganza is a percussion instrument used in samba music.

  a. Find the surface area of each of the two labeled ganzas.

  b. The weight of the smaller ganza is 1.1 pounds. Assume that the surface area is proportional to the weight. What is the weight of the larger ganza?

10 cm

24.5 cm

3.5 cm

5.5 cm

19. BRIE CHEESE The cut wedge represents one-eighth of the cheese.

  a. Find the surface area of the cheese before it is cut.

  b. Find the surface area of the remaining cheese after the wedge is removed. Did the surface area increase, decrease, or remain the same?

├─ 3 in. ─┤

1 in.

20. **Critical Thinking** The lateral surface area of a cylinder is 184 square centimeters. The radius is 9 centimeters. What is the surface area of the cylinder? Explain how you found your answer.

Fair Game Review *What you learned in previous grades & lessons*

Evaluate the expression. *(Skills Review Handbook)*

21. $\frac{1}{2}(26)(9)$

22. $\frac{1}{2}(8.24)(3) + 8.24$

23. $\frac{1}{2}(18.84)(3) + 28.26$

24. MULTIPLE CHOICE A store pays $15 for a basketball. The percent of markup is 30%. What is the selling price? *(Section 4.3)*

   Ⓐ $10.50   Ⓑ $19.50   Ⓒ $30   Ⓓ $34.50

You can use a **four square** to organize information about a topic. Each of the four squares can be a category, such as *definition*, *vocabulary*, *example*, *non-example*, *words*, *algebra*, *table*, *numbers*, *visual*, *graph*, or *equation*. Here is an example of a four square for a three-dimensional figure.

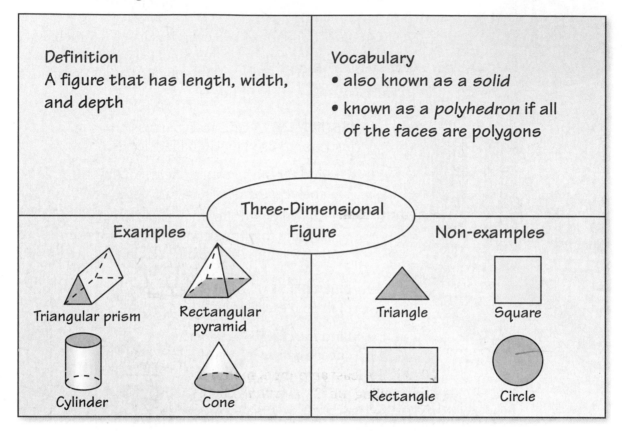

On Your Own

Make a four square to help you study these topics.

1. polyhedron
2. prism
3. pyramid
4. cylinder
5. cone
6. drawing a solid
7. surface area

   a. of a prism   **b.** of a cylinder

After you complete this chapter, make four squares for the following topics.

8. surface area

   a. of a pyramid   **b.** of a cone   **c.** of a composite solid

"My four square shows that my new red skateboard is faster than my old blue skateboard."

Check It Out
Progress Check
BigIdeasMath.com

Draw the front, side, and top views of the solid.   *(Section 6.1)*

1.

2.

3.

Find the surface area of the cylinder. Round your answer to the nearest tenth.   *(Section 6.3)*

4.
10 ft
3 ft

5.
5 m
6 m

Find the surface area of the prism.   *(Section 6.2)*

6.
3 cm   4 cm
10 cm
5 cm

7.
4 mm
2 mm
7 mm

8. MAILING TUBE What is the least amount of material needed to make the mailing tube?   *(Section 6.3)*

3 ft
3 in.

9. GEOMETRY Consider a prism that has *n* faces. Write an expression that represents the number of lateral faces.   *(Section 6.2)*

1.5 in.
1 in.
5 in.
3 in.

10. TOMATO PASTE How much more paper is used for the label of the large can of tomato paste than for the label of the small can?   *(Section 6.3)*

11. WOODEN CHEST All the faces of the wooden chest will be painted except for the bottom. Find the area to be painted, in *square inches*.   *(Section 6.2)*

2 ft
4 ft
1.5 ft

6.4 Surface Areas of Pyramids

Essential Question How can you find the surface area of a pyramid?

Even though many well-known **pyramids** have square bases, the base of a pyramid can be any polygon.

Triangular Base

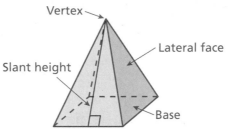

Vertex

Lateral face

Slant height

Base

Square Base

Hexagonal Base

1 ACTIVITY: Making a Scale Model

Work with a partner. Each pyramid has a square base.

- **Draw a net for a scale model of one of the pyramids. Describe your scale.**
- **Cut out the net and fold it to form a pyramid.**
- **Find the lateral surface area of the real-life pyramid.**

a. Cheops Pyramid in Egypt

Side = 230 m, Slant height ≈ 186 m

b. Muttart Conservatory in Edmonton

Side = 26 m, Slant height ≈ 27 m

c. Louvre Pyramid in Paris

Side = 35 m, Slant height ≈ 28 m

d. Pyramid of Caius Cestius in Rome

Side = 22 m, Slant height ≈ 29 m

2 ACTIVITY: Estimation

Work with a partner. There are many different types of gemstone cuts. Here is one called a brilliant cut.

Top View   *Side View*   *Bottom View*

Crown

Pavilion

The size and shape of the pavilion can be approximated by an octagonal pyramid.

a. What does octagonal mean?

b. Draw a net for the pyramid.

c. Find the lateral surface area of the pyramid.

2 mm

Slant height
4 mm

3 ACTIVITY: Building a Skylight

Work with a partner. The skylight has 12 triangular pieces of glass. Each piece has a base of 1 foot and a slant height of 3 feet.

a. How much glass will you need to make the skylight?

b. Can you cut the 12 glass triangles from a sheet of glass that is 4 feet by 8 feet? If so, draw a diagram showing how this can be done.

What Is Your Answer?

4. IN YOUR OWN WORDS How can you find the surface area of a pyramid? Draw a diagram with your explanation.

Practice

Use what you learned about the surface area of a pyramid to complete Exercises 4–6 on page 274.

Check It Out
Lesson Tutorials
BigIdeasMath.com

Key Vocabulary
regular pyramid,
    p. 272
slant height, p. 272

A **regular pyramid** is a pyramid whose base is a regular polygon. The lateral faces are triangles. The height of each triangle is the **slant height** of the pyramid.

 Key Idea

Surface Area of a Pyramid

The surface area S of a pyramid is the sum of the areas of the base and the lateral faces.

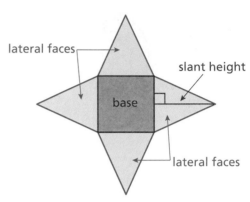

S = area of base + areas of lateral faces

Remember

In a regular polygon, all of the sides have the same length and all of the angles have the same measure.

EXAMPLE 1   Finding the Surface Area of a Square Pyramid

Find the surface area of the regular pyramid.

Draw a net.

Area of base	*Area of a lateral face*
$5 \cdot 5 = 25$	$\frac{1}{2} \cdot 5 \cdot 8 = 20$

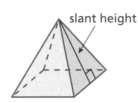

Find the sum of the areas of the base and the lateral faces.

S = area of base + areas of lateral faces

$= 25 + 20 + 20 + 20 + 20$

$= 105$

There are 4 identical lateral faces. Count the area 4 times.

∴ The surface area is 105 square inches.

On Your Own

1. What is the surface area of a square pyramid with a base side length of 9 centimeters and a slant height of 7 centimeters?

Multi-Language Glossary at BigIdeasMath.com.

EXAMPLE 2 Finding the Surface Area of a Triangular Pyramid

Find the surface area of the regular pyramid.

Draw a net.

Area of base

$$\frac{1}{2} \cdot 10 \cdot 8.7 = 43.5$$

Area of a lateral face

$$\frac{1}{2} \cdot 10 \cdot 14 = 70$$

Find the sum of the areas of the base and the lateral faces.

S = area of base + areas of lateral faces

$= 43.5 + \underbrace{70 + 70 + 70}$

$= 253.5$

> There are 3 identical lateral faces. Count the area 3 times.

∴ The surface area is 253.5 square meters.

EXAMPLE 3 Real-Life Application

A roof is shaped like a square pyramid. One bundle of shingles covers 25 square feet. How many bundles should you buy to cover the roof?

The base of the roof does not need shingles. So, find the sum of the areas of the lateral faces of the pyramid.

Area of a lateral face

$$\frac{1}{2} \cdot 18 \cdot 15 = 135$$

There are four identical lateral faces. So, the sum of the areas of the lateral faces is

$$135 + 135 + 135 + 135 = 540.$$

Because one bundle of shingles covers 25 square feet, it will take $540 \div 25 = 21.6$ bundles to cover the roof.

∴ So, you should buy 22 bundles of shingles.

On Your Own

Now You're Ready
Exercises 4–12

2. What is the surface area of the pyramid at the right?

3. **WHAT IF?** In Example 3, one bundle of shingles covers 32 square feet. How many bundles should you buy to cover the roof?

Check It Out
Help with Homework
BigIdeasMath ✓com

 Vocabulary and Concept Check

1. **VOCABULARY** Which of the polygons could be the base for a regular pyramid?

2. **VOCABULARY** Can a pyramid have rectangles as lateral faces? Explain.

3. **CRITICAL THINKING** Why is it helpful to know the slant height of a pyramid to find its surface area?

 Practice and Problem Solving

Use the net to find the surface area of the regular pyramid.

4.
3 in.
4 in.

5.
9 mm
10 mm
Area of base
is 43.3 mm².

6.
6 m
6 m
Area of base
is 61.9 m².

In Exercises 7–11, find the surface area of the regular pyramid.

1 2 7.

9 ft
6 ft

8.
6 cm
4 cm

9.

10 yd
9 yd
7.8 yd

10.

10 in.
15 in.
13 in.

11.

20 mm
16 mm
Area of base
is 440.4 mm².

10 in.

3 12. **LAMPSHADE** The base of the lampshade is a regular hexagon with a side length of 8 inches. Estimate the amount of glass needed to make the lampshade.

13. **GEOMETRY** The surface area of a square pyramid is 85 square meters. The base length is 5 meters. What is the slant height?

14. BMX You are building a bike ramp that is shaped like a square pyramid. You use two 4-foot by 8-foot sheets of plywood. How much plywood do you have left over?

3 ft

5 ft   5 ft

5 ft

4 ft

15. UMBRELLA You are making an umbrella that is shaped like a regular octagonal pyramid.

a. Estimate the amount of fabric that is needed to make the umbrella.

b. The fabric comes in rolls that are 72 inches wide. You don't want to cut the fabric "on the bias". Find out what this means. Then, draw a diagram of how you can cut the fabric most efficiently.

c. How much fabric is wasted?

16. REASONING The *height* of a pyramid is the distance between the base and the top of the pyramid. Which is greater, the height of a pyramid or the slant height? Explain your reasoning.

Pyramid height

17. TETRAHEDRON A tetrahedron is a triangular pyramid whose four faces are identical equilateral triangles. The total lateral surface area is 93 square centimeters. Find the surface area of the tetrahedron.

18. Reasoning Is the total area of the lateral faces of a pyramid *greater than*, *less than*, or *equal* to the area of the base? Explain.

 Fair Game Review What you learned in previous grades & lessons

Find the area and circumference of the circle. Use 3.14 for π. *(Skills Review Handbook)*

19.

12

20.

8

21.

27

22. MULTIPLE CHOICE A youth baseball diamond is similar to a professional baseball diamond. The ratio of the perimeters is 2 : 3. The distance between bases on a youth diamond is 60 feet. What is the distance between bases on a professional diamond? *(Section 5.3)*

(A) 40 ft   (B) 90 ft   (C) 120 ft   (D) 180 ft

Essential Question How can you find the surface area of a cone?

A cone is a solid with one circular base and one vertex.

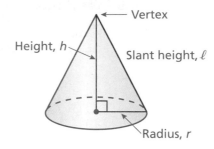

Vertex

Height, h

Slant height, ℓ

Radius, r

1 ACTIVITY: Finding the Surface Area of a Cone

Work with a partner.

- Draw a circle with a radius of 3 inches.

- Mark the circumference of the circle into six equal parts.

- The circumference of the circle is $2(\pi)(3) = 6\pi$. So each of the six parts on the circle has a length of π. Label each part.

- Cut out one part as shown. Then, make a cone.

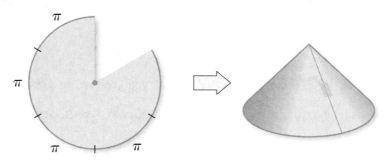

a. The base of the cone should be a circle. Explain why the circumference of the base is 5π.

b. Find the radius of the base.

c. What is the area of the original circle?

d. What is the area of the circle with one part missing?

e. Describe the surface area of the cone. Use your description to find the surface area, including the base.

2 ACTIVITY: Experimenting with Surface Area

Work with a partner.

- Cut out another part from the circle in Activity 1 and make a cone.
- Find the radius of the base and the surface area of the cone.
- Record your results in the table.
- Repeat this three times.
- Describe the pattern.

Shape					
Radius of Base					
Slant Height					
Surface Area					

3 ACTIVITY: Writing a Story

Write a story that uses real-life cones. Include a diagram and label the dimensions. In your story, explain why you would want to know the surface area of the cone. Then, estimate the surface area.

What Is Your Answer?

4. **IN YOUR OWN WORDS** How can you find the surface area of a cone? Draw a diagram with your explanation.

Practice Use what you learned about the surface area of a cone to complete Exercises 4–6 on page 280.

Key Vocabulary
slant height, *p. 278*

The distance from the vertex of a cone to any point on the edge of its base is called the **slant height** of the cone.

🔑 Key Idea

Surface Area of a Cone

Words The surface area S of a cone is the sum of the areas of the base and the lateral surface.

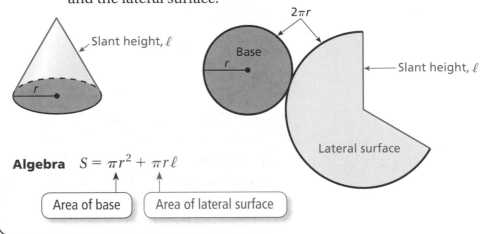

Algebra $S = \pi r^2 + \pi r \ell$

$\uparrow$ Area of base $\uparrow$ Area of lateral surface

EXAMPLE **1** **Finding the Surface Area of a Cone**

Find the surface area of the cone. Round your answer to the nearest tenth.

Draw a net.

$S = \pi r^2 + \pi r \ell$

$\quad = \pi(1)^2 + \pi(1)(3)$

$\quad = \pi + 3\pi$

$\quad = 4\pi \approx 12.6$

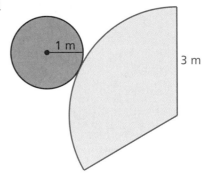

∴ The surface area is about 12.6 square meters.

⬤ On Your Own

Now You're Ready
Exercises 4–9

Find the surface area of the cone. Round your answer to the nearest tenth.

1.

2.

EXAMPLE ② **Finding the Slant Height of a Cone**

The surface area of the cone is 100π square meters. What is the slant height ℓ of the cone?

$$S = \pi r^2 + \pi r \ell \qquad \text{Write formula.}$$

$$100\pi = \pi(5)^2 + \pi(5)(\ell) \qquad \text{Substitute.}$$

$$100\pi = 25\pi + 5\pi\ell \qquad \text{Simplify.}$$

$$75\pi = 5\pi\ell \qquad \text{Subtract } 25\pi \text{ from each side.}$$

$$15 = \ell \qquad \text{Divide each side by } 5\pi.$$

∴ The slant height is 15 meters.

EXAMPLE ③ **Real-Life Application**

You design a party hat. You attach a piece of elastic along a diameter. (a) How long is the elastic? (b) How much paper do you need to make the hat?

a. To find the length of the elastic, find the diameter of the base.

$$C = \pi d \qquad \text{Write formula.}$$

$$22 \approx (3.14)d \qquad \text{Substitute.}$$

$$7.0 \approx d \qquad \text{Solve for } d.$$

∴ The elastic is about 7 inches long.

5 in.

C = 22 in.

b. To find how much paper you need, find the lateral surface area.

Remember

The diameter d of a circle is two times the radius r.

$$d = 2r$$

$$S = \pi r \ell \qquad \longleftarrow \boxed{\text{Do not include the area of the base in the formula.}}$$

$$= \pi(3.5)(5) \qquad \text{Substitute.}$$

$$= 17.5\pi \approx 55 \qquad \text{Multiply.}$$

∴ You need about 55 square inches of paper to make the hat.

● **On Your Own**

Now You're Ready
Exercises 10–14

3. **WHAT IF?** In Example 2, the surface area is 50π square meters. What is the slant height of the cone?

4. **WHAT IF?** In Example 3, the slant height of the party hat is doubled. Does the amount of paper used double? Explain.

✓ Vocabulary and Concept Check

1. **VOCABULARY** Is the base of a cone a polygon? Explain.

2. **CRITICAL THINKING** In the formula for the surface area of a cone, what does $\pi r \ell$ represent? What does πr^2 represent?

3. **REASONING** Write an inequality comparing the slant height ℓ and the radius r of a cone.

Practice and Problem Solving

Find the surface area of the cone. Round your answer to the nearest tenth.

① 4.

6 in.
3 in.

5.

5 m
4 m

6.

9 mm
5 mm

7.
10 ft
7 ft

8.

5 cm
11 cm

9.
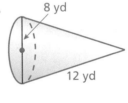
8 yd
12 yd

Find the slant height ℓ of the cone.

② 10. $S = 33\pi$ in.^{2}

ℓ
3 in.

11. $S = 126\pi$ cm^2
12 cm
ℓ

12. $S = 60\pi$ ft^2

ℓ
5 ft

③ 13. NÓN LÁ How much material is needed to make the Nón Lá Vietnamese leaf hat?

14. **PAPER CUP** A paper cup shaped like a cone has a diameter of 6 centimeters and a slant height of 7.5 centimeters. How much paper is needed to make the cup?

13 in.
20 in.

Find the surface area of the cone with diameter d and slant height ℓ.

15. $d = 2$ ft

$\ell = 18$ in.

16. $d = 12$ cm

$\ell = 85$ mm

17. $d = 4$ yd

$\ell = 10$ ft

18. ROOF A roof is shaped like a cone with a diameter of 12 feet. One bundle of shingles covers 32 square feet. How many bundles should you buy to cover the roof?

19. MEGAPHONE Two stickers are placed on opposite sides of the megaphone. Estimate the percent of the surface area of the megaphone covered by the stickers. Round your answer to the nearest percent.

20. REASONING The height of a cone is the distance between the base and the vertex. Which is greater, the height of a cone or the slant height? Explain your reasoning.

21. GEOMETRY The surface area of a cone is also given as $S = \frac{1}{2}C\ell + B$, where C is the circumference and ℓ is the slant height. What does $\frac{1}{2}C\ell$ represent?

22. Critical Thinking A cone has a diameter of x millimeters and a slant height of y millimeters. A square pyramid has a base side length of x millimeters and a slant height of y millimeters. Which has the greater surface area? Explain.

Fair Game Review What you learned in previous grades & lessons

Find the area of the shaded region. Use 3.14 for π. *(Skills Review Handbook)*

23.

6 in.   4 in.   15 in.

24.

3 m   5 m

25.

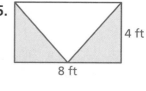

4 ft   8 ft

26. MULTIPLE CHOICE Which best describes a translation? *(Section 5.5)*

  Ⓐ a flip

  Ⓒ a turn

  Ⓑ a slide

  Ⓓ an enlargement

Essential Question How can you find the surface area of a composite solid?

Share Your Work at... My.BigIdeasMath.com

1 ACTIVITY: Finding a Surface Area

Work with a partner. You are manufacturing scale models of old houses.

a. Name the four basic solids of this composite figure.

b. Determine a strategy for finding the surface area of this model. Would you use a scale drawing? Would you use a net? Explain.

Many castles have cylindrical towers with conical roofs. These are called turrets.

Front View

18 in.

60 in.

36 in.   16 in.

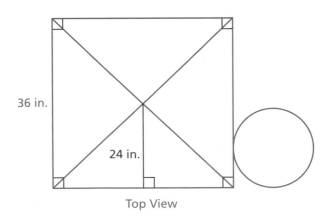

36 in.

24 in.

Top View

2 ACTIVITY: Finding and Using a Pattern

Work with a partner.

- Find the surface area of each figure.
- Use a table to organize your results.
- Describe the pattern in the table.
- Use the pattern to find the surface area of the figure that has a base of 10 blocks.

3 ACTIVITY: Finding and Using a Pattern

Work with a partner. You own a roofing company. Each building has the same base area. Which roof would be cheapest? Which would be the most expensive? Explain your reasoning.

flat   lean-to   gable   hip

cross-hipped   gambrel   mansard   cross-gabled

What Is Your Answer?

4. **IN YOUR OWN WORDS** How can you find the surface area of a composite solid?

5. Design a building that has a turret and also has a mansard roof. Find the surface area of the roof.

Practice Use what you learned about the surface area of a composite solid to complete Exercises 6–8 on page 286.

Check It Out
Lesson Tutorials
BigIdeasMath ✓ com

Key Vocabulary 🔊
composite solid,
p. 284

A **composite solid** is a figure that is made up of more than one solid.

composite solid

cone
cylinder

EXAMPLE **1** **Identifying Solids**

Identify the solids that make up Fort Matanzas.

Rectangular prism

Cylinder

Approximately a rectangular prism

EXAMPLE **2** **Standardized Test Practice**

20 in. 7 in.
10 in.
7 in.
24 in.

You painted the steps to an apartment green. What is the surface area that you painted?

Ⓐ 210 in.²   Ⓑ 408 in.²   Ⓒ 648 in.²   Ⓓ 1056 in.²

Find the area of each green face.

20 in.
24 in.   7 in.

10 in.
7 in.
24 in.

Green area on top step:
$A = 20(24) + 7(24) = 648$ in.²

Green area on bottom step:
$A = 10(24) + 7(24) = 408$ in.²

You painted $648 + 408 = 1056$ square inches.

∴ The correct answer is Ⓓ.

⚫ **On Your Own**

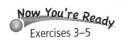
Now You're Ready
Exercises 3–5

1. **WHAT IF?** In Example 2, you also painted the sides of the steps green. What is the surface area that you painted?

🔊 Multi-Language Glossary at BigIdeasMath ✓ com.

EXAMPLE 3   Finding the Surface Area of a Composite Solid

8 m

4 m

6 m

6 m

Find the surface area of the composite solid.

The solid is made up of a square prism and a square pyramid. Use the surface area formulas for a prism and a pyramid, but do not include the areas of the sides that overlap.

Do not include the top base of the prism in the surface area.

4 m

6 m

6 m

Do not include the base of the pyramid in the surface area.

8 m

6 m

6 m

Square prism

$$S = \ell w + 2\ell h + 2wh \qquad \text{Write formula.}$$

$$= 6(6) + 2(6)(4) + 2(6)(4) \qquad \text{Substitute.}$$

$$= 36 + 48 + 48 \qquad \text{Multiply.}$$

$$= 132 \qquad \text{Add.}$$

Square pyramid

$$S = \text{areas of lateral faces} \qquad \text{Write formula.}$$

$$= 4\left(\frac{1}{2} \cdot 6 \cdot 8\right) \qquad \text{Substitute.}$$

$$= 96 \qquad \text{Multiply.}$$

Find the sum of the surface areas: $132 + 96 = 228$.

∴ The surface area is 228 square meters.

On Your Own

Now You're Ready
Exercises 6–11

Identify the solids that make up the composite solid. Then find the surface area. Round your answer to the nearest tenth.

2.

5 yd

3 yd

5 yd

3.

4 cm

5 cm

3 cm

5 cm

3 cm

Vocabulary and Concept Check

7 in.

10 in.

4 in.

1. **OPEN-ENDED** Draw a composite solid formed by a triangular prism and a cone.

2. **REASONING** Explain how to find the surface area of the composite solid.

Practice and Problem Solving

Identify the solids that form the composite solid.

3.

4.

5.

Identify the solids that form the composite solid. Then find the surface area. Round your answer to the nearest tenth.

6.
4 ft
3 ft
6 ft
6 ft

7.
8 m
8 m
4 m
10 m

8.
4 in.
4 in.
5 in.
5 in.
5 in.

9.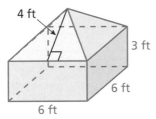
2 cm
2.5 cm
2.5 cm
2 cm
3 cm
6 cm
5 cm

10.
7 in.
8 in.
8 in.
10 in.
8 in.
6.9 in.

11.
8 ft
2 ft
4 ft
12 ft
5 ft

12. OPEN-ENDED The solid is made using eight cubes with side lengths of 1 centimeter.

a. Draw a new solid using eight cubes that has a surface area less than that of the original solid.

b. Draw a new solid using eight cubes that has a surface area greater than that of the original solid.

13. BATTERIES What is the percent increase in the surface area of the AAA battery to the AA battery? Round your answer to the nearest tenth of a percent.

AAA battery   AA battery

0.8 mm
3.8 mm
43 mm
10 mm

1 mm
5.5 mm
49 mm
14 mm

1.75 in.   5 in.
1.5 in.
20 lbs.
20 lbs.
2 in.
3.5 in.

14. BARBELL The diameter of the handle of a barbell is 1 inch. The hexagonal weights are identical. What is the surface area of the barbell?

REASONING Find the surface area of the solid. Round your answer to the nearest tenth.

15.

4 in.   2 in.
10 in.

16.

1 ft   4 ft
5 ft
8 ft   4 ft

17.

7 mm
24 mm
25 mm
10 mm

18. **Critical Thinking** The cube is made with 27 identical cubes. All cubes that cannot be seen are orange. Is the surface area of the solid formed without the purple cubes *greater than*, *less than*, or *equal to* the surface area of the solid formed without the green cubes? Explain your reasoning.

Fair Game Review What you learned in previous grades & lessons

Find the area. *(Skills Review Handbook)*

19.

2 ft
5 ft

20.

4 cm
8 cm

21.

7 in.
5 in.
12 in.

22. MULTIPLE CHOICE A cliff swallow nest is 86 meters above a canyon floor. The elevation of the nest is −56 meters. What is the elevation of the canyon floor? *(Section 2.4)*

(A) −142   (B) −30   (C) 30   (D) 142

Check It Out
Progress Check
BigIdeasMath ✓com

Identify the solids that form the composite solid.   *(Section 6.6)*

1.

2.

3.

Find the surface area of the regular pyramid.   *(Section 6.4)*

4.

12 m

Area of base is 65 m².

5 m

5.

6 cm

2 cm

Find the surface area of the cone. Round your answer to the nearest tenth.
(Section 6.5)

6.

3 m   8 m

7.

7 mm

6 mm

Find the surface area of the composite solid. Round your answer to the nearest tenth.   *(Section 6.6)*

8.

3 m   1 m

2 m

9.

4 mm   5 mm

3 mm

3 mm   2 mm

99 cm

12 cm

12 cm

25 cm

10. **TRAFFIC CONE** A square reflective sticker is placed on a traffic cone to make it more visible at night. Estimate the percent of the surface area of the traffic cone covered by the sticker to the nearest percent.   *(Section 6.5)*

11. **GEOMETRY** The surface area of a cone is 150π square inches. The radius of the base is 10 inches. What is the slant height?   *(Section 6.5)*

5 in.

1.4 in.

8 in.

9.6 in.

18 in.

12. **TOOLBOX** Find the surface area of the toolbox.   *(Section 6.6)*

Check It Out
Vocabulary Help
BigIdeasMath ✓com

Review Key Vocabulary

three-dimensional figure, *p. 252*	surface area, *p. 256*	slant height, *pp. 272, 278*
polyhedron, *p. 252*	net, *p. 256*	composite solid, *p. 284*
lateral face, *p. 252*	regular pyramid, *p. 272*	

Review Examples and Exercises

6.1 **Drawing 3-Dimensional Figures** *(pp. 250–255)*

Draw a triangular prism.

Draw identical triangular bases.	Connect corresponding vertices.	Change any *hidden* lines to dashed lines.

Exercises

Draw the solid.

1. Square pyramid   **2.** Hexagonal prism   **3.** Cylinder

6.2 **Surface Areas of Prisms** *(pp. 256–261)*

Find the surface area of the prism.

Draw a net.

$$S = 2\ell w + 2\ell h + 2wh$$
$$= 2(6)(4) + 2(6)(5) + 2(4)(5)$$
$$= 48 + 60 + 40$$
$$= 148$$

∴ The surface area is 148 square feet.

Exercises

Find the surface area of the prism.

4.

5.

6.

6.3 Surface Areas of Cylinders (pp. 262–267)

Find the surface area of the cylinder. Round your answer to the nearest tenth.

Draw a net.

$$S = 2\pi r^2 + 2\pi rh$$
$$= 2\pi(8)^2 + 2\pi(8)(9)$$
$$= 128\pi + 144\pi$$
$$= 272\pi \approx 854.1$$

The surface area is about 854.1 square millimeters.

Exercises

Find the surface area of the cylinder. Round your answer to the nearest tenth.

7.
   7 in.
   2 in.

8. 3 cm 1 cm

9. 4 m 5 m

6.4 Surface Areas of Pyramids (pp. 270–275)

Find the surface area of the regular pyramid.

10 yd
6 yd
5.2 yd

10 yd
6 yd
5.2 yd

Draw a net.

Area of base
$$\frac{1}{2} \cdot 6 \cdot 5.2 = 15.6$$

Area of a lateral face
$$\frac{1}{2} \cdot 6 \cdot 10 = 30$$

Find the sum of the areas of the base and all 3 lateral faces.

$$S = 15.6 + 30 + 30 + 30 = 105.6$$

The surface area is 105.6 square yards.

Exercises

Find the surface area of the regular pyramid.

10.
    3 in.
    2 in.

11.
    10 m
    8 m 6.9 m

12.
    9 cm
    7 cm
    Area of base is 84.3 cm².

6.5 **Surface Areas of Cones** *(pp. 276–281)*

Find the surface area of the cone. Round your answer to the nearest tenth.

Draw a net.

$$S = \pi r^2 + \pi r \ell$$
$$= \pi(3)^2 + \pi(3)(5)$$
$$= 9\pi + 15\pi$$
$$= 24\pi \approx 75.4$$

⋮ The surface area is about 75.4 square millimeters.

Exercises

Find the surface area of the cone. Round your answer to the nearest tenth.

13.

4 in.

1 in.

14.

4 cm

3 cm

15.

8 m   4 m

6.6 **Surface Areas of Composite Solids** *(pp. 282–287)*

Find the surface area of the composite solid. Round your answer to the nearest tenth.

The solid is made of a cone and a cylinder. Use the surface area formulas. Do not include the areas of the bases that overlap.

10 in.

8 in.

6 in.

Cone

$$S = \pi r \ell$$
$$= \pi(6)(10)$$
$$= 60\pi \approx 188.4$$

Cylinder

$$S = \pi r^2 + 2\pi r h$$
$$= \pi(6)^2 + 2\pi(6)(8)$$
$$= 36\pi + 96\pi$$
$$= 132\pi \approx 414.5$$

⋮ The surface area is about 188.4 + 414.5 = 602.9 square inches.

Exercises

Find the surface area of the composite solid. Round your answer to the nearest tenth.

16.

4 ft

6 ft

6 ft

6 ft

17.

10 yd

6 yd

1 yd

8 yd   2 yd

18.

3 m

5 m

10 m

Check It Out
Test Practice
BigIdeasMath ✓.com

Draw the solid.

1. Square prism   **2.** Pentagonal pyramid   **3.** Cone

Find the surface area of the prism or regular pyramid.

4.

3 ft
2 ft
5 ft

5.

2 in.
1 in.

6.

15 m
11 m
9.5 m

Find the surface area of the cylinder or cone. Round your answer to the nearest tenth.

7.

8 m
2 m

8.

10 in.
7 in.

9. Draw the front, side, and top views of the solid in Exercise 8.

Identify the solids that form the composite solid. Then find the surface area. Round your answer to the nearest tenth.

10.

9 ft
7 ft
1 ft

11.

13 cm
5 cm
6 cm
12 cm
1 cm

4 in.
5 in.

Chestnut Grove
Fresh Ground
Cornmeal
NET WT. 16 OZ.

12. CORN MEAL How much paper is used for the label of the corn meal container?

13. CRACKER BOX Find the surface area of the cracker box.

Cheezy
CRACKERS
Swiss cheese flavor

10 in.
8 in.
3 in.

14. COSTUME The cone-shaped hat will be part of a costume for a school play. What is the least amount of material needed to make this hat?

11 in.
6 in.

15.2 ft
19.5 ft
6 ft
14 ft

15. SKATEBOARD RAMP A quart of paint covers 80 square feet. How many quarts should you buy to paint the ramp with two coats? (Assume you will not paint the bottom of the ramp.)

1. In the figure below, $\triangle PQR \sim \triangle STU$.

What is the value of x?

A. 9.6 cm

B. $10\frac{2}{3}$ cm

C. 13.5 cm

D. 15 cm

2. The rectangle below is divided into six regions.

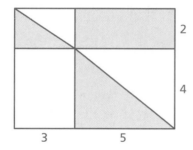

What is the area of the part of the figure that is shaded?

F. 23 units²

G. 24 units²

H. 25 units²

I. 28 units²

3. A right rectangular prism and its dimensions are shown below.

What is the total surface area, in square inches, of the right rectangular prism?

4. You rode your bicycle 0.8 mile in 2 minutes. You want to know how many miles you could ride in 1 hour, if you ride at the same rate. Which proportion could you use to get your answer?

A. $\dfrac{0.8}{2} = \dfrac{60}{x}$

C. $\dfrac{0.8}{2} = \dfrac{30}{x}$

B. $\dfrac{0.8}{2} = \dfrac{x}{60}$

D. $\dfrac{0.8}{2} = \dfrac{x}{30}$

5. A right square pyramid is shown below.

The square base and one of the triangular faces of the right square pyramid are shown below with their dimensions.

5 in.

3 in.   3 in.

Square Base   **A Triangular Face**

What is the total surface area of the right square pyramid?

F. 16.5 in.^{2}

H. 39 in.^{2}

G. 31.5 in.^{2}

I. 69 in.^{2}

6. A right circular cylinder with a radius of 3 centimeters and a height of 7 centimeters will be carved out of wood.

Part A   Draw and label a right circular cylinder with a radius of 3 centimeters and a height of 7 centimeters.

The two bases of the right circular cylinder will be painted blue. The rest of the cylinder will be painted red.

Part B   What is the surface area, in square centimeters, that will be painted blue? Show your work and explain your reasoning. (Use 3.14 for π.)

Part C   What is the surface area, in square centimeters, that will be painted red? Show your work and explain your reasoning. (Use 3.14 for π.)

7. Anna was simplifying the expression in the box below.

$$-\frac{3}{8} \cdot \left[\frac{2}{5} \div (-4)\right] = -\frac{3}{8} \cdot \left[\frac{2}{5} \cdot \left(-\frac{1}{4}\right)\right]$$

$$= -\frac{3}{8} \cdot \left(-\frac{1}{10}\right)$$

$$= -\frac{3}{80}$$

What should Anna do to correct the error that she made?

A. Make the product inside the brackets positive.

B. Multiply by -10 instead of $-\frac{1}{10}$.

C. Make the final product positive.

D. Multiply by 4 instead of $-\frac{1}{4}$.

8. Which equation has the greatest solution?

F. $-3x + 9 = -15$

G. $12 = 2x + 28$

H. $\frac{x}{2} - 13 = -7$

I. $6 = \frac{x}{3} + 10$

9. A cube has a total surface area of 600 square inches. What is the length, in inches, of each edge of the cube?

10. A line contains the two points plotted in the coordinate plane below.

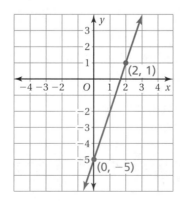

Another point on this line can be represented by the ordered pair $(-1, y)$. What is the value of y?

A. -11

B. -8

C. -6

D. -2

7 Volumes of Solids

"I petitioned my owner for a dog house with greater volume."

"Add a bunk bed and we can have a sleep over."

"And this is what he built for me."

"This setup is too good to be true."

"Do you know why the volume of a cone is one-third the volume of the cylinder with the same height and base?"

What You Learned Before

Number one on America's list of 10 worst ideas.

"I just figured out how to find your volume. We'll immerse you in a barrel of water and measure the water that overflows."

Identifying Similar Figures

Example 1 Which rectangle is similar to Rectangle A?

Rectangle A
8
18

Rectangle B
8
27

Rectangle C
12
27

Rectangle A and Rectangle B

$$\frac{\text{Length of A}}{\text{Length of B}} = \frac{18}{27} = \frac{2}{3} \qquad \frac{\text{Width of A}}{\text{Width of B}} = \frac{8}{8} = 1 \qquad \text{Not proportional}$$

Rectangle A and Rectangle C

$$\frac{\text{Length of A}}{\text{Length of C}} = \frac{18}{27} = \frac{2}{3} \qquad \frac{\text{Width of A}}{\text{Width of C}} = \frac{8}{12} = \frac{2}{3} \qquad \text{Proportional}$$

∴ So, Rectangle C is similar to Rectangle A.

Finding Measures in Similar Figures

Example 2 The two triangles are similar. Find the value of *x*.

5 cm
10 cm
x
y
17.5 cm
24.5 cm

$$\frac{5}{17.5} = \frac{x}{24.5}$$ Write a proportion.

$$122.5 = 17.5x$$ Use Cross Products Property.

$$7 = x$$ Divide each side by 17.5.

∴ So, *x* is 7 centimeters.

Try It Yourself

1. Construct two more rectangles that are similar to Rectangle A in Example 1.

2. Find the value of *y* in Example 2.

Essential Question How can you find the volume of a prism?

---

1 ACTIVITY: Pearls in a Treasure Chest

Work with a partner. A treasure chest is filled with valuable pearls. Each pearl is about 1 centimeter in diameter and is worth about $80.

Use the diagrams below to describe two ways that you can estimate the number of pearls in the treasure chest.

a.

1 cm

60 cm

120 cm

60 cm

b.

c. Use the method in part (a) to estimate the value of the pearls in the chest.

---

2 ACTIVITY: Finding a Formula for Volume

Work with a partner. You know that the formula for the volume of a rectangular prism is $V = \ell wh$.

a. Find a new formula that gives the volume in terms of the area of the base B and the height h.

b. Use both formulas to find the volume of each prism. Do both formulas give you the same volumes?

3 ACTIVITY: Finding a Formula for Volume

Work with a partner. Use the concept in Activity 2 to find a formula that gives the volume of any prism.

Triangular Prism

Rectangular Prism

Pentagonal Prism

Triangular Prism

Hexagonal Prism

Octagonal Prism

4 ACTIVITY: Using a Formula

Work with a partner. A ream of paper has 500 sheets.

a. Does a single sheet of paper have a volume? Why or why not?

b. If so, explain how you can find the volume of a single sheet of paper.

What Is Your Answer?

5. IN YOUR OWN WORDS How can you find the volume of a prism?

6. Draw a prism that has a trapezoid as its base. Use your formula to find the volume of the prism.

 Practice

Use what you learned about the volumes of prisms to complete Exercises 4–6 on page 302.

Check It Out
Lesson Tutorials
BigIdeasMath.com

Key Vocabulary
volume, p. 300

The **volume** of a three-dimensional figure is a measure of the amount of space that it occupies. Volume is measured in cubic units.

Key Idea

Volume of a Prism

Words The volume V of a prism is the product of the area of the base and the height of the prism.

area of base, B

height, h

area of base, B

height, h

Algebra $V = Bh$

Area of base   Height of prism

EXAMPLE 1 Finding the Volume of a Prism

Study Tip

The area of the base of a rectangular prism is the product of the length ℓ and the width w.

You can use $V = \ell wh$ to find the volume of a rectangular prism.

Find the volume of the prism.

$V = Bh$ Write formula for volume.

$\quad = 6(8) \cdot 15$ Substitute.

$\quad = 48 \cdot 15$ Simplify.

$\quad = 720$ Multiply.

15 yd

8 yd

6 yd

∴ The volume is 720 cubic yards.

EXAMPLE 2 Finding the Volume of a Prism

Find the volume of the prism.

$V = Bh$ Write formula for volume.

$\quad = \dfrac{1}{2}(5.5)(2) \cdot 4$ Substitute.

$\quad = 5.5 \cdot 4$ Simplify.

$\quad = 22$ Multiply.

2 in.

4 in.

5.5 in.

∴ The volume is 22 cubic inches.

 Multi-Language Glossary at BigIdeasMath.com.

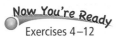

On Your Own

Find the volume of the prism.

Now You're Ready
Exercises 4–12

1.

2.

EXAMPLE 3 **Real-Life Application**

A movie theater designs two bags to hold 96 cubic inches of popcorn.
(a) Find the height of each bag. (b) Which bag should the theater
choose to reduce the amount of paper needed? Explain.

a. Find the height of each bag.

Bag A	**Bag B**
$V = Bh$	$V = Bh$
$96 = 4(3)(h)$	$96 = 4(4)(h)$
$96 = 12h$	$96 = 16h$
$8 = h$	$6 = h$

∴ The height is 8 inches.   ∴ The height is 6 inches.

b. To determine the amount of paper needed, find the surface
area of each bag. Do not include the top base.

Bag A	**Bag B**
$S = \ell w + 2\ell h + 2wh$	$S = \ell w + 2\ell h + 2wh$
$= 4(3) + 2(4)(8) + 2(3)(8)$	$= 4(4) + 2(4)(6) + 2(4)(6)$
$= 12 + 64 + 48$	$= 16 + 48 + 48$
$= 124 \text{ in.}^2$	$= 112 \text{ in.}^2$

∴ The surface area of Bag B is less than the surface area of Bag A.
So, the theater should choose Bag B.

On Your Own

Bag C

3. You design Bag C that has a volume of
96 cubic inches. Should the theater in
Example 3 choose your bag? Explain.

✓ Vocabulary and Concept Check

1. **VOCABULARY** What type of units are used to describe volume?

2. **CRITICAL THINKING** What is the difference between volume and surface area?

3. **CRITICAL THINKING** You are ordering packaging for a product. Should you be more concerned with volume or surface area? Explain.

Practice and Problem Solving

Find the volume of the prism.

 4.

7 in.
8 in.
9 in.

5.

8 cm
12 cm
6 cm

6.

8 m
7 m
4 m

7.

5 yd
4 yd
8 yd

8.

6 ft
9 ft
4.5 ft

9.

8 mm
10 mm
10.5 mm

 10.

4.8 m
10 m
7.2 m

 11.

15 mm
$B = 43$ mm^2

 12.

20 ft
$B = 166$ ft^2

13. **ERROR ANALYSIS** Describe and correct the error in finding the volume of the triangular prism.

7 cm
10 cm
5 cm

✗
$V = Bh$
$= 10(5)(7)$
$= 50 \cdot 7$
$= 350$ cm^3

School Locker

Gym Locker

60 in.
48 in.
12 in.
12 in.
10 in.
15 in.

14. **LOCKER** Each locker is shaped like a rectangular prism. Which has more storage space? Explain.

15. **CEREAL BOX** A cereal box is 9 inches by 2.5 inches by 10 inches. What is the volume of the box?

Find the volume of the prism.

16.

12 in.
12 in.   10 in.

17.

24 ft
30 ft
20 ft

18. **REASONING** Two prisms have the same volume. Do they *always*, *sometimes*, or *never* have the same surface area? Explain.

19. **CUBIC UNITS** How many cubic inches are in a cubic foot? Use a sketch to explain your reasoning.

20. **CAPACITY** As a gift, you fill the calendar with packets of chocolate candy. Each packet has a volume of 2 cubic inches. Find the maximum number of packets you can fit inside the calendar.

6 in.
8 in.   4 in.

21. **HEIGHT** Two liters of water are poured into an empty vase shaped like an octagonal prism. The base area is 100 square centimeters. What is the height of the water? (1 L = 1000 cm^3)

22. **GAS TANK** The gas tank is 20% full. Use the current price of gas in your community to find the cost to fill the tank. (1 gal = 231 in.^{3})

23. **OPEN-ENDED** You visit an aquarium. One of the tanks at the aquarium holds 450 gallons of water. Draw a diagram to show one possible set of dimensions of the tank. (1 gal = 231 in.^{3})

11 in.
1.25 ft   1.75 ft
15 in   21 in

24. **Critical Thinking** What is the volume of the rectangular prism?

40 cm^2
30 cm^2 48 cm^2

Identify the transformation. (*Section 5.5, Section 5.6, and Section 5.7*)

25.

26.

27.

28. **MULTIPLE CHOICE** What is the approximate surface area of a cylinder with a radius of 3 inches and a height of 10 inches? (*Section 6.3*)

Ⓐ 30 in.^{2} Ⓑ 87 in.^{2} Ⓒ 217 in.^{2} Ⓓ 245 in.^{2}

7.2 Volumes of Cylinders

Essential Question How can you find the volume of a cylinder?

Share Your Work at...
My.BigIdeasMath.com

1 ACTIVITY: Finding a Formula Experimentally

Work with a partner.

   a. Find the area of the face of a coin.

   b. Find the volume of a stack of a dozen coins.

   c. Generalize your results to find the volume of a cylinder.

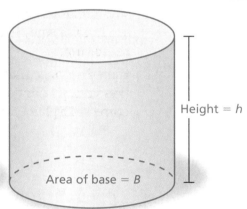

Height = h

Area of base = B

2 ACTIVITY: Making a Business Plan

Work with a partner. You are planning to make and sell 3 different sizes of cylindrical candles. You buy 1 cubic foot of candle wax for $20 to make 8 candles of each size.

   a. Design the candles. What are the dimensions of each size?

   b. You want to make a profit of $100. Decide on a price for each size.

   c. Did you set the prices so that they are proportional to the volume of each size of candle? Why or why not?

3 ACTIVITY: Science Experiment

Work with a partner. Use the diagram to describe how you can find the volume of a small object.

4 ACTIVITY: Comparing Cylinders

Work with a partner.

a. Just by looking at the two cylinders, which one do you think has the greater volume? Explain your reasoning.

b. Find the volume of each cylinder. Was your prediction in part (a) correct? Explain your reasoning.

What Is Your Answer?

5. **IN YOUR OWN WORDS** How can you find the volume of a cylinder?

6. Compare your formula for the volume of a cylinder with the formula for the volume of a prism. How are they the same?

"Here's how I remember how to find the volume of <u>any</u> prism or cylinder."

"Base times tall, will fill 'em all."

Math: A
Poetry: C

Practice

Use what you learned about the volumes of cylinders to complete Exercises 3–5 on page 308.

Key Idea

Volume of a Cylinder

Words The volume V of a cylinder is the product of the area of the base and the height of the cylinder.

area of base, B

height, h

Algebra $V = Bh$

Area of base — Height of cylinder

EXAMPLE 1 Finding the Volume of a Cylinder

Study Tip

Because $B = \pi r^2$, you can use $V = \pi r^2 h$ to find the volume of a cylinder.

Find the volume of the cylinder. Round your answer to the nearest tenth.

$V = Bh$ Write formula for volume.

$\quad = \pi(3)^2(6)$ Substitute.

$\quad = 54\pi \approx 169.6$ Simplify.

∴ The volume is about 169.6 cubic meters.

3 m

6 m

EXAMPLE 2 Finding the Height of a Cylinder

Find the height of the cylinder. Round your answer to the nearest whole number.

The diameter is 10 inches. So, the radius is 5 inches.

$V = Bh$ Write formula for volume.

$314 = \pi(5)^2(h)$ Substitute.

$314 = 25\pi h$ Simplify.

$4 \approx h$ Divide each side by 25π.

∴ The height is about 4 inches.

h

10 in.

Volume = 314 in.³

On Your Own

Now You're Ready
Exercises 3–11
and 13–15

Find the volume V or height h of the cylinder. Round your answer to the nearest tenth.

1.

15 ft

4 ft

$V \approx$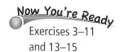

2.

8 cm

$h \approx$

Volume = 176 cm³

EXAMPLE 3 **Real-Life Application**

How much salsa is missing from the jar?

The missing salsa fills a cylinder with a height of $10 - 4 = 6$ centimeters and a radius of 5 centimeters.

5 cm

10 cm

4 cm

$$V = Bh \qquad \text{Write formula for volume.}$$
$$= \pi(5)^2(6) \qquad \text{Substitute.}$$
$$= 150\pi \approx 471 \qquad \text{Simplify.}$$

∴ About 471 cubic centimeters of salsa are missing from the jar.

EXAMPLE 4 **Standardized Test Practice**

1.7 ft

1 ft

About how many gallons of water does the water cooler bottle contain? (1 ft³ ≈ 7.5 gal)

(A) 5.3 gal   (B) 10 gal   (C) 17 gal   (D) 40 gal

Find the volume of the cylinder. The diameter is 1 foot. So, the radius is 0.5 foot.

$$V = Bh \qquad \text{Write formula for volume.}$$
$$= \pi(0.5)^2(1.7) \qquad \text{Substitute.}$$
$$= 0.425\pi \approx 1.3345 \qquad \text{Simplify.}$$

So, the cylinder contains about 1.3345 cubic feet of water. To find the number of gallons it contains, multiply by $\dfrac{7.5 \text{ gal}}{1 \text{ ft}^3}$.

$$1.3345 \, \cancel{\text{ft}^3} \times \frac{7.5 \text{ gal}}{1 \, \cancel{\text{ft}^3}} \approx 10 \text{ gal}$$

∴ The water cooler bottle contains about 10 gallons of water. The correct answer is (B).

● **On Your Own**

Now You're Ready
Exercise 12

3. **WHAT IF?** In Example 3, the height of the salsa in the jar is 5 centimeters. How much salsa is missing from the jar?

4. A cylindrical water tower has a diameter of 15 meters and a height of 5 meters. About how many gallons of water can the tower contain? (1 m³ ≈ 264 gal)

Vocabulary and Concept Check

1. **DIFFERENT WORDS, SAME QUESTION** Which is different? Find "both" answers.

   How much does it take to fill the cylinder?

   What is the capacity of the cylinder?

   How much does it take to cover the cylinder?

   How much does the cylinder contain?

   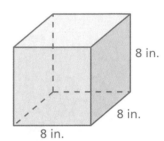

2. **REASONING** Without calculating, which of the solids has the greater volume? Explain.

 Practice and Problem Solving

Find the volume of the cylinder. Round your answer to the nearest tenth.

① **3.**
9 ft
6 ft

4. 3 m
3 m

5. 7 ft
5 ft

6. 5 ft
10 ft

7. 10 mm
3 mm

8. 2 ft
1 ft

9. 7 in.
3 in.

10. 15 m
5 m

11. 16 cm
8 cm

④ **12. SWIMMING POOL** A cylindrical swimming pool has a diameter of 16 feet and a height of 4 feet. About how many gallons of water can the pool contain? Round your answer to the nearest whole number. (1 ft^3 ≈ 7.5 gal)

Find the height of the cylinder. Round your answer to the nearest whole number.

② 13. Volume = 250 ft³

8 ft

h

14. Volume = 32,000 in.³

32 in.

h

15. Volume = 600,000 cm³

100 cm

h

16. CRITICAL THINKING How does the volume of a cylinder change when its diameter is halved? Explain.

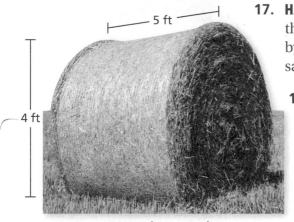

5 ft

4 ft

Round Hay Bale

17. HAY BALES A traditional "square" bale of hay is actually in the shape of a rectangular prism. Its dimensions are 2 feet by 2 feet by 4 feet. How many "square" bales contain the same amount of hay as one large "round" bale?

18. ROAD ROLLER A tank on the road roller is filled with water to make the roller heavy. The tank is a cylinder that has a height of 6 feet and a radius of 2 feet. One cubic foot of water weighs 62.5 pounds. Find the weight of the water in the tank.

19. VOLUME A cylinder has a surface area of 1850 square meters and a radius of 9 meters. Estimate the volume of the cylinder to the nearest whole number.

20. **Critical Thinking** Water flows at 2 feet per second through a pipe with a diameter of 8 inches. A cylindrical tank with a diameter of 15 feet and a height of 6 feet collects the water.

   a. What is the volume, in cubic inches, of water flowing out of the pipe every second?

   b. What is the height, in inches, of the water in the tank after 5 minutes?

   c. How many minutes will it take to fill 75% of the tank?

Fair Game Review What you learned in previous grades & lessons

Write and solve an equation to answer the question. *(Section 4.1)*

21. 50% of 200 is what number?

22. 80% of 400 is what number?

23. MULTIPLE CHOICE The variables x and y vary directly. When x is 18, y is 24. Which equation relates x and y? *(Section 3.7)*

  Ⓐ $y = \frac{3}{4}x$ Ⓑ $y = 2x - 12$ Ⓒ $y = 4x - 3$ Ⓓ $y = \frac{4}{3}x$

Essential Question

How can you find the volume of a pyramid?

1 ACTIVITY: Finding a Formula Experimentally

Work with a partner.

- Draw the two nets on cardboard and cut them out.

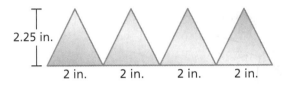

2.25 in.

2 in. 2 in. 2 in. 2 in.

2 in. 2 in. 2 in.

2 in.

2 in.

2 in.

- Fold and tape the nets to form an open square box and an open pyramid.

- Both figures should have the same size square base and the same height.

- Fill the pyramid with pebbles. Then pour the pebbles into the box. Repeat this until the box is full. How many pyramids does it take to fill the box?

- Use your result to find a formula for the volume of a pyramid.

2 ACTIVITY: Comparing Volumes

Work with a partner. You are an archeologist studying two ancient pyramids. What factors would affect how long it took to build each pyramid? Given similar conditions, which pyramid took longer to build? Explain your reasoning.

Cholula Pyramid in Mexico
Height: about 217 ft
Base: about 1476 ft by 1476 ft

Cheops Pyramid in Egypt
Height: about 480 ft
Base: about 755 ft by 755 ft

3 ACTIVITY: Finding and Using a Pattern

Work with a partner.

- Find the volumes of the pyramids.
- Organize your results in a table.
- Describe the pattern.
- Use your pattern to find the volume of a pyramid with a side length and height of 20.

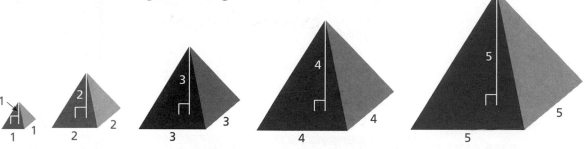

4 ACTIVITY: Breaking a Prism into Pyramids

Work with a partner. The rectangular prism can be cut to form three pyramids. Show that the sum of the volumes of the three pyramids is equal to the volume of the prism.

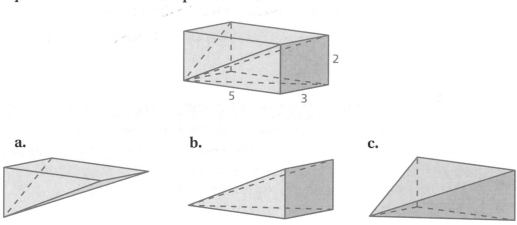

a.   b.   c.

What Is Your Answer?

5. IN YOUR OWN WORDS How can you find the volume of a pyramid?

6. Write a general formula for the volume of a pyramid.

Use what you learned about the volumes of pyramids to complete Exercises 4–6 on page 314.

7.3   Lesson

Check It Out
Lesson Tutorials
BigIdeasMath ✓com

Key Idea

Volume of a Pyramid

Words The volume V of a pyramid is one-third the product of the area of the base and the height of the pyramid.

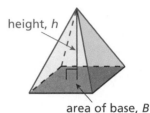

Area of base

Algebra $V = \frac{1}{3}Bh$

Height of pyramid

EXAMPLE 1 Finding the Volume of a Pyramid

Find the volume of the pyramid.

$$V = \frac{1}{3}Bh \qquad \text{Write formula for volume.}$$

$$= \frac{1}{3}(48)(9) \qquad \text{Substitute.}$$

$$= 144 \qquad \text{Multiply.}$$

∴ The volume is 144 cubic millimeters.

EXAMPLE 2 Finding the Volume of a Pyramid

Find the volume of the pyramid.

> **Study Tip**
> The area of the base of a rectangular pyramid is the product of the length ℓ and the width w.
> You can use $V = \frac{1}{3}\ell wh$ to find the volume of a rectangular pyramid.

a.

$$V = \frac{1}{3}Bh$$

$$= \frac{1}{3}(3)(4)(7)$$

$$= 28$$

∴ The volume is 28 cubic feet.

b.

$$V = \frac{1}{3}Bh$$

$$= \frac{1}{3}\left(\frac{1}{2}\right)(17.5)(6)(10)$$

$$= 175$$

∴ The volume is 175 cubic meters.

312   Chapter 7   Volumes of Solids

On Your Own

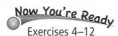

Now You're Ready
Exercises 4–12

Find the volume of the pyramid.

1.

6 ft

$B = 21 \text{ ft}^2$

2.

7 in.

8 in.

10 in.

3.

11 cm

18 cm

7 cm

EXAMPLE 3 **Real-Life Application**

(a) The volume of sunscreen in Bottle B is how many times the volume in Bottle A?

(b) Which is the better buy?

Bottle A
$9.96

6 in.

1 in.

2 in.

Bottle B
$14.40

4 in.

1.5 in.

3 in.

a. Use the formula for the volume of a pyramid to estimate the amount of sunscreen in each bottle.

Bottle A

$$V = \frac{1}{3}Bh$$

$$= \frac{1}{3}(2)(1)(6)$$

$$= 4 \text{ in.}^3$$

Bottle B

$$V = \frac{1}{3}Bh$$

$$= \frac{1}{3}(3)(1.5)(4)$$

$$= 6 \text{ in.}^3$$

So, the volume of sunscreen in Bottle B is $\frac{6}{4}$, or 1.5 times the volume in Bottle A.

b. Find the unit cost for each bottle.

Bottle A

$$\frac{\text{cost}}{\text{volume}} = \frac{\$9.96}{4 \text{ in.}^3}$$

$$= \frac{\$2.49}{1 \text{ in.}^3}$$

Bottle B

$$\frac{\text{cost}}{\text{volume}} = \frac{\$14.40}{6 \text{ in.}^3}$$

$$= \frac{\$2.40}{1 \text{ in.}^3}$$

The unit cost of Bottle B is less than the unit cost of Bottle A. So, Bottle B is the better buy.

On Your Own

Now You're Ready
Exercise 18

4. Bottle C is on sale for $13.20. Is Bottle C a better buy than Bottle B in Example 3? Explain.

Bottle C

3 in.

2 in.

3 in.

Vocabulary and Concept Check

1. **WRITING** How is the formula for the volume of a pyramid different from the formula for the volume of a prism?

2. **OPEN-ENDED** Describe a real-life situation that involves finding the volume of a pyramid.

3. **REASONING** A triangular pyramid and a triangular prism have the same base and height. The volume of the prism is how many times the volume of the pyramid?

 Practice and Problem Solving

Find the volume of the pyramid.

1 2 **4.**

2 ft
2 ft
1 ft

5.

4 mm
$B = 15 \text{ mm}^2$

6.

8 yd
4 yd
5 yd

7.

8 in.
10 in.
6 in.

8.

7 cm
3 cm
1 cm

9.

12 mm
$B = 63 \text{ mm}^2$

10.

7 ft
8 ft
6 ft

11.

15 mm
14 mm
20 mm

12. **PARACHUTE** In 1483, Leonardo da Vinci designed a parachute. It is believed that this was the first parachute ever designed. In a notebook, he wrote "If a man is provided with a length of gummed linen cloth with a length of 12 yards on each side and 12 yards high, he can jump from any great height whatsoever without injury." Find the volume of air inside Leonardo's parachute.

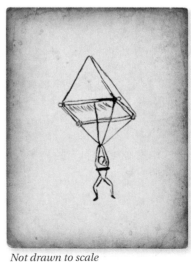

Not drawn to scale

Copy and complete the table to find the area of the base B or the height h of the pyramid.

	Volume, V	Area of Base, B	Height, h
13.	60 in.^{3}		6 in.
14.	144 cm^3	48 cm^2	
15.	135 ft^3	54 ft^2	

4 in.

3 in.

3 in.

Paperweight

16. TEEPEE Use the photo of the teepee.

    a. What is the shape of the base? How can you tell?

    b. The teepee's height is about 10 feet. Estimate the volume of the teepee.

17. PAPERWEIGHT How much glass is needed to manufacture 1000 paperweights? Explain your reasoning.

③ 18. SPIRE Which sandcastle spire has a greater volume? How much more sand is required to make the spire with the greater volume?

6 in.

8 in.

$B = 30$ in.^{2}

$B = 24$ in.^{2}

Spire A   Spire B

19. OPEN-ENDED A pyramid has a volume of 40 cubic feet and a height of 6 feet. Find one possible set of dimensions of the rectangular base.

20. Reasoning Do the two solids have the same volume? Explain.

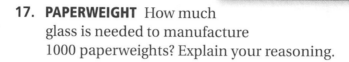

z y x $3z$ y x

Fair Game Review What you learned in previous grades & lessons

Simplify the expression. *(Skills Review Handbook)*

21. $\frac{1}{3} \times 12 \times 7$ **22.** $\frac{1}{3} \times 8 \times 27$ **23.** $\frac{1}{3} \times 6^2 \times 5$ **24.** $\frac{1}{3} \times 2^2 \times 15$

25. MULTIPLE CHOICE You spend 25% of your money on a shirt. Then you spend $\frac{1}{6}$ of the remainder on lunch. Lunch costs $8. What percent of your money is spent on lunch? *(Section 4.1)*

    A 4.2%   **B** 12.5%   **C** 16.7%   **D** 32%

Essential Question How can you remember the formulas for surface area and volume?

You discovered that the volume of a pyramid is one-third the volume of a prism that has the same base and same height. You can use a similar activity to discover that the volume of a cone is one-third the volume of a cylinder that has the same base and height.

Volume of a Cone = $\frac{1}{3}$(Area of Base) × (Height)

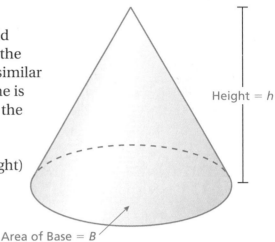

Height = h

Area of Base = B

1 ACTIVITY: Summarizing Volume Formulas

Work with a partner. You can remember the volume formulas for all of the solids shown with just two concepts.

Volumes of Prisms and Cylinders

Volume = (Area of Base) × (Height)

Volumes of Pyramids and Cones

Volume = $\frac{1}{3}$ (Volume of Prism or Cylinder with same base and height)

Make a list of all the formulas you need to remember to find the area of a base. Talk about strategies for remembering these formulas.

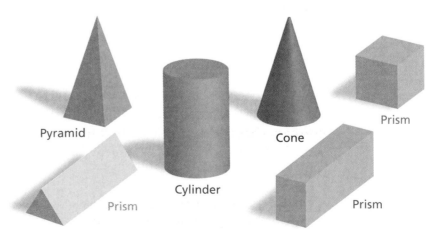

Pyramid

Prism

Cylinder

Cone

Prism

Prism

ACTIVITY: Volumes of Oblique Solids

Work with a partner. Think of a stack of paper. If you adjust the stack so that the sides are oblique (slanted), do you change the volume of the stack? If the volume of the stack does not change, then the formulas for volumes of right solids also apply to oblique solids.

| Right cylinder | Oblique cylinder | Right cone | Oblique cone |

3

ACTIVITY: Summarizing Surface Area Formulas

Work with a partner. Make a list of the formulas for surface area that you studied in Chapter 6. Organize these formulas in a way similar to what you did in Activity 1.

Surface Area of a Right Prism =

Surface Area of a Right Pyramid =

Surface Area of a Right Cylinder =

Surface Area of a Right Cone =

What Is Your Answer?

4. IN YOUR OWN WORDS How can you remember the formulas for surface area and volume? Write all of the surface area and volume formulas on a summary sheet. Make the list short so that you do not have to memorize many formulas.

Practice

Use what you learned about the volumes of cones to complete Exercises 4–6 on page 320.

Key Idea

Volume of a Cone

Words The volume V of a cone is one-third the product of the area of the base and the height of the cone.

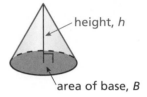

height, h

area of base, B

Algebra $V = \dfrac{1}{3}Bh$

Area of base

Height of cone

EXAMPLE **1** **Finding the Volume of a Cone**

Study Tip

Because $B = \pi r^2$, you can use $V = \dfrac{1}{3}\pi r^2 h$ to find the volume of a cone.

Find the volume of the cone. Round your answer to the nearest tenth.

The diameter is 4 meters. So, the radius is 2 meters.

$$V = \frac{1}{3}Bh \qquad \text{Write formula.}$$

$$= \frac{1}{3}\pi(2)^2(6) \qquad \text{Substitute.}$$

$$= 8\pi \approx 25.1 \qquad \text{Simplify.}$$

∴ The volume is about 25.1 cubic meters.

6 m

4 m

EXAMPLE **2** **Finding the Height of a Cone**

Find the height of the cone. Round your answer to the nearest tenth.

$$V = \frac{1}{3}Bh \qquad \text{Write formula.}$$

$$956 = \frac{1}{3}\pi(9)^2(h) \qquad \text{Substitute.}$$

$$956 = 27\pi h \qquad \text{Simplify.}$$

$$11.3 \approx h \qquad \text{Divide each side by } 27\pi.$$

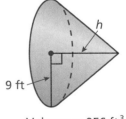

h

9 ft

Volume = 956 ft³

∴ The height is about 11.3 feet.

Now You're Ready
Exercises 4–17

On Your Own

Find the volume V or height h of the cone. Round your answer to the nearest tenth.

1.

6 cm

15 cm

$V \approx$ ◻

2.

$h \approx$ ◻

15 yd

Volume = 7200 yd³

EXAMPLE **3** **Real-Life Application**

30 mm

10 mm

24 mm

You must answer a trivia question before the sand in the timer falls to the bottom. The sand falls at a rate of 50 cubic millimeters per second. How much time do you have to answer the question?

Use the formula for the volume of a cone to find the volume of the sand in the timer.

$$V = \frac{1}{3}Bh \qquad\qquad \text{Write formula.}$$

$$= \frac{1}{3}\pi(10)^2(24) \qquad\qquad \text{Substitute.}$$

$$= 800\pi \approx 2512 \qquad\qquad \text{Simplify.}$$

The volume of the sand is about 2512 cubic millimeters. To find the amount of time you have to answer the question, multiply the volume by the rate at which the sand falls.

$$2512 \text{ mm}^3 \times \frac{1 \text{ sec}}{50 \text{ mm}^3} = 50.24 \text{ sec}$$

∴ You have about 50 seconds to answer the question.

On Your Own

3. **WHAT IF?** In Example 3, the sand falls at a rate of 60 cubic millimeters per second. How much time do you have to answer the question?

4. **WHAT IF?** In Example 3, the height of the sand in the timer is 12 millimeters and the radius is 5 millimeters. How much time do you have to answer the question?

Vocabulary and Concept Check

1. **VOCABULARY** Describe the height of a cone.

2. **WRITING** Compare and contrast the formulas for the volume of a pyramid and the volume of a cone.

3. **REASONING** You know the volume of a cylinder. How can you find the volume of a cone with the same base and height?

 ## Practice and Problem Solving

Find the volume of the cone. Round your answer to the nearest tenth.

1 4.

4 in.
2 in.

5.

3 m
6 m

6.

10 mm
5 mm

7.

2 ft   1 ft

8.

5 cm
8 cm

9.

9 yd
6 yd

10.

7 ft
3 ft

11.

10 in.
5 in.

12.

4 cm
8 cm

13. **ERROR ANALYSIS** Describe and correct the error in finding the volume of the cone.

8 m
6 m

$$\times \quad V = \frac{1}{3}Bh$$

$$= \frac{1}{3}(\pi)(6)^2(8)$$

$$= 96\pi \text{ m}^3$$

3 cm
4 cm
10 cm
8 cm
Glass A   Glass B

14. **GLASS** The inside of each glass is shaped like a cone. Which glass can hold more liquid? How much more?

Find the height of the cone. Round your answer to the nearest tenth.

2 **15.** Volume = $\frac{1}{18}\pi$ ft³

$\frac{2}{3}$ ft

16. Volume = 225 cm³

├─ 10 cm ─┤

17. Volume = 3.6 in.³

1.8 in.

18. REASONING The volume of a cone is 20π cubic meters. What is the volume of a cylinder having the same base and same height?

4.8 in.

10 in.

19. VASE Water leaks from a crack in a vase at a rate of 0.5 cubic inch per minute. How long does it take for 20% of the water to leak from a full vase?

20. LEMONADE STAND You have 10 gallons of lemonade to sell. (1 gal ≈ 3785 cm³)

├─ 8 cm ─┤

11 cm

a. Each customer uses one paper cup. How many paper cups will you need?

b. The cups are sold in packages of 50. How many packages should you buy?

c. How many cups will be left over if you sell 80% of the lemonade?

21. REASONING The cylinder and the cone have the same volume. What is the height of the cone?

x

y

?

2x

22. **Critical Thinking** Cone A has the same height but twice the radius of Cone B. What is the ratio of the volume of Cone A to the volume of Cone B?

Fair Game Review *What you learned in previous grades & lessons*

Find the volume of the solid. *(Section 7.1, Section 7.2, and Section 7.3)*

23.

9 m

7 m

5 m

24.

15 cm

8 cm

10 cm

25. 4 ft

9.5 ft

26. MULTIPLE CHOICE Which scale has a scale factor of 3 : 1? *(Section 5.4)*

Ⓐ 1 in. : 2 ft   Ⓑ 3 cm : 1 mm   Ⓒ 5 ft : 15 yd   Ⓓ 0.5 ft : 2 in.

You can use a **formula triangle** to arrange variables and operations of a formula. Here is an example of a formula triangle for volume of a prism.

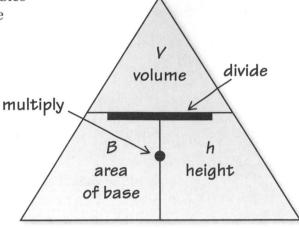

To find an unknown variable, use the other variables and the operation between them. For example, to find the area *B* of the base, cover up the *B*. Then you can see that you divide the volume *V* by the height *h*.

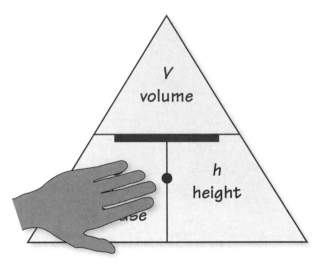

On Your Own

Make a formula triangle to help you study these topics. *Hint:* Your formula triangles may have a different form than what is shown in the example.

1. volume of a cylinder

2. volume of a pyramid

3. volume of a cone

After you complete this chapter, make formula triangles for the following topics.

4. volume of a composite solid

5. surface areas of similar solids

6. volumes of similar solids

"See how a formula triangle works? Cover any variable and you get its formula."

Find the volume of the prism. *(Section 7.1)*

1.
8 in.
3 in.
7 in.

2.
6 ft
8 ft
15 ft

3.
25 mm
$B = 197 \text{ mm}^2$

Find the volume of the solid. Round your answer to the nearest tenth.
(Section 7.2, Section 7.3, and Section 7.4)

4.
4 yd
3.5 yd

5.
3 m
2 m
5 m

6.
12 ft
$B = 166 \text{ ft}^2$

7.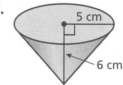
5 cm
6 cm

8. PAPER CONE The paper cone can hold 84.78 cubic centimeters of water. What is the height of the cone?   *(Section 7.4)*

6 cm
h

9. ROOF A pyramid hip roof is a good choice for a house in a hurricane area. What is the volume of the roof to the nearest tenth?   *(Section 7.3)*

20 ft
40 ft   40 ft

10. CUBIC UNITS How many cubic feet are there in a cubic yard? Use a sketch to explain your reasoning. *(Section 7.1)*

11. JUICE CAN You are buying two cylindrical cans of juice. Each can holds the same amount of juice. What is the height of Can B?   *(Section 7.2)*

4 in.
Harvest Grown
made with 100%
FRUIT JUICE
h
6 in.
6 in.
Apple Ridge
FRUIT JUICE
100% Natural
Can A   Can B

Essential Question How can you estimate the volume of a composite solid?

1 ACTIVITY: Estimating Volume

Work with a partner. You work for a toy company and need to estimate the volume of a Minifigure that will be molded out of plastic.

a. Estimate the number of cubic inches of plastic that is needed to mold the Minifigure's head. Show your work.

b. Estimate the number of cubic inches of plastic that is needed to mold one of the Minifigure's legs. Show your work.

One unit = $\frac{1}{10}$ inch

Work with a partner.

a. Make a plan for estimating the amount of plastic it takes to make a standard eight-stud LEGO® Brick.

© 2008 The LEGO Group, used with permission

b. How much water, in cubic inches, would it take to make ten LEGO® Brick ice cubes?

What Is Your Answer?

3. **IN YOUR OWN WORDS** How can you estimate the volume of a composite solid? Try thinking of some alternative strategies.

Practice   Use what you learned about the volumes of composite solids to complete Exercises 4–6 on page 328.

Check It Out
Lesson Tutorials
BigIdeasMath ✓com

EXAMPLE 1 **Finding the Volume of a Composite Solid**

Find the volume of the composite solid.

The solid is made up of a square prism and a square pyramid. Find each volume.

Square prism

Square pyramid

$$V = Bh$$
$$= 15(15)(10)$$
$$= 2250$$

$$V = \frac{1}{3}Bh$$
$$= \frac{1}{3}(15)(15)(8)$$
$$= 600$$

Find the sum: $2250 + 600 = 2850$ in.^{3}.

❖ The volume of the composite solid is 2850 cubic inches.

EXAMPLE 2 **Finding the Volume of a Composite Solid**

Find the volume of the composite solid. Round your answer to the nearest tenth.

The solid is a cylinder with a cylinder-shaped hole. Find each volume.

Entire Cylinder

Cylinder-Shaped Hole

$$V = Bh$$
$$= \pi(9)^2(3)$$
$$= 243\pi$$

$$V = Bh$$
$$= \pi(5)^2(3)$$
$$= 75\pi$$

Find the difference: $243\pi - 75\pi = 168\pi \approx 527.5$ m^3.

❖ The volume of the composite solid is about 527.5 cubic meters.

On Your Own

Now You're Ready
Exercises 4–11

Find the volume of the composite solid. Round your answer to the nearest tenth.

1.

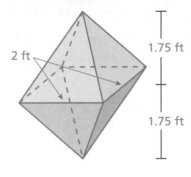

2 ft

1.75 ft

1.75 ft

2.

2 in.

12 in.

14 in.

10 in.

EXAMPLE 3 **Real-Life Application**

8.5 mm

11.5 mm

2.2 mm

What is the volume of the silver ring in an Argentine peso? Round your answer to the nearest tenth.

The coin is a cylinder. The silver ring is the portion remaining when the inner cylinder is removed. Find the volume of each cylinder.

Entire cylinder

11.5 mm

2.2 mm

Inner cylinder

8.5 mm

2.2 mm

$V = Bh$

$\quad = \pi(11.5)^2(2.2)$

$\quad = 290.95\pi$

$V = Bh$

$\quad = \pi(8.5)^2(2.2)$

$\quad = 158.95\pi$

Subtract the volume of the inner cylinder from the volume of the entire cylinder: $290.95\pi - 158.95\pi = 132\pi \approx 414.5$ mm^3.

∴ The volume of the silver ring is about 414.5 cubic millimeters.

On Your Own

3. WHAT IF? In Example 3, how would the volume of the silver ring change if the coin were only half as thick?

4. Find the volume of the composite solid. Round your answer to the nearest tenth.

3 ft

4 ft

5 ft

Vocabulary and Concept Check

1. **VOCABULARY** What is a composite solid?

2. **WRITING** Explain how to find the volume of the composite solid.

3. **CRITICAL THINKING** Explain how finding the volume in Example 2 is different from finding the volume in Example 1.

 Practice and Problem Solving

Find the volume of the composite solid. Round your answer to the nearest tenth.

1 2 4.

5.

6.

7.

8.

9.

10.

11.

12. **BIRD FEEDER** The cedar waxwing measures about 6 inches from head to tail. The green hexagonal part of the bird feeder has a base area of 18 square inches. Estimate how much bird seed the bird feeder will hold. Explain how you found your estimate.

13. **CAKE** The raspberry layer cake has a diameter of 10 inches and a height of 5 inches.

    a. About what percent of the cake is remaining?

    b. Estimate the volume of the remaining cake.

5.5 in.

0.6 in.
2 in.
0.6 in.

12 in.

1.25 in.

11 in.

14. **KICKBOARD** A foam kickboard used for swimming has two identical hand grips.

    a. Find the volume of the kickboard.

    b. One cubic inch of foam weighs about 0.007 pound. How much does the kickboard weigh?

$B = 6$ in.²

3 in.

0.75 in.

$B = 10.5$ in.²

15. **PAPERWEIGHT** Estimate the amount of glass in the paperweight. Explain how you found your estimate.

16. 🎇 **Puzzle** 🎇 The volume of each group of solids is given. Find the volume of each of the four types of blocks.

$V = 8\pi + 8$

$V = 8\pi + 28$

$V = 8\pi + 20$

 Fair Game Review What you learned in previous grades & lessons

The two figures are similar. Find the ratio (red to blue) of the areas. *(Section 5.2)*

17.

    A
    10
    C   B
    D
    6
    F   E

18.

    P   Q
    9
    S   R
    W   X
    7
    Z   Y

19. **MULTIPLE CHOICE** A fire hydrant releases 1200 gallons of water in 4 minutes. What is the rate of release in gallons per second? *(Section 3.1)*

    Ⓐ 3 gal/sec   Ⓑ 5 gal/sec   Ⓒ 30 gal/sec   Ⓓ 300 gal/sec

Surface Areas and Volumes of Similar Solids

Essential Question When the dimensions of a solid increase by a factor of k, how does the surface area change? How does the volume change?

1 ACTIVITY: Comparing Volumes and Surface Areas

Work with a partner. Copy and complete the table. Describe the pattern. Are the solids similar? Explain your reasoning.

a.

Radius	1	1	1	1	1
Height	1	2	3	4	5
Surface Area					
Volume					

b.

Radius	1	2	3	4	5
Height	1	2	3	4	5
Surface Area					
Volume					

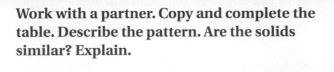

2 ACTIVITY: Comparing Volumes and Surface Areas

Work with a partner. Copy and complete the table. Describe the pattern. Are the solids similar? Explain.

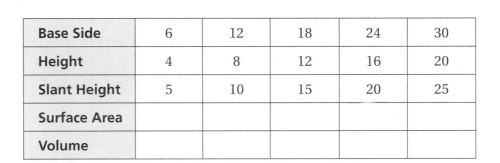

Base Side	6	12	18	24	30
Height	4	8	12	16	20
Slant Height	5	10	15	20	25
Surface Area					
Volume					

What Is Your Answer?

3. **IN YOUR OWN WORDS** When the dimensions of a solid increase by a factor of k, how does the surface area change?

4. **IN YOUR OWN WORDS** When the dimensions of a solid increase by a factor of k, how does the volume change?

5. All the dimensions of a cone increase by a factor of 5.

   a. How many times greater is the surface area? Explain.

   | 5 | 10 | 25 | 125 |

   b. How many times greater is the volume? Explain.

   | 5 | 10 | 25 | 125 |

Practice

Use what you learned about the surface areas and volumes of similar solids to complete Exercises 4–6 on page 335.

7.6 Lesson

Check It Out
Lesson Tutorials
BigIdeasMath.com

Key Vocabulary
similar solids, *p. 332*

Solids of the same type that have proportional corresponding linear measures are **similar solids**.

EXAMPLE 1 Identifying Similar Solids

Which cylinder is similar to Cylinder A?

Cylinder B
5 m
3 m

Cylinder C

7.5 m
5 m

Cylinder A
6 m
4 m

Check to see if corresponding linear measures are proportional.

Cylinder A and Cylinder B

$$\frac{\text{Height of A}}{\text{Height of B}} = \frac{4}{3} \qquad \frac{\text{Radius of A}}{\text{Radius of B}} = \frac{6}{5}$$

Not proportional

Cylinder A and Cylinder C

$$\frac{\text{Height of A}}{\text{Height of C}} = \frac{4}{5} \qquad \frac{\text{Radius of A}}{\text{Radius of C}} = \frac{6}{7.5} = \frac{4}{5}$$

Proportional

So, Cylinder C is similar to Cylinder A.

EXAMPLE 2 Finding Missing Measures in Similar Solids

The cones are similar. Find the missing slant height ℓ.

Cone X
13 yd
5 yd

Cone Y
ℓ
7 yd

$$\frac{\text{Radius of X}}{\text{Radius of Y}} = \frac{\text{Slant height of X}}{\text{Slant height of Y}}$$

$$\frac{5}{7} = \frac{13}{\ell} \qquad \text{Substitute.}$$

$$5\ell = 91 \qquad \text{Use Cross Products Property.}$$

$$\ell = 18.2 \qquad \text{Divide each side by 5.}$$

The slant height is 18.2 yards.

On Your Own

Now You're Ready
Exercises 4–9

1. Cylinder D has a radius of 7.5 meters and a height of 4.5 meters. Which cylinder in Example 1 is similar to Cylinder D?

2. The prisms are similar. Find the missing width and length.

Prism A
20 in.
8 in.
11 in.

Prism B
8 in.
ℓ
w

Multi-Language Glossary at BigIdeasMath.com.

Key Ideas

Linear Measures

Surface Areas of Similar Solids

If two solids are similar, then the ratio of their surface areas is equal to the square of the ratio of their corresponding linear measures.

Solid A

Solid B

$$\frac{\text{Surface Area of A}}{\text{Surface Area of B}} = \left(\frac{a}{b}\right)^2$$

EXAMPLE ③ **Finding Surface Area**

Pyramid A

6 ft

Pyramid B

10 ft

Surface Area = 600 ft²

The pyramids are similar. What is the surface area of Pyramid A?

$$\frac{\text{Surface Area of A}}{\text{Surface Area of B}} = \left(\frac{\text{Height of A}}{\text{Height of B}}\right)^2$$

$$\frac{S}{600} = \left(\frac{6}{10}\right)^2 \qquad \text{Substitute.}$$

$$\frac{S}{600} = \frac{36}{100} \qquad \text{Evaluate power.}$$

$$\frac{S}{600} \cdot 600 = \frac{36}{100} \cdot 600 \qquad \text{Multiply each side by 600.}$$

$$S = 216 \qquad \text{Simplify.}$$

∴ The surface area of Pyramid A is 216 square feet.

 On Your Own

The solids are similar. Find the surface area of the red solid. Round your answer to the nearest tenth.

3.

8 m

5 m

Surface Area = 608 m²

4.

5 cm

4 cm

Surface Area = 110 cm²

Key Idea

Volumes of Similar Solids

If two solids are similar, then the ratio of their volumes is equal to the cube of the ratio of their corresponding linear measures.

$$\frac{\text{Volume of A}}{\text{Volume of B}} = \left(\frac{a}{b}\right)^3$$

Solid A a

Solid B b

EXAMPLE 4 **Standardized Test Practice**

Original Tank

Volume = 2000 ft³

The dimensions of the touch tank at an aquarium are doubled. What is the volume of the new touch tank?

(A) 150 ft³   (B) 4000 ft³

(C) 8000 ft³   (D) 16,000 ft³

The dimensions are doubled, so the ratio of the dimensions in the original tank to the dimensions in the new tank is 1 : 2.

$$\frac{\text{Original volume}}{\text{New volume}} = \left(\frac{\text{Original dimension}}{\text{New dimension}}\right)^3$$

$$\frac{2000}{V} = \left(\frac{1}{2}\right)^3 \qquad \text{Substitute.}$$

$$\frac{2000}{V} = \frac{1}{8} \qquad \text{Evaluate power.}$$

$$16{,}000 = V \qquad \text{Use Cross Products Property.}$$

Study Tip

When the dimensions of a solid are multiplied by k, the surface area is multiplied by k^2 and the volume is multiplied by k^3.

∴ The volume of the new tank is 16,000 cubic feet. The correct answer is (D).

⬤ **On Your Own**

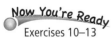
Now You're Ready
Exercises 10–13

The solids are similar. Find the volume of the red solid. Round your answer to the nearest tenth.

5.

5 cm

12 cm

Volume = 288 cm³

6.

3 in.
Volume = 9 in.³

4 in.

Vocabulary and Concept Check

1. **VOCABULARY** What are similar solids?

2. **OPEN-ENDED** Draw two similar solids and label their corresponding linear measures.

3. **REASONING** The ratio of the corresponding linear measures of Cube A to Cube B is $\frac{2}{3}$.

   a. Find the ratio of the area of one face of Cube A to the area of one face of Cube B.

   b. Find the ratio of the volume of Cube A to the volume of Cube B.

Practice and Problem Solving

Determine whether the solids are similar.

4.

3 in.
9 in.
2 in. 1 in.
3 in.
6 in.

5.

4 in.
4 in.
4 in. 2 in.
2 in. 1 in.

6.

6 ft   6.5 ft   12 ft   13 ft
5 ft
5 ft   10 ft
10 ft

7.

21 m   20 m
15 m
9 m
12 m
29 m

The solids are similar. Find the missing dimension(s).

8.

10 ft
4 ft
d
10 in.

9.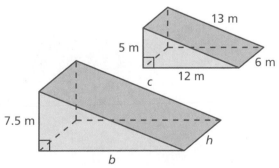

13 m
5 m
6 m
12 m
c
7.5 m
h
b

The solids are similar. Find the surface area S or volume V of the red solid. Round your answer to the nearest tenth.

③ ④ 10.

4 m

Surface Area = 336 m²

6 m

11.

20 in.

Surface Area = 1800 in.²

15 in.

12.

21 mm

21 mm

Volume = 5292 mm³

7 mm

7 mm

13.

10 ft

12 ft

Volume = 7850 ft³

14. ERROR ANALYSIS The ratio of the corresponding linear measures of two similar solids is 3 : 5. The volume of the smaller solid is 108 cubic inches. Describe and correct the error in finding the volume of the larger solid.

✗
$$\frac{108}{V} = \left(\frac{3}{5}\right)^2$$
$$\frac{108}{V} = \frac{9}{25}$$
$$300 = V$$

The volume of the larger solid is 300 cubic inches.

15. MIXED FRUIT The ratio of the corresponding linear measures of two similar cans of fruit is 4 to 7. The smaller can has a surface area of 220 square centimeters. Find the surface area of the larger can.

16. CLASSIC MUSTANG The volume of a 1968 Ford Mustang GT engine is 390 cubic inches. Which scale model of the Mustang has the greater engine volume, a 1 : 18 scale model or a 1 : 24 scale model? How much greater?

17. **Critical Thinking** You and a friend make paper cones to collect beach glass.
You cut out the largest possible three-fourths circle from each piece of paper.

   a. Are the cones similar? Explain your reasoning.

   b. Your friend says that because your sheet of paper is twice as large, your cone will hold exactly twice the volume of beach glass. Is this true? Explain your reasoning.

Friend's paper   Your paper

8.5 in.   11 in.

11 in.   17 in.

18. **MARBLE STATUE** You have a small marble statue of Wolfgang Mozart that is 10 inches tall and weighs 16 pounds. The original statue in Vienna is 7 feet tall.

   a. Estimate the weight of the original statue. Explain your reasoning.

   b. If the original statue were 20 feet tall, how much would it weigh?

19. **RUSSIAN DOLLS** The largest doll is 7 inches tall. Each of the other dolls is 1 inch shorter than the next larger doll. Make a table that compares the surface areas and volumes of the seven dolls.

Wolfgang Mozart

 Fair Game Review *What you learned in previous grades & lessons*

Add. *(Section 1.2)*

20. $69 + (-31) + 7 + (-6)$ **21.** $-2 + (-5) + (-12) + 20$ **22.** $10 + (-6) + (-5) + 1$

23. **MULTIPLE CHOICE** What is the mean of the numbers below?
(Skills Review Handbook)

      14, 6, 21, 8, 14, 19, 30

   (**A**) 6   (**B**) 15   (**C**) 16   (**D**) 56

1. Determine whether the solids are similar. *(Section 7.6)*

6 cm
4 cm
7.5 cm
5 cm

2. The prisms are similar. Find the missing width and height. *(Section 7.6)*

h
2 in.
10 in.
4 in.   1 in.
w

Find the volume of the composite solid. Round your answer to the nearest tenth.
(Section 7.5)

3.

9 ft
8 ft
12 ft

4.

2 mm
2 mm
2 mm
4 mm
4.5 mm
4.5 mm

5. The solids are similar. Find the surface area of the red solid. *(Section 7.6)*

2 m
4 m

Surface Area = 18.84 m²

6. **ARCADE** You win a token after playing an arcade game. What is the volume of the gold ring? Round your answer to the nearest tenth. *(Section 7.5)*

KING ARCADE
1 TOKEN
9 mm
10 mm
2 mm

7. **SHED** What is the volume of the storage shed? *(Section 7.5)*

1 ft
8 ft
7 ft   7 ft

8. **JEWELRY BOXES** The ratio of the corresponding linear measures of two similar jewelry boxes is 2 to 3. The larger box has a volume of 162 cubic inches. Find the volume of the smaller jewelry box. *(Section 7.6)*

9. **GELATIN** You make a dessert with lemon gelatin and lime gelatin. What percent of the dessert is lime-flavored? Explain. *(Section 7.5)*

1 in.
1 in.
0.5 in.
13 in.
9 in.

Review Key Vocabulary

volume, *p. 300*   similar solids, *p. 332*

Review Examples and Exercises

7.1 **Volumes of Prisms** *(pp. 298–303)*

Find the volume of the prism.

$V = Bh$ Write formula for volume.

$= \dfrac{1}{2}(7)(3) \cdot 5$ Substitute.

$= 52.5$ Multiply.

∴ The volume is 52.5 cubic feet.

Exercises

Find the volume of the prism.

1.   **2.**   **3.**

6 in.
8 in.   2 in.

7.5 m
4 m   8 m

9 mm
15 mm   4.5 mm

7.2 **Volumes of Cylinders** *(pp. 304–309)*

Find the height of the cylinder. Round your answer to the nearest whole number.

$V = Bh$ Write formula for volume.

$565 = \pi(6)^2(h)$ Substitute.

$565 = 36\pi h$ Simplify.

$5 \approx h$ Divide each side by 36π.

∴ The height is about 5 centimeters.

6 cm
h
Volume = 565 cm³

Exercises

Find the volume V or height h of the cylinder. Round your answer to the nearest tenth.

4.   10 in.   **5.**   4 m   **6.**   15 ft

2 in.
$V \approx$ ▮

$h \approx$ ▮
$V = 150$ m³

7 ft
$V \approx$ ▮

Find the volume of the pyramid.

$$V = \frac{1}{3}Bh \qquad \text{Write formula for volume.}$$

$$= \frac{1}{3}(6)(5)(10) \qquad \text{Substitute.}$$

$$= 100 \qquad \text{Multiply.}$$

The volume is 100 cubic yards.

10 yd

5 yd

6 yd

Exercises

Find the volume of the pyramid.

7.

20 ft

17 ft 15 ft

8.

30 in.

$B = 210 \text{ in.}^2$

9.

9 mm

8 mm

8 mm

Find the height of the cone. Round your answer to the nearest tenth.

$$V = \frac{1}{3}Bh \qquad \text{Write formula for volume.}$$

$$900 = \frac{1}{3}\pi(6)^2(h) \qquad \text{Substitute.}$$

$$900 = 12\pi h \qquad \text{Simplify.}$$

$$23.9 \approx h \qquad \text{Divide each side by } 12\pi.$$

The height is about 23.9 millimeters.

6 mm

h

Volume = 900 mm³

Exercises

Find the volume V or height h of the cone. Round your answer to the nearest tenth.

10.

12 m

8 m

$V \approx$

11.

4 cm

10 cm

$V \approx$

12.

$h \approx$

9 in.

$V = 3052 \text{ in.}^3$

7.5 Volumes of Composite Solids (pp. 324–329)

Find the volume of the composite solid. Round your answer to the nearest tenth.

Square Prism	**Cylinder**
$V = Bh$	$V = Bh$
$= (12)(12)(9)$	$= \pi(5)^2(9)$
$= 1296$	$= 225\pi \approx 706.5$

Find the difference: $1296 - 706.5 = 589.5$.

∴ The volume of the composite solid is about 589.5 cubic feet.

Exercises

Find the volume of the composite solid. Round your answer to the nearest tenth.

13.

14.

15.

7.6 Surface Areas and Volumes of Similar Solids (pp. 330–337)

The cones are similar. What is the volume of the red cone? Round your answer to the nearest tenth.

$$\frac{\text{Volume of A}}{\text{Volume of B}} = \left(\frac{\text{Height of A}}{\text{Height of B}}\right)^3$$

$$\frac{V}{157} = \left(\frac{4}{6}\right)^3 \quad \text{Substitute.}$$

$$\frac{V}{157} = \frac{64}{216} \quad \text{Evaluate power.}$$

$$V \approx 46.5 \quad \text{Multiply each side by 157.}$$

Cone A   Cone B

Volume = 157 in.³

∴ The volume is about 46.5 cubic inches.

Exercises

The solids are similar. Find the surface area S or volume V of the red solid.

16.

Pyramid C   Pyramid D

Volume = 4608 m³

17.

Prism F   Prism G

Surface Area = 154 yd²

Check It Out
Test Practice
BigIdeasMath Vcom

Find the volume of the solid. Round your answer to the nearest tenth.

1.

6 in.
9 in.
12 in.

2.

20 mm
30 mm

3.

6 m
8 m
3 m

4.

6 cm
3 cm

5.

4 mm
18 mm
12 mm   12 mm

6.

10 m
6 m
12 m

7. The pyramids are similar.

   a. Find the missing dimension.

   b. Find the surface area of the red pyramid.

4 cm   5 cm
6 cm   ℓ
Surface Area = 96 cm²

5 in.
3 in.
5 in.
5.5 in.

8. **SMOOTHIES** You are making smoothies. You will use either the cone-shaped glass or the cylindrical glass. Which glass holds more? About how much more?

9. **CAPACITY** A baseball team uses a heated tub to treat injuries. What is the capacity of the tub in liters? (1 L = 1000 cm³)

80 cm
150 cm   150 cm

10. **WAFFLE CONES** The ratio of the corresponding linear measures of two similar waffle cones is 3 to 4. The smaller cone has a volume of about 18 cubic inches. Find the volume of the larger cone. Round your answer to the nearest tenth.

11. **OPEN-ENDED** Draw two different composite solids that have the same volume, but different surface areas. Explain your reasoning.

1. What is the value of the expression below when $h = \frac{1}{2}$ and $k = -\frac{1}{6}$?

$$h \div 3 + 3 \div k$$

A. $-17\frac{5}{6}$

B. $-\frac{1}{3}$

C. 1

D. $17\frac{5}{6}$

2. A right circular cone and its dimensions are shown below.

20 cm

14 cm

What is the volume of the right circular cone? $\left(\text{Use } \frac{22}{7} \text{ for } \pi.\right)$

F. $1,026\frac{2}{3}$ cm³

G. $3,080$ cm³

H. $4,106\frac{2}{3}$ cm³

I. $12,320$ cm³

3. A right triangular prism and its dimensions are shown below.

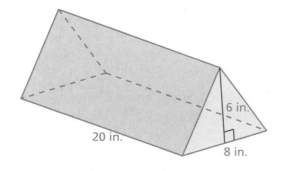

6 in.

20 in.

8 in.

What is the volume of the right triangular prism?

4. A tropical storm has maximum sustained surface winds of at least 39 miles per hour but less than 74 miles per hour. Which graph correctly represents the possible wind speeds of a tropical storm?

A.

B.

C.

D.

5. Use the coordinate plane to answer the question below.

Which point does *not* lie on the same line as the other three?

F. $(-5, 3)$ **H.** $(-1, -1)$

G. $(-3, 2)$ **I.** $(1, -4)$

6. Olga was solving an equation in the box shown.

What should Olga do to correct the error that she made?

A. Multiply both sides by $-\dfrac{5}{2}$ instead of $-\dfrac{2}{5}$.

B. Multiply both sides by $\dfrac{2}{5}$ instead of $-\dfrac{2}{5}$.

C. Distribute $-\dfrac{2}{5}$ to get $-4x - 6$.

D. Add 15 to -30.

$$-\frac{2}{5}(10x - 15) = -30$$

$$10x - 15 = -30\left(-\frac{2}{5}\right)$$

$$10x - 15 = 12$$

$$10x - 15 + 15 = 12 + 15$$

$$10x = 27$$

$$\frac{10x}{10} = \frac{27}{10}$$

$$x = \frac{27}{10}$$

7. It has been raining at a rate of 0.08 inch per hour. At this rate, how much rain will fall in $2\frac{1}{2}$ hours?

   F. 0.032 in.   **H.** 0.3125 in.

   G. 0.2 in.   **I.** 0.33 in.

8. A right circular cylinder has a volume of 1296 cubic inches. If the radius of the cylinder is divided by 12, what would be the volume, in cubic inches, of the smaller cylinder?

9. If 9 friends share equally a large box of baseball cards, each friend gets 240 cards. If 6 friends share equally the same box of cards, how many cards does each friend get?

   A. 80   **C.** 360

   B. 160   **D.** 400

10. All students in a class were surveyed to find out their preferences for writing instruments. The survey found that 12 students prefer to write with a pencil and 20 students prefer to write with a pen. What percent of students in the class prefer to write with a pencil?

   F. 12%   **H.** 60%

   G. 37.5%   **I.** 62.5%

11. The figure below is a diagram for making a tin lantern.

3 in.

8 in.

2 in.

The figure consists of a right circular cylinder without its top base and a right circular cone without its base. What is the volume, in cubic inches, of the entire lantern? Show your work and explain your reasoning. (Use 3.14 for π.)

8 Data Analysis and Samples

"I took a survey of pet owners on how many times per day you should treat your dog to a biscuit."

You just couldn't resist participating yourself, could you?

"What do you think?"

For the sake of privacy, can't we label the 2% part as "Other."

Use litter box 2%
Claw furniture 6.3%
Eat 8.3%
Sleep 66.7%
Play with friends 16.7%

"I've completed a circle graph analyzing what you do each day."

What You Learned Before

"Mom, my owner, and Fluffy have agreed to participate in my random survey. Will you be my fourth participant?"

FLUFFY! You asked Fluffy before you asked me!

● Finding Mean, Median, Mode, and Range

The table shows the top ten Olympic pole vault heights for men and women.

Olympic Pole Vault Heights (meters)	
Men	**Women**
5.45	4.55
5.60	5.05
5.96	4.75
5.70	4.65
5.45	4.65
5.70	4.55
5.60	4.70
5.70	4.75
5.85	4.80
5.70	4.45

Example 1 What is the mean of the men's data?

$$\text{mean} = \frac{\text{sum of data}}{\text{number of data values}}$$

$$= \frac{56.71}{10} \approx 5.67$$

⋮• So, the mean height is about 5.67 meters.

Example 2 What is the median of the women's data?

$$4.45, \ 4.55, \ 4.55, \ 4.65, \ \underbrace{4.65, \ 4.70}, \ 4.75, \ 4.75, \ 4.80, \ 5.05$$

$$\frac{4.65 + 4.70}{2} \approx 4.68$$

⋮• So, the median is about 4.68 meters.

Example 3 What is the mode of the men's data?

⋮• Because it occurs most often, the mode is 5.70 meters.

Example 4 What is the range of the men's data?

$$\text{range} = \text{greatest data value} - \text{least data value}$$

$$= 5.96 - 5.45 = 0.51$$

⋮• So, the range is 0.51 meter.

Try It Yourself

Use the table to answer the question. Round your answer to the nearest hundredth.

1. What is the mean of the women's data?

2. What is the median of the men's data?

3. What is the mode(s) of the women's data?

4. What is the range of the women's data?

Essential Question How can you use a stem-and-leaf plot to organize a set of numbers?

1 ACTIVITY: Decoding a Graph

Work with a partner. You intercept a secret message that contains two different types of plots. You suspect that each plot represents the same data. The graph with the dots indicates only ranges for the numbers.

a. How many numbers are in the data set? How can you tell?

b. How many numbers are greater than or equal to 90? How can you tell?

c. Is 91 in the data set? If so, how many times is it in the set? How can you tell?

d. Make a list of all of the numbers in the data set.

e. You intercept a new secret message. Use the secret code shown below to decode the message.

Secret Code

A = 29	F = 31	K = 18	P = 4	U = 19
B = 33	G = 8	L = 26	Q = 10	V = 17
C = 7	H = 16	M = 22	R = 21	W = 12
D = 20	I = 5	N = 3	S = 2	X = 25
E = 15	J = 11	O = 9	T = 32	Y = 13
				Z = 1

$\overline{32}\ \overline{16}\ \overline{15}\quad \overline{2}\ \overline{32}\ \overline{15}\ \overline{22}\quad \overline{2}\ \overline{16}\ \overline{9}\ \overline{12}\ \overline{2}\quad \overline{32}\ \overline{16}\ \overline{15}\quad \overline{32}\ \overline{15}\ \overline{3}\ \overline{2}$

$\overline{32}\ \overline{16}\ \overline{15}\quad \overline{26}\ \overline{15}\ \overline{29}\ \overline{17}\ \overline{15}\ \overline{2}\quad \overline{2}\ \overline{16}\ \overline{9}\ \overline{12}\quad \overline{32}\ \overline{16}\ \overline{15}\quad \overline{9}\ \overline{3}\ \overline{15}\ \overline{2}$

2 ACTIVITY: Organizing Data

Work with a partner. You are working on an archeological dig. You find several arrowheads.

50 mm

18	61	62
42	42	42
23	41	40
45	45	45
37	28	50
35	39	34
37	32	26
63	24	54
58	58	60
52	53	72
17	73	

As you find each arrowhead, you measure its length (in millimeters) and record it in a notebook.

a. Use a stem-and-leaf plot to organize the lengths.

b. Find the mean length.

c. Find the median length.

d. Describe the distribution of the data.

3 ACTIVITY: Conducting an Experiment

Work with a partner. Use two number cubes to conduct the following experiment.

- Toss the cubes four times and total the results.

  Sample: $2 + 3 \; + \; 2 + 2 \; + \; 3 + 5 \; + \; 6 + 3 \; = 26$

  | 1st toss | 2nd toss | 3rd toss | 4th toss |

  So, 26 is the first number.

- Repeat this process 29 more times.
- Use a stem-and-leaf plot to organize your results.
- Describe your results.

What Is Your Answer?

4. IN YOUR OWN WORDS How can you use a stem-and-leaf plot to organize a set of numbers?

5. RESEARCH Find a career in which a person collects and organizes data. Describe how data are collected and organized in that career.

Practice →

Use what you learned about stem-and-leaf plots to complete Exercises 4–7 on page 352.

Check It Out
Lesson Tutorials
BigIdeasMath.com

Key Vocabulary
stem-and-leaf plot, *p. 350*
stem, *p. 350*
leaf, *p. 350*

Key Idea

Stem-and-Leaf Plots

A **stem-and-leaf plot** uses the digits of data values to organize a data set. Each data value is broken into a **stem** (digit or digits on the left) and a **leaf** (digit or digits on the right).

A stem-and-leaf plot shows how data are distributed.

Stem	Leaf
2	0 0 1 2 5 7
3	1 4 8
4	2
5	8 9

Key: 2|0 = 20

The *key* explains what the stems and leaves represent.

EXAMPLE 1 Making a Stem-and-Leaf Plot

Make a stem-and-leaf plot of the length of the 12 cell phone calls.

Step 1: Order the data.

2, 3, 5, 6, 10, 14, 18, 23, 23, 30, 36, 55

Step 2: Choose the stems and leaves. Because the data values range from 2 to 55, use the *tens* digits for the stems and the *ones* digits for the leaves.

Step 3: Write the stems to the *left* of the vertical line.

Step 4: Write the leaves for each stem to the *right* of the vertical line.

	A	B
1	DATE	MINUTES
2	JULY 9	55
3	JULY 9	3
4	JULY 9	6
5	JULY 10	14
6	JULY 10	18
7	JULY 10	5
8	JULY 10	23
9	JULY 11	30
10	JULY 11	23
11	JULY 11	10
12	JULY 11	2
13	JULY 11	36

Phone call lengths

Order the stems vertically. The stem for data values less than 10 is 0.

Include stems without leaves.

Write the leaves horizontally.

Stem	Leaf
0	2 3 5 6
1	0 4 8
2	3 3
3	0 6
4	
5	5

Key: 1|4 = 14 minutes

On Your Own

Now You're Ready
Exercises 8–11

1. Make a stem-and-leaf plot of the hair lengths.

Hair Length (centimeters)									
5	1	20	12	27	2	30	5	7	38
40	47	1	2	1	32	4	44	33	23

Multi-Language Glossary at BigIdeasMath.com.

EXAMPLE 2 Interpreting a Stem-and-Leaf Plot

Test Scores

Stem	Leaf
6	6
7	0 5 7 8
8	1 1 3 4 4 6 8 8 9
9	0 2 9
10	0

Key: 9|2 = 92 points

The stem-and-leaf plot shows student test scores. (a) How many students scored less than 80 points? (b) How many students scored at least 90 points? (c) How are the data distributed?

a. There are five scores less than 80 points: 66, 70, 75, 77, and 78.

⋮ Five students scored less than 80 points.

b. There are four scores of at least 90 points: 90, 92, 99, and 100.

⋮ Four students scored at least 90 points.

c. There are few low test scores and few high test scores. So, most of the scores are in the middle.

On Your Own

Exercises 16–19

2. Use the grading scale at the right.

a. How many students received a B on the test?

b. How many students received a C on the test?

A: 90–100
B: 80–89
C: 70–79
D: 60–69
F: 59 and below

EXAMPLE 3 Standardized Test Practice

Which statement is *not* true?

(A) Most of the plants are less than 20 inches tall.

(B) The median plant height is 11 inches.

(C) The range of the plant heights is 35 inches.

(D) The plant height that occurs most often is 11 inches.

Plant Heights

Stem	Leaf
0	1 2 4 5 6 8 9
1	0 1 1 5 7
2	2 5
3	6

Key: 1|5 = 15 inches

There are 15 plant heights. So, the median is the eighth data value, 10 inches.

⋮ The correct answer is **(B)**.

On Your Own

3. You are told that three plants are taller than 20 inches. Is the statement true? Explain.

Vocabulary and Concept Check

1. **VOCABULARY** The key for a stem-and-leaf plot is $3|4 = 34$. Which number is the stem? the leaf?

2. **WRITING** Describe how to make a stem-and-leaf plot for the data values 14, 22, 9, 13, 30, 8, 25, and 29.

3. **WRITING** How does a stem-and-leaf plot show the distribution of data?

 Practice and Problem Solving

Use the stem-and-leaf plot at the right.

4. How many data values are in the set?

5. What is the least value? greatest value?

6. What is the median? range?

7. Is the value 32 in the set? Explain.

Stem	Leaf
0	4 6 8
1	0
2	3 4
3	0 6 6 9
4	2

Key: $3|6 = 36$

Make a stem-and-leaf plot of the data.

 8.

Books Read			
26	15	20	9
31	25	29	32
17	26	19	40

9.

Hours Online			
8	12	21	14
18	6	15	24
12	17	2	0

10.

Test Scores (%)				
87	82	95	91	69
88	68	87	65	81
97	85	80	90	62

11.

Points Scored				
58	50	42	71	75
45	51	43	38	71
42	70	56	58	43

12. **ERROR ANALYSIS** Describe and correct the error in making a stem-and-leaf plot of the data.

51, 25, 47, 42, 55, 26, 50, 44, 55

Stem	Leaf
2	5 6
4	2 4 7
5	0 1 5 5

Key: $4|2 = 42$

13. **PUPPIES** The weights (in pounds) of eight puppies at a pet store are 12, 24, 17, 8, 18, 31, 24, and 15. Make a stem-and-leaf plot of the data. Describe the distribution of the data.

Make a stem-and-leaf plot of the data.

14.

Bikes Sold			
78	112	105	99
86	96	115	100
79	81	99	108

15.

Minutes in Line			
4.0	2.6	1.9	3.1
3.6	2.2	2.7	3.8
1.6	2.0	3.1	2.9

VOLLEYBALL The stem-and-leaf plot shows the number of digs for the top 15 players at a volleyball tournament.

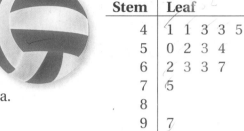

Stem	Leaf
4	1 1 3 3 5
5	0 2 3 4
6	2 3 3 7
7	5
8	
9	7

Key: 5|0 = 50 digs

② 16. How many players had more than 60 digs?

17. Find the mean, median, mode, and range of the data.

18. Describe the distribution of the data.

19. Which data value is the outlier? Describe how the outlier affects the mean.

20. **RESEARCH** Use the Internet to find the heights of the players on your favorite professional sports team.

    a. Make a stem-and-leaf plot of the data.

    b. Analyze the stem-and-leaf plot and make two conclusions about the heights.

21. **OPEN-ENDED** Describe a real-life situation with eight data values that has a median of 33. Make a stem-and-leaf plot of the data.

22. Make a frequency table and a stem-and-leaf plot of the bowling scores in the table. Compare and contrast the two data displays. Which display is better for showing how the data are distributed? Explain.

Bowling Scores					
131	108	115	140	152	122
120	118	156	142	112	107
136	85	127	119	136	125

Fair Game Review What you learned in previous grades & lessons

Draw the solid. *(Section 6.1)*

23. Square pyramid

24. Hexagonal prism

25. Cone

26. Cylinder

27. **MULTIPLE CHOICE** In a bar graph, what determines the length of each bar? *(Skills Review Handbook)*

    Ⓐ Frequency   Ⓑ Data value   Ⓒ Leaf   Ⓓ Change in data

Essential Question How do histograms show the differences in distributions of data?

1 ACTIVITY: Analyzing Distributions

Work with a partner. The graphs (histograms) show four different types of distributions.

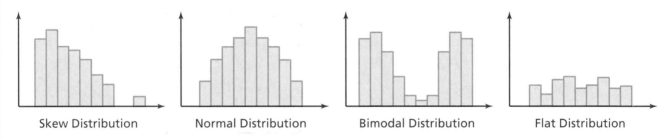

Skew Distribution   Normal Distribution   Bimodal Distribution   Flat Distribution

a. Describe a real-life example of each distribution.

b. Describe the mean, median, and mode of each distribution.

c. In which distributions are the mean and median about equal? Explain your reasoning.

d. How did each type of distribution get its name?

2 ACTIVITY: Analyzing Distributions

Work with a partner. A survey asked 100 adult men and 100 adult women to answer the following questions.

Question 1: What is your ideal weight?
Question 2: What is your ideal age?

Match the histogram to the question.

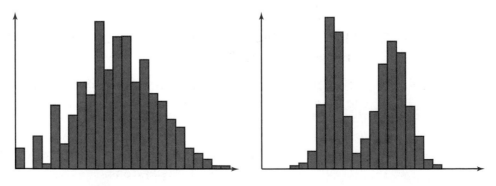

3 **ACTIVITY: Conducting Experiments**

Work with a partner. Conduct two experiments.
Make a frequency table and a histogram for
each experiment. Compare and contrast the
results of the two experiments.

a. Toss one number cube 36 times.
Record the numbers.

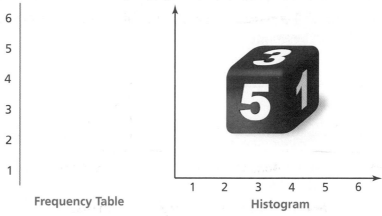

Frequency Table   **Histogram**

b. Toss two number cubes 36 times. Record the sums of the two numbers.

Frequency Table   **Histogram**

What Is Your Answer?

4. **IN YOUR OWN WORDS** How do histograms show the differences in
distributions of data?

5. Describe an experiment that you can conduct to collect data. Predict
the type of data distribution the results will create.

Practice

Use what you learned about histograms to complete
Exercises 4 and 5 on page 358.

8.2 Lesson

Check It Out
Lesson Tutorials
BigIdeasMath.com

Key Vocabulary
histogram, *p. 356*

Key Idea

Histograms

A **histogram** is a bar graph that shows the frequency of data values in intervals of the same size.

The height of a bar represents the frequency of the values in the interval.

CDs Owned

EXAMPLE 1 Making a Histogram

The frequency table shows the number of pairs of shoes that each person in a class owns. Display the data in a histogram.

Step 1: Draw and label the axes.

Step 2: Draw a bar to represent the frequency of each interval.

Pairs of Shoes	Frequency
1–3	11
4–6	4
7–9	0
10–12	3
13–15	6

Remember

A *frequency table* groups data values into intervals. The *frequency* is the number of data values in an interval.

Shoes Owned

Include any interval with a frequency of 0. The bar height is 0.

There is no space between the bars of a histogram.

On Your Own

Now You're Ready
Exercises 6–8

1. The frequency table shows the ages of people riding a roller coaster. Display the data in a histogram.

Age	10–19	20–29	30–39	40–49	50–59
Frequency	16	11	5	2	4

Multi-Language Glossary at BigIdeasMath.com.

EXAMPLE 2 Using a Histogram

The histogram shows the winning speeds at the Daytona 500.
(a) Which interval contains the most data values? (b) How many of the winning speeds are less than 140 miles per hour? (c) How many of the winning speeds are at least 160 miles per hour?

Daytona 500 Winning Speeds

a. The interval with the tallest bar contains the most data values.

⋮• So, the 150–159 miles per hour interval contains the most data values.

b. One winning speed is in the 120–129 miles per hour interval and four winning speeds are in the 130–139 miles per hour interval.

⋮• So, 1 + 4 = 5 winning speeds are less than 140 miles per hour.

c. Seven winning speeds are in the 160–169 miles per hour interval and five winning speeds are in the 170–179 miles per hour interval.

⋮• So, 7 + 5 = 12 winning speeds are at least 160 miles per hour.

● On Your Own

Now You're Ready
Exercises 9–11

2. The histogram shows the number of hours that students in a class slept last night.

    a. How many students slept at least 8 hours?

    b. How many students slept less than 12 hours?

Amount of Sleep

Vocabulary and Concept Check

1. **VOCABULARY** Which graph is a histogram? Explain your reasoning.

2. **REASONING** Describe the outliers in the histogram.

3. **CRITICAL THINKING** How can you tell when an interval of a histogram has a frequency of zero?

 ## Practice and Problem Solving

Determine the type of distribution shown by the histogram.

4.

5.

Display the data in a histogram.

① 6.

States Visited	
States	Frequency
1–5	12
6–10	14
11–15	6
16–20	3

7.

Chess Team	
Wins	Frequency
10–13	3
14–17	4
18–21	4
22–25	2

8.

Movies Watched	
Movies	Frequency
0–1	5
2–3	11
4–5	8
6–7	1

② 9. **MAGAZINES** The histogram shows the number of magazines read last month by students in a class.

   a. Which interval contains the fewest data values?

   b. How many students are in the class?

   c. What percent of the students read less than six magazines?

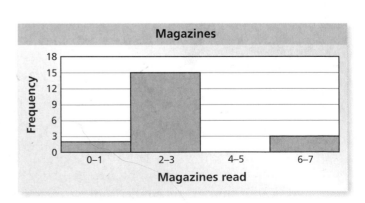

10. **VOTING** The histogram shows the percent of the voting age population that voted in a recent presidential election. Explain whether each statement is supported by the graph.

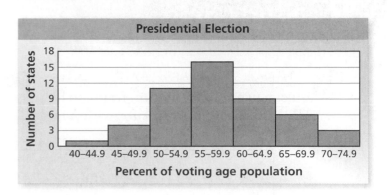

a. Only 40% of one state voted.

b. Most states had between 50% and 64.9% that voted.

11. **AREA** The histograms show the areas of counties in Pennsylvania and Indiana. Which state do you think has the greater area? Explain.

12. **REASONING** Can you find the mean, median, mode, and range of the data in Exercise 7? If so, find them. If not, explain why.

13. **Critical Thinking** The table shows the weights of guide dogs enrolled in a training program.

Weight (lb)					
81	88	57	82	70	85
71	51	82	77	79	77
83	80	54	80	81	73
59	84	75	76	68	78
83	78	55	67	85	79

a. Make a histogram of the data starting with the interval 51–55.

b. Make another histogram of the data using a different sized interval.

c. Compare and contrast the two histograms.

 Fair Game Review What you learned in previous grades & lessons

Find the percent of the number. *(Section 4.1)*

14. 25% of 180

15. 30% of 90

16. 16% of 140

17. 64% of 80

18. **MULTIPLE CHOICE** Two rectangles are similar. The smaller rectangle has a length of 8 feet. The larger rectangle has a length of 14 feet. What is the ratio of the area of the smaller rectangle to the area of the larger rectangle? *(Section 5.3)*

Ⓐ 7 : 4   Ⓑ 4 : 7   Ⓒ 9 : 16   Ⓓ 16 : 49

You can use an **information frame** to help you organize and remember concepts. Here is an example of an information frame for a stem-and-leaf plot.

Definition
A *stem-and-leaf plot* is a data display that uses the digits of data values to organize the data. Stem-and-leaf plots show how data are distributed.

Example
Make a stem-and-leaf plot of the data.

Patient Ages			
32	21	5	43
28	27	16	9
42	13	16	24

Stem-and-Leaf Plot

Visual

Stem	Leaf
0	5 9
1	3 6 6
2	1 4 7 8
3	2
4	2 3

Key: 2 | 4 = 24

Making a stem-and-leaf plot

Order the data.

Choose the stems and leaves.

Write the stems to the *left* of the vertical line.

Write the leaves for each stem to the *right* of the vertical line.

On Your Own

Make an information frame to help you study the topic.

1. histogram

After you complete this chapter, make information frames for the following topics.

2. circle graph

3. making a prediction about a population

4. Pick three other topics that you studied earlier in this course. Make an information frame for each topic.

"I'm having trouble thinking of a good title for my information frame."

Make a stem-and-leaf plot of the data.   *(Section 8.1)*

1.

Cans Collected Each Month			
80	90	84	92
76	83	79	59
68	55	58	61

2.

Miles Driven Each Day				
21	18	12	16	10
16	9	15	20	28
35	50	37	20	11

3.

Ages of Tortoises			
86	99	100	124
92	85	110	130
115	129	83	104

4.

Kilometers Run Each Day				
6.0	5.6	6.2	3.0	2.5
3.5	2.0	5.0	3.9	3.1
6.2	3.1	4.5	3.8	6.1

Display the data in a histogram.   *(Section 8.2)*

5.

Soccer Team Goals	
Goals per Game	Frequency
0–1	5
2–3	4
4–5	0
6–7	1

6.

Minutes Practiced	
Minutes	Frequency
0–19	8
20–39	10
40–59	11
60–79	2

7.

Poems Written for Class	
Poems	Frequency
0–4	6
5–9	16
10–14	4
15–19	2
20–24	2

8. WEIGHTS The weights (in ounces) of nine packages are 7, 22, 16, 12, 6, 18, 15, 13, and 25. Make a stem-and-leaf plot of the data. Describe the distribution of the data.   *(Section 8.1)*

9. REBOUNDS The histogram shows the number of rebounds per game for a middle school basketball player this season.   *(Section 8.2)*

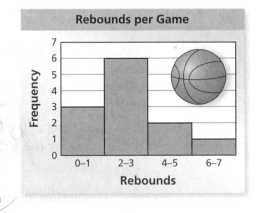

a. Which interval contains the most data values?

b. How many games were played by the player this season?

c. What percent of the games did the player have 4 or more rebounds?

Stem	Leaf
0	6 8 8 9
1	0 1 2 3 7 8
2	0

Key: 0|9 = 9 hours

10. STAGE CREW The stem-and-leaf plot shows the number of hours 11 stage crew members spent building sets. Find the mean, median, mode, and range of the data.   *(Section 8.1)*

8.3 Circle Graphs

Essential Question How can you use a circle graph to show the results of a survey?

Share Your Work at...
My.BigIdeasMath.com

1 ACTIVITY: Reading a Circle Graph

Work with a partner. Six hundred middle school students were asked "What is your favorite sport?" The circle graph shows the results of the survey.

Baseball
Other
Football
Skating
Basketball
Gymnastics
Swimming
Wrestling
Track
Soccer
Hockey

a. Use a protractor to find the angle measure (in degrees) of the section (pie piece) for football.

b. How many degrees are in a full circle?

c. Write and solve a proportion to determine the number of students who said that football is their favorite sport.

d. Repeat the process for the other sections of the circle graph.

ACTIVITY: Making a Circle Graph

Work with a partner.

a. Conduct a survey in your class. Each student should check his or her favorite sport on a piece of paper similar to the one shown below.

What is your favorite sport?

Baseball	❏	Skating	❏
Basketball	❏	Soccer	❏
Football	❏	Swimming	❏
Gymnastics	❏	Track	❏
Hockey	❏	Wrestling	❏
		Other	❏

b. Organize the results on the board.

c. Display the results in a circle graph.

d. Compare and contrast your class survey with the survey in Activity 1.

What Is Your Answer?

3. **IN YOUR OWN WORDS** How can you use a circle graph to show the results of a survey?

4. Find a circle graph in a newspaper, in a magazine, or on the Internet. Copy it and describe the results that it shows.

"I conducted a survey and asked 30 people if they would like a million dollars."

"I organized the results in a circle graph."

Practice

Use what you learned about circle graphs to complete Exercises 5–7 on page 366.

Check It Out
Lesson Tutorials
BigIdeasMath ✓.com

Key Vocabulary 🔊
circle graph, p. 364

 Key Idea

Circle Graphs

A **circle graph** displays data as sections of a circle. The sum of the angle measures in a circle graph is 360°.

Favorite Fruit

The percents total 100%.

The circle represents all of the data.

Each section represents part of the data.

40%
35%
25%

When the data are given in percents, multiply the decimal form of each percent by 360° to find the angle measure for each section.

EXAMPLE **1** **Making a Circle Graph**

Favorite Amusement Park	People
Disney World	25
Busch Gardens	15
Universal Studios	12
Marineland	8

The table shows the results of a survey. Display the data in a circle graph.

Step 1: Find the total number of people.

$$25 + 15 + 12 + 8 = 60$$

Step 2: Find the angle measure for each section of the graph. Multiply the fraction of people that chose each park by 360°.

Check

$$\frac{25}{60} + \frac{15}{60} + \frac{12}{60} + \frac{8}{60} = 1$$

$$150° + 90° + 72° + 48° = 360° ✓$$

Disney World
$$\frac{25}{60} \cdot 360° = 150°$$

Busch Gardens
$$\frac{15}{60} \cdot 360° = 90°$$

Universal Studios
$$\frac{12}{60} \cdot 360° = 72°$$

Marineland
$$\frac{8}{60} \cdot 360° = 48°$$

Step 3: Use a protractor to draw the angle measures found in Step 2 on a circle. Then label the sections.

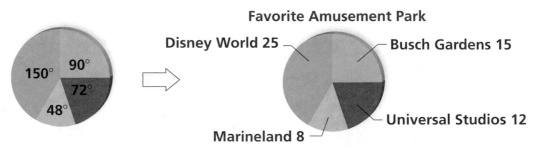

Favorite Amusement Park

150°
90°
72°
48°

Disney World 25
Busch Gardens 15
Universal Studios 12
Marineland 8

🔊 Multi-Language Glossary at BigIdeasMath ✓.com.

Now You're Ready
Exercises 8–14

On Your Own

1. The table shows the dog and cat ownership among teachers in a school. Display the data in a circle graph.

Kind of pet	Dogs only	Cats only	Both	Neither
Percent	30%	30%	15%	25%

EXAMPLE **2** **Using a Circle Graph**

Students chose one of four topics for their science projects. **(a) What fraction of the students chose *Biotechnology*? (b) How many students are in the class? (c) How many students chose *Plate Tectonics*?**

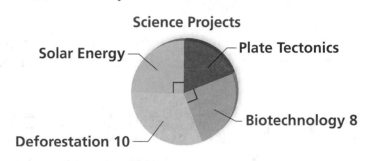

Science Projects

Solar Energy — Plate Tectonics

Deforestation 10 — Biotechnology 8

a. Because the *Biotechnology* section has a right angle, this section represents $\dfrac{90°}{360°} = \dfrac{1}{4}$ of the data.

∴ One-fourth of the students chose *Biotechnology*.

b. Let x be the number of students.

$\dfrac{1}{4}x = 8$ Use the circle graph and the results of part (a) to write an equation.

$x = 32$ Multiply each side by 4.

∴ There are 32 students in the class.

c. Because the *Solar Energy* and *Biotechnology* sections have the same angle measure, the same number of students chose each project. So, 8 students chose *Solar Energy*. Subtract to find the number of students who chose *Plate Tectonics*.

$32 - 8 - 8 - 10 = 6$

∴ Six students chose *Plate Tectonics*.

On Your Own

2. What percent chose *Deforestation*? What percent chose either *Biotechnology* or *Solar Energy*?

✓ **Vocabulary and Concept Check**

1. **VOCABULARY** How do you make a circle graph when the data are given in percents?

2. **REASONING** Can one section of a circle graph be 110%? Explain.

3. **WHICH ONE DOESN'T BELONG?** Which one does *not* belong with the other three? Explain your reasoning.

$$360° \qquad 100\% \qquad 1 \qquad \frac{1}{2}$$

4. **DIFFERENT WORDS, SAME QUESTION** Which is different? Find "both" answers.

How many people chose drama?

What is 25% of 120?

What is 90% of 120?

What is $\frac{1}{4}$ of 120?

Favorite Movie

Total: 120

 Practice and Problem Solving

The circle graph shows the results of a survey on favorite fruit.

5. Which fruit is the most popular?

6. Compare the number of students who chose oranges with the number of students who chose apples.

7. The survey included 80 students. How many students chose bananas?

Find the angle measure that corresponds to the percent of a circle.

 8. 20%   **9.** 15%   **10.** 70%   **11.** 3%

Favorite Fruit

Display the data in a circle graph.

12.

Season	Rainfall (inches)
Spring	9
Summer	18
Fall	6
Winter	3

13.

Expense	Cost (dollars)
Play rights	400
Costume rental	650
Programs/tickets	300
Advertising	250
Other	400

14. **LAND AREA** The table shows the land areas, in millions of square miles, of all the countries in North America.

Country	United States	Mexico	Canada	Other
Land area	3.72	0.76	3.85	1.12
Percent				
Angle in circle graph				

    a. Copy and complete the table. Round each angle to the nearest 5 degrees.

    b. Display the data in a circle graph.

    c. Find a map of North America. Do Canada and the United States appear to have the same area? Explain why or why not.

15. **REASONING** A survey asks a group of students what they like to do during summer vacation. The results show that 68% like to go to the beach, 45% like to go camping, 72% like to go to amusement parks, and 29% like to go to the mall. Can a circle graph be used to display these data? Explain your reasoning.

Department Store Sales

140°   80°   Other 75°

16. **RETAIL** A department store had $7200 in sales.

    a. Find the amount collected for each category.

    b. Long sleeve shirts were $\frac{1}{4}$ of the shirt sales. Find the angle measure of the section that would represent long sleeve shirts on the circle graph.

17. **WRITING** What math skills are needed to interpret data in a circle graph?

18. **Critical Thinking** Make a circle graph and a bar graph of the data in the table. Compare and contrast the two data displays. Which of the two better represents the data? Explain your reasoning.

Favorite Subject	Students
Art	12
English	56
Math	82
Music	28
Science	22

![Fair Game Review] **Fair Game Review** What you learned in previous grades & lessons

Solve the proportion. *(Section 3.5)*

19. $\dfrac{5}{8} = \dfrac{x}{64}$ **20.** $\dfrac{6}{n} = \dfrac{51}{127.5}$ **21.** $\dfrac{138}{23} = \dfrac{9}{w}$

22. MULTIPLE CHOICE Which formula gives the surface area of a prism? *(Section 6.2)*

    Ⓐ $S = 2\ell w + 2\ell h + 2wh$ **Ⓑ** $S = Ch + 2B$

    Ⓒ $S = 2\pi r^2 + 2\pi rh$ **Ⓓ** $S = \frac{1}{2}C\ell + B$

8.4 Samples and Populations

Essential Question How can you use a survey to make conclusions about the general population?

Share Your Work at... My.BigIdeasMath.com

1 ACTIVITY: Interpreting a Survey

Work with a partner. Read the newspaper article. Analyze the survey by answering the following questions.

a. The article does not say how many "teens and young adults" were surveyed. How many do you think need to be surveyed so that the results can represent all teens and young adults in your state? in the United States? Explain your reasoning.

b. Outline the newspaper article. List all of the important points.

c. Write a questionnaire that could have been used for the survey. Do not include leading questions. For example, "Do you think your cell phone plan is restrictive?" is a leading question.

The Daily Ti...

VOL 01   No. 279   WEDNESDAY, OCTOBER 6, 2010

TEXT MESSAGING SURVEY RESULTS

A survey reports that almost one-third of teens and young adults believe that their text messaging plans are restrictive.

About 40% say their plans lead to higher cell phone bills. According to those participating in the survey, the average number of text messages sent per day is between 6 and 7.

The majority of survey participants say they would send more text messages if their cell phone plans were not as restrictive.

2 ACTIVITY: Conducting a Survey

Work with a partner. The newspaper article in Activity 1 states that the average number of text messages sent per day is between 6 and 7.

a. Does this statement seem correct to you? Explain your reasoning.

b. Plan a survey to check this statement. How will you conduct the survey?

c. Survey your classmates. Organize your data using one of the types of graphs you have studied in this chapter.

d. Write a newspaper article summarizing the results of your survey.

Work with a partner.

- Plan a survey to determine how many of the following texting shortcuts people know.

- Write a questionnaire to use in your survey.

- In the survey, try to determine whether *teenagers* or *people over 30* know more of the shortcuts.

- Conduct your survey. What can you conclude from the results? Do the results confirm your prediction?

Texting Shortcuts

R	Are	U	You
4	For	L8R	Later
SUP	What's up	TTYL	Talk to you later
PLZ	Please	BRB	Be right back
C	See	LOL	Laugh out loud
IDK	I don't know	BFF	Best friends forever
JK	Just kidding	THX	Thanks
2NITE	Tonight	GR8	Great
QPSA?	Que Pasa?	4COL	For crying out loud

What Is Your Answer?

4. **IN YOUR OWN WORDS** How can you use a survey to make conclusions about the general population?

5. Find a survey in a newspaper, in a magazine, or on the Internet. Decide whether you think the conclusion of the survey is correct. Explain your reasoning.

"I'm sending my Mom a text message for Mother's Day."

"2 GR8 2 ME 2 EVR B 4GOT10. XX00"

Use what you learned about samples and populations to complete Exercises 3–5 on page 372.

Check It Out
Lesson Tutorials
BigIdeasMath com

Key Vocabulary 🔊)
population, *p. 370*
sample, *p. 370*

🔑 Key Idea

Samples and Population

A **population** is an entire group of people or objects. A **sample** is a part of the population.

A class is a part of an entire school.

All of the students in a school are a population.

All of the students in a class are a sample.

EXAMPLE 1   Identifying a Population and a Sample

Response	Residents
Favor road	533
Oppose road	267

An agency wants to know the opinions of county residents on the construction of a new road. The agency surveys 800 residents. Identify the population and the sample.

The population is all county residents. The sample consists of the 800 residents surveyed by the agency.

🔘 On Your Own

Now You're Ready
Exercises 6–9

1.   You want to know how many students in your school are going to the volleyball game. You survey 50 students. Ten are going to the game. The rest are not going to the game. Identify the population and the sample.

🔑 Key Idea

Reasonable Samples

A reasonable sample is
 • selected at random,
 • representative of the population, and
 • large enough to provide accurate data.

The results of a reasonable sample are proportional to the results of the population. So, reasonable samples can be used to make predictions about the population.

🔊) Multi-Language Glossary at BigIdeasMath✓com.

EXAMPLE 2 **Standardized Test Practice**

You want to estimate the number of students in a high school who ride the school bus. Which sample is best?

Ⓐ 4 students in the hallway

Ⓑ All students in the marching band

Ⓒ 50 seniors at random

Ⓓ 100 students at random during lunch

Choice A is not large enough to provide accurate data.

Choice B is not selected at random.

Choice C is not representative of the population because seniors are more likely to drive to school than other students.

∴ Choice Ⓓ is best. It is large and random.

EXAMPLE 3 **Making Predictions**

Movies per Week

1 movie 21
0 movies 30
2 or more movies 24

You ask 75 randomly chosen students how many movies they watch each week. There are 1200 students in the school. **(a) Predict the number *n* of students in the school who watch one movie each week. (b) Is the prediction appropriate? Explain.**

a. Find the fraction of students in the sample who watch one movie.

$$\frac{\text{Students who watch one movie}}{\text{Number of students in sample}} = \frac{21}{75}$$

Multiply to find *n*.

$$n = \frac{21}{75}(1200) = 336$$

∴ About 336 students watch one movie each week.

b. The sample is selected at random, representative of the population, and large enough to provide accurate data.

∴ The sample is reasonable, so the prediction is appropriate.

● **On Your Own**

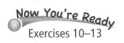

Now You're Ready
Exercises 10–13

2. WHAT IF? In Example 2, you want to estimate the number of seniors in a high school who ride the school bus. Which sample should you use to make a prediction?

3. In Example 3, predict the number *n* of students in the school who watch two or more movies each week.

✓ Vocabulary and Concept Check

1. **VOCABULARY** Why would you survey a sample instead of a population?

2. **CRITICAL THINKING** What should you consider when conducting a survey?

Practice and Problem Solving

The circle graph shows the results of a survey of 960 adults randomly chosen from different parts of the United States. In the survey, each adult was asked to name his or her favorite nut.

Almonds
Pistachios
Pecans
Peanuts
Cashews

3. Do you think the results would be similar if the survey were conducted using middle school students? children in first grade? Explain your reasoning.

4. What other type of data display could be used to show the data?

5. Plan a survey to check the results of the survey. How could you conduct the survey so that the people surveyed would be chosen at random?

Identify the population and the sample.

① 6.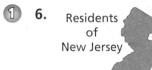

Residents of New Jersey   Residents of Ocean County

7.

150 Quarters   All quarters in circulation

8.

5 Ants   Colony of ants

9.

All books in library   10 library books

③ 10. **ERROR ANALYSIS** Consider the information given in Example 3. Describe and correct the error in predicting the number n of students in the school who watch zero movies each week.

$$n = \frac{45}{75}(1200)$$
$$n = 720$$

② 11. **INSTRUMENT** You want to know the number of students in your school who play a musical instrument. You survey the first 15 students who arrive at a band class.

    a. What is the population of your survey? the sample?

    b. Is the sample reasonable? Explain.

Which sample is better for making a prediction? Explain.

12.

Predict the number of students in a school who like gym class.	
Sample A	A random sample of 8 students from the yearbook
Sample B	A random sample of 80 students from the yearbook

13.

Predict the number of defective pencils produced per day.	
Sample A	A random sample of 500 pencils from 20 machines
Sample B	A random sample of 500 pencils from 1 machine

Determine whether you would survey the population or a sample. Explain.

14. You want to know the average height of seventh-graders in the United States.

15. You want to know the favorite types of music of students in your homeroom.

16. You want to know the number of students in your state who have summer jobs.

Ticket Sales	
Adults	**Students**
522	210

17. **THEATER** A survey asked 72 randomly chosen students if they were going to attend the school play. Twelve said yes. Predict the number of students who attend the school.

18. **CRITICAL THINKING** Explain why 200 people with email addresses may not be a random sample.

19. **Reasoning** A guidance counselor surveys a random sample of 60 out of 900 high school students. Using the survey results, the counselor predicts that approximately 675 students plan to attend college. Do you agree with her prediction? Explain.

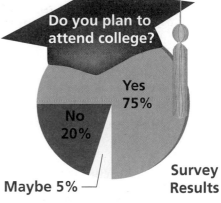

Do you plan to attend college?

Yes 75%

No 20%

Maybe 5%

Survey Results

Fair Game Review What you learned in previous grades & lessons

Write the fraction as a percent. *(Skills Review Handbook)*

20. $\frac{5}{8}$

21. $\frac{5}{16}$

22. $\frac{21}{27}$

23. $\frac{36}{44}$

24. **MULTIPLE CHOICE** What is the volume of the cone? *(Section 7.4)*

    (A) 16π cm^3

    (B) 108π cm^3

    (C) 48π cm^3

    (D) 144π cm^3

4 cm

9 cm

Check It Out
Progress Check
BigIdeasMath.com

Identify the population and the sample. *(Section 8.4)*

1.
Passengers on a train

Passengers in the first train car

2.
DVDs in a video store   DVDs in the comedy section

3. Display the data in a circle graph. *(Section 8.3)*

Favorite Book Genre	Students
Fantasy	20
Historical Fiction	10
Mystery	15
Nonfiction	5

Which sample is better for making a prediction? Explain. *(Section 8.4)*

4.
Predict the number of people who plan to vote in this year's election.	
Sample A	A random sample of 5000 registered voters
Sample B	A random sample of 50,000 United States citizens

5.
Predict the number of defective light bulbs produced per day.	
Sample A	A sample of the last 1000 light bulbs produced during a day
Sample B	A random sample of 1000 light bulbs produced throughout a day

6. **EXERCISE EQUIPMENT** You want to know how many students in your school support the purchase of new exercise equipment for the gym this year. You survey the first 20 students who arrive for football team tryouts. *(Section 8.4)*

   a. What is the population for your survey? the sample?

   b. Is the sample reasonable? Explain.

7. **WORLD LANGUAGES** Every student in a middle school takes one world language class. *(Section 8.3)*

   a. What fraction of the students take French?

   b. How many students are in the school?

   c. How many students take Spanish?

World Language Classes
French 125
German 100
Spanish

8. **NEWSPAPERS** A survey asks 48 randomly chosen students if they plan to buy a school newspaper this week. Of the 48 surveyed, 32 plan to buy a school newspaper. Predict the number of students enrolled at the school. *(Section 8.4)*

Newspaper Sales	
Faculty	Students
18	360

8 Chapter Review

Check It Out
Vocabulary Help
BigIdeasMath √com

Review Key Vocabulary

stem-and-leaf plot, *p. 350*   histogram, *p. 356*   population, *p. 370*
stem, *p. 350*   circle graph, *p. 364*   sample, *p. 370*
leaf, *p. 350*

Review Examples and Exercises

8.1 Stem-and-Leaf Plots *(pp. 348–353)*

Make a stem-and-leaf plot of the number of DVDs rented each day at a store.

Day	DVDs Rented
Sun.	50
Mon.	19
Tue.	25
Wed.	28
Thu.	39
Fri.	53
Sat.	50

Step 1: Order the data. 19, 25, 28, 39, 50, 50, 53

Step 2: Choose the stems and leaves. Because the data range from 19 to 53, use the *tens* digits for the stems and the *ones* digits for the leaves.

Step 3: Write the stems to the *left* of the vertical line.

Step 4: Write the leaves for each stem to the *right* of the vertical line.

DVDs Rented

Order the stems vertically. The stem for data values less than 10 is 0.

Include stems without leaves.

Stem	Leaf
1	9
2	5 8
3	9
4	
5	0 0 3

Write the leaves horizontally.

Key: 2 | 5 = 25 DVDs

Exercises

Make a stem-and-leaf plot of the data.

1.

Hats Sold Each Day			
5	18	12	15
21	30	8	12
13	9	14	25

2.

Ages of Park Volunteers			
13	17	40	15
48	21	19	52
13	55	60	20

The stem-and-leaf plot shows the weights (in pounds) of yellowfin tuna caught during a fishing contest.

3. How many tuna weigh less than 90 pounds?

4. What is the median weight of the tuna?

Weights of Tuna

Stem	Leaf
7	6
8	0 2 5 7 9
9	5 6
10	2

Key: 8 | 5 = 85 pounds

Histograms *(pp. 354–359)*

The frequency table shows the number of crafts each member of the Craft Club made for a fundraiser. Display the data in a histogram.

Crafts	Frequency
0–2	10
3–5	8
6–8	5
9–11	0
12–14	2

Step 1: Draw and label the axes.

Step 2: Draw a bar to represent the frequency of each interval.

Exercises

Display the data in a histogram.

5.

Heights of Gymnasts	
Heights (in.)	**Frequency**
50–54	1
55–59	8
60–64	5
65–69	2

6.

Minutes Studied	
Minutes	**Frequency**
0–19	5
20–39	9
40–59	12
60–79	3

8.3 **Circle Graphs** *(pp. 362–367)*

The table shows the results of a survey of 50 students. Display the data in a circle graph.

Favorite P.E. Activity	Students
Badminton	15
Volleyball	10
Kickball	25

Step 1: Find the angle measure for each section of the graph.

Multiply the fraction of students who chose each activity by 360°.

Badminton

$$\frac{15}{50} \cdot 360° = 108°$$

Volleyball

$$\frac{10}{50} \cdot 360° = 72°$$

Kickball

$$\frac{25}{50} \cdot 360° = 180°$$

Step 2: Use a protractor to draw the angle measures on a circle. Label the sections.

Kickball 25 — Badminton 15

180°   108°

72°

Volleyball 10

Exercises

Display the data in a circle graph.

7.

Singing Part	Students
Soprano	12
Alto	20
Tenor	18
Bass	10

8.

Candidate	Votes
Jon	60
Isabelle	35
Carmen	50
Ernesto	55

8.4 **Samples and Populations** *(pp. 368–373)*

You ask 80 randomly chosen students how many pets they have. There are 600 students in the school. (a) Predict the number n of students in the school who have exactly one pet. (b) Is the prediction appropriate? Explain.

a. Find the fraction of students in the sample who have exactly one pet.

$$\frac{\text{Students who have exactly one pet}}{\text{Number of students in sample}} = \frac{42}{80}$$

Multiply to find n.

$$n = \frac{42}{80}(600) = 315$$

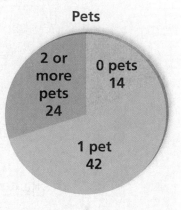

Pets

❖ About 315 students in the school have exactly one pet.

b. The sample is selected at random, is representative of the population, and is large enough to provide accurate data.

❖ The sample is reasonable, so the prediction is appropriate.

Exercises

9. Use the information in the Example above. Predict the number x of students in the school who have two or more pets.

10. Your principal wants to know how many parents plan to attend Back-to-School Night. The principal surveys 50 parents and finds that 40 plan to attend. Identify the population and the sample.

11. Which sample is better for making a prediction? Explain.

Predict the number of people in your town who support building a new library.	
Sample A	A random sample of 500 people in your town
Sample B	A random sample of 5000 people in your state

Make a stem-and-leaf plot of the data.

1.

Quiz Scores (%)			
96	88	80	72
80	94	92	100
76	80	68	90

2.

CDs Sold Each Day				
45	31	29	38	38
67	40	62	45	60
40	39	60	43	48

3. Display the data in a histogram.

Television Watched Per Week	
Hours	**Frequency**
0–9	14
10–19	16
20–29	10
30–39	8

4. Display the data in a circle graph.

Category	Amount Spent ($)
Clothing	30
Entertainment	10
Food	5
Savings	15

5. Which sample is better for making a prediction? Explain.

Predict the number of students in your school who play at least one sport.	
Sample A	A random sample of 10 students from the school student roster
Sample B	A random sample of 80 students from the school student roster

6. WATER The histogram shows the number of glasses of water that the students in a class drink in one day.

   a. Which interval contains the fewest data values?

   b. How many students are in the class?

   c. Health experts recommend drinking at least 8 glasses of water per day. What percent of the students drink the recommended amount?

7. FIELD TRIP Of 60 randomly chosen students surveyed, 16 chose the aquarium as their favorite field trip. There are 720 students in the school. Predict the number of students in the school who would choose the aquarium as their favorite field trip.

8. MALL There are 240 stores in a mall.

   a. Find the number of stores in each category.

   b. Electronics stores make up $\frac{1}{5}$ of the "Other" category. Find the angle measure of the section that would represent electronics.

1. Which deposit will earn the most simple interest for the given terms and annual interest rates?

   A. $3300 for 1 year at 4%

   B. $2000 for 1 year at 5.5%

   C. $2500 for 6 months at 8%

   D. $3000 for 18 months at 3%

2. The band instructor made the circle graph below to show the percent of students in each section of the Jazz Band.

Jazz Band Sections

Trumpet ?

Saxophone 20%

Trombone 20%

Rhythm 16%

   There are 4 students in the rhythm section. What is the number of students in the trumpet section?

   F. 11

   G. 12

   H. 28

   I. 44

Test-Taking Strategy
Use Intelligent Guessing

What is the mean length of these hyena fangs: 4 in., 3 in., 3 in., 4 in., 5 in., 5 in.?

Ⓐ 6 in.   Ⓑ $\frac{1}{3}$ ft   Ⓒ 2 in.   Ⓓ 5 in.

MEOW!

"The mean can't be 6 or 2 or 5 inches. So, you can use intelligent guessing to find that the answer is $\frac{1}{3}$ ft, or 4 in."

3. One of the leaves is missing in the stem-and-leaf plot.

   The median of the data set represented by the stem-and-leaf plot is 38. What is the value of the missing leaf?

Stem	Leaf
1	3 4
2	
3	4 5 7 7 ? 9
4	0 1 1 4
5	0 2 3

Key: 1|4 = 14

4. Mario was solving the equation in the box below.

$$3y + 4 + y = 5 - 11$$
$$3y + 4 = -6$$
$$3y = -10$$
$$y = -\frac{10}{3}$$

What should Mario do to correct the error that he made?

A. Divide -6 by 3 to get 2.

B. Add $3y$ and y to get $4y$.

C. Subtract 4 from -6 to get -2.

D. Simplify $3y + 4 + y$ to get $7y$.

5. The president of a service organization made a large bowl of fruit punch for a party. She needs to decide whether to serve the punch in 6-ounce servings or 4-ounce servings. She determined that she could serve 96 guests with 6-ounce servings. How many more guests could she serve with 4-ounce servings than with 6-ounce servings?

F. 144

H. 48

G. 64

I. 32

6. At the end of the school year, your teacher counted up the number of absences for each student. The results are shown in the histogram below.

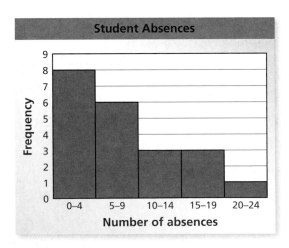

Based on the histogram, how many students had fewer than 10 absences?

7. What is the value of the expression below when $a = -6$ and $b = 4$?

$$\frac{|2 - a|}{-|b|}$$

A. -2 **C.** 1

B. -1 **D.** 2

8. A right square pyramid and its dimensions are shown below.

12 cm

10 cm

10 cm

What is the surface area of the pyramid?

F. 160 cm^2 **H.** 340 cm^2

G. 240 cm^2 **I.** 400 cm^2

9. Suppose that the volume of a right rectangular prism is V. The lengths of all the edges of the prism are then doubled. What is the volume of the new prism that is created?

A. $2V$ **C.** $6V$

B. $4V$ **D.** $8V$

10. A stem-and-leaf plot is shown.

For Parts A–D, explain how the stem-and-leaf plot can help to find each measure. Then find each measure using the stem-and-leaf plot. Show your work and explain your reasoning for each answer.

Part A range

Part B mode

Part C median

Part D mean

Stem	Leaf
4	5 8 8
5	2 7 7 7 8
6	0 1 6 8
7	
8	3 3 4 8 9 9
9	0 8

Key: 5|2 = 52

9 Probability

"If there are 7 cats in a sack and I draw one at random,..."

"... what is the probability that I will draw you?"

"I'm just about finished making my two number cubes."

"Now, here's how the game works. You toss the two cubes."

"If the sum is even I win. If it's odd, you win."

What You Learned Before

M = Mouse
B = Dog Biscuit

Why do we always have to use this spinner?

"Let's spin to decide what we will have for lunch."

● Simplifying Fractions

Example 1   Simplify $\dfrac{12}{36}$.

$$\dfrac{12 \div 12}{36 \div 12} = \dfrac{1}{3}$$

> Simplify fractions by using the Greatest Common Factor.

Example 2   Simplify $\dfrac{33}{60}$.

$$\dfrac{33 \div 3}{60 \div 3} = \dfrac{11}{20}$$

● Writing Ratios

Example 3

a. Write the ratio of girls to boys in Classroom A.

$$\dfrac{\text{Girls in Classroom A}}{\text{Boys in Classroom A}} = \dfrac{11}{14}$$

	Boys	Girls
Classroom A	14	11
Classroom B	12	8

∴ So, the ratio of girls to boys in Classroom A is $\dfrac{11}{14}$.

b. Write the ratio of boys in Classroom B to the total number of students in both classes.

$$\dfrac{\text{Boys in Classroom B}}{\text{Total number of students}} = \dfrac{12}{14 + 11 + 12 + 8} = \dfrac{12}{45} = \dfrac{4}{15}$$

← Write in simplest form.

∴ So, the ratio of boys in Classroom B to the total students is $\dfrac{4}{15}$.

Try It Yourself
Write the ratio in simplest form.

1. Baseballs to footballs
2. Footballs to total pieces of equipment

3. Sneakers to ballet slippers
4. Sneakers to total number of shoes

Essential Question How can you predict the results of spinning a spinner?

1 **ACTIVITY: Helicopter Flight**

Play with a partner.

- You begin flying the helicopter at (0, 0) on the coordinate plane. Your goal is to reach the cabin at (20, 14).

- Spin any one of the spinners. Move one unit in the indicated direction.

- If the helicopter encounters any obstacles, you must start over.

- Record the number of moves it takes to land exactly on (20, 14).

- After you have played once, it is your partner's turn to play.

- The player who finishes in the fewest moves wins.

Spinner A   **Spinner B**   **Spinner C**   **Spinner D**

ACTIVITY: Analyzing the Spinners

Work with a partner.

a. How are the spinners in Activity 1 alike? How are they different?

b. Which spinner will advance the helicopter to the finish fastest? Why?

c. If you want to move up, which spinner should you spin? Why?

d. Spin each spinner 50 times and record the results.

Spinner A	
Up	
Down	
Reverse	
Forward	

Spinner B	
Up	
Down	
Reverse	
Forward	

Spinner C	
Up	
Down	
Reverse	
Forward	

Spinner D	
Up	
Down	
Reverse	
Forward	

e. Organize the results from part (d) in a bar graph for each spinner.

f. After analyzing the results, would you change your strategy in the helicopter flight game? Explain why or why not.

What Is Your Answer?

3. **IN YOUR OWN WORDS** How can you predict the results of spinning a spinner?

Use what you learned about probability and spinners to complete Exercises 4 and 5 on page 388.

Check It Out
Lesson Tutorials
BigIdeasMath ✓com

Key Vocabulary 🔊
experiment, *p. 386*
outcomes, *p. 386*
event, *p. 386*
probability, *p. 387*

Key Ideas

Outcomes and Events

An **experiment** is an activity with varying results. The possible results of an experiment are called **outcomes**. A collection of one or more outcomes is an **event**. The outcomes of a specific event are called *favorable outcomes*.

For example, randomly selecting a marble from a group of marbles is an experiment. Each marble in the group is an outcome. Selecting a green marble from the group is an event.

Possible outcomes   *Event: Choosing a green marble*
                              Number of favorable outcomes: 2

EXAMPLE **1** **Identifying Outcomes**

You roll the number cube.

a. What are the possible outcomes?

   The six possible outcomes are rolling a 1, 2, 3, 4, 5, and 6.

b. What are the favorable outcomes of rolling an even number?

even	*not* even
2, 4, 6	1, 3, 5

∴ The favorable outcomes of the event are rolling a 2, 4, and 6.

c. What are the favorable outcomes of rolling a number greater than 5?

greater than 5	*not* greater than 5
6	1, 2, 3, 4, 5

∴ The favorable outcome of the event is rolling a 6.

● On Your Own

Now You're Ready
Exercises 6–12

1. You randomly choose a letter from a hat that contains the letters A through K. (a) What are the possible outcomes? (b) What are the favorable outcomes of choosing a vowel?

🔊 Multi-Language Glossary at BigIdeasMath✓com.

EXAMPLE 2   Counting Outcomes

You spin the spinner.

a. How many possible outcomes are there?

The spinner has 6 sections. So, there are 6 possible outcomes.

b. In how many ways can spinning red occur?

The spinner has 3 red sections. So, spinning red can occur in 3 ways.

c. In how many ways can spinning *not* purple occur? What are the favorable outcomes of spinning *not* purple?

The spinner has 5 sections that are *not* purple. So, spinning *not* purple can occur in 5 ways.

purple	*not* purple
purple	red, red, red, green, blue

The favorable outcomes of the event are red, red, red, green, and blue.

On Your Own

Now You're Ready
Exercises 13–18

2. You randomly choose a marble.

   a. How many possible outcomes are there?

   b. In how many ways can choosing blue occur?

   c. In how many ways can choosing *not* yellow occur? What are the favorable outcomes of choosing *not* yellow?

 Key Idea

Probability

The **probability** of an event is a number that measures the likelihood that the event will occur. Probabilities are between 0 and 1, including 0 and 1. The diagram relates likelihoods (above the diagram) and probabilities (below the diagram).

Study Tip

Probabilities can be written as fractions, decimals, or percents.

Impossible		Equally likely to happen or not happen		Certain
	Unlikely		Likely	
0	$\frac{1}{4}$	$\frac{1}{2}$	$\frac{3}{4}$	1
0	0.25	0.5	0.75	1
0%	25%	50%	75%	100%

9.1 Exercises

 ## Vocabulary and Concept Check

1. **VOCABULARY** Is rolling an even number on a number cube an *outcome* or an *event*? Explain.

2. **REASONING** Can the probability of an event be 1.5? Explain.

3. **OPEN-ENDED** Give a real-life example of an event that is impossible. Give a real-life example of an event that is certain.

 ## Practice and Problem Solving

Use the spinners shown.

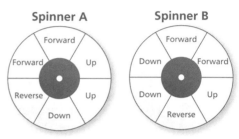

4. You want to move down. Which spinner should you spin? Explain.

5. You want to move forward. Does it matter which spinner you spin? Explain.

6. What are the possible outcomes of randomly choosing one of the tiles shown below?

You randomly choose one of the tiles shown above. Find the favorable outcomes of the event.

7. Choosing a 6

8. Choosing an odd number

9. Choosing a number greater than 5

10. Choosing an odd number less than 5

11. Choosing a number less than 3

12. Choosing a number divisible by 3

You randomly choose one marble from the bag. (a) Find the number of ways the event can occur. (b) Find the favorable outcomes of the event.

13. Choosing blue

14. Choosing green

15. Choosing purple

16. Choosing yellow

17. Choosing *not* red

18. Choosing *not* blue

19. **ERROR ANALYSIS** Describe and correct the error in finding the number of ways that choosing *not* purple can occur.

✗	purple	*not* purple
	purple	red, blue, green, yellow

Choosing *not* purple can occur in 4 ways.

Color Distinguishment Help at BigIdeasMath✓com.

20. COINS You have 10 coins in your pocket. Five are Susan B. Anthony Dollars, two are Golden Dollars, and three are Presidential Dollars. You randomly choose a coin. In how many ways can choosing *not* a Presidential Dollar occur?

Susan B. Anthony Dollar

Golden Dollar

Presidential Dollar

Spinner A

Spinner B

Tell whether the statement is *true* or *false*. If it is false, change the italicized word to make the statement true.

21. There are *three* possible outcomes of spinning Spinner A.

22. Spinning *red* can occur in four ways on Spinner B.

23. Spinning blue and spinning *green* are equally likely on Spinner A.

24. It is *impossible* to spin purple on Spinner B, so it is certain to spin not purple on spinner B.

25. LIKELIHOOD There are more red sections on Spinner B than on Spinner A. Does this mean that you are more likely to spin red on Spinner B? Explain.

Baker
Dancer
Pirate
Fireman
Bellhop

26. MUSIC A bargain bin contains classical and rock CDs. There are 60 CDs in the bin. You are equally likely to randomly choose a classical CD or a rock CD from the bin. How many of the CDs are classical CDs?

27. **Reasoning** You randomly choose one of the cards. Then, you randomly choose a second card. Describe how the number of possible outcomes changes after the first card is chosen.

 Fair Game Review What you learned in previous grades & lessons

Multiply. *(Section 2.3)*

28. $\frac{1}{2} \times 2$

29. $\frac{5}{6} \times 36$

30. $-\frac{4}{5} \times 25$

31. $\frac{1}{8} \times (-28)$

32. MULTIPLE CHOICE You are making half of a recipe that requires $\frac{3}{4}$ cup of sugar. How much sugar should you use? *(Section 2.3)*

Ⓐ $\frac{3}{8}$ cup

Ⓑ $\frac{5}{8}$ cup

Ⓒ $\frac{5}{4}$ cups

Ⓓ $\frac{3}{2}$ cups

Essential Question How can you find a theoretical probability?

Share Your Work at...
My.BigIdeasMath.com

1 ACTIVITY: Black and White Spinner Game

Work with a partner. You work for a game company. You need to create a game that uses the spinner below.

a. Write rules for a game that uses the spinner. Then play it.

b. After playing the game, do you want to revise the rules? Explain.

c. Each pie-shaped section of the spinner is the same size. What is the measure of the central angle of each section?

d. What is the probability that the spinner will land on 1? Explain.

ACTIVITY: Changing the Spinner

Work with a partner. For each spinner, find the probability of landing on each number. Do your rules from Activity 1 make sense for these spinners? Explain.

a.

b.

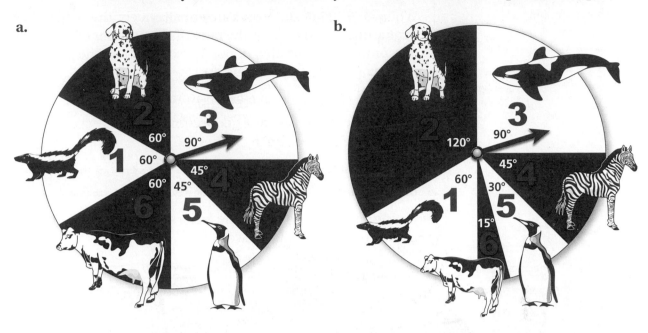

3 ACTIVITY: Is This Game Fair?

Work with a partner. Apply the following rules to each spinner in Activities 1 and 2. Is the game fair? If not, who has the better chance of winning?

- **Take turns spinning the spinner.**
- **If the spinner lands on an odd number, Player 1 wins.**
- **If the spinner lands on an even number, Player 2 wins.**

What Is Your Answer?

4. **IN YOUR OWN WORDS** How can you find a theoretical probability?

5. Find and describe a career in which probability is used. Explain why probability is used in that career.

6. Two people play the following game.

   Each player has 6 cards numbered 1, 2, 3, 4, 5, and 6. At the same time, each player holds up one card. If the product of the two numbers is odd, Player 1 wins. If the product is even, Player 2 wins. Continue until both players are out of cards. Which player is more likely to win? Why?

Practice

Use what you learned about theoretical probability to complete Exercises 4–7 on page 394.

Check It Out
Lesson Tutorials
BigIdeasMath .com

Key Vocabulary 🔊
theoretical probability,
  p. 392
fair experiment,
  p. 393

 Key Idea

Theoretical Probability

When all possible outcomes are equally likely, the **theoretical probability** of an event is the ratio of the number of favorable outcomes to the number of possible outcomes. The probability of an event is written as $P(\text{event})$.

$$P(\text{event}) = \frac{\text{number of favorable outcomes}}{\text{number of possible outcomes}}$$

EXAMPLE 1 **Finding a Theoretical Probability**

You randomly choose one of the letters shown. What is the theoretical probability of choosing a vowel?

$$P(\text{event}) = \frac{\text{number of favorable outcomes}}{\text{number of possible outcomes}}$$

$$P(\text{vowel}) = \frac{3}{7}$$

There are 3 vowels.

There is a total of 7 letters.

∴ The probability of choosing a vowel is $\frac{3}{7}$ or about 43%.

EXAMPLE 2 **Using a Theoretical Probability**

The theoretical probability that you randomly choose a green marble from a bag is $\frac{3}{8}$. There are 40 marbles in the bag. How many are green?

$$P(\text{green}) = \frac{\text{number of green marbles}}{\text{total number of marbles}}$$

$$\frac{3}{8} = \frac{n}{40} \qquad \text{Substitute. Let } n \text{ be the number of green marbles.}$$

$$15 = n \qquad \text{Multiply each side by 40.}$$

∴ There are 15 green marbles in the bag.

On Your Own

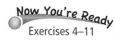
Exercises 4–11

1. In Example 1, what is the theoretical probability of choosing an X?

2. The theoretical probability that you spin an odd number on a spinner is 0.6. The spinner has 10 sections. How many sections have odd numbers?

An experiment is **fair** if all of its possible outcomes are equally likely.

The spinner is equally likely to land on 1 or 2. The spinner is fair.

The spinner is more likely to land on 1 than on either 2 or 3. The spinner is *not* fair.

EXAMPLE 3 **Making a Prediction**

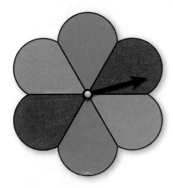

Scoring Rules:

- You get one point when the spinner lands on blue or green.

- Your friend gets one point when the spinner lands on red.

- The first person to get 10 points wins.

You and your friend play the game. (a) Is the spinner fair? (b) Is the game fair? (c) Predict the number of turns it will take you to win.

a. Yes, the spinner is fair because it is equally likely to land on red, blue, or green.

b. Find and compare the theoretical probabilities of the events.

You: $P(\text{blue or green}) = \dfrac{\text{number of blue or green sections}}{\text{total number of sections}}$

$$= \frac{4}{6} = \frac{2}{3}$$

Your friend: $P(\text{red}) = \dfrac{\text{number of red sections}}{\text{total number of sections}}$

$$= \frac{2}{6} = \frac{1}{3}$$

⁞• It is more likely that the spinner will land on blue or green than on red. Because your probability is greater, the game is *not* fair.

c. Write and solve an equation using $P(\text{blue or green})$ found in part (b). Let x be the number of turns it will take you to win.

$\dfrac{2}{3}x = 10$ Write equation.

$x = 15$ Multiply each side by $\dfrac{3}{2}$.

⁞• So, you can predict that it will take you 15 turns to win.

● On Your Own

Now You're Ready
Exercises 12–14

3. **WHAT IF?** In Example 3, you get one point when the spinner lands on blue or green. Your friend gets one point when the spinner lands on red or blue. The first person to get 5 points wins. Is the game fair? Explain.

Vocabulary and Concept Check

1. **VOCABULARY** An event has a theoretical probability of 0.5. What does this mean?

2. **OPEN-ENDED** Describe an event that has a theoretical probability of $\frac{1}{4}$.

3. **WHICH ONE DOESN'T BELONG?** Which spinner does *not* belong with the other three? Explain your reasoning.

| Spinner 1 | Spinner 2 | Spinner 3 | Spinner 4 |

 Practice and Problem Solving

Use the spinner to determine the theoretical probability of the event.

4. Spinning red

5. Spinning a 1

6. Spinning an odd number

7. Spinning a multiple of 2

8. Spinning a number less than 7

9. Spinning a 7

10. **LETTERS** Each letter of the alphabet is printed on an index card. What is the theoretical probability of randomly choosing any letter except Z?

11. **GAME SHOW** On a game show, a contestant randomly chooses a chip from a bag that contains numbers and strikes. The theoretical probability of choosing a strike is $\frac{3}{10}$. There are 30 chips in the bag. How many are strikes?

A number cube is rolled. Determine if the game is fair. If it is *not* fair, who has the greater probability of winning?

12. You win if the number is odd. Your friend wins if the number is even.

13. You win if the number is less than 3. If it is not less than 3, your friend wins.

14. **SCORING POINTS** You get one point if a 1 or a 2 is rolled on the number cube. Your friend gets one point if a 5 or a 6 is rolled. The first person to 5 points wins.

   a. Is the number cube fair? Is the game fair? Explain.

   b. Predict the number of turns it will take you to win.

15. **HISTORY** You write a report about your favorite president. Your friend writes a report on a randomly chosen president. What is the theoretical probability that you write reports on the same president?

16. **BIRTHDAYS** The bar graph shows the birthday months of all 200 employees at a local business.

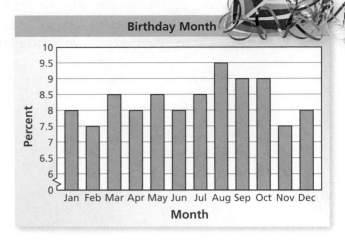

a. What is the theoretical probability of randomly choosing a person at the business who was born in a month with an R in its name?

b. What is the theoretical probability of randomly choosing a person at the business who has a birthday in the first half of the year?

17. **SCHEDULING** There are 16 females and 20 males in a class.

a. What is the theoretical probability of randomly choosing a female from the class?

b. One week later, there are 45 students in the class. The theoretical probability of randomly selecting a female is the same as last week. How many males joined the class?

A Punnett square is a grid used to show possible gene combinations for the offspring of two parents. In the Punnett square shown, a boy is represented by *XY*. A girl is represented by *XX*.

18. Complete the Punnett square.

19. Explain why the probability of two parents having a boy or having a girl is equally likely.

20. **Critical Thinking** Two parents each have the gene combination *Cs*. The gene *C* is for curly hair. The gene *s* is for straight hair.

a. Make a Punnett square for the two parents. If all outcomes are equally likely, what is the probability of a child having the gene combination *CC*?

b. Any gene combination that includes a *C* results in curly hair. If all outcomes are equally likely, what is the probability of a child having curly hair?

Fair Game Review What you learned in previous grades & lessons

Multiply. *(Section 2.3)*

21. $\dfrac{1}{2} \times \dfrac{1}{2}$

22. $-\dfrac{1}{6} \times \dfrac{2}{3}$

23. $-\dfrac{3}{5} \times \dfrac{7}{8}$

24. $\dfrac{4}{5} \times \dfrac{1}{36}$

25. **MULTIPLE CHOICE** What is the mean of the numbers 11, 6, 12, 22, 7, 8, and 4? *(Skills Review Handbook)*

    (A) 4   (B) 8   (C) 10   (D) 70

You can use a **word magnet** to organize information associated with a vocabulary word or term. Here is an example of a word magnet for probability.

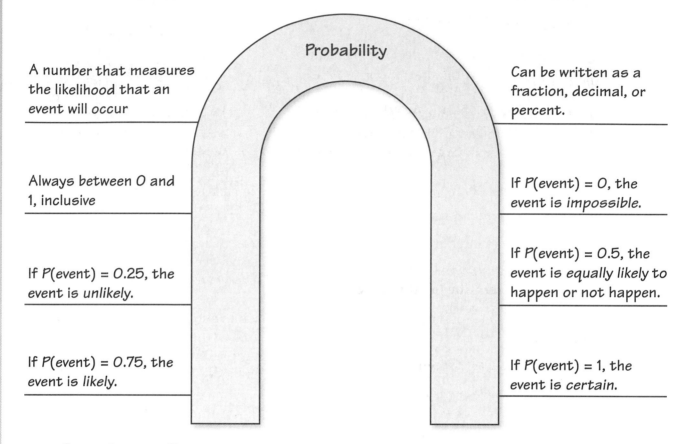

Probability

A number that measures the likelihood that an event will occur

Always between 0 and 1, inclusive

If $P(event) = 0.25$, the event is *unlikely*.

If $P(event) = 0.75$, the event is *likely*.

Can be written as a fraction, decimal, or percent.

If $P(event) = 0$, the event is *impossible*.

If $P(event) = 0.5$, the event is *equally likely to happen or not happen*.

If $P(event) = 1$, the event is *certain*.

On Your Own

Make a word magnet to help you study these topics.

1. event

2. outcome

3. theoretical probability

After you complete this chapter, make word magnets for the following topics.

4. experimental probability

5. independent events

6. dependent events

7. Choose three other topics that you studied earlier in this course. Make a word magnet for each topic.

"I'm going to sell my word magnet poster at the Fraidy Cat Festival."

Check It Out
Progress Check
BigIdeasMath ✓.com

You spin the spinner. Find the favorable outcomes of the event. *(Section 9.1)*

1. Spinning an even number

2. Spinning a number divisible by 4

3. Spinning a number greater than or equal to 3

You randomly choose one butterfly. Find the number of ways the event can occur. *(Section 9.1)*

4. Choosing red

5. Choosing brown

6. Choosing *not* blue

You randomly choose one push pin from the jar. Determine the theoretical probability of the event. *(Section 9.2)*

12 Green
6 White
8 Red
4 Blue
10 Yellow

7. Choosing a yellow pin

8. *Not* choosing a blue pin

9. Choosing a green or red pin

The spinner is spun. Determine if the game is fair. If it is *not* fair, who has the greater probability of winning? *(Section 9.2)*

10. You win if the number is even. Your friend wins if the number is odd.

11. You win if the number is less than 4. Your friend wins if the number is 4 or greater.

12. **TICKETS** The theoretical probability that your ticket will be drawn from a bucket to win a bicycle is $\frac{1}{35}$. There are 665 tickets in the bucket. How many tickets are yours? *(Section 9.2)*

13. **APPLES** There are 104 apples in a bushel. The probability of randomly choosing a Granny Smith apple from the bushel is 25%. How many of the apples are *not* Granny Smith apples? *(Section 9.2)*

Essential Question What is meant by experimental probability?

1 ACTIVITY: Throwing Sticks

Play with a partner. This game is based on an Apache game called "Throw Sticks."

- Take turns throwing three sticks into the center of the circle and moving around the circle according to the chart.

- If your opponent lands on or passes your playing piece, you must start over.

- The first player to pass his or her starting point wins.

MOVE CHART

3 Decorated	10 stones
3 Plain	5 stones
2 Plain, 1 Decorated	3 stones
2 Decorated, 1 Plain	2 stones

Each stick has one plain side and one decorated side.

The game board has 40 stones arranged in a circle. The stones are placed in groups of 10.

Players start on opposite sides of the circle.

Player 1 Starting Point

Player 2 Starting Point

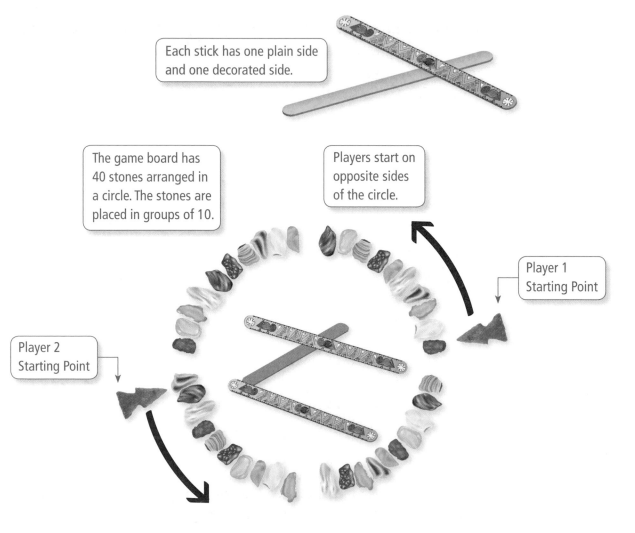

2 ACTIVITY: Conducting an Experiment

Work with a partner. Throw the 3 sticks 32 times. Tally the results using the outcomes listed below. Organize the results in a bar graph. Use the bar graph to estimate the probability of each outcome. These are called experimental probabilities.

a. PPP

b. DPP

c. DDP

d. DDD

3 ACTIVITY: Analyzing the Possibilities

Work with a partner. A tree diagram helps you see different ways that the same outcome can occur.

a. Find the number of ways that each outcome can occur.

- Three Ps
- One D and two Ps
- Two Ds and one P
- Three Ds

b. Find the theoretical probability of each outcome.

c. Compare and contrast your experimental and theoretical probabilities.

What Is Your Answer?

4. IN YOUR OWN WORDS What is meant by experimental probability?

5. Give a real-life example of experimental probability.

Practice

Use what you learned about experimental probability to complete Exercises 3–6 on page 402.

🔑 Key Idea

Experimental Probability

Probability that is based on repeated trials of an experiment is called **experimental probability**.

$$P(\text{event}) = \frac{\text{number of times the event occurs}}{\text{total number of trials}}$$

EXAMPLE 1 **Standardized Test Practice**

Thirteen out of 20 emails in your inbox are junk emails. What is the experimental probability that your next email is junk?

Ⓐ 35%   Ⓑ 45%   Ⓒ 55%   Ⓓ 65%

$$P(\text{event}) = \frac{\text{number of times the event occurs}}{\text{total number of trials}}$$

$$P(\text{junk}) = \frac{13}{20}$$

You have 13 emails that are junk.

You have a total of 20 emails.

∴ The probability is $\frac{13}{20}$, 0.65, or 65%. The correct answer is Ⓓ.

EXAMPLE 2 **Making a Prediction**

"April showers bring May flowers." Old Proverb, 1557

It rains 2 out of the last 12 days in March. If this trend continues, how many rainy days would you expect in April?

Find the experimental probability of a rainy day.

$$P(\text{event}) = \frac{\text{number of times the event occurs}}{\text{total number of trials}}$$

$$P(\text{rain}) = \frac{2}{12} = \frac{1}{6}$$

It rains 2 days.

There is a total of 12 days.

To make a prediction, multiply the probability of a rainy day by the number of days in April.

$$\frac{1}{6} \cdot 30 = 5$$

∴ You can predict that there will be 5 rainy days in April.

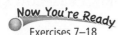
On Your Own

1. In Example 1, what is the experimental probability that your next email is *not* junk?

2. At a clothing company, an inspector finds 5 defective pairs in a shipment of 200 jeans.

   a. What is the experimental probability of a pair of jeans being defective?

   b. About how many would you expect to be defective in a shipment of 5000 pairs of jeans?

EXAMPLE 3 Comparing Experimental and Theoretical Probabilities

Rolling a Number Cube

The bar graph shows the results of rolling a number cube 50 times. What is the experimental probability of rolling an odd number? How does this compare with the theoretical probability of rolling an odd number?

Find the experimental probability of rolling a 1, 3, or 5.

The bar graph shows 10 ones, 8 threes, and 8 fives. So, an odd number was rolled $10 + 8 + 8 = 26$ times in a total of 50 rolls.

Experimental Probability

$$P(\text{event}) = \frac{\text{number of times the event occurs}}{\text{total number of trials}}$$

$P(\text{odd}) = \dfrac{26}{50}$ ← An odd number was rolled 26 times.
← There was a total of 50 rolls.

$= \dfrac{13}{25}$

Theoretical Probability

$$P(\text{event}) = \frac{\text{number of favorable outcomes}}{\text{number of possible outcomes}}$$

$P(\text{odd}) = \dfrac{3}{6}$ ← There are 3 odd numbers.
← There is a total of 6 numbers.

$= \dfrac{1}{2}$

⋮• The experimental probability is $\dfrac{13}{25} = 0.52 = 52\%$. The theoretical probability is $\dfrac{1}{2} = 0.5 = 50\%$. The experimental and theoretical probabilities are similar.

On Your Own

3. In Example 3, what is the experimental probability of rolling a number greater than 1? How does this compare with the theoretical probability of rolling a number greater than 1?

Vocabulary and Concept Check

1. **VOCABULARY** Describe how to find the experimental probability of an event.

2. **REASONING** You flip a coin 10 times and find the experimental probability of flipping tails to be 0.7. Does this seem reasonable? Explain.

 Practice and Problem Solving

You have three sticks. Each stick has one red side and one blue side. You throw the sticks 10 times and record the results. Use the table to find the experimental probability of the event.

Outcome	Frequency
3 red	4
3 blue	0
2 blue, 1 red	2
2 red, 1 blue	4

3. Tossing 3 red

4. Tossing 2 blue, 1 red

5. Tossing 2 red, 1 blue

6. *Not* tossing all red

Use the bar graph to find the experimental probability of the event.

Spinning a Spinner

7. Spinning a 6

8. Spinning an even number

9. *Not* spinning a 1

10. Spinning a number less than 3

11. Spinning a 1 or a 3

12. Spinning a 7

13. **ERROR ANALYSIS** Describe and correct the error in finding $P(4)$ using the bar graph.

$$P(4) = \frac{\text{number of favorable outcomes}}{\text{number of possible outcomes}} = \frac{1}{6}$$

14. **EGGS** You check 20 cartons of eggs. Three of the cartons have at least one cracked egg. What is the experimental probability that a carton of eggs has at least one cracked egg?

15. **BOARD GAME** There are 105 lettered tiles in a board game. You choose the tiles shown. How many of the 105 tiles would you expect to be vowels?

16. **CARDS** You have a package of 20 assorted thank-you cards. You pick the four cards shown. How many of the 20 cards would you expect to have flowers on them?

17. **QUALITY CONTROL** An inspector estimates that $\frac{1}{2}$% of MP3 players are defective. In a shipment of 5000 MP3 players, predict the number that are defective.

18. **MUSIC** During a 24-hour period, the ratio of pop songs played to rap songs played on a radio station is 60 : 75.

    a. What is the experimental probability that the next song played is rap?

    b. Out of the next 90 songs, how many would you expect to be pop?

③ 19. **FLIPPING A COIN** You flip a coin 20 times. You flip heads 12 times. Compare your experimental probability of flipping heads with the theoretical probability of flipping heads.

You roll a pair of number cubes 60 times. You record your results in the bar graph shown.

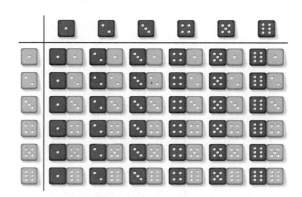

20. Use the bar graph to find the experimental probability of rolling each sum. Which sum is most likely?

21. Use the table to find the theoretical probability of rolling each sum. Which sum is most likely?

22. Compare the probabilities you found in Exercises 20 and 21.

23. **Critical Thinking** You roll two number cubes. Describe and perform an experiment to find the probability that the product of the two numbers rolled is at least 12. How many times did you roll the number cubes?

Fair Game Review What you learned in previous grades & lessons

Solve the equation. *(Section 2.5)*

24. $5x = 100$

25. $75 = 15x$

26. $2x = -26$

27. $-4x = -96$

28. **MULTIPLE CHOICE** What is the least common denominator of the fractions $\frac{1}{16}$, $\frac{2}{19}$, and $\frac{3}{76}$? *(Skills Review Handbook)*

Ⓐ 16　　　　Ⓑ 76　　　　Ⓒ 304　　　　Ⓓ 1216

Essential Question What is the difference between dependent and independent events?

1 ACTIVITY: Dependent Events

Work with a partner. You have three marbles in a bag. There are two green marbles and one purple marble. You randomly draw two marbles from the bag.

a. Use the tree diagram to find the probability that both marbles are green.

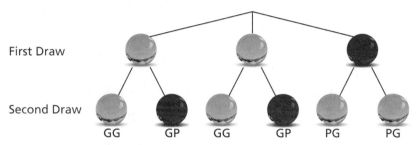

First Draw

Second Draw

GG GP GG GP PG PG

b. In the tree diagram, does the probability of getting a green marble on the second draw *depend* on the color of the first marble? Explain.

2 ACTIVITY: Independent Events

Work with a partner. Using the same marbles from Activity 1, randomly draw a marble from the bag. Then put the marble back in the bag and draw a second marble.

a. Use the tree diagram to find the probability that both marbles are green.

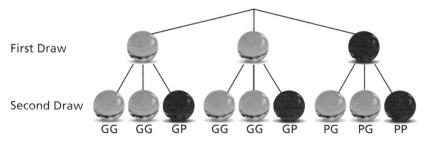

First Draw

Second Draw

GG GG GP GG GG GP PG PG PP

b. In the tree diagram, does the probability of getting a green marble on the second draw *depend* on the color of the first marble? Explain.

Work with a partner. Conduct two experiments.

a. In the first experiment, randomly draw two marbles from the bag 36 times. Record each result as GG or GP. Make a bar graph of your results.

b. What is the experimental probability of drawing two green marbles? Does this answer seem reasonable? Explain.

c. In the second experiment, randomly draw one marble from the bag. Put it back. Draw a second marble. Repeat this 36 times. Record each result as GG, GP, or PP. Make a bar graph of your results.

d. What is the experimental probability of drawing two green marbles? Does this answer seem reasonable? Explain.

1st Experiment

GG	
GP	

2nd Experiment

GG	
GP	
PP	

What Is Your Answer?

4. IN YOUR OWN WORDS What is the difference between dependent and independent events? Describe a real-life example of each.

Practice

Use what you learned about independent and dependent events to complete Exercises 5 and 6 on page 409.

Check It Out
Lesson Tutorials
BigIdeasMath ✓com

Two events are **independent events** if the occurrence of one event *does not* affect the likelihood that the other event will occur.

Two events are **dependent events** if the occurrence of one event *does* affect the likelihood that the other event will occur.

EXAMPLE **1** **Identifying Independent and Dependent Events**

Tell whether the events are *independent* or *dependent*. Explain.

a. You flip heads on one coin and tails on another coin.

The outcome of flipping one coin does not affect the outcome of flipping the other coin.

∴ So, the events are independent.

b. Your teacher chooses one student to lead a group, and then chooses another student to lead another group.

The teacher cannot pick the same student to lead both groups. So, there are fewer students to choose from when the leader of the second group is chosen.

∴ So, the events are dependent.

On Your Own

Now You're Ready
Exercises 5–9

Tell whether the events are *independent* or *dependent*. Explain.

1. You choose a blue marble from a bag and set it aside. Then you choose a green marble from the bag.

2. You roll a 5 on a number cube and spin blue on a spinner.

🔑 Key Idea

Probability of Independent Events

Words The probability of two independent events A and B is the probability of A times the probability of B.

Symbols $P(A \text{ and } B) = P(A) \cdot P(B)$

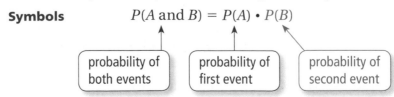

| probability of both events | probability of first event | probability of second event |

🔊 Multi-Language Glossary at BigIdeasMath✓com.

EXAMPLE 2 **Finding the Probability of Independent Events**

You flip two quarters. What is the probability that you flip two heads?

Method 1: Use a tree diagram to find the probability.

Let H = Heads and T = Tails.

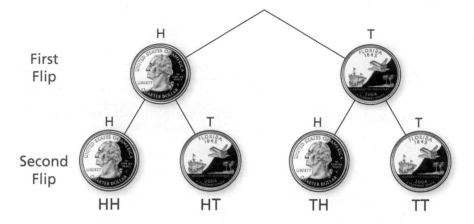

First Flip

Second Flip

HH   HT   TH   TT

$$P(\text{two heads}) = \frac{\text{number of times two heads occur}}{\text{total number of outcomes}}$$

$$= \frac{1}{4}$$

∴ The probability that you flip two heads is $\frac{1}{4}$.

Method 2: Use the formula for independent events.

$$P(A \text{ and } B) = P(A) \cdot P(B)$$

$$P(\text{heads and heads}) = P(\text{heads}) \cdot P(\text{heads})$$

$$= \frac{1}{2} \cdot \frac{1}{2} \qquad \text{Substitute.}$$

$$= \frac{1}{4} \qquad \text{Multiply.}$$

∴ The probability that you flip two heads is $\frac{1}{4}$.

On Your Own

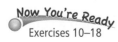
Now You're Ready
Exercises 10–18

3. You flip two coins. What is the probability that you flip one heads and one tails?

4. You flip a coin and roll a number cube. What is the probability that you flip tails and roll a number less than 5?

Key Idea

Probability of Dependent Events

Words The probability of two dependent events A and B is the probability of A times the probability of B after A occurs.

Symbols $P(A \text{ and } B) = P(A) \cdot P(B \text{ after } A)$

probability of both events   probability of first event   probability of second event after first event occurs

EXAMPLE ③ **Finding the Probability of Dependent Events**

You randomly choose a flower from the vase to take home. Your friend randomly chooses another flower from the vase to take home. What is the probability that you choose a purple flower and your friend chooses a yellow flower?

Purple: 7
Yellow: 9
Pink: 12

Choosing a flower changes the number of flowers left in the vase. So, the events are dependent.

$$P(\text{first is purple}) = \frac{7}{28} = \frac{1}{4}$$

There are 7 purple flowers.

There is a total of 28 flowers.

$$P(\text{second is yellow}) = \frac{9}{27} = \frac{1}{3}$$

There are 9 yellow flowers.

There is a total of 27 flowers left.

Use the formula to find the probability.

$$P(A \text{ and } B) = P(A) \cdot P(B \text{ after } A)$$

$$P(\text{purple and yellow}) = P(\text{purple}) \cdot P(\text{yellow after purple})$$

$$= \frac{1}{4} \cdot \frac{1}{3} \qquad \text{Substitute.}$$

$$= \frac{1}{12} \qquad \text{Simplify.}$$

∴ The probability of choosing a purple flower and then a yellow flower is $\frac{1}{12}$, or about 8%.

● **On Your Own**

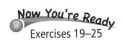
Exercises 19–25

5. WHAT IF? In Example 3, what is the probability that both flowers are purple?

9.4 Exercises

✓ Vocabulary and Concept Check

1. **VOCABULARY** Events A and B are independent. Describe two ways to find $P(A \text{ and } B)$.

2. **FILL IN THE BLANKS** Copy and complete the tree diagram to find the possible outcomes for flipping a coin three times.

3. **OPEN-ENDED** Describe a real-life example of two independent events. Describe a real-life example of two dependent events.

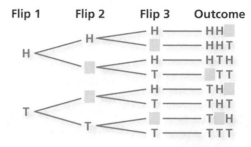

4. **DIFFERENT WORDS, SAME QUESTION** Which is different? Find "both" answers.

   Find the probability of rolling a 1 and then a 2, 4, or 6.

   Find the probability of rolling a 1 and then an even number.

   Find the probability of rolling an odd number and then an even number.

   Find the probability of rolling a number less than 2 and then an even number.

✐ Practice and Problem Solving

Tell whether the events are *independent* or *dependent*. Explain.

 5. You roll a number cube twice.

   First Roll: You roll a 4.
   Second Roll: You roll an even number.

6. You flip a coin twice.

   First Flip: Heads
   Second Flip: Heads

7. You randomly draw a marble from a bag containing 2 red marbles and 5 green marbles. You put the marble back and then draw a second marble.

   First Draw: Green   Second Draw: Red

8. You randomly draw a marble from a bag containing 2 red marbles and 5 green marbles. You keep the marble and then draw a second marble.

   First Draw: Green   Second Draw: Red

9. You and your friend are in a drawing for two door prizes. You can win only one prize.

   First Draw: Your name is drawn.   Second Draw: Your friend's name is drawn.

A spinner has three equal sections numbered 1, 2, and 3. You spin it twice. Use the tree diagram to find the probability of the events.

② 10. Spinning a 1 and then a 3

11. Spinning an odd number and then a 2

12. Spinning a 3 and then an even number

13. Spinning an even number and then an odd number

14. Spinning an odd number on each spin

First Spin   1   2   3

Second Spin 1 2 3 1 2 3 1 2 3

You spin the spinner and flip a coin. Find the probability of the events.

15. Spinning a 4 and flipping heads

16. Spinning an even number and flipping tails

17. Spinning a multiple of 3 and flipping heads

18. Spinning white and *not* flipping tails

You randomly choose one of the lettered tiles. Without replacing the first tile, you choose a second tile. Find the probability of choosing the first tile, then the second tile.

③ 19. R and N

20. A and L

21. D and O

22. N and yellow

23. O and *not* yellow

24. *Not* O and O

25. If you randomly choose all seven tiles in order, what is the probability that you will spell the name of a popular vacation destination in Florida?

26. EARRINGS A jewelry box contains two gold hoop earrings and two silver hoop earrings. You randomly choose two earrings. What is the probability that both are silver hoop earrings?

27. PASSWORD You forgot the last two digits of your password for a website.

    a. You choose a two-digit number at random. What is the probability that your choice is correct?

    b. Suppose you remember that both digits are even numbers. How does this change the probability that your choice is correct?

28. FISH You randomly choose two fish from the bowl. What is the probability that the first is red and the second is gold?

29. TAKING A TEST You are guessing at two questions on a multiple choice test. Each question has three choices: A, B, and C.

  a. What is the probability that you guess the correct answers to both questions?

  b. Suppose you can eliminate one of the choices for each question. How does this change the probability that your guesses are correct?

30. REASONING The probability of winning a spelling bee *and* winning a checkers game is 10%. The probability of winning a checkers game is $\frac{1}{2}$. (a) What is the probability of winning a spelling bee? (b) You enter 10 spelling bees. How many do you expect to win?

31. SHOES Twenty percent of the shoes manufactured by a company are black. One shoe is chosen and replaced. Then a second shoe is chosen. What is the probability that *neither* shoe is black?

32. **Critical Thinking** You randomly choose a pair of sunglasses from the shelf below. Then you randomly choose a second pair of sunglasses without replacing the first pair. List all of the possible outcomes.

| Blue (B) | Green (G) | White (W) | Green (G) | Blue (B) |

ODDS The *odds in favor of* an event is the ratio of the number of favorable outcomes to the number of unfavorable outcomes. The *odds against* an event is the ratio of the number of unfavorable outcomes to the number of favorable outcomes. Find the *odds in favor of* and the *odds against* the event when rolling a number cube.

33. Rolling a 6

34. Rolling a number less than 5

35. Rolling a 6, then rolling a 3

 Fair Game Review What you learned in previous grades & lessons

Solve the equation. *(Section 2.4, Section 2.5, and Section 2.6)*

36. $6 = 9.3 + x$

37. $\frac{n}{2} = -5.4$

38. $-4p + 6 = -10$

39. MULTIPLE CHOICE Which intervals can be used to make a histogram? *(Section 8.2)*

  (A) 16–18, 19–21, 22–26, 27–32

  (B) 91–110, 111–130, 131–150

  (C) 11–20, 21–40, 41–50, 51–70

  (D) 50–60, 60–70, 70–80, 80–90

Check It Out
Progress Check
BigIdeasMath ✓com

Use the bar graph to find the experimental probability of the event. *(Section 9.3)*

1. Rolling a 4

2. Rolling a multiple of 3

3. Rolling a 2 or a 3

4. Rolling a number less than 7

Rolling a Number Cube

You randomly choose a playing piece and flip a coin. Find the probability of the events. *(Section 9.4)*

5. Choosing red and flipping tails

6. Choosing black and flipping heads

7. *Not* choosing red and *not* flipping heads

You randomly choose one of the letter blocks. Without replacing the first block, you choose a second block. Find the probability of choosing the first block, then the second block. *(Section 9.4)*

8. E and M   **9.** M and *not* E   **10.** Red and blue

11. PENS There are 30 pens in a box. You choose the five pens shown. How many of the 30 pens would you expect to have red ink? *(Section 9.3)*

12. SWEATERS A drawer contains three tan sweaters and two black sweaters. You randomly choose two sweaters. What is the probability that both sweaters are black? *(Section 9.4)*

13. SPINNER You spin the spinner 40 times. It lands on red 32 times. Compare the experimental probability of the spinner landing on red with the theoretical probability of the spinner landing on red. *(Section 9.3)*

14. FISH You randomly choose one fish from each bowl for your aquarium. What is the probability of choosing two gold fish? *(Section 9.4)*

Review Key Vocabulary

experiment, *p. 386*
outcomes, *p. 386*
event, *p. 386*
probability, *p. 387*
theoretical probability, *p. 392*

fair experiment, *p. 393*
experimental
    probability, *p. 400*
independent events, *p. 406*
dependent events, *p. 406*

Review Examples and Exercises

9.1 Introduction to Probability *(pp. 384–389)*

You randomly choose one toy racecar.

a. In how many ways can choosing a green car occur?

b. In how many ways can choosing a car that is *not* green occur? What are the favorable outcomes of choosing a car that is *not* green?

a. There are 5 green cars. So, choosing a green car can occur in 5 ways.

b. There are 2 cars that are *not* green. So, choosing a car that is *not* green can occur in 2 ways.

green	*not* green
green, green, green, green, green	blue, red

∴ The favorable outcomes of the event are blue and red.

Exercises

You spin the spinner. Find the number of ways the event can occur.

1. Spinning a 1

2. Spinning a 3

3. Spinning an odd number

4. Spinning a number greater than 0

5. On the spinner, what are the favorable outcomes of spinning a number less than 3?

9.2 **Theoretical Probability** *(pp. 390–395)*

The theoretical probability that you choose a purple grape from a bag is $\frac{2}{9}$. There are 36 grapes in the bag. How many are purple?

$$P(\text{purple}) = \frac{\text{number of purple grapes}}{\text{total number of grapes}}$$

$\frac{2}{9} = \frac{n}{36}$ Substitute. Let *n* be the number of purple grapes.

$8 = n$ Multiply each side by 36.

∴ There are 8 purple grapes in the bag.

Exercises

6. You get one point when the spinner at the right lands on an odd number. Your friend gets one point when it lands on an even number. The first person to get 5 points wins. Is the game fair? If it is not fair, who has the greater probability of winning?

7. The probability that you spin an even number on a spinner is $\frac{2}{3}$. The spinner has 12 sections. How many sections have even numbers?

9.3 **Experimental Probability** *(pp. 398–403)*

The bar graph shows the results of spinning the spinner 70 times. What is the experimental probability of spinning a 2?

The bar graph shows 14 ones, 12 twos, 16 threes, 15 fours, and 13 fives. So, a two was spun 12 times in 70 spins.

$$P(\text{event}) = \frac{\text{number of times the event occurs}}{\text{total number of trials}}$$

$P(2) = \frac{12}{70}$ A 2 was spun 12 times.   There was a total of 70 spins.

$= \frac{6}{35}$

∴ The experimental probability is $\frac{6}{35}$, or about 17%.

Exercises

Use the bar graph on page 414 to find the experimental probability of the event.

8. Spinning a 3

9. Spinning an odd number

10. *Not* spinning a 5

11. Spinning a number greater than 3

9.4 **Independent and Dependent Events** *(pp. 404–411)*

You randomly choose a marble without replacing it. Your friend then chooses another marble. What is the probability that you choose a red marble and your friend chooses a blue marble?

Choosing a marble changes the number of marbles left. So, the events are dependent.

$$P(\text{first is red}) = \frac{5}{12}$$

There are 5 red marbles.

There is a total of 12 marbles.

$$P(\text{second is blue}) = \frac{3}{11}$$

There are 3 blue marbles.

There is a total of 11 marbles left.

Use the formula to find the probability.

$$P(\text{red and blue}) = P(\text{red}) \cdot P(\text{blue after red})$$

$$= \frac{5}{12} \cdot \frac{3}{11} \qquad \text{Substitute.}$$

$$= \frac{5}{44} \qquad \text{Simplify.}$$

∴ The probability of choosing a red marble followed by a blue marble is $\frac{5}{44}$, or about 11%.

Exercises

You randomly choose one of the lettered tiles. Without replacing the first tile, you choose a second tile. Find the probability of choosing the first tile, then the second tile.

12. R and A

13. A and A

14. R and *not* D

15. You choose one of the lettered tiles and flip a coin. What is the probability of choosing an A and flipping heads?

You randomly choose one game piece. (a) Find the number of ways the event can occur. (b) Find the favorable outcomes of the event.

1. Choosing green

2. Choosing *not* yellow

The spinner is spun. Determine if the game is fair. If it is *not* fair, who has the greater probability of winning?

3. You win if the number is odd. Your friend wins if the number is even.

4. You win if the number is less than 5. Your friend wins if the number is greater than 5. If the number is 5, nobody wins.

Use the bar graph to find the experimental probability of the event.

5. Rolling a 1 or a 2

6. Rolling an odd number

7. *Not* rolling a 5

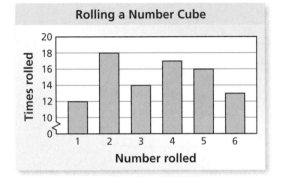

You randomly choose one chess piece. Without replacing the first piece, you choose a second piece. Find the probability of choosing the first piece, then the second piece.

8. Bishop and bishop

9. King and queen

10. King and pawn

11. King and *not* pawn

12. **MINTS** You have a bag of 60 assorted mints. You randomly choose six mints. Two of the mints you choose are peppermints. How many of the 60 mints would you expect to be peppermints?

13. **NAMES** The names of 49 middle school students are placed in a hat. The probability of randomly drawing the name of a seventh-grade student is $\frac{3}{7}$. How many seventh-grade students' names are in the hat?

14. **BEADS** Thirty percent of the beads in a bag are blue. One bead is randomly chosen and replaced. Then a second bead is chosen. What is the probability that *neither* bead is blue?

1. A school athletic director asked each athletic team member to name his or her favorite professional sports team. The results are below:

- Columbus Crew: 3
- Detroit Shock: 4
- Florida Marlins: 20
- Florida Panthers: 8
- Jacksonville Jaguars: 26
- Miami Dolphins: 22
- Miami Heat: 15
- New York Buzz: 5
- Orlando Magic: 18
- Pensacola Power: 7
- Tampa Bay Buccaneers: 17
- Tampa Bay Lightning: 12
- Tampa Bay Rays: 28
- Other: 6

One athletic team member is picked at random. What is the likelihood that this team member's favorite professional sports team is *not* located in Florida?

A. certain

B. likely, but not certain

C. unlikely, but not impossible

D. impossible

2. Trapezoid *KLMN* is graphed in the coordinate plane shown.

Rotate trapezoid *KLMN* 90° clockwise about the origin. What are the coordinates of point *M'*, the image of point *M* after the rotation?

F. $(-3, -2)$

G. $(-2, -3)$

H. $(-2, 3)$

I. $(3, 2)$

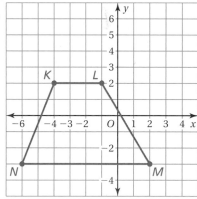

3. Each student in your class voted for his or her favorite day of the week. Their votes are shown below:

- Sunday: 6
- Saturday: 10
- Friday: 8
- Other day: 6

A student from your class is picked at random. What is the probability that this student's favorite day of the week is Sunday?

4. A formula for converting a temperature in degrees Celsius C to a temperature in degrees Fahrenheit F is shown below.

$$F = \frac{9}{5}C + 32$$

When the temperature in degrees Celsius is $-9°$, what is the temperature, to the nearest degree, in degrees Fahrenheit?

A. $-27°$ **C.** $16°$

B. $-16°$ **D.** $27°$

5. A nutritionist calculated the calories in a meal that came from three sources, as shown below.

- Calories from carbohydrates: 240
- Calories from fat: 180
- Calories from protein: 180

The nutritionist wants to make a circle graph to display this data. What should be the angle measure for the section labeled "carbohydrates"?

F. $120°$ **H.** $180°$

G. $144°$ **I.** $240°$

6. A right circular cone has a diameter of 10 centimeters and a slant height of 13 centimeters. Stan was computing its surface area in the box below.

$$\pi r^2 + \pi r \ell = 3.14 \cdot 5^2 + 3.14 \cdot 5 \cdot 13$$
$$= 15.7^2 + 15.7 \cdot 13$$
$$= 246.49 + 204.1$$
$$= 450.59 \text{ cm}^2$$

What should Stan do to correct the error that he made?

A. Use the formula $\frac{1}{3}\pi r^2 h$.

B. Label the answer with the unit cm^3.

C. Square the 5 before multiplying by 3.14.

D. Distribute the 3.14 to get $3.14 \cdot 5 + 3.14 \cdot 13$.

7. Which expression is *not* equal to the other three?

F. 6 **H.** $|6|$

G. -6 **I.** $|-6|$

8. A spinner is divided into 8 congruent sections, as shown below.

You spin the spinner twice. What is the probability that the arrow will stop in a yellow section both times?

9. For a vacation trip, 4 cousins decided to rent a minivan and share the cost equally. They determined that each cousin would have to pay $300.

The minivan had 2 unused seats, so 2 additional cousins joined them. If the larger group of cousins now share the cost equally, what would each cousin have to pay?

A. $150   **C.** $300

B. $200   **D.** $450

10. A travel store has 16 umbrellas in stock. Ten of the umbrellas are black. What percent of the umbrellas are black?

F. 1.6%   **H.** 58%

G. 10%   **I.** 62.5%

11. A professional golfer hit 1125 tee shots, of which 675 landed in the fairway. A statistic called "driving accuracy" is found by using the formula below.

$$\text{driving accuracy} = \frac{\text{number of fairways hit}}{\text{number of tee shots}}$$

Part A   What was the golfer's driving accuracy, expressed as a percent? Show your work and explain your reasoning.

Part B   Based only on your answer to Part A, how many of the golfer's next 500 tee shots would you expect to land in the fairway? Explain your reasoning.

Appendix A
My Big Ideas Projects

"I'm analyzing our new business. When the income line intersects the expense line, we will start making a profit. How many months will it take?"

"Let x be the number of my dog biscuits that I am sharing with you."

"Now, double that number and add 4 and you get 4 times the sum of 1 and the number."

"How many biscuits do you get?"

Appendix B
Exploring Equations and Functions

The Mathematics of Jules Verne

1 Project Overview

Jules Verne (1828–1905) was a famous French science fiction writer. He wrote about space, air, and underwater travel before aircraft and submarines were commonplace, and before any means of space travel had been devised.

For example, in his 1865 novel *From the Earth to the Moon*, he wrote about three astronauts who were launched from Florida and recovered through a splash landing. The first actual moon landing wasn't until 1969.

Essential Question How does the knowledge of mathematics influence science fiction writing?

Read one of Jules Verne's science fiction novels. Then write a book report about some of the mathematics used in the novel.

> **Sample:** A league is an old measure of distance. It is approximately equal to 4 kilometers. You can convert 20,000 leagues to miles as follows.
>
> $$20{,}000 \text{ leagues} \cdot \frac{4 \text{ km}}{1 \text{ league}} \cdot \frac{1 \text{ mile}}{1.6 \text{ km}} = 50{,}000 \text{ miles}$$

2 Things to Include

- Describe the major events in the plot.

- Write a brief paragraph describing the setting of the story.

- List and identify the main characters. Explain the contribution of each character to the story.

- Explain the major conflict in the story.

- Describe at least four examples of mathematics used in the story.

- Which of Jules Verne's scientific predictions have come true since he wrote the novel?

Jules Verne (1828–1905)

3 Things to Remember

- You can download one of Jules Verne's novels at *My.BigIdeasMath.com*.

- Add your own illustrations to your project.

- Organize your report in a folder, and think of a title for your report.

A.2 History Project

Mathematics in Ancient Greece

Corinthian Helmet

1 Getting Started

The ancient Greek period began around 1100 B.C. and lasted until the Roman conquest of Greece in 146 B.C.

The civilization of the ancient Greeks influenced the languages, politics, educational systems, philosophy, science, mathematics, and arts of Western Civilization. It was a primary force in the birth of the Renaissance in Europe between the 14th and 17th centuries.

Essential Question How do you use mathematical knowledge that was originally discovered by the Greeks?

Sample: Ancient Greek symbols for the numbers from 1 through 10 are shown in the table.

I	II	III	IIII	Γ	ΓI	ΓII	ΓIII	ΓIIII	△
1	2	3	4	5	6	7	8	9	10

These same symbols were used to write the numbers between 11 and 39. Here are some examples.

$$\triangle\ \Gamma\ |||\ = 18 \qquad \triangle\ \triangle\ \triangle\ \Gamma = 35 \qquad \triangle\ \triangle\ ||||\ = 24$$

Alexander the Great

Parthenon

2 Things to Include

- Describe at least one contribution that each of the following people made to mathematics.

  Pythagoras (c. 570 B.C.–c. 490 B.C.)

  Aristotle (c. 384 B.C.–c. 322 B.C.)

  Euclid (c. 300 B.C.)

  Archimedes (c. 287 B.C.–c. 212 B.C.)

  Eratosthenes (c. 276 B.C.–c. 194 B.C.)

- Which of the people listed above was the teacher of Alexander the Great? What subjects did Alexander the Great study when he was in school?

- How did the ancient Greeks represent fractions?

- Describe how the ancient Greeks used mathematics. How does this compare with the ways in which mathematics is used today?

A α	alpha	N ν	nu
B β	beta	Ξ ξ	xi
Γ γ	gamma	O o	omicron
Δ δ	delta	Π π	pi
E ε	epsilon	P ρ	rho
Z ζ	zeta	Σ σ	sigma
H η	eta	T τ	tau
Θ θ	theta	Υ υ	upsilon
I ι	iota	Φ φ	phi
K κ	kappa	X χ	chi
Λ λ	lambda	Ψ ψ	psi
M μ	mu	Ω ω	omega

3 Things to Remember

- Add your own illustrations to your project.

- Try to include as many different math concepts as possible. Your goal is to include at least one concept from each of the chapters you studied this year.

- Organize your report in a folder, and think of a title for your report.

Greek Pottery

Trireme Greek Warship

Building a Kaleidoscope

Mirrors
set at 60°

1 Getting Started

A kaleidoscope is a tube of mirrors
containing loose colored beads, pebbles,
or other small colored objects. You look
in one end and light enters the other end,
reflecting off the mirrors.

Essential Question How does the knowledge of mathematics help
you create a kaleidoscope?

If the angle between the mirrors is 45°, you see 8 duplicate images.
If the angle is 60°, you see 6 duplicate images. If the angle is 90°, you
see 4 duplicate images. As the tube is rotated, the colored objects
tumble, creating various patterns.

Write a report about kaleidoscopes. Discuss the mathematics you
need to know in order to build a kaleidoscope.

Sample: A kaleidoscope
whose mirrors meet at 60°
angles has reflective symmetry
and rotational symmetry.

Reflect

Rotate
120°

Antique Kaleidoscope

- How does the angle at which the mirrors meet affect the number of duplicate images that you see?

- What angles can you use other than 45°, 60°, and 90°? Explain your reasoning.

- Research the history of kaleidoscopes. Can you find examples of kaleidoscopes being used before they were patented by David Brewster in 1816?

- Make your own kaleidoscope.

- Describe the mathematics you used to create your kaleidoscope.

Mirrors set at 90°

Mirrors set at 60°

3 **Things to Think About**

- Add your own drawings and pattern creations to your project.

- Organize your report in a folder, and think of a title for your report.

Giant Kaleidoscope, San Diego harbor

Mirrors set at 45°

Classifying Animals

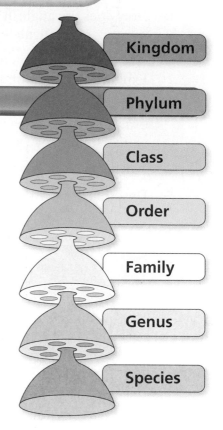

Kingdom

Phylum

Class

Order

Family

Genus

Species

1   Getting Started

Biologists classify animals by placing them in phylums, or groups, with similar characteristics. Latin names, such as Chordata (having a spinal cord) or Arthropoda (having jointed limbs and rigid bodies) are used to describe these groups.

Biological classification is difficult, and scientists are still developing a complete system. There are seven main ranks of life on Earth; kingdom, phylum, class, order, family, genus, and species. However, scientists usually use more than these seven ranks to classify organisms.

Essential Question How does the classification of living organisms help you understand the similarities and differences of animals?

Write a report about how animals are classified. Choose several different animals and list the phylum, class, and order of each animal.

Wasp
Phylum: Arthropoda
Class: Insecta
Order: Hymenoptera
(membranous wing)

Sample: A bat is classified as an animal in the phylum Chordata, class Mammalia, and order Chiroptera. *Chiroptera* is a Greek word meaning "hand-wing."

Bat
Phylum: Chordata
Class: Mammalia
Order: Chiroptera
(hand-wing)

Monkey
Phylum: Chordata
Class: Mammalia
Order: Primate (large brain)

Kangaroo
Phylum: Chordata
Class: Mammalia
Order: Diprotodontia
(two front teeth)

② Things to Include

- List the different classes of phylum Chordata. Have you seen a member of each class?

- List the different classes of phylum Arthropoda. Have you seen a member of each class?

- Show how you can use graphic organizers to help classify animals. Which types of graphic organizers seem to be most helpful? Explain your reasoning.

- Summarize the number of species in each phlyum in an organized way. Be sure to include fractions, decimals, and percents.

Parrot
Phylum: Chordata
Class: Aves
Order: Psittaciformes
(strong, curved bill)

Frog
Phylum: Chordata
Class: Amphibia
Order: Anura (no tail)

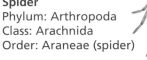

Spider
Phylum: Arthropoda
Class: Arachnida
Order: Araneae (spider)

③ Things to Remember

- Organize your report in a folder, and think of a title for your report.

Lobster
Phylum: Arthropoda
Class: Malacostraca
Order: Decopada (ten footed)

Crocodile
Phylum: Chordata
Class: Reptilia
Order: Crocodilia
(pebble-worm)

Cougar
Phylum: Chordata
Class: Mammalia
Order: Carnivora (meat eater)

Essential Question How can you convert temperatures between the Fahrenheit and Celsius scales?

1 ACTIVITY: Comparing Fahrenheit and Celsius

Work with a partner. The temperature scales show the relationship between the Fahrenheit and Celsius scales. Use the two scales to complete the table.

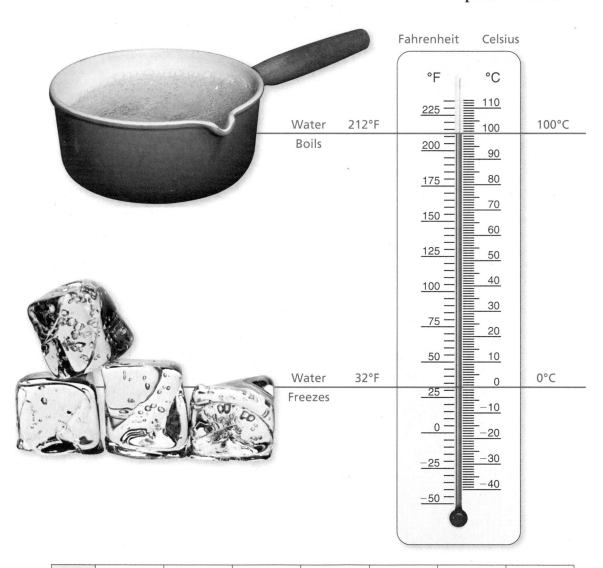

F	0°	32°	70°	80°	90°	100°	212°
C							

2 ACTIVITY: Comparing Fahrenheit and Celsius

Work with a partner.

   a. Plot the points from the table in Activity 1.

   b. Draw a line through the points.

   c. Find the slope of the line. Write the slope as a fraction in simplest form.

   d. Which of the following shows the relationship between C and F?

$$C = \frac{5}{9}(F + 32)$$

$$C = \frac{5}{9}(F - 32)$$

$$C = \frac{9}{5}(F + 32)$$

$$C = \frac{9}{5}(F - 32)$$

3 ACTIVITY: Converting Temperatures

Work with a partner. You have email pals in four countries that use the Celsius scale. Write each temperature in degrees Fahrenheit. Then use the scale in Activity 1 to check that your answer is reasonable.

   a. Canada: 19°C

   b. Mexico: 35°C

   c. Japan: 28°C

   d. Russia: 6°C

What Is Your Answer?

   4. IN YOUR OWN WORDS How can you convert temperatures between the Fahrenheit and Celsius scales? Give two examples.

Practice

Use what you learned about multi-step equations to complete Exercises 3–5 on page A14.

B.1 Lesson

EXAMPLE 1 **Combining Like Terms to Solve an Equation**

Solve $-2x + 4x - 12 = 40$. Check your solution.

Check

$-2x + 4x - 12 = 40$

$-2(26) + 4(26) - 12 \stackrel{?}{=} 40$

$-52 + 104 - 12 \stackrel{?}{=} 40$

$40 = 40$ ✓

$-2x + 4x - 12 =$	40	Write the equation.
$2x - 12 =$	40	Combine like terms.
$\underline{+12 \quad +12}$		Undo the subtraction by adding 12 to each side.
$2x =$	52	Simplify.
$\dfrac{2x}{2} = \dfrac{52}{2}$		Undo the multiplication by dividing each side by 2.
$x = 26$		Simplify.

∴ The solution is $x = 26$.

EXAMPLE 2 **Using the Distributive Property to Solve an Equation**

Solve $4(2x - 7) + 5 = -39$.

$4(2x - 7) + 5 = -39$	Write the equation.
$4(2x) - 4(7) + 5 = -39$	Use Distributive Property.
$8x - 28 + 5 = -39$	Multiply.
$8x - 23 = -39$	Combine like terms.
Undo the subtraction. ⟶ $+23 \quad +23$	Add 23 to each side.
$8x = -16$	Simplify.
Undo the multiplication. ⟶ $\dfrac{8x}{8} = \dfrac{-16}{8}$	Divide each side by 8.
$x = -2$	Simplify.

∴ The solution is $x = -2$.

On Your Own

Exercises 6–11

Solve the equation. Check your solution.

1. $51 - 2z - 8z = 23$

2. $2 + \dfrac{1}{2}y - 34 = -12$

3. $-2(x + 5) - 4x = 11$

4. $3 - 2.5(3 - 2d) = 5.5$

EXAMPLE ③ **Using a Formula**

$S = 684$ in.²

20 in.

8 in.

ℓ

The surface area of a rectangular prism can be found using the formula $S = 2\ell w + 2\ell h + 2wh$. What is the length of the prism?

$$S = 2\ell w + 2\ell h + 2wh$$ Write the formula.

$$684 = 2\ell(8) + 2\ell(20) + 2(8)(20)$$ Substitute.

$$684 = 16\ell + 40\ell + 320$$ Simplify.

$$684 = 56\ell + 320$$ Combine like terms.

$$\underline{-320 \qquad\qquad -320}$$ Subtract 320 from each side.

$$364 = 56\ell$$ Simplify.

$$\frac{364}{56} = \frac{56\ell}{56}$$ Divide each side by 56.

$$6.5 = \ell$$ Simplify.

⋰ The length is 6.5 inches.

EXAMPLE ④ **Real-Life Application**

Your order for concert tickets is shown. You receive one free song download per ticket. How many song downloads do you receive?

Let x be the number of tickets.

Each ticket has a $6.50 service charge.

The order has a $3.30 processing fee.

Each ticket is $37.

The total is $220.80.

Review Order	
Item	Charge
TICKET PRICE	$37.00 per ticket
Service Charges	$6.50 per ticket
Processing Fee	**$3.30**
Will Call	**Free**
TOTAL	**$220.80**

$$37x + 6.5x + 3.3 = 220.8$$ Write an equation.

$$43.5x + 3.3 = 220.8$$ Combine like terms.

$$\underline{-3.3 \qquad -3.3}$$ Subtract 3.3 from each side.

$$43.5x = 217.5$$ Simplify.

$$\frac{43.5x}{43.5} = \frac{217.5}{43.5}$$ Divide each side by 43.5.

$$x = 5$$ Simplify.

⋰ You purchase 5 tickets. So, you receive 5 song downloads.

● **On Your Own**

5. **WHAT IF?** In Example 3, the surface area of the prism is 656 square inches. What is the length of the prism?

6. **WHAT IF?** In Example 4, you change your order. The total is $133.80. How many song downloads do you receive?

B.1 Exercises

Vocabulary and Concept Check

1. REASONING Describe the steps you would use to solve the equation $6x + 3x + 2 = 8$.

2. REASONING Describe the steps you would use to solve the equation $2(4x - 5) + 11 = -63$.

Practice and Problem Solving

Use the temperature scales to convert between Celsius and Kelvin.

3. Kelvin is a temperature scale used by scientists. Convert 40°C to Kelvin.

4. Water boils at 100°C. At what temperature does water boil on the Kelvin scale?

5. Write an equation that describes the relationship between Kelvin and Celsius.

Solve the equation. Check your solution.

6. $-3x + 7x = 17 + 11$

7. $3x + 12x - 20 = 25$

8. $-5n + 6n + 15 - 3n = -3$

9. $3(2m + 9) - 1 = 2$

10. $4(x - 3) + 7 - 10x = 5$

11. $\frac{2}{3}(y - 12) = -6$

12. ERROR ANALYSIS Describe and correct the error in solving the equation.

$$2x - 6x + 4 = 12$$
$$-4x + 4 = 12$$
$$x + 4 = -3$$
$$x = -7$$

13. PUZZLE Twenty-five more than 3 times the quantity of a number decreased by 9 is 43. Find the number.

14. CYLINDER What is the diameter of a soup can if the lateral surface area is 188.4 square centimeters and the height is 10 centimeters?

15. MOVIES You and three friends go to the movies.

a. Your group purchases 2 specials, 2 single tickets, and one additional box of popcorn. The total is $36.50. What is the price of a single ticket?

b. The price of 2 boxes of popcorn and 3 drinks is fifty cents more than purchasing one special. What is the price of a drink?

Single Ticket	x
Popcorn	$2.50
Drink	y
Special-Includes single ticket, popcorn, and drink	$9.75

16. **PUZZLE** During a recent season, there were 18 girls on the high school softball team. There were equal numbers of freshmen, sophomores, and seniors on the team. The number of juniors was two less than the number of seniors. How many juniors were on the team?

17. **SALE** A store is having a clearance sale. The total for a skirt, a pair of shoes, and a pair of socks is $25.60 before tax. The pair of socks costs $3.50. The original prices of the skirt and the shoes were the same. What is the sale price of the skirt?

18. **RUNNING** Use the clues given by the table.

   a. You ran a total of 12 miles this week. Make a table showing the number of miles you ran each day.
   b. Did you run every day? Explain.

Day	Mon.	Tues.	Wed.	Thurs.	Fri.
Distance	x	$\frac{1}{6}x$	$1 - \frac{1}{4}x$	$x - \frac{2}{3}$	x

19. **Critical Thinking** Use the graphic organizer to solve the equation in two different ways. What are the advantages and disadvantages of each way?

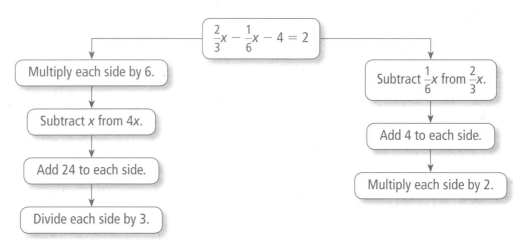

$$\frac{2}{3}x - \frac{1}{6}x - 4 = 2$$

Multiply each side by 6.

Subtract x from $4x$.

Add 24 to each side.

Divide each side by 3.

Subtract $\frac{1}{6}x$ from $\frac{2}{3}x$.

Add 4 to each side.

Multiply each side by 2.

Fair Game Review What you learned in previous grades & lessons

Simplify. *(Skills Review Handbook)*

20. $12[10 - (3 + 6)] + 14$

21. $2[4 + (3 + 6)] - 12 - 2$

22. **MULTIPLE CHOICE** What is the value of the expression below? *(Section 1.4)*

$$-4^2 - (-3)^2 + 1$$

Ⓐ -24 Ⓑ -6 Ⓒ 3 Ⓓ 6

B.2 Solving Equations with Variables on Both Sides

Essential Question How can you solve an equation that has variables on both sides?

1 ACTIVITY: Using a Table, Graph, and Algebra

Work with a partner. You have an email pal in Antarctica. Your email pal tells you the temperature in McMurdo. You ask whether he gave the temperature in Celsius or Fahrenheit. He says "It's the same on both scales." What is the temperature?

a. **TABLE** Use "Guess, Check, and Revise" with a table to find the only temperature that is the same on both scales.

F							
C							

b. **GRAPH** Draw the line given by $C = F$ in the coordinate plane. Locate the point at which the graph of $C = F$ intersects the graph of

$$C = \frac{5}{9}(F - 32).$$

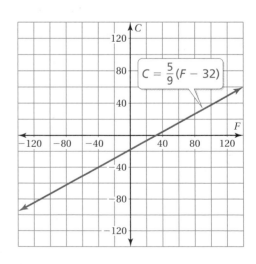

Antarctic Peninsula

Atlantic Ocean

South Pole

McMurdo

South Pacific Ocean

Indian Ocean

c. **ALGEBRA** Let x be the temperature that is the same on both scales. Substitute x for C and F in the equation

$$C = \frac{5}{9}(F - 32).$$

Then solve for x.

d. Compare your solutions from parts (a)–(c). Did you get the same solution with each method? Which method do you prefer? Why?

$$C = \frac{5}{9}(F - 32)$$

2 GAME: Race to the South Pole

Play with a partner.

- Write each expression on a scrap of brown or blue paper. Place the brown pieces of paper in one bag and the blue pieces of paper in another bag.

- Draw an expression from each bag and set them equal to each other.

- If you can solve the equation, you move one space. If you cannot solve the equation, your partner gets a chance to solve it and move one space.

- Put the expressions back into their bags.

- Take turns. The first person to reach the South Pole wins.

Brown Papers	Blue Papers
x	$2x$
$x + 1$	$2x + 4$
$x - 1$	$-2x$
$x + 2$	$-2x + 4$
$x - 2$	$3x$
$x + 3$	$3x + 6$
$x - 3$	$-3x$
	$-3x + 6$

$$x + 1 \quad = \quad 3x$$

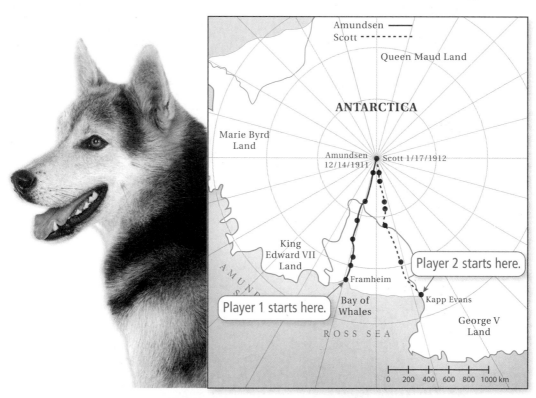

What Is Your Answer?

3. **IN YOUR OWN WORDS** How can you solve an equation that has variables on both sides? Give an example and solve it.

Practice ➤ Use what you learned about solving equations with variables on both sides to complete Exercises 4–9 on page A20.

To solve an equation with variables on both sides, collect the variable terms on one side and the constant terms on the other side.

EXAMPLE 1 Solving an Equation with Variables on Both Sides

Solve $-4y = 9 - y$. Check your solution.

$-4y = 9 - y$		Write the equation.
Collect the variable terms. → $\underline{+y \qquad +y}$		Add y to each side.
$-3y = 9$		Simplify.
$\dfrac{-3y}{-3} = \dfrac{9}{-3}$		Divide each side by -3.
$y = -3$		Simplify.

Check
$$-4y = 9 - y$$
$$-4(-3) \stackrel{?}{=} 9 - (-3)$$
$$12 = 12 \checkmark$$

EXAMPLE 2 Using the Distributive Property to Solve an Equation

Solve $-4\left(\dfrac{7}{2}x + 1\right) = 2(x - 4)$.

$-4\left(\dfrac{7}{2}x + 1\right) = 2(x - 4)$		Write the equation.
$-14x - 4 = 2x - 8$		Use Distributive Property.
Collect the variable terms. → $\underline{-2x \qquad -2x}$		Subtract $2x$ from each side.
$-16x - 4 = -8$		Simplify.
Collect the constant terms. → $\underline{+4 \qquad +4}$		Add 4 to each side.
$-16x = -4$		Simplify.
$\dfrac{-16x}{-16} = \dfrac{-4}{-16}$		Divide each side by -16.
$x = \dfrac{1}{4}$		Simplify.

⬤ On Your Own

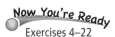
Now You're Ready
Exercises 4–22

Solve the equation. Check your solution.

1. $-5x = x + 12$
2. $15 - 4z = z - 8$
3. $6x = 2(7x + 3)$
4. $-3(1 - x) = \dfrac{1}{2}(2x + 1)$

EXAMPLE **3**

The polygons have the same perimeter. What is the area of the rectangle?

A 12 in. **B** 8 in.^{2} **C** 12 in.^{2} **D** 24 in.^{2}

The perimeter of the rectangle is $x + x + 4 + 4 = 2x + 8$.

The perimeter of the triangle is $4 + 2x + x + 2 = 3x + 6$.

Perimeter of rectangle	Perimeter of triangle

$$2x + 8 = 3x + 6 \qquad \text{Write an equation.}$$

$$8 = x + 6 \qquad \text{Subtract } 2x \text{ from each side.}$$

$$2 = x \qquad \text{Subtract 6 from each side.}$$

⋮• So, the area of the rectangle is $2(4) = 8$ square inches. The correct answer is **B**.

EXAMPLE 4 **Real-Life Application**

A boat travels x miles per hour from Toledo to Buffalo. The boat travels 3 miles per hour slower on the return trip. What is the distance from Toledo to Buffalo?

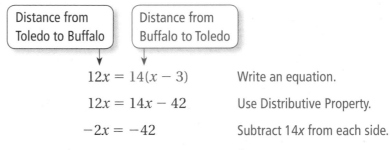

The speed, or rate, of the boat on the return trip is $(x - 3)$ miles per hour.

Distance from Toledo to Buffalo	Distance from Buffalo to Toledo

$$12x = 14(x - 3) \qquad \text{Write an equation.}$$

$$12x = 14x - 42 \qquad \text{Use Distributive Property.}$$

$$-2x = -42 \qquad \text{Subtract } 14x \text{ from each side.}$$

$$x = 21 \qquad \text{Divide each side by } -2.$$

The boat travels 21 miles per hour from Toledo to Buffalo in 12 hours. So, the boat travels $12(21) = 252$ miles.

⋮• The distance from Toledo to Buffalo is 252 miles.

● **On Your Own**

Now You're Ready
Exercises 25–27

5. In Example 3, what is the perimeter of the triangle?

6. In Example 4, what is the speed of the boat on the return trip?

✓ Vocabulary and Concept Check

1. **REASONING** Describe the steps you would use to solve $5x = 3x + 4$.

2. **OPEN-ENDED** Write an equation with variables on both sides that has a solution of -1.

3. **WRITING** To solve $-3x + 4 = -2x$, is it easier to add $3x$ to each side or add $2x$ to each side? Explain.

 ## Practice and Problem Solving

Solve the equation. Check your solution.

① 4. $2x = -x - 6$

5. $-9 + c = 4c$

6. $-3y = 7y$

7. $-5a = 2 - a$

8. $6w - 5 = 8w$

9. $3z = 14 + 10z$

10. $4f + 8 = 9f - 12$

11. $3p - 11 = 5p + 6$

12. $-7k + 10 = 9k + 18$

13. $-2 + 2d = 6d + 6$

14. $8b - 7 = -11 + 3b$

15. $12h - 7 = 6h + 8$

16. **ERROR ANALYSIS** Describe and correct the error in solving the equation.

$$3x - 7 = -2x + 8$$
$$3x + (-2x) = 8 + 7$$
$$x = 15$$

Solve the equation. Check your solution.

② 17. $2k - 8 = 4(k + 1)$

18. $3(g - 3) = 2(6 - 2g)$

19. $-5(f + 7) = 3(3f - 1)$

20. $9.2 - 4w = -2(3w + 5)$

21. $2.5(3b - 4) = 3.5b - 6b$

22. $6(1.5h - 1) = 5(2.2h + 3)$

23. **ERROR ANALYSIS** Describe and correct the error in solving the equation.

✗
$$2(v - 5) = -(3v + 5)$$
$$2v - 10 = -3v + 5$$
$$5v = 15$$
$$v = 3$$

24. **MUSIC LESSONS** It costs $50 to be a member of a music club. A member of the club pays $10 per music lesson. A nonmember pays $20 per music lesson. How many music lessons must a member and a nonmember take so that the cost for each is the same?

In a regular polygon each side has the same length. Find the perimeter of the regular polygon.

❸ 25.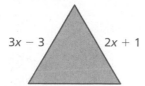

3x − 3   2x + 1

26.

x − 8

$\frac{1}{3}x$

27.

7 − 2x

4x − 5

Write an equation that describes the situation. Then solve the equation.

28. Two more than the product of a number n and 3 is equal to the product of the number n and 4.

29. Three less than 5 times a number n is equal to 8 more than negative 6 times the number n.

30. **SAVINGS** The table shows the beginning balance in each savings account. You save $10 per week and your friend saves $17 per week. How many weeks will it take for you and your friend to have the same balance?

Savings Account Balance	
You	Your Friend
$126	$84

31. **FLIGHT** A nonstop flight from Billings to Minneapolis takes x hours. The return flight takes 30 minutes longer. What is the distance from Billings to Minneapolis?

32. **PLAYGROUND** There are 87 children at a playground. There are 23 more boys than girls. How many of each are at the playground?

33. **GEOMETRY** △ABC is similar to △DEF. The ratio of AC to DF is 3 : 5. What is the perimeter of each triangle?

B
x $x + 3$
A $18 − x$ C

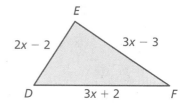

E
$2x − 2$ $3x − 3$
D $3x + 2$ F

34. **Critical Thinking** Is it possible for an equation with variables on both sides to have no solution? If so, give an example.

Fair Game Review What you learned in previous grades & lessons

Graph the function. *(Skills Review Handbook)*

35. $y = 2x − 1$

36. $y = 4 − x$

37. $y = 0.5x + 2$

38. **MULTIPLE CHOICE** What is the theoretical probability of rolling an even number on a number cube? *(Section 9.2)*

Ⓐ $\frac{1}{6}$ Ⓑ $\frac{1}{3}$ Ⓒ $\frac{1}{2}$ Ⓓ $\frac{2}{3}$

B.3 Solving Equations Using Tables and Graphs

Essential Question How can you use tables and graphs to solve equations?

Share Your Work at...
My.BigIdeasMath.com

1 ACTIVITY: Using a Table, Graph, and Algebra

Work with a partner. You start a website design company. How many sites must you design before you start making a profit?

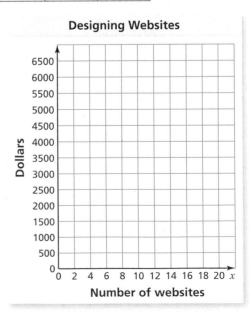

- You pay $4000 for a new computer and software.
- It costs you $100 to design each website.
- You charge $500 to design each website.

Let x represent the number of sites you design.

$$C = 4000 + 100x \qquad \text{Cost of designing } x \text{ sites}$$

$$R = 500x \qquad \text{Income for designing } x \text{ sites}$$

You will start making a profit when $C = R$. That is, when you have designed enough websites to cover your start-up cost of $4000 and $100 for each site.

a. **TABLE** Use "Guess, Check, and Revise" with a table to find the value of x for which $C = R$.

x							
C							
R							

b. **GRAPH** Graph $C = 4000 + 100x$ and $R = 500x$ in the same coordinate plane. Find the value of x for which the two lines intersect.

c. **ALGEBRA** Set C equal to R.

$$C = R$$
$$4000 + 100x = 500x$$

Solve for x.

d. The point at which the two lines intersect is called the "break-even" point. Why is it called this?

Designing Websites

Dollars

6500
6000
5500
5000
4500
4000
3500
3000
2500
2000
1500
1000
500
0
0 2 4 6 8 10 12 14 16 18 20 x

Number of websites

ACTIVITY: Planning Your Own Business

Make a plan to start your own business.

- Describe your business.
- Are you providing a product or a service?
- Make a list of the things you need to start the business. Find the cost of each item or service.
- Write an equation that represents the cost of making x items. Write an equation that represents the income for selling x items.
- Use a table to compare the cost and income for several values of x.

x						
C						
R						

- Draw a graph that shows when your company will reach the break-even point.

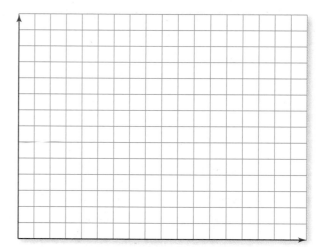

- Organize all of your planning in a folder. Include your company name, logo, and a plan for advertising and selling your product or service.

What Is Your Answer?

3. **IN YOUR OWN WORDS** How can you use tables and graphs to solve equations? Describe a real-life example.

Practice

Use what you learned about solving equations using tables and graphs to complete Exercises 4–6 and 13–15 on page A26.

Key Idea

Solving Equations

Method 1 **Use algebra.** *(Section B.1 and Section B.2)*

Method 2 **Use a table.** Find the value of the variable that makes the value of each side of the equation the same. *(Section B.3)*

Method 3 **Use a graph.** Graph each side of the equation. The *x*-coordinate of the point of intersection is the solution of the equation. *(Section B.3)*

EXAMPLE **1** **Solving an Equation Using a Table**

Use a table to solve $4x + 2 = 5x$. Check your solution.

Find the *x*-value that makes $4x + 2$ equal to $5x$.

Try different values of *x*.

Check

$$4x + 2 = 5x$$
$$\underline{-4x \qquad -4x}$$
$$2 = x \ ✓$$

x	4x + 2	5x
−1	$4(-1) + 2 = -2$	$5(-1) = -5$
0	$4(0) + 2 = 2$	$5(0) = 0$
1	$4(1) + 2 = 6$	$5(1) = 5$
2	$4(2) + 2 = 10$	$5(2) = 10$

Each side of the equation equals 10 when $x = 2$.

∴ The solution is $x = 2$.

EXAMPLE **2** **Solving an Equation Using Graphs**

Use a graph to solve $x + 1 = 5 - x$. Check your solution.

Check

$$x + 1 = 5 - x$$
$$2 + 1 \overset{?}{=} 5 - 2$$
$$3 = 3 \ ✓$$

Write equations for each side of the original equation.

$$x + 1 = 5 - x$$

$$\boxed{y = x + 1} \qquad \boxed{y = 5 - x}$$

Use a graphing calculator to graph $y = x + 1$ and $y = 5 - x$.

∴ The lines intersect at (2, 3). So, the solution is $x = 2$.

On Your Own

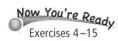
Now You're Ready
Exercises 4–15

Use a table or a graph to solve the equation. Check your solution. Then explain your choice of method.

1. $1 - 2z = 2z - 3$

2. $-3x + 2 = x + 18$

3. $-x = 2x - 3$

4. $x + 2 = 2x - 3$

EXAMPLE 3 Real-Life Application

Hourly Rentals	
Canoe	Kayak
$15	$10

You pay $30 for a workshop on environmental conservation. Then you rent a canoe for x hours. Your friend pays $45 for a kayak paddling lesson, then rents a kayak for x hours. At the end of the day, you both spent the same amount. How many hours did you rent the canoe?

Write equations for your total cost and your friend's total cost.

Your total cost	*Your friend's total cost*
$y = 15x + 30$	$y = 10x + 45$

canoe cost   workshop cost   kayak cost   lesson cost

Use a graphing calculator to graph each equation.

X=3   Y=75

⁛ The lines intersect at (3, 75). So, you rented the canoe for 3 hours and paid a total of $75.

Check Find the total costs for 3 hours.

Your total cost	*Your friend's total cost*
$y = 15x + 30$	$y = 10x + 45$
$= 15(3) + 30$	$= 10(3) + 45$
$= 75$	$= 75$ ✓

On Your Own

5. WHAT IF? In Example 3, your friend receives a $5 discount on the paddling lesson. At the end of the day, you both spent the same amount. How many hours did you rent the canoe?

Check It Out
Help with Homework
BigIdeasMath.com

 Vocabulary and Concept Check

1. **REASONING** What equation is being solved by the table? What is the solution?

2. **VOCABULARY** You graph each side of an equation. The point of intersection is $(4, -2)$. What is the solution of the equation?

3. **WRITING** Would you rather use a table or a graph to solve an equation? Explain.

x	$3x - 2$	$x + 2$
0	-2	2
1	1	3
2	4	4

 Practice and Problem Solving

Use a table to solve the equation. Check your solution.

4. $4x = 3x + 1$ **5.** $7h - 6 = 4h$ **6.** $-3k - 4 = k$

7. $9 = 3g - 6$ **8.** $6z = 8z + 2$ **9.** $3a + 5 = -11 - 5a$

10. $3 - 4q = 2q - 21$ **11.** $-5p - 3 = 2p + 18$ **12.** $-7w + 15 = 3w - 5$

Use the graph to solve the equation. Check your solution.

13. $-2x - 6 = x + 3$ **14.** $2x - 4 = -3x + 11$ **15.** $x - 1 = 4x + 5$

16. **SHOPPING** You buy 5 shirts and your friend buys 8 shirts. You spend $48 on shoes. You both spend the same amount of money. All the shirts cost the same amount. Use a table to find the cost of each shirt.

17. **CELL PHONE** A wireless carrier offers a free cell phone with Plan A or a $120 cell phone with Plan B. Use a graph to find the number of months it takes for the cost of Plan A to equal the cost of Plan B.

Find *x*. Then find the perimeter of the square.

18.
0.5x + 0.5

2x − 7

19.
x − 10

$\frac{1}{4}x + 2$

20.
$\frac{1}{3}(4x + 7)$

2.5x

21. CRITICAL THINKING Explain how to solve the equation $5x + 1 = 10x − 10$ using a table and "Guess, Check, and Revise." What is the solution?

22. RIBBON You cut a piece of ribbon into two pieces so that one piece is 24 inches longer than the other. The longer piece is four times as long as the shorter piece.

   a. How long is each piece of ribbon?

   b. How long was the original ribbon?

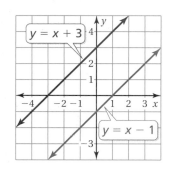

23. BICYCLING You and a friend are participating in a bicycling fundraiser. Both of you start at the same location. You leave 30 minutes before your friend. How many hours will it take for your friend to catch you?

Cycling Rate (mi/h)	
You	**Your Friend**
15	18

24. REASONING Use the graph to determine whether the equation $x + 3 = x − 1$ has a solution. Explain your reasoning.

y = x + 3

y = x − 1

25. *Geometry* The area of the rectangle is twice the area of the triangle. Find the area of each figure.

3x

3x + 3

3x

5x − 1

 Fair Game Review *What you learned in previous grades & lessons*

Find the slope of the line that passes through the two points. *(Section 3.2)*

26. $(0, 0), (4, 6)$ **27.** $(2, 1), (6, 3)$ **28.** $(−3, −1), (6, 2)$

29. MULTIPLE CHOICE Your backpack contains 3 blue pens and 2 black pens. You randomly choose one pen to give to a friend and then you randomly choose another pen to use yourself. What is the probability that both pens are blue? *(Section 9.4)*

   A $\frac{6}{25}$ **B** $\frac{3}{10}$ **C** $\frac{9}{25}$ **D** $\frac{3}{5}$

Check It Out
Graphic Organizer
BigIdeasMath ✓.com

You can use a **concept circle** to organize information about a concept. Here is an example of a concept circle for combining like terms to solve an equation.

Combining Like Terms to Solve an Equation

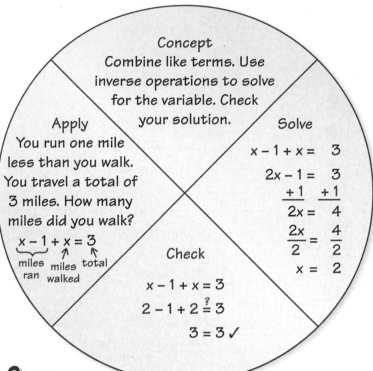

On Your Own

Make a concept circle to help you study these topics.

1. using the distributive property to solve an equation

2. solving an equation with variables on both sides

3. solving an equation using a table

4. solving an equation using a graph

After you complete this chapter, make concept circles for the following topics.

5. finding the slope of a line

6. graphing a line using a point and a slope

7. identifying slope and *y*-intercept

8. graphing a line using slope-intercept form

9. graphing a linear function

"Do you think this concept circle will help my owner understand that 'Speak' and 'Sit' need motivation?"

Solve the equation. Check your solution.   *(Section B.1 and Section B.2)*

1. $-9x + 5x - 18 = 2$

2. $5(2t - 5) - 6 = 9$

3. $-5y = 8 - y$

4. $3a - 8 = 2(6 - a)$

Use a table to solve the equation. Check your solution.   *(Section B.3)*

5. $2x + 1 = 3x$

6. $-7w - 4 = 2 - 4w$

Use the graph to solve the equation. Check your solution.   *(Section B.3)*

7. $-2x + 7 = 3x - 3$

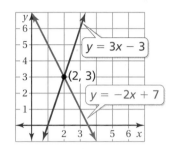

$y = 3x - 3$
$(2, 3)$
$y = -2x + 7$

8. $\frac{1}{2}x + 3 = -2x - 2$

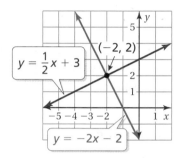

$y = \frac{1}{2}x + 3$
$(-2, 2)$
$y = -2x - 2$

9. The rectangles have the same perimeter. What is the area of the red rectangle? *(Section B.2)*

x

6 cm

$2x$

$2x$

10. PUZZLE Sixteen more than 5 times the quantity of a number minus 6 is 20. Find the number. *(Section B.1)*

11. WOOD You cut a piece of wood into two smaller pieces so that one piece is 40 centimeters longer than the other piece. The longer piece is three times as long as the shorter piece. *(Section B.3)*

   a. What are the lengths of the pieces of wood?

   b. How long was the original piece of wood?

12. BETTAS An aquarium store sells red, blue, and orange bettas. There are 14 bettas in the store. Two bettas are orange. The number of blue bettas is 3 times the number of red bettas. Find the number of blue bettas in the store. *(Section B.1)*

B.4 Slope of a Line

Essential Question How can the slope of a line be used to describe the line?

You studied the following definition of the slope of a line.

Slope is the rate of change between any two points on a line. It is a measure of the *steepness* of a line. To find the slope of a line, find the ratio of the change in y (vertical change) to the change in x (horizontal change).

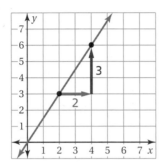

$$\text{slope} = \frac{\text{change in } y}{\text{change in } x}$$

$$= \frac{3}{2}$$

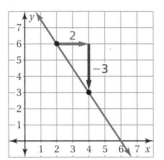

$$\text{slope} = \frac{\text{change in } y}{\text{change in } x}$$

$$= \frac{-3}{2} = -\frac{3}{2}$$

1 ACTIVITY: Extending the Concept of a Slope

Work with a partner. Find the slope of each line.

a.

b.

c.

d.

e.

f.
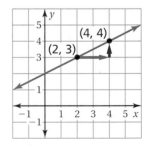

Inductive Reasoning

Work with a partner. Copy and complete the table.

	Two Points	Change in y	Change in x	Slope of Line
1a	**2.** $(2, 2)$, $(4, 4)$	2	2	
1b	**3.** $(1, 2)$, $(2, 1)$	-1	1	
1c	**4.** $(2, 3)$, $(4, 4)$			
1d	**5.** $(-3, 4)$, $(1, 2)$			
1e	**6.** $(-4, -1)$, $(-2, 3)$			
1f	**7.**			
	8. $(-4, 0)$, $(0, 1)$			
	9. $(-3, 4)$, $(6, -2)$			
	10. $(-4, 2)$, $(8, -1)$			
	11. $(-6, -1)$, $(3, 5)$			
	12. $(-5, 7)$, $(10, -5)$			
	13. $(0, 1)$, $(4, 1)$			
	14. $(-4, -2)$, $(-3, -6)$			

What Is Your Answer?

15. IN YOUR OWN WORDS How can the slope of a line be used to describe the line?

    a. Draw three lines that have positive slopes.

    b. Draw three lines that have negative slopes.

16. Compare a slope of 1 with a slope of 2. Show your comparison on a graph.

17. Compare a slope of -1 with a slope of -2. Show your comparison on a graph.

Practice Use what you learned about the slope of a line to complete Exercises 4–7 on page A34.

Key Vocabulary ◀))
slope, p. A32
rise, p. A32
run, p. A32

🔑 Key Idea

Slope

The **slope** of a line is a ratio of the change in y (the **rise**) to the change in x (the **run**) between any two points on the line.

$$\text{slope} = \frac{\text{change in } y}{\text{change in } x} = \frac{\text{rise}}{\text{run}}$$

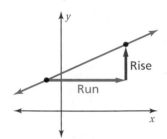

EXAMPLE ① **Real-Life Application**

What is the slope of the stairs when walking up to the apartment?

$$\text{slope} = \frac{\text{rise}}{\text{run}} \qquad \text{Write formula for slope.}$$

$$= \frac{8 \text{ ft}}{12 \text{ ft}} \qquad \text{Substitute.}$$

$$= \frac{2}{3} \qquad \text{Simplify.}$$

∴ The slope of the stairs is $\frac{2}{3}$.

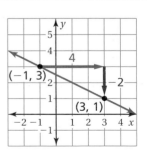

⬤ On Your Own

1. **WHAT IF?** The rise of the stairs is 9 feet. What is the slope of the stairs?

EXAMPLE ② **Finding the Slope of a Line**

Study Tip

A line that rises from left to right has a *positive* slope.
A line that falls from left to right has a *negative* slope.

Find the slope of the line.

$$\text{slope} = \frac{\text{rise}}{\text{run}} \qquad \text{Write formula for slope.}$$

$$= \frac{-2}{4} \qquad \text{Substitute.}$$

$$= -\frac{1}{2} \qquad \text{Simplify.}$$

∴ The slope is $-\frac{1}{2}$.

On Your Own

Now You're Ready
Exercises 8–10

Find the slope of the line.

2.

3.

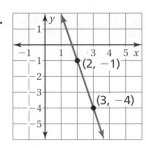

EXAMPLE ③ **Graphing Lines Using a Point and a Slope**

a. **Graph the line with a slope of 3 that passes through $(-3, -4)$.**

Step 1: Plot $(-3, -4)$.

Step 2: Find the rise and the run.

$$\text{slope} = \frac{\text{rise}}{\text{run}} = \frac{3}{1}$$

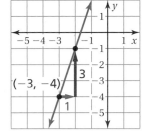

Step 3: Plot the point that is 1 unit right and 3 units up from $(-3, -4)$.

Step 4: Draw a line through the two points.

∴ The graph is shown at the left.

b. **Graph the line with a slope of $-\dfrac{4}{3}$ that passes through $(2, 3)$.**

Step 1: Plot $(2, 3)$.

Step 2: Find the rise and the run.

$$\text{slope} = \frac{\text{rise}}{\text{run}} = \frac{-4}{3}$$

Step 3: Plot the point that is 3 units right and 4 units down from $(2, 3)$.

Step 4: Draw a line through the two points.

∴ The graph is shown at the left.

On Your Own

Now You're Ready
Exercises 11–14

Graph the line with the given slope that passes through the given point.

4. slope = 1; $(1, 3)$

5. slope = $\dfrac{2}{5}$; $(2, -1)$

6. slope = -2; $(0, -2)$

7. slope = $-\dfrac{3}{2}$; $(-4, -4)$

Check It Out
Help with Homework
BigIdeasMath com

 Vocabulary and Concept Check

1. **OPEN-ENDED** How could you measure the slope of the roof of a house?

2. **REASONING** The slope of a line is $\frac{1}{2}$. What do you know about the graph of the line?

3. **OPEN-ENDED** A line with slope $-\frac{2}{3}$ passes through the point $(2, -6)$. Find two additional points on the line.

 Practice and Problem Solving

Copy and complete the table.

	Two Points	Change in y	Change in x	Slope of Line
4.	$(0, 5), (2, 7)$			
5.	$(-10, 4), (5, -20)$			
6.	$(-8, -4), (-6, 5)$			
7.	$(1, 9), (7, 6)$			

Find the slope of the line.

 8.

9.

10.
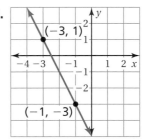

Graph the line with the given slope that passes through the given point.

 11. slope $= 3$; $(1, 1)$

12. slope $= \frac{1}{5}$; $(-2, 2)$

13. slope $= -2$; $(4, 7)$

14. slope $= -\frac{3}{7}$; $(-6, 1)$

15. POINTS What point is 3 units right and 5 units down from $(-6, -2)$?

16. **ERROR ANALYSIS** Describe and correct the error made in finding the slope of the line.

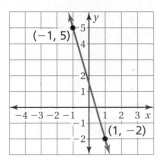

17. **RACING** The bankings of two race tracks are shown.

    a. What is the slope of each track?

    b. Which track has the steeper slope?

    c. Why are the tracks sloped and not flat?

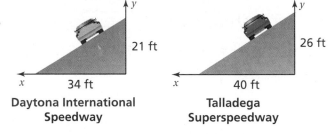

Daytona International Speedway

Talladega Superspeedway

18. **SKIING** What is the slope of the ski hill?

19. **ROADWAY** A construction company is hired to build the roadway shown at the right.

    a. The gradient of a hill can be calculated by converting its slope to a percent. What is the gradient of the roadway?

    b. The gradient of the new roadway cannot exceed 18%. What changes could you make to accommodate this restriction?

20. **Reasoning** A line has a slope of 0.5 and passes through the point $(-4, 5)$. Does the line also pass through the point $(2, 7)$? Explain.

Fair Game Review What you learned in previous grades & lessons

Solve. *(Section 2.6)*

21. $4x - 8 = -24$

22. $2x - 19 = 5$

23. $15 - 3x = -6$

24. **MULTIPLE CHOICE** What is the solution of the equation? *(Section B.1)*

$$6[4(3 + x) - 14] + 2^2 = 0$$

A $\frac{1}{2}$ B $\frac{1}{3}$ C $\frac{4}{3}$ D $\frac{5}{3}$

Essential Question
How can you describe the graph of an equation of the form $y = mx + b$?

The Meaning of a Word ● Function

Your score on a test is usually a **function** of how much you study.
If you study a lot, your score is usually high.
If you study a little, your score is usually low.

1 ACTIVITY: Using an Input-Output Table

Work with a partner.

a. Copy and complete the input-output table for the equation $y = -\frac{1}{2}x + 2$.

Input, x	−3	−2	−1	0	1	2	3
Output, y							

b. Plot the points from the table.

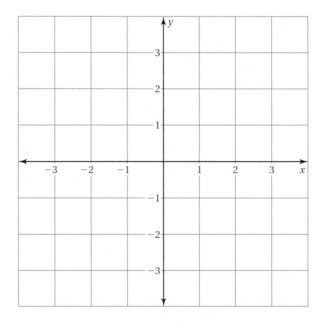

c. Describe the pattern of the points. Draw a graph that represents the pattern.

d. Choose three values of x that are not in the table. Find their corresponding y-values and plot the points. Do the points lie on the graph you made in part (c)?

Inductive Reasoning

Work with a partner. Sketch the graph of each equation. Then copy and complete the table.

Equation	Description of Graph	Point of Intersection with y-axis	Slope of Graph
2. $y = -\dfrac{1}{2}x + 2$	Line	$(0, 2)$	$-\dfrac{1}{2}$
3. $y = -x + 2$			
4. $y = -x + 1$			
5. $y = -\dfrac{1}{2}x + 1$			
6. $y = x + 1$			
7. $y = x - 1$			
8. $y = \dfrac{1}{2}x - 1$			
9. $y = \dfrac{1}{2}x + 1$			
10. $y = 2x + 1$			
11. $y = 2x - 2$			
12. $y = -2x + 3$			

What Is Your Answer?

13. **IN YOUR OWN WORDS** How can you describe the graph of an equation of the form $y = mx + b$?

    a. How does the value of m affect the graph?

    b. How does the value of b affect the graph?

    c. Test your answers to parts (a) and (b) with three equations that are not in the table.

14. Why is an equation of the form $y = mx + b$ called a linear function? What does the word *linear* mean? What does the word *function* mean?

Practice

Use what you learned about linear functions to complete Exercises 12–17 on page A40.

A **linear function** is a function whose graph is a line. The **y-intercept** is the *y*-coordinate of the point where the line crosses the *y*-axis.

Key Vocabulary
linear function,
   p. A38
y-intercept, p. A38
slope-intercept form,
   p. A38

Key Idea

Slope-Intercept Form

Words   A linear function written in the form $y = mx + b$ is in
slope-intercept form. The graph of the function is a line
whose slope is m and whose *y*-intercept is b.

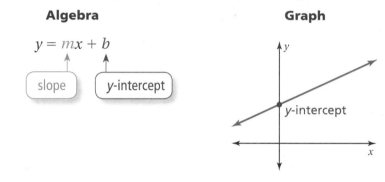

Algebra   **Graph**

$y = mx + b$

slope   *y*-intercept

EXAMPLE 1   **Identifying Slopes and y-Intercepts**

Find the slope and *y*-intercept of the graph of each function.

a. $y = -x - 5$

$y = -1x + (-5)$ Write in slope-intercept form.

∴ The slope is -1 and the *y*-intercept is -5.

Common Error

The *y*-intercept of
$y = -x - 5$ is not 5.
Be sure to write
equations in the form
$y = mx + b$.

b. $y - 2 = -\dfrac{1}{3}x$

$y = -\dfrac{1}{3}x + 2$ Add 2 to each side.

∴ The slope is $-\dfrac{1}{3}$ and the *y*-intercept is 2.

c. $4y - 5x = 12$

$4y = 5x + 12$ Add 5*x* to each side.

$y = \dfrac{5}{4}x + 3$ Divide each side by 4.

∴ The slope is $\dfrac{5}{4}$ and the *y*-intercept is 3.

On Your Own

Now You're Ready
Exercises 6–11

Find the slope and y-intercept of the graph of the linear function.

1. $y = -3x + 10$

2. $-5y + x = 25$

EXAMPLE 2 **Graphing Lines Using Slope-Intercept Form**

a. Graph $y = -2x + 3$.

Step 1: Find the slope and y-intercept.

$$y = {}^-2x + 3$$

slope   y-intercept

Step 2: The y-intercept is 3. So, plot (0, 3).

Step 3: Find the rise and the run.

$$\text{slope} = \frac{\text{rise}}{\text{run}} = \frac{-2}{1}$$

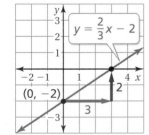

Step 4: Plot the point that is 1 unit right and 2 units down from (0, 3).

Step 5: Draw a line through the two points.

b. Graph $y = \frac{2}{3}x - 2$

Step 1: Find the slope and y-intercept.

$$y = \frac{2}{3}x + (-2)$$

slope   y-intercept

Step 2: The y-intercept is −2. So, plot (0, −2).

Step 3: Find the rise and the run.

$$\text{slope} = \frac{\text{rise}}{\text{run}} = \frac{2}{3}$$

Step 4: Plot the point that is 3 units right and 2 units up from (0, −2).

Step 5: Draw a line through the two points.

On Your Own

Now You're Ready
Exercises 12–23

Graph the linear function using slope-intercept form.

3. $y = -x - 1$

4. $y = \frac{3}{2}x - 5$

Vocabulary and Concept Check

1. **VOCABULARY** What is the y-intercept of a line?

2. **WRITING** Why is $y = mx + b$ called the slope-intercept form of a line?

MATCHING Match the linear function with its graph.

3. $y = 2x$

4. $y = 2x - 1$

5. $y = -2x + 1$

 Practice and Problem Solving

Find the slope and y-intercept of the graph of the linear function.

① 6. $y = 4x + 1$

7. $y = -2x + 6$

8. $y = \frac{2}{3}x - 3$

9. $5x + y = 3$

10. $9x - 3y = 24$

11. $-4y + 10x = 36$

Graph the linear function using slope-intercept form.

② 12. $y = 3x - 3$

13. $y = 2x + 5$

14. $y = -x + 4$

15. $y = -\frac{3}{2}x - 1$

16. $y = -\frac{1}{5}x + 2$

17. $y = \frac{1}{4}x - 4$

18. $y = -4x + 1$

19. $y = 6x - 5$

20. $y = -3x - 2$

21. $5y - 4x = -15$

22. $5x + 3y = -6$

23. $3x + 4y = 12$

24. **ERROR ANALYSIS** Describe and correct the error in graphing the linear function $y = \frac{1}{4}x - 1$.

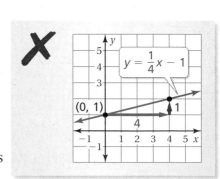

25. **CARTOONIST** The number c of cartoons a cartoonist plans to complete by the nth day of the month is given by $c = 24 + 4n$. What does the y-intercept represent?

Write an equation of the linear function in slope-intercept form.

26.

27.

28.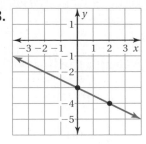

29. **PERIMETER** The perimeter of the rectangle can be modeled by the linear function $y = 2x + 7$.

3.5
x

    a. Find the slope and y-intercept of the graph of the linear function.

    b. Graph the linear function.

    c. Is it possible for the rectangle to have a perimeter of 5 units? Examine the graph and explain.

30. **ESCALATOR** To get from the second floor to the first floor in a mall, you can either ride the escalator or take the stairs. The graph shows the vertical distance y (in feet) you have left to travel on the escalator after x seconds.

    a. Write an equation in slope-intercept form of the linear function representing the amount of time you have left on the escalator.

    b. How long does it take to ride the escalator from the second floor to the first floor?

    c. The equation $y = -1.6x + 20$ represents the vertical distance y (in feet) you have left to travel on the stairs after x seconds. How much time do you save by taking the stairs?

31. **Reasoning** Find the slope and y-intercept of the graph of $Ax + By = C$ in terms of A, B, and C.

Fair Game Review   What you learned in previous grades & lessons

Solve the equation. *(Section B.2)*

32. $3x - 6 = 9 - 2x$

33. $5 - 8v = 3v - \dfrac{1}{2}$

34. $-5w - 4 = 4(w - 7)$

35. **MULTIPLE CHOICE** Which does *not* describe the sum of the sections of a circle graph? *(Section 8.3)*

    (A) $\dfrac{1}{2}$ (B) 1   (C) 100%   (D) 360°

Check It Out
Progress Check
BigIdeasMath.com

Graph the line with the given slope that passes through the given point. *(Section B.4)*

1. slope $= -3$; $(2, 4)$

2. slope $= \dfrac{2}{3}$; $(-1, 0)$

3. Find the slope of the line. *(Section B.4)*

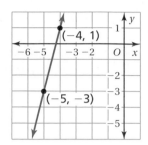

Find the slope and *y*-intercept of the graph of the linear function. *(Section B.5)*

4. $y = 2x + 9$

5. $y = -5x + 4$

6. $y = \dfrac{3}{5}x - 6$

7. $3x - y = 8$

8. $2x + 8y = -16$

9. $4x - 3y = 15$

Graph the linear function using slope-intercept form. *(Section B.5)*

10. $y = -x + 2$

11. $y = \dfrac{3}{2}x - 4$

12. $-x + 3y = 3$

13. PERIMETER The perimeter of the rectangle can be modeled by the linear function $y = 2x + 11$. *(Section B.5)*

   a. Find the slope and *y*-intercept of the graph of the linear function.

   b. Graph the linear function.

   c. Is it possible for the rectangle to have a perimeter of 9 units? Explain.

5.5

x

14. RAMP What is the slope of the skateboard ramp? What is the slope of the skateboard ramp if the length is doubled? *(Section B.4)*

2 ft

4 ft

B Appendix Review

Check It Out
Vocabulary Help
BigIdeasMath com

Review Key Vocabulary

slope, *p. A32*   run, *p. A32*   *y*-intercept, *p. A38*
rise, *p. A32*   linear function, *p. A38*   slope-intercept form, *p. A38*

Review Examples and Exercises

B.1 **Solving Multi-Step Equations**   *(pp. A10–A15)*

a. Solve $-5x + 9x + 30 = 14$. Check your solution.

$-5x + 9x + 30 =$	14	Write the equation.
$4x + 30 =$	14	Combine like terms.
$\underline{-\ 30}$	$\underline{-\ 30}$	Subtract 30 from each side.
$4x =$	-16	Simplify.
$\dfrac{4x}{4} =$	$\dfrac{-16}{4}$	Divide each side by 4.
$x =$	-4	Simplify.

Check

$$-5x + 9x + 30 = 14$$
$$-5(-4) + 9(-4) + 30 \overset{?}{=} 14$$
$$20 - 36 + 30 \overset{?}{=} 14$$
$$14 = 14 \ \checkmark$$

⋮• The solution is $x = -4$.

b. Solve $2(n + 5) - 3 = 9$. Check your solution.

$2(n + 5) - 3 =$	9	Write the equation.
$2(n) + 2(5) - 3 =$	9	Use Distributive Property.
$2n + 10 - 3 =$	9	Multiply.
$2n + 7 =$	9	Subtract.
$\underline{-\ 7}$	$\underline{-\ 7}$	Subtract 7 from each side.
$2n =$	2	Simplify.
$\dfrac{2n}{2} =$	$\dfrac{2}{2}$	Divide each side by 2.
$n =$	1	Simplify.

Check

$$2(n + 5) - 3 = 9$$
$$2(1 + 5) - 3 \overset{?}{=} 9$$
$$2(1) + 2(5) - 3 \overset{?}{=} 9$$
$$2 + 10 - 3 \overset{?}{=} 9$$
$$9 = 9 \ \checkmark$$

⋮• The solution is $n = 1$.

Exercises

Solve the equation. Check your solution.

1. $-4x + 6x - 15 = -25$ **2.** $11k - 8k - 3 = 9$

3. $3(2n - 7) - 3 = 36$ **4.** $7 - 1.5(4 - 10d) = 31$

Solving Equations with Variables on Both Sides *(pp. A16–A21)*

Solve $z - 42 = -6z$. Check your solution.

$$z - 42 = -6z \qquad \text{Write the equation.}$$

$$\underline{-z \qquad\qquad -z} \qquad \text{Subtract } z \text{ from each side.}$$

$$-42 = -7z \qquad \text{Simplify.}$$

$$\frac{-42}{-7} = \frac{-7z}{-7} \qquad \text{Divide each side by } -7.$$

$$6 = z \qquad \text{Simplify.}$$

Check

$$z - 42 = -6z$$

$$6 - 42 \overset{?}{=} -6(6)$$

$$-36 = -36 \checkmark$$

∴ The solution is $z = 6$.

Exercises

Solve the equation. Check your solution.

5. $3x = x - 18$

6. $-5n + 4 = 24 - n$

7. $8s = 3(s + 5)$

8. $-2(1 - 2a) = 4\left(\dfrac{5}{4}a - 2\right)$

9. $5w + 6 = -4 - 5w$

10. $-6(m + 2) = m - 2$

Solving Equations Using Tables and Graphs *(pp. A22–A27)*

Use a table to solve $7x = 6x + 1$. Check your solution.

Find the x-value that makes $7x$ equal to $6x + 1$.

Try different values of x.

x	$7x$	$6x + 1$
-1	$7(-1) = -7$	$6(-1) + 1 = -5$
0	$7(0) = 0$	$6(0) + 1 = 1$
1	$7(1) = 7$	$6(1) + 1 = 7$

Check

$$7x = \quad 6x + 1$$

$$\underline{-6x \quad\; -6x}$$

$$x = 1 \checkmark$$

Each side of the equation equals 7 when $x = 1$.

∴ The solution is $x = 1$.

Exercises

Use a table to solve the equation. Check your solution.

11. $6x - 4 = 8x$

12. $x + 7 = 3x + 1$

13. $-13 - 2b = b - 7$

14. $4 + 4m = m + 13$

B.4 **Slope of a Line** *(pp. A30–A35)*

Find the slope of the line.

$$\text{slope} = \frac{\text{rise}}{\text{run}} \qquad \text{Write formula for slope.}$$

$$= \frac{1}{3} \qquad \text{Substitute.}$$

∴ The slope is $\frac{1}{3}$.

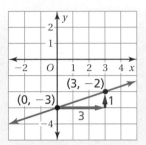

Exercises

Find the slope of the line.

15.

16.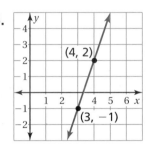

B.5 **Linear Functions** *(pp. A36–A41)*

Find the slope and y-intercept of the graph of the function $3x + 4y = 8$.

$3x + 4y = 8$ Write the equation.

$4y = -3x + 8$ Subtract $3x$ from each side.

$y = -\dfrac{3}{4}x + 2$ Divide each side by 4.

∴ The slope is $-\dfrac{3}{4}$ and the y-intercept is 2.

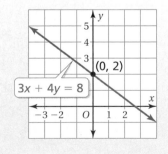

Exercises

17. Find the slope and y-intercept of the graph of the function $5x + 5y = 10$.

18. Graph the linear function $y = 4x - 1$ using slope-intercept form.

B Appendix Test

Solve the equation. Check your solution.

1. $-3x + 6x - 17 = 10$

2. $-7x - 5x + 2 = -22$

3. $2(k + 4) - 6 = -12$

4. $-3y = 8 - y$

5. Use a table to solve $5x + 2 = 4x$. Check your solution.

6. Use the graph to solve the equation $x + 6 = -2x - 9$. Check your solution.

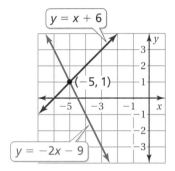

7. Find the slope of the line.

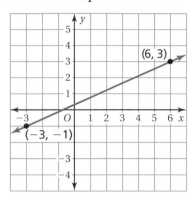

Graph the line with the given slope that passes through the given point.

8. slope $= 2$; $(-3, 0)$

9. slope $= -\dfrac{3}{4}$; $(1, 2)$

Find the slope and *y*-intercept of the graph of the linear function.

10. $y = 3x - 6$

11. $y = -2x + 3$

Graph the linear function using slope-intercept form.

12. $y = -x + 3$

13. $2x + 6y = 12$

14. DRIVING Two cars are driving on the same highway. Car A is 5 miles ahead of Car B and is traveling at a speed of 45 miles per hour. Car B is traveling at a speed of 55 miles per hour. How many minutes will it take for Car B to catch up with Car A?

15. RAMP What is the slope of the accessibility ramp?

Photo Credits

Selected Answers

Section 1.1

Integers and Absolute Value
(pages 6 and 7)

1. $9, -1, 15$

3. -6; All of the other expressions are equal to 6.

5. 6   **7.** 10   **9.** 13   **11.** 12   **13.** 8   **15.** 18

17. 45   **19.** 125   **21.** $|-4| < 7$ **23.** $|-4| > -6$ **25.** $|5| = |-5|$

27. Because $|-5| = 5$, the statement is incorrect. $|-5| > 4$

29. $-8, 5$ **31.** $-7, -6, |5|, |-6|, 8$ **33.** $-17, |-11|, |20|, 21, |-34|$

35. -4

37. a. MATE   **b.** TEAM

39. $n \geq 0$ **41.** The number closer to 0 is the greater integer.

43. a. Player 3   **b.** Player 2   **c.** Player 1

45. false; The absolute value of zero is zero, which is neither positive nor negative.

47. 144   **49.** 3170

Section 1.2

Adding Integers
(pages 12 and 13)

1. Change the sign of the integer.

3. positive; 20 has the greater absolute value and is positive.

5. negative; The common sign is a negative sign.

7. false; A positive integer and its absolute value are equal, not opposites.

9. -10 **11.** 7   **13.** 0   **15.** 10

17. -7 **19.** -11 **21.** -4 **23.** -34

25. -10 and -10 are not opposites. $-10 + (-10) = -20$

27. \$48   **29.** -27 **31.** 21   **33.** -85

35. Use the Associate Property to add 13 and -13 first. -8

37. Use the Commutative Property to switch two terms. Then use the Associative Property to add 7 and -7 first. -12

39. Use the Commutative Property to switch the order of two terms. Then use the Associative Property to add the two positive numbers first. 11

41. -13 **43.** *Sample answer:* $-26 + 1; -12 + (-13)$

45. $b = 2$ **47.** $6 + (-3) + 8$

49. Find the number in each row or column that already has two numbers in it before guessing.

51. 8   **53.** 183

Section 1.3

Subtracting Integers
(pages 18 and 19)

1. You add the integer's opposite.

3. What is 3 less than -2?; -5; 5

5. C

7. B

9. 13

11. -5

13. -10

15. 3

17. 17

19. 1

21. -22

23. -20

25. $-3 - 9$

27. 6

29. 9

31. 7

33. $m = 14$

35. $c = 15$

37. 2

39. 3

41. *Sample answer:* $x = -2, y = -1$; $x = -3, y = -2$

43. sometimes; It's positive only if the first integer is greater.

45. always; It's always positive because the first integer is always greater.

47. all values of a and b

49. when $|a| > |b|$ or $|a| = |b|$

51. -45

53. 468

55. 2378

Section 1.4

Multiplying Integers
(pages 26 and 27)

1. a. They are the same.   **b.** They are different.

3. negative; different signs

5. negative; different signs

7. false; The product of the first two negative integers is positive. The product of the positive result and the third negative integer is negative.

9. -21

11. 12

13. 27

15. 12

17. 0

19. -30

21. 78

23. 121

25. $-240,000$

27. 54

29. -105

31. 0

33. -1

35. -36

37. 54

39. The answer should be negative. $-10^2 = -(10 \cdot 10) = -100$

41. 32

43. $-7500, 37,500$

45. -12

47. a.

Month	Price of Skates	
June	165	= $165
July	$165 + (-12)$	= $153
August	$165 + 2(-12)$	= $141
September	$165 + 3(-12)$	= $129

b. The price drops $12 every month.

c. no; yes; In August you have $135 but the cost is $141. In September you have $153 and the cost is only $129.

49. 3

51. 14

53. D

Section 1.5

Dividing Integers
(pages 32 and 33)

1. They have the same sign. They have different signs. The dividend is zero.

3. *Sample answer:* $-4, 2$ **5.** negative **7.** negative

9. -3 **11.** 3 **13.** 0 **15.** -6 **17.** 7 **19.** -10

21. undefined **23.** 12

25. The quotient should be 0. $0 \div (-5) = 0$ **27.** 15 pages

29. -8 **31.** 65 **33.** 5

35. 4 **37.** -400 ft/min **39.** 5

41. *Sample answer:* $-20, -15, -10, -5, 0$; Start with -10, then pair -15 with -5 and -20 with 0.

43.

45. B

Section 1.6

The Coordinate Plane
(pages 38 and 39)

1. 4

3. $(2, -2)$ is in Quadrant IV, $(-2, 2)$ is in Quadrant II.

5. $(3, 1)$ **7.** $(-2, 4)$ **9.** $(2, -2)$ **11.** $(-4, 2)$ **13.** $(4, 0)$

15–25. See graph below.

15. Quadrant I

17. y-axis

19. Quadrant IV

21. Quadrant II

23. Quadrant III

25. Quadrant II

27. The numbers are reversed. To plot $(4, 5)$, start at $(0, 0)$ and move 4 units right and 5 units up.

29. $(-2, 1)$ **31.** sometimes; It is true only for $(0, 0)$.

33. always; The x-coordinate of a point in Quadrant II is negative, and so is the y-coordinate of a point in Quadrant IV.

35. Flamingo Café

Hint

37. Because the rainforest is in Quadrant IV, the x-coordinate of the point will be positive and the y-coordinate of the point will be negative.

39. $(2, 2)$

41–43. See graph below.

41. Quadrant II

43. x-axis

45. $-\dfrac{16}{2} < -\dfrac{12}{3}$

47. $3.45 > 3\dfrac{3}{8}$

Rational Numbers
(pages 54 and 55)

1. A number is rational if it can be written as $\dfrac{a}{b}$ where a and b are integers and $b \neq 0$.

3. rational numbers, integers

5. rational numbers, integers, whole numbers

7. repeating

9. terminating

11. 0.875

13. $-0.\overline{7}$

15. $1.8\overline{3}$

17. $-5.58\overline{3}$

19. The bar should be over both digits to the right of the decimal point. $-\dfrac{7}{11} = -0.\overline{63}$

21. $\dfrac{9}{20}$

23. $-\dfrac{39}{125}$

25. $-1\dfrac{16}{25}$

27. $-12\dfrac{81}{200}$

29. $-2.5, -1.1, -\dfrac{4}{5}, 0.8, \dfrac{9}{5}$

31. $-\dfrac{9}{4}, -0.75, -\dfrac{6}{10}, \dfrac{5}{3}, 2.1$

33. $-2.4, -2.25, -\dfrac{11}{5}, \dfrac{15}{10}, 1.6$

35. spotted turtle

37. $-1.82 < -1.81$

39. $-4\dfrac{6}{10} > -4.65$

41. $-2\dfrac{13}{16} < -2\dfrac{11}{14}$

43. Michelle

45. No; The base of the skating pool is at -10 feet, which is deeper than $-9\dfrac{5}{6}$ feet.

47. **a.** when a is negative

　　b. when a and b have the same sign, $a \neq 0 \neq b$

49. $\dfrac{7}{30}$

50. 21.15

Adding and Subtracting Rational Numbers
(pages 60 and 61)

1. Because $|-8.46| > |5.31|$, subtract $|5.31|$ from $|-8.46|$ and the sign is negative.

3. What is 3.9 less than -4.8?; -8.7; -0.9

5. $-\dfrac{5}{14}$

7. $2\dfrac{3}{10}$

9. -0.9

11. 1.844

13. $1\dfrac{1}{2}$

15. $\dfrac{1}{18}$

17. $-18\dfrac{13}{24}$

19. -2.6

21. 14.963

23. $\dfrac{3}{8} - \dfrac{5}{6} = -\dfrac{11}{24}$

25. $\dfrac{1}{18}$

27. $-3\dfrac{9}{10}$

29. No, the cook needs $\dfrac{1}{12}$ cup more.

Hint

31–33. Subtract the least number from the greatest number.

35. $-\dfrac{n}{4}$

37. $-\dfrac{b}{24}$

39. 35.88

41. $8\dfrac{2}{3}$

43. C

Multiplying and Dividing Rational Numbers
(pages 66 and 67)

1. The same rules for signs of integers are applied to rational numbers.

3. $-\dfrac{1}{3}$

5. $-\dfrac{3}{7}$

7. negative

9. positive

11. $-\dfrac{2}{3}$

13. $-\dfrac{1}{100}$

15. $2\dfrac{5}{14}$

17. $3.\overline{63}$

19. -6

21. -2.5875

23. $\dfrac{1}{3}$

25. $2\dfrac{1}{2}$

27. $-4\dfrac{17}{27}$

29. 0.025

31. 47.43

33. -0.064

35. The wrong fraction was inverted.

$$-\dfrac{1}{4} \div \dfrac{3}{2} = -\dfrac{1}{4} \times \dfrac{2}{3}$$

$$= -\dfrac{2}{12}$$

$$= -\dfrac{1}{6}$$

37. 8 packages

39. 1.3

41. $-4\dfrac{14}{15}$

43. $-1\dfrac{11}{36}$

45. $191\dfrac{11}{12}$ yd

47. How many spaces are between the boards?

49. a. -2, 4, -8, 16, -32, 64

b. When -2 is raised to an odd power, the product is negative. When -2 is raised to an even power, the product is positive.

c. negative

51. -5.4

53. $-8\dfrac{5}{18}$

Section 2.4 — Solving Equations Using Addition or Subtraction (pages 74 and 75)

1. Subtraction Property of Equality

3. No, $m = -8$ not -2 in the first equation.

5. $a = 19$

7. $k = -20$

9. $c = 3.6$

11. $q = -\frac{1}{6}$

13. $g = -10$

15. $y = -2.08$

17. $q = -\frac{7}{18}$

19. $w = -1\frac{13}{24}$

21. The 8 should have been subtracted rather than added.

$$x + 8 = 10$$
$$\underline{-8 \quad -8}$$
$$x = 2$$

23. $c + 10 = 3;\ c = -7$

25. $p - 6 = -14;\ p = -8$

27. $P + 2.54 = 1.38;\ -\$1.16$ million

29. $x + 8 = 12;\ 4$ cm

31. $x + 22.7 = 34.6;\ 11.9$ ft

33. Because your first jump is higher, your second jump went a farther distance than your first jump.

35. $m + 30.3 + 40.8 = 180;\ 108.9°$

37. -9

39. $6, -6$

41. -56

43. -9

45. B

Section 2.5 — Solving Equations Using Multiplication or Division (pages 80 and 81)

1. Multiplication is the inverse operation of division, so it can undo division.

3. dividing by 5

5. multiplying by -8

7. $h = 5$

9. $n = -14$

11. $m = -2$

13. $x = -8$

15. $p = -8$

17. $n = 8$

19. $g = -16$

21. $f = 6\frac{3}{4}$

23. They should divide by -4.2.

$$-4.2x = 21$$
$$\frac{-4.2x}{-4.2} = \frac{21}{-4.2}$$
$$x = -5$$

25. $\frac{2}{5}x = \frac{3}{20};\ x = \frac{3}{8}$

27. $\frac{x}{-1.5} = 21;\ x = -31.5$

29. $\frac{x}{30} = 12\frac{3}{5};\ 378$ ft

31–33. Sample answers are given.

31. a. $-2x = 4.4$ **b.** $\frac{x}{1.1} = -2$

33. a. $4x = -5$ **b.** $\frac{x}{5} = -\frac{1}{4}$

35. $-1.26n = -10.08;\ 8$ days

37. -50 ft

39. $-5, 5$

41. -7

43. 12

45. B

Solving Two-Step Equations
(pages 86 and 87)

1. Eliminate the constants on the side with the variable. Then solve for the variable using either division or multiplication.

3. D

5. A

7. $b = -3$

9. $t = -4$

11. $g = 4.22$

13. $p = 3\dfrac{1}{2}$

15. $h = -3.5$

17. $y = -6.4$

19. Each side should be divided by -3, not 3.

$$-3x + 2 = -7$$
$$-3x = -9$$
$$\frac{-3x}{-3} = \frac{-9}{-3}$$
$$x = 3$$

21. $a = 1\dfrac{1}{3}$

23. $b = 13\dfrac{1}{2}$

25. $v = -\dfrac{1}{30}$

27. $2.5 + 2.25x = 9.25$; 3 games

29. $v = -5$

31. $d = -12$

33. $m = -9$

35. *Sample answer:* You travel halfway up a ladder. Then you climb down two feet and are 8 feet above the ground. How long is the ladder? $x = 20$

37. the initial fee

39. Find the number of insects remaining and then find the number of insects you caught.

41. decrease the length by 10 cm; $2(25 + x) + 2(12) = 54$

43. $-6\dfrac{2}{3}$

45. -6.2

Section 3.1

Ratios and Rates
(pages 102 and 103)

1. It has a denominator of 1.

3. *Sample answer:* A basketball player runs 10 ft down the court in 2 sec.

5. $0.10 per fl oz

7. $72

9. 840 MB

11. $\dfrac{5}{9}$

13. $\dfrac{7}{3}$

15. $\dfrac{4}{3}$

17. 60 mi/h

19. $2.40 per lb

21. 54 words per min

23. 90 calories per serving

25. 4.5 servings per package

27. 4.8 MB per min

29. **a.** It costs $122 for 4 tickets.

b. $30.50 per ticket

c. $305

31. The 9-pack is the best buy at $2.55 per container.

33. Try searching for "fire hydrant colors."

35–37.

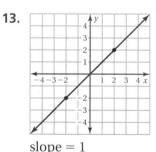

Section 3.2 Slope
(pages 108 and 109)

1. yes; Slope is the rate of change of a line.

3. 5; A ramp with a slope of 5 increases 5 units vertically for every 1 unit horizontally. A ramp with a slope of $\frac{1}{5}$ increases 1 unit vertically for every 5 units horizontally.

5. $\frac{3}{2}$

7. 1

9. $\frac{4}{5}$

11.

slope = 32.5

13.

slope = 1

15. The change in y should be in the numerator. The change in x should be in the denominator.

Slope $= \frac{5}{4}$

17. **a.**

b. 2.5; Every millimeter represents 2.5 miles.

c. 120 mi

d. 90 mm

19. $y = 6$

21. <

23. $-\frac{4}{5}$

25. 3

Proportions
(pages 114 and 115)

1. Both ratios are equal.

3. *Sample answer:* $\frac{6}{10}, \frac{12}{20}$

5. yes **7.** no **9.** yes **11.** no **13.** yes

15. yes **17.** yes **19.** no **21.** yes

23. yes; Both can do 45 sit-ups per minute.

25. yes **27.** yes **29.** yes; They are both $\frac{4}{5}$.

31. a. Pitcher 3 **b.** Pitcher 2 and Pitcher 4

33. a. no

b. *Sample answer:* If the collection has 50 quarters and 30 dimes, when 10 of each coin are added, the new ratio of quarters to dimes is 3:2.

35. -13 **37.** -18 **39.** D

Writing Proportions
(pages 120 and 121)

1. You can use the columns or the rows of the table to write a proportion.

3. *Sample answer:* $\frac{x}{12} = \frac{5}{6}$; $x = 10$

5. $\frac{x}{50} = \frac{78}{100}$

7. $\frac{x}{150} = \frac{96}{100}$

9. $\frac{n \text{ winners}}{85 \text{ entries}} = \frac{34 \text{ winners}}{170 \text{ entries}}$

11. $\frac{100 \text{ meters}}{x \text{ seconds}} = \frac{200 \text{ meters}}{22.4 \text{ seconds}}$

13. $\frac{\$24}{3 \text{ shirts}} = \frac{c}{7 \text{ shirts}}$

15. $\frac{5 \text{ 6th grade swimmers}}{16 \text{ swimmers}} = \frac{s \text{ 6th grade swimmers}}{80 \text{ swimmers}}$

17. $y = 16$ **19.** $c = 24$ **21.** $g = 14$

23. $\frac{1}{200} = \frac{19.5}{x}$; Dimensions for the model are in the numerators and the corresponding dimensions for the actual space shuttle are in the denominators.

25. Draw a diagram of the given information.

27. $x = 9$

29. $x = 140$

Solving Proportions
(pages 126 and 127)

1. mental math; Multiplication Property of Equality; Cross Products Property

3. yes; Both cross products give the equation $3x = 60$.

5. $h = 80$ 7. $n = 15$ 9. $y = 7\frac{1}{3}$ 11. $k = 5.6$

13. $n = 10$ 15. $d = 5.76$ 17. $m = 20$ 19. $d = 15$

21. $k = 5.4$ 23. 108 pens   25. $x = 1.5$ 27. $k = 4$

29. $769.50   31. **a.** 16 mo   **b.** 40 mo

33. Make a table to solve the problem.

35. $2; \dfrac{1/2}{1/4} = \dfrac{1}{2} \times \dfrac{4}{1} = 2$

37. 6400   39. 7920

Converting Measures Between Systems
(pages 134 and 135)

1. To convert between measurements, multiply by the ratio of the given relationship such that the desired unit is in the numerator, or set up and solve a proportion using the given relationship as one of the ratios.

3. Find the number of inches in 5 cm; 5 cm ≈ 1.97 in.; 5 in. ≈ 12.7 cm

5. >   7. >   9. <   11. 9.5

13. 21.08   15. 3.13   17. 121.92   19. 64.96

21. 2.38   23. about 584 km   25. >   27. >

29. <   31. 72   33. 4.72   35. 77,400 kg

37. A kilometer is shorter than a mile. So, the given speed when converted should be greater than 110.

39. about 3.7 gal

41.

slope $= \dfrac{3}{2}$

43. C

1. As one quantity increases, the other quantity increases.

3. the second graph; The points do not lie on a line.

5. no; The line does not pass through the origin.

7. yes; The points lie on a line that passes through the origin.

9. no; The line does not pass through the origin.

11. yes; The line passes through the origin.

13. yes; The line passes through the origin.

15. yes; The equation can be written as $y = kx$.

17. no; The equation cannot be written as $y = kx$.

19. yes; The equation can be written as $y = kx$.

21. no; The equation cannot be written as $y = kx$.

23. yes

25. $y = 5x$

27. $y = 24x$

29. $y = \dfrac{9}{8}x$

Hint

31. You can draw the ramp on a coordinate plane and write a direct variation equation.

33. no

35. Every graph of direct variation is a line; however, not all lines show direct variation because the line must pass through the origin.

37. $y = -60$

39. $d = -59\dfrac{1}{2}$

1. As x increases, y decreases.

3. *Sample answer:* The wingspan of a bird varies inversely with its wing beat frequency.

5. inverse variation; The equation can be written as $y = \dfrac{k}{x}$.

7. direct variation; The equation can be written as $y = kx$.

9. neither; The equation cannot be written as $y = kx$ or $y = \dfrac{k}{x}$.

11. direct variation; The equation can be written as $y = kx$.

13. inverse variation; The equation can be written as $y = \dfrac{k}{x}$.

15. neither; The equation cannot be written as $y = kx$ or $y = \dfrac{k}{x}$.

17.

direct variation

19.

inverse variation

21. inverse variation; The equation can be written as $y = \dfrac{k}{x}$.

23. $y = \dfrac{4}{x}$

25. **a.** yes; $t = \dfrac{12}{s}$ **b.** 3 h

27. decreases

29. 88

31. 63

33. yes

35. yes

37. B

Section 4.1

The Percent Equation
(pages 162 and 163)

1. A part of the whole is equal to a percent times the whole.

3. 55 is 20% of what number?; 275; 11

5. 37.5%

7. 84

9. 64

11. $45 = p \cdot 60$; 75%

13. $a = 0.32 \cdot 25$; 8

15. $12 = 0.005 \cdot w$; 2400

17. $102 = 1.2 \cdot w$; 85

19. 30 represents the part of the whole.

$30 = 0.6 \cdot w$

$50 = w$

21. $5400

23. 26 years old

25. 56 signers

27. If the percent is less than 100%, the percent of a number is less than the number. If the percent is equal to 100%, the percent of a number will equal the number. If the percent is greater than 100%, the percent of a number is greater than the number.

29. Remember when writing a proportion that either the units are the same on each side of the proportion, or the numerators have the same units and the denominators have the same units.

31. 92%

33. 0.88

35. 0.36

Percents of Increase and Decrease
(pages 168 and 169)

1. If the original amount decreases, the percent of change is a percent of decrease. If the original amount increases, the percent of change is a percent of increase.

3. The new amount is now 0.

5. decrease; 66.7%   7. increase; 225%   9. decrease; 12.5%   11. decrease; 37.5%

13. 10 m   15. 37 points   17. 153 students   19. 42.16 kg

21. They should have subtracted 10 in the last step because 25 is decreased by 40%.

    40% of 25 = 0.4 • 25 = 10

    So, 25 − 10 = 15.

23. increase; 100%   25. increase; 133.3%

27. Increasing 20 to 40 is the same as increasing 20 by 20. So, it is a 100% increase. Decreasing 40 to 20 is the same as decreasing 40 by one-half of 40. So, it is a 50% decrease.

29. **a.** 100% increase   **b.** 300% increase

31. less than; *Sample answer:* Let x represent the number. A 10% increase is equal to $x + 0.1x$, or $1.1x$. A 10% decrease of this new number is equal to $1.1x − 0.1(1.1x)$, or $0.99x$. Because $0.99x < x$, the result is less than the original number.

33. 10 girls   35. 35%   37. 56.25

Discounts and Markups
(pages 176 and 177)

1. *Sample answer:* Multiply the original price by 100% − 25% = 75% to find the sale price.

3. **a.** 6% tax on a discounted price; The discounted price is less, so the tax is less.

   b. 30% markup on a $30 shirt; 30% of $30 is less than $30.

5. $35.70   7. $76.16   9. $53.33   11. $450   13. $172.40   15. 20%

17. no; Only the amount of markup should be in the numerator, $\dfrac{105 − 60}{60} = 0.75$.

    So, the markup is 75%.

19. $36

21. "Multiply $45.85 by 0.1" and "Multiply $45.85 by 0.9, then subtract from $45.85." Both will give the sale price of $4.59. The first method is easier because it is only one step.

23. no; $31.08   25. $30   27. 180   29. C

Section 4.4 — Simple Interest
(pages 182 and 183)

1. I = simple interest, P = principal, r = annual interest rate (in decimal form), t = time (in years)

3. You have to change 6% to a decimal and 8 months to years.

5. **a.** $300 **b.** $1800

7. **a.** $292.50 **b.** $2092.50

9. **a.** $308.20 **b.** $1983.20

11. **a.** $1722.24 **b.** $6922.24

13. 3% 15. 4% 17. 2 yr 19. 1.5 yr 21. $1440 23. 2 yr

25. $2720 27. $6700.80 29. $8500 31. 5.25% 33. 4 yr

35. 12.5 yr; Substitute $2000 for P and I, 0.08 for r, and solve for t.

37. Year 1 = $520; Year 2 = $540.80; Year 3 = $562.43

39. $n = 5$ 41. $z = 9$

Section 5.1 — Identifying Similar Figures
(pages 198 and 199)

1. They have the same measure.

3. *Sample answer:* A photograph of size 3 in. × 5 in. and another photograph of size 6 in. × 10 in.

5. $\angle A$ and $\angle W$, $\angle B$ and $\angle X$, $\angle C$ and $\angle Y$, $\angle D$ and $\angle Z$;
   Side AB and Side WX, Side BC and Side XY, Side CD and Side YZ, Side AD and Side WZ

7.   A and B; Corresponding side lengths are proportional and corresponding angles have the same measure.

9. similar; Corresponding angles have the same measure. Because $\frac{4}{6} = \frac{6}{9} = \frac{8}{12}$, the corresponding side lengths are proportional.

11. no 13. 48° 15. 42°

17. Simplify the ratios of length to width for each photo to see if any of the photos are similar.

19. yes; One could be a trapezoid and the other could be a parallelogram.

21. **a.** yes

   b. yes; It represents the fact that the sides are proportional because you can split the isosceles triangles into smaller right triangles that will be similar.

23. $\frac{16}{81}$ 25. $\frac{49}{16}$ 27. B

Perimeters and Areas of Similar Figures
(pages 204 and 205)

1. The ratio of the perimeters is equal to the ratio of the corresponding side lengths.

3. 120 in.^{2}; Because the ratio of the corresponding side lengths is $\frac{1}{2}$, the ratio of the areas is equal to $\left(\frac{1}{2}\right)^2$. To find the area, solve the proportion $\frac{30}{x} = \frac{1}{4}$.

5. $\frac{5}{8}$; $\frac{25}{64}$

7. $\frac{14}{9}$; $\frac{196}{81}$

9. perimeter triples

11. Area is 16 times larger.

13. 45 in.

15. false; $\dfrac{\text{Area of } \triangle ABC}{\text{Area of } \triangle DEF} = \left(\dfrac{AB}{DE}\right)^2$

17. 6300%; The ratio of the corresponding lengths is $\dfrac{15 \text{ in.}}{120 \text{ in.}} = \dfrac{1}{8}$. So, the ratio of the areas is $\dfrac{1}{64}$ and the area of the actual merry-go-round is 4928 square inches. The percent of increase is $\dfrac{4928 - 77}{77} = 63 = 6300\%$.

19. $\frac{3}{4}$

21. 25% increase

23. 42.7% decrease

Finding Unknown Measures in Similar Figures
(pages 210 and 211)

1. You can set up a proportion and solve for the unknown measure.

3. 15

5. 14.4

7. 8.4

9. 35 ft

11. 108 yd

13. 3 times

15. 12.5 bottles

17. 31.75

19. 3.88

21. 41.63

Scale Drawings
(pages 216 and 217)

1. A scale is the ratio that compares the measurements of the drawing or model with the actual measurements. A scale factor is a scale without any units.

3. Convert one of the lengths into the same units as the other length. Then, form the scale and simplify.

5. 10 ft by 10 ft

7. 112.5%

9. 50 mi

11. 110 mi

13. 15 in.

15. 21.6 yd

17. The 5 cm should be in the numerator.
$$\frac{1 \text{ cm}}{20 \text{ m}} = \frac{5 \text{ cm}}{x \text{ m}}$$
$$x = 100 \text{ m}$$

19. 2.4 cm; 1 cm : 10 mm

21. a. *Answer should include, but is not limited to:* Make sure words and picture match the product.

   b. Answers will vary.

23. Find the size of the object that would represent the model of the Sun.

25–27.

29. C

Section 5.5

Translations
(pages 224 and 225)

1. A

3. yes; Translate the letters T and O to the end.

5. no

7. yes

9. no

11. $A'(-3, 0)$, $B'(0, -1)$, $C'(1, -4)$, $D'(-3, -5)$

13.

15.

17. 2 units left and 2 units up

19. 6 units right and 3 units down

21. a. 5 units right and 1 unit up

   b. no; It would hit the island.

   c. 4 units right and 4 units up

23. If you are doing more than 10 moves and have not moved the knight to g5, you might want to start over.

25. no

27. yes

Section 5.6

Reflections
(pages 230 and 231)

1. The third one because it is not a reflection.

3. Quadrant IV

5. yes

7. no

9. no

11. $M'(-2, -1)$, $N'(0, -3)$, $P'(2, -2)$

13. $D'(-2, 1)$, $E'(0, 2)$, $F'(1, 5)$, $G'(-1, 4)$

15. $T'(-1, -1)$, $U'(-4, 2)$, $V'(-6, -2)$

17. $J'(-2, 2)$, $K'(-7, 4)$, $L'(-9, -2)$, $M'(-3, -1)$

19. *x*-axis

21. *y*-axis

Reflections *(continued)*
(pages 230 and 231)

23.

25. the first one; The left side of the face is a mirror image of the right side.

27.

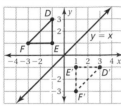

The *x*-coordinate and *y*-coordinate for each point are switched in the image.

29. straight   **31.** acute

Rotations
(pages 236 and 237)

1. a. reflection   **b.** rotation   **c.** translation

3. Quadrant I   **5.** Quadrant III   **7.** No

9. yes; 180° clockwise or counterclockwise

11. It only needs to rotate 90° to produce an identical image.

13. $A'(-1, -4)$, $B'(-4, -3)$,
     $C'(-4, -1)$, $D'(-1, -2)$

15. $A'(0, 1)$, $B'(-1, -2)$,
     $C'(-3, -2)$, $D'(-2, 1)$

17. because both ways will produce the same image

19. Use Guess, Check, and Revise to solve this problem.

21. triangular prism   **23.** C

1. Prisms and cylinders both have two parallel, identical bases. The bases of a cylinder are circles. The bases of a prism are polygons. A prism has lateral faces that are parallelograms or rectangles. A cylinder has one smooth, round lateral surface.

3. *Sample answer:* Prisms: A cereal box is a rectangular prism. A pup tent with parallel triangular bases at the front and back is a triangular prism.

   Pyramids: The Egyptian pyramids are rectangular pyramids. A house roof forms a pyramid if it has lateral faces that are triangles that meet at a common vertex.

   Cylinders: Some examples of cylinders are a soup can, a tuna fish can, and a new, unsharpened, round pencil.

   Cones: some examples of cones are a traffic cone, an ice cream sugar cone, a party hat, and the sharpened end of a pencil.

5. base: circle; solid: cylinder

7. front: side: top:

   surface area: 34 units^2; volume: 10 units^3

9. front: side: top:

   surface area: 38 units^2; volume: 9 units^3

11.

13.

15.

17. front:

    side:

    top: ⬤

19. front: △

    side: △

    top: ▽

21. front:

    side:

    top:

23. The Washington Monument is an *obelisk*. It consists of a pyramid sitting on top of a solid that tapers as it rises.

25.

27. Use cubes to create solids that are possible.

29. 28 m^2

31. 15 ft^2

1. *Sample answer:* You want to paint a large toy chest in the form of a rectangular prism, and in order to know how much paint to buy, you need to know the surface area.

3. 18 cm^2

5. 108 cm^2

7.

72 cm^2

9. 130 ft^2 11. 76 yd^2 13. 136 m^2

15. 448 in.^2; The surface area of the box is 448 square inches, so that is the least amount of paper needed to cover the box.

17. 156 in.^2 19. 83 ft^2 21. 2 qt

23. $S = 2B + Ph$ 25. 48 units   27. C

1. $2\pi rh$

3. $36\pi \approx 113.0 \text{ cm}^2$

5.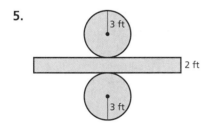

$30\pi \approx 94.2 \text{ ft}^2$

7.

$168\pi \approx 527.5 \text{ ft}^2$

9. $156\pi \approx 489.8 \text{ ft}^2$ 11. $120\pi \approx 376.8 \text{ ft}^2$ 13. $28\pi \approx 87.9 \text{ m}^2$

15. The error is that only the lateral surface area is found. The areas of the bases should be added;
$$S = 2\pi r^2 + 2\pi rh$$
$$= 2\pi (6)^2 + 2\pi (6)(11)$$
$$= 72\pi + 132\pi$$
$$= 204\pi \text{ ft}^2$$

Hmmm.

17. The surface area of the cylinder with the height of 8.5 inches is greater than the surface area of the cylinder with the height of 11 inches.

19. After removing the wedge, is there any new surface area added?

21. 117   23. 56.52

Section 6.4 — Surface Areas of Pyramids
(pages 274 and 275)

1. the triangle and the hexagon

3. Knowing the slant height helps because it represents the height of the triangle that makes up each lateral face. So, the slant height helps you to find the area of each lateral face.

5. 178.3 mm² **7.** 144 ft² **9.** 170.1 yd²

11. 1240.4 mm² **13.** 6 m

15. Determine how long the fabric needs to be so you can cut the fabric most efficiently.

17. 124 cm²

19. $A \approx 452.16$ units²; $C \approx 75.36$ units

21. $A \approx 572.265$ units²; $C \approx 84.78$ units

Section 6.5 — Surface Areas of Cones
(pages 280 and 281)

1. no; The base of a cone is a circle. A circle is not a polygon.

3. $\ell > r$ **5.** $36\pi \approx 113.0$ m² **7.** $119\pi \approx 373.7$ ft²

9. $64\pi \approx 201.0$ yd² **11.** 15 cm **13.** $130\pi \approx 408.2$ in.²

15. $360\pi \approx 1130.4$ in.²; $2.5\pi \approx 7.85$ ft² **17.** $96\pi \approx 301.44$ ft²; $\frac{32}{3}\pi \approx 33.49\overline{3}$ yd²

19. 12% **21.** the lateral surface area

23. 45 in.² **25.** 16 ft²

Section 6.6 — Surface Areas of Composite Solids
(pages 286 and 287)

1. *Sample answer:*

3. three cylinders

5. rectangular prism, half of a cylinder

7. cones; $104\pi \approx 326.6$ m²

9. trapezoidal prism, rectangular prism; 152 ft² **11.** two rectangular prisms; 308 ft²

13. 63.4% **15.** $144\pi \approx 452.2$ in.² **17.** $806\pi \approx 2530.84$ mm²

19. 10 ft² **21.** 47.5 in.²

Section 7.1 — Volumes of Prisms
(pages 302 and 303)

1. cubic units

3. *Sample answers:* Volume because you want to make sure the product will fit inside the package. Surface area because of the cost of packaging.

5. 288 cm^3

7. 160 yd^3

9. 420 mm^3

11. 645 mm^3

13. The area of the base is wrong.
$$V = \frac{1}{2}(7)(5) \cdot 10$$
$$= 175 \text{ cm}^3$$

15. 225 in.^3

17. 7200 ft^3

19. 1728 in.^3

$1 \times 1 \times 1 = 1 \text{ ft}^3$ $12 \times 12 \times 12 = 1728 \text{ in.}^3$

21. 20 cm

23. You can write the volume in cubic inches and use prime factorization to find the dimensions.

Hint

25. reflection

27. rotation

Section 7.2 — Volumes of Cylinders
(pages 308 and 309)

1. How much does it take to cover the cylinder?; $170\pi \approx 533.8 \text{ cm}^2$; $300\pi \approx 942 \text{ cm}^3$

3. $486\pi \approx 1526.0 \text{ ft}^3$

5. $245\pi \approx 769.3 \text{ ft}^3$

7. $90\pi \approx 282.6 \text{ mm}^3$

9. $63\pi \approx 197.8 \text{ in.}^3$

11. $256\pi \approx 803.8 \text{ cm}^3$

13. $\frac{125}{8\pi} \approx 5 \text{ ft}$

15. $\frac{240}{\pi} \approx 76 \text{ cm}$

Hint

17. Divide the volume of one round bale by the volume of one square bale.

19. $8325 - 729\pi \approx 6036 \text{ m}^3$

21. $a = 0.5 \cdot 200$; 100

23. D

Section 7.3 — Volumes of Pyramids
(pages 314 and 315)

1. The volume of a pyramid is $\frac{1}{3}$ times the area of the base times the height. The volume of a prism is the area of the base times the height.

3. 3 times greater

5. 20 mm^3

7. 80 in.^3

9. 252 mm^3

11. 700 mm^3

13. 30 in.^2

15. 7.5 ft

17. 12,000 in.^{3}; The volume of one paperweight is 12 cubic inches. So, 12 cubic inches of glass is needed to make one paperweight. So it takes $12 \times 1000 = 12{,}000$ cubic inches to make 1000 paperweights.

19. *Sample answer:* 5 ft by 4 ft

21. 28   **23.** 60   **25.** B

Section 7.4

Volumes of Cones
(pages 320 and 321)

1. The height of a cone is the distance from the vertex to the center of the base.

3. Divide by 3.

5. $9\pi \approx 28.3$ m^3

7. $\dfrac{2\pi}{3} \approx 2.1$ ft^3

9. $27\pi \approx 84.8$ yd^3

11. $\dfrac{125\pi}{6} \approx 65.4$ in.^{3}

13. The diameter was used instead of the radius.

$$V = \frac{1}{3}(\pi)(3)^2(8)$$

$$= 24\pi \text{ m}^3$$

15. 1.5 ft

17. $\dfrac{40}{3\pi} \approx 4.2$ in.

19. 24.1 min

21. $3y$

23. 315 m^3

25. $152\pi \approx 477.28$ ft^3

Section 7.5

Volumes of Composite Solids
(pages 328 and 329)

1. A composite solid is a solid that is made up of more than one solid.

3. In Example 2, you had to subtract the volume of the cylinder-shaped hole from the volume of the entire cylinder. In Example 1, you had to find the volumes of the square prism and the square pyramid and add them together.

5. $125 + 16\pi \approx 175.2$ in.^{3}

7. 220 cm^3

9. 173.3 ft^3

11. $216 - 24\pi \approx 140.6$ m^3

13. **a.** *Sample answer:* 80%

    b. *Sample answer:* $100\pi \approx 314$ in.^{3}

15. 13.875 in.^{3}; The volume of the hexagonal prism is 10.5(0.75) and the volume of the hexagonal pyramid is $\dfrac{1}{3}(6)(3)$.

17. $\dfrac{25}{9}$

19. B

1. Similar solids are solids of the same type that have proportional corresponding linear measures.

3. **a.** $\frac{4}{9}$ **b.** $\frac{8}{27}$ 5. no   7. no

9. $b = 18$ m; $c = 19.5$ m; $h = 9$ m

11. 1012.5 in.^{2} 13. 13,564.8 ft^3 15. 673.75 cm^2

17. **a.** yes; Because all circles are similar, the slant height and the circumference of the base of the cones are proportional.

   b. no; because the ratio of the volumes of similar solids is equal to the cube of the ratio of their corresponding linear measures

19. Choose two variables, one to represent the surface area of the smallest doll and one to represent the volume of the smallest doll. Use these variables to find the surface areas and volumes of the other dolls.

Hint

21. 1   23. C

1. 3 is the stem; 4 is the leaf

3. From the leaves, you can see where most of the data lies and whether there are many values that are low or high.

5. 4; 42   7. no; There is no 2 as a leaf for the stem 3.

9. **Hours Online**

Stem	Leaf
0	0 2 6 8
1	2 2 4 5 7 8
2	1 4

Key: 2 | 1 = 21 hours

11. **Points Scored**

Stem	Leaf
3	8
4	2 2 3 3 5
5	0 1 6 8 8
6	
7	0 1 1 5

Key: 3 | 8 = 38 points

13. **Weights**

Stem	Leaf
0	8
1	2 5 7 8
2	4 4
3	1

Key: 2 | 4 = 24 pounds

Most of the weights are in the middle.

15. **Minutes in Line**

Stem	Leaf
1	6 9
2	0 2 6 7 9
3	1 1 6 8
4	0

Key: 4 | 0 = 4.0 minutes

17. mean: 56.6; median: 53; modes: 41, 43, 63; range: 56

19. 97; It increases the mean.

21. *Sample answer:* Points by a basketball player in his first 8 games

Points

Stem	Leaf
2	1 3 4
3	2 4
4	0 1 5

Key: 3 | 2 = 32 points

23.

25.

27. B

Section 8.2

Histograms
(pages 358 and 359)

1. The *Test Scores* graph is a histogram because the number of students (frequency) achieving the test scores are shown in intervals of the same size (20).

3. No bar is shown on that interval.

5. flat

7.

9. a. 4–5

  b. 20 students

  c. 85%

11. Pennsylvania; You can see from the intervals and frequencies that Pennsylvania counties are greater in area, which makes up for it having fewer counties.

13. Don't use a smaller interval because the distribution will appear flat.

15. 27   **17.** 51.2

Section 8.3

Circle Graphs
(pages 366 and 367)

1. Multiply the decimal form of each percent by 360° to find the angle measure for each section.

3. $\frac{1}{2}$ does not belong because it does not represent an entire circle.

5. orange   **7.** 20 students   **9.** 54°   **11.** 10.8°

13.

Expenses

Other $400
Play rights $400
Programs/tickets $300
Advertising $250
Costume rental $650

15. no; The sum of the percentages is greater than 100%. This would occur when students like more than one of these activities.

17. *Sample answer:* Knowledge of percentages, proportions, and degrees of a circle. How to convert from one form to another.

19. $x = 40$

21. $w = 1.5$

Section 8.4

Samples and Populations
(pages 372 and 373)

1. Samples are easier to obtain.

3. *Sample answer:* The results may be similar for middle school students, but not for children in first grade. Children in first grade probably do not know all of these nuts.

5. *Sample answer:* You could send a survey home with your classmates and have them ask one of their parents what their favorite nut is.

7. Population: All quarters in circulation
Sample: 150 quarters

9. Population: All books in library
Sample: 10 books

11. a. Population: All students at your school
Sample: First 15 students at band class

b. no; Your sample includes 15 students arriving at band class, and students who take band class play a musical instrument.

13. Sample A because it is representative of the population.

15. A population because there are few enough students in your homeroom to not make the surveying difficult.

17. 1260 students

19. Use the survey results to find the number of students in the school that plan to attend college.

21. 31.25%

23. $81.\overline{81}\%$

Section 9.1 — Introduction to Probability
(pages 388 and 389)

1. event; It is a collection of several outcomes.

3. *Sample answer:* flipping a coin and getting both heads and tails; rolling a number cube and getting a number between 1 and 6

5. no; They both have the same number of forward outcomes.

7. 6

9. 6, 7, 8, 9

11. 1, 2

13. **a.** 2 ways **b.** blue, blue

15. **a.** 2 ways **b.** purple, purple

17. **a.** 6 ways **b.** yellow, green, blue, blue, purple, purple

19. There are 7 marbles that are *not* purple, even though there are only 4 colors. Choosing *not* purple could be red, red, red, blue, blue, green, or yellow.

21. false; five

23. false; red

25. no; More sections on a spinner does not necessarily mean you are more likely to spin red. It depends on the size of the sections of the spinner.

27. Do the number of outcomes increase, decrease, or stay the same? Hmmm.

29. 30

31. $-3\frac{1}{2}$

Section 9.2 — Theoretical Probability
(pages 394 and 395)

1. There is a 50% chance you will get a favorable outcome.

3. Spinner 4; The other three spinners are fair.

5. $\frac{1}{6}$ or about 16.7%

7. $\frac{1}{2}$ or 50%

9. 0 or 0%

11. 9 chips

13. not fair, your friend

15. $\frac{1}{44}$ or about 2.3%

17. **a.** $\frac{4}{9}$ or about 44.4% **b.** 5 males

19. There are 2 combinations for each.

21. $\frac{1}{4}$

23. $-\frac{21}{40}$

25. C

Section 9.3

Experimental Probability
(pages 402 and 403)

1. Perform an experiment several times. Count how often the event occurs and divide by the number of trials.

3. $\frac{2}{5}$ or 40%   5. $\frac{2}{5}$ or 40%   7. $\frac{7}{50}$ or 14%   9. $\frac{21}{25}$ or 84%   11. $\frac{17}{50}$ or 34%

13. The theoretical probability was found, not the experimental probability. $P(4) = \frac{11}{50}$

15. 45 tiles   17. 25

19. The experimental probability of 60% is close to the theoretical probability of 50%.

21. Make a list of all the possible ways to get each sum.

23. *Sample answer:* Roll two number cubes 50 times and find each product. Record how many times the product is at least 12. Divide this number by 50 to find the experimental probability.

25. $x = 5$ 27. $x = 24$

Section 9.4

Independent and Dependent Events
(pages 409–411)

1. Draw a tree diagram or multiply $P(A)$ by $P(B)$.

3. *Sample answer:* independent events: a traffic jam and a sunny day; dependent events: temperatures below freezing and ice

5. independent; The outcome of the first roll does not affect the outcome of the second roll.

7. independent; You replace the marble, so the probability doesn't change.

9. dependent; There is one less person to choose from on the second draw.

11. $\frac{2}{9}$ 13. $\frac{2}{9}$ 15. $\frac{1}{20}$ or 5%   17. $\frac{3}{20}$ or 15%

19. $\frac{1}{42}$ or about 2.4%   21. $\frac{1}{21}$ or about 4.8%   23. $\frac{4}{21}$ or about 19%   25. $\frac{1}{2520}$ or about 0.04%

27. **a.** $\frac{1}{100}$ or 1%

  b. It increases the probability that your choice is correct to $\frac{1}{25}$ or 4%, because each digit could be 0, 2, 4, 6, or 8.

29. **a.** $\frac{1}{9}$ or about 11.1%

  b. It increases the probability that your guesses are correct to $\frac{1}{4}$ or 25%, because you are only choosing between 2 choices for each question.

31. $\frac{16}{25}$ or 64%   33. $1:5; 5:1$ 35. $1:35; 35:1$

37. $n = -10.8$ 39. B

Solving Multi-Step Equations
(pages A14 and A15)

1. Add $6x$ and $3x$, subtract 2 from each side, and divide each side by 9.

3. 313 K

5. $K = C + 273$

7. $x = 3$

9. $m = -4$

11. $y = 3$

13. 15

15. a. $7.25 **b.** $1.75

17. The question asks for the sale price of the skirt, not the original price of the skirt.

19. $x = 12$; *Sample answer:* The left side has more steps, but does not deal with fractions like the right side does.

21. 12

Solving Equations with Variables on Both Sides *(pages A20 and A21)*

1. Subtract $3x$ from each side and divide each side by 2.

3. Add $3x$ to each side so the constant is by itself.

5. $c = -3$

7. $a = -\dfrac{1}{2}$

9. $z = -2$

11. $p = -8\dfrac{1}{2}$

13. $d = -2$

15. $h = 2\dfrac{1}{2}$

17. $k = -6$

19. $f = -2\dfrac{2}{7}$

21. $b = 1$

23. They did not distribute the negative sign on the right side.
$$2(v - 5) = -(3v + 5)$$
$$2v - 10 = -3v - 5$$
$$5v = 5$$
$$v = 1$$

25. 27

27. 18

29. $5n - 3 = 8 - 6n$; $n = 1$

31. Use $d = rt$ and the fact that the distance is the same to write an equation with variables on both sides.

33. perimeter of $\triangle ABC$: 27; perimeter of $\triangle DEF$: 45

35–37.

1. $3x - 2 = x + 2; x = 2$

3. *Sample answer:* A table because graphs have to be accurate to find the point of intersection.

5. $h = 2$ **7.** $g = 5$ **9.** $a = -2$ **11.** $p = -3$

13. $x = -3$ **15.** $x = -2$ **17.** 3 months   **19.** $x = 16; P = 24$ units

21. *Sample answer:* From the table, you can see that the solution is between 2 and 3. Then, you can use *Guess, Check, and Revise* to find the solution, which is 2.2.

23. Use $d = rt$ and the fact that both of you will have travelled the same distance when your friend catches you to write an equation with variables on both sides.

25. triangle: 27 square units; rectangle: 54 square units

27. $\dfrac{1}{2}$ **29.** B

Section B.4

Slope of a Line
(pages A34 and A35)

1. *Sample answer:* The rise is the difference of the distance from the ground to the peak of the roof and the distance from the ground to the lowest point on the roof. The run is the horizontal distance from the peak to the lowest point on the roof. The slope is the ratio of the rise to the run.

3. *Sample answer:* $(5, -8), (-1, -4)$

Two Points	Change in y	Change in x	Slope of Line
5. $(-10, 4), (5, -20)$	-24	15	$-\dfrac{8}{5}$
7. $(1, 9), (7, 6)$	-3	6	$-\dfrac{1}{2}$

9. $-\dfrac{5}{2}$ **11.**   **13.**

15. $(-3, -7)$

17. **a.** Daytona: $\dfrac{21}{34}$; Talladega: $\dfrac{13}{20}$

     b. Talladega Superspeedway

     c. *Sample answer:* So they can maintain a high speed through turns.

19. In part (b), you can change the height or the length of the roadway.

21. $x = -4$ **23.** $x = 7$

1. the y-coordinate of the point where the line crosses the y-axis

3. B

5. A

7. slope: -2; y-intercept: 6

9. slope: -5; y-intercept: 3

11. slope: $\dfrac{5}{2}$; y-intercept: -9

13.

15.

17.

19.

21.

23.

25. the number of cartoons the cartoonist has already completed

27. $y = -3x + 2$

29. a. slope: 2; y-intercept: 7

b.

c. no; The value of y is 5 when $x = -1$. The value of x cannot be negative because the side length of a rectangle is never negative.

31. slope: $-\dfrac{A}{B}$, y-intercept: $\dfrac{C}{B}$

33. $v = \dfrac{1}{2}$

35. A

Student Index

This student-friendly index will help you find vocabulary, key ideas, and concepts. It is easily accessible and designed to be a reference for you whether you are looking for a definition, real-life application, or help with avoiding common errors.

Absolute value, 2–7
  comparing, 5
  defined, 4
  error analysis, 6
  finding, 4
  opposites, 10
  practice problems, 6
  real-life application, 5
Addition
  of integers, 8–13, 14–15
    error analysis, 12
    practice problems, 12
  Property of Equality, 72
  of rational numbers, 56–61
  to solve equations, 70–75
Additive inverse, defined, 10
Additive Inverse Property, 10
Algebra
  area of a cylinder, 264
  cross products, 113
  equations
    direct variation, 138–141
    error analysis, A14
    inverse variation, 142–147
    multi-step, A10–A15
    percent, 158–163
    practice problems, A14, A20
    simple interest, 178, 180–183
    solving by addition, 70–75
    solving by division, 76–81
    solving by multiplication,
      76–81
    solving by subtraction, 70–75
    solving two-step, 82–87
    solving using tables and
      graphs, A22–A27
    with variables on both sides,
      A16–A21
  formulas, *See* Formula(s)
  integers, 13, 18
  surface area of a prism, 258
    formula for, 258
Algebra tiles, 70–71, 76, 82–83
Angle(s)
  corresponding, 196–199
    practice problems, 198

  practice problems, 366
  of rotation, 234
  symbol for, 196
Angle of rotation, defined, 234
Arc
  symbol for, 197
Area
  of a circle, 264
  of a similar figure, 200–205, 209
    practice problems, 204
  of a triangle, 259

Base(s)
  of a cone, 278
  of a cylinder, 262, 264
  inverse variation with height, 142
  of a prism, 256, 258–259
  of a pyramid, 270
  of a regular pyramid, 272

Center of rotation, defined, 234
Circle graph(s), 362–367
  defined, 364
  making, 363–364
  practice problems, 366, 372
  reasoning, 367
Circle(s)
  area of, 264
  diameter of, 279
Common errors
  linear functions, A38
  percent equation, 160
  rotations, 235
  similar figures, 197
  y-intercept, A38
Comparing
  absolute values, 5
  direct and inverse variation, 143
  probabilities, 401
  similar solids, 330–331
  units of measure, 131
  volumes, 310
    and surface areas, 330–331

Composite solids
  defined, 284
  open-ended, 286
  surface area of, 282–287
  volume of, 324–329
    formula for, 326
    real-life application, 327
Concept circle, A28
Cone(s), 276–281
  defined, 252
  drawing, 276–277
  height of, 318
  similar, 332
  slant height, 278–279
    practice problems, 280
  surface area of, 276–281
    formula for, 278
    real-life application, 279
  volume of, 316–321
    error analysis, 320
    formula for, 316, 318
    practice problems, 320
    real-life application, 319
    reasoning, 320–321
    writing, 320
Connections to math strands,
    Throughout. For example,
    see:
  algebra, 27, 32, 61, A16, A22
    integers, 13, 19
  geometry, 38, 75, 87, 115, 169,
    199, 205, 274, 281, A21
Conversion
  between metric and customary
    units, 130–135
Coordinate plane(s), 34–39
  defined, 36
  error analysis, 38
  graphing, 34–35, 105–109,
    137–140
  ordered pairs, 34–39
    practice problems, 38
  origin, 36
  quadrants, 36
  real-life application, 37
  reflections in, 229–231
  rotations in, 235–237
  translations in, 223–225

with variables on both sides,
A16–A21
error analysis, A20
practice problems, A20
real-life application, A19
writing, 87
Equivalent equations, defined, 72
Error analysis
algebra, 74, 80
converting units of measure, 134
coordinate planes, 38
direct variation, 140
division
of integers, 32
equations
multi-step, A14
percent, 162
solving, 74, 80, 86
two-step, 86
with variables on both sides,
A20
integers
absolute value of, 6
adding, 12
dividing, 32
multiplying, 26
subtracting, 18
interest, simple, 182
inverse variation, 146
linear functions, A40
percents, 162
of change, 168
of decrease, 168
prisms
volume of, 302
probability, 388
outcomes, 402
proportions, 120, 126
rational numbers
as decimals, 54
dividing, 66
multiplying, 66
subtracting, 60
samples and populations, 372
similar solids, 336
slope, 108, A35
stem-and-leaf plots, 352
surface area of a cylinder, 267
volume
of a cone, 320
of a prism, 302
of similar solids, 336

Event(s), *See also* Probability
defined, 386
dependent, 404–411
defined, 406
practice problems, 409
independent, 404–411
defined, 406
practice problems, 409
Example and non-example chart,
218
Experiment(s), *See also* Probability
defined, 386
Experimental probability, *See also*
Probability
defined, 400
Exponent(s)
using, 25
Expression(s)
equivalent
defined, 72
error analysis, 26
evaluating, 31

F

Fair experiment, defined, 393
Financial literacy, 57, 179
Formula(s)
area
of a circle, 264
of a lateral surface, 265
of a triangle, 259
interest, simple, 178
surface area
of a square prism, 285
of a square pyramid, 285
for surface area of
a cone, 279
a cylinder, 264
a rectangular prism, 258
a regular pyramid, 272
volume
of a composite solid, 326
of a cone, 316, 318
of a cylinder, 306
of a prism, 298–299
of a pyramid, 312
of a square prism, 326
of a square pyramid, 326
Formula triangle, 422
Four square, 268

Fraction(s)
adding
practice problems, 60
decimals as, 53
dividing
practice problems, 66
multiplying
practice problems, 66
simplifying
practice problems, 60, 66
subtracting
practice problems, 60
Frequency table(s), 356
Function(s), *See also* Linear
function(s), Equation(s)
input-output tables and, A36

G

Graph(s), 105
circle, 362–367
in a coordinate plane, 101,
106–109, 137–140
of direct variation, 137–140
drawing, 137
of equations, A16, A36–A41
practice problems, A26
histograms, 354–359
linear, A30–A35
practice problems, A34, A40
using slope-intercept forms,
A38–A41
of rates, 101
for solving equations, A22–A27
practice problems, A26
real-life application, A25
stem-and-leaf plots, 348–353
Graphic organizer(s)
concept circle, A28
example and non-example
chart, 218
formula triangle, 422
four square, 268
idea and examples chart, 20
information frame, 360
information wheel, 128
process diagram, 68
summary triangle, 170
word magnet, 396

H

Height
of a cone, 318
inverse variation with base, 142

O

Open-ended, *Throughout. For example, see:*
  absolute value, 7
  composite solids, 286
  decimals
    repeating, 55
    terminating, 55
  drawing a composite solid, 286
  equations
    solving, 81
    with variables on both sides, A20
  fractions
    multiplying, 67
  integers, 18
    adding, 13
    dividing, 32
    subtracting, 19
  inverse operations, 80
  inverse variation, 146
  measurements
    converting, 134
  probability, 388
    dependent events, 409
    independent events, 409
    theoretical, 394
  proportions, 120
    solving, 126
  rates, 102
  rational numbers
    adding, 60
    multiplying, 67
  ratios, 114
  scale factor, 217
  similar figures, 198
  similar solids, 335
  slope, A34
  stem-and-leaf plots, 353
  surface area of a prism, 260
  volume of a pyramid, 314, 315
Opposites, defined, 10
Order of operations, 31
Ordering
  rational numbers, 50, 53
Origin, of a coordinate plane, defined, 36
Outcomes, *See also* Probability
  defined, 386

P

Pattern(s)
  area
    of a similar figure, 201
  finding
    of surface areas, 283
  perimeter
    of a similar figure, 201
  reflections, 226–227
  volume of a pyramid, 311
Percent(s)
  of change, 166
    defined, 166
    error analysis, 168
  of decrease, 164–169
    defined, 166
    error analysis, 168
    finding, 167
    practice problems, 168
  defined, 160
  equation, 158–163
    error analysis, 162
    practice problems, 162
    real-life application, 161
    reasoning, 163
  estimating, 158–159
  of increase, 164–169
    defined, 166
    finding, 166
    practice problems, 168
  interest, simple, 178–183
    defined, 178
    error analysis, 182
    formula for, 178
    modeling, 178
    practice problems, 182
    reasoning, 183
  modeling, 158–159
  prices
    practice problems, 176
Perimeter
  of a similar figure, 200–205, 208
    practice problems, 204
Pi, 264
Polygon(s)
  regular, 272
Polyhedron(s), defined, 252
Population(s)
  defined, 370
  practice problems, 372
  and samples, 368–373

Practice problems, *Throughout. For example, see:*
  algebra, 74, 80
  angles, 366
  circle graphs, 366, 372
  converting units of measure, 134
  coordinate planes
    ordered pairs, 38
  Cross Products Property, 126
  direct variation, 140, 146
  equations
    graphing, A26
    multi-step, A14
    percent, 162
    solving, 74, 80, 86, A14, A26
    two-step, 86
    with variables on both sides, A20
  fractions
    dividing, 66
    multiplying, 66
    simplifying, 60, 66
  histograms, 358
  integers
    absolute value of, 6
    adding, 12
    dividing, 32
    multiplying, 26
    subtracting, 18
  interest, simple, 182
  inverse variation, 146
  lateral faces, 266
  linear functions
    graphing, A40
  nets, 266
  percents, 162
    of decrease, 168
    of increase, 168
    prices, 176
  populations, 372
  prisms
    nets of, 260
    surface area of, 260
    volume of, 302
  probability
    dependent events, 409
    experimental, 402
    independent events, 409
    outcomes, 388
    theoretical, 394
  proportions, 120
    solving, 126

Q

Conversions

U.S. Customary
1 foot = 12 inches
1 yard = 3 feet
1 mile = 5280 feet
1 acre ≈ 43,560 square feet
1 cup = 8 fluid ounces
1 pint = 2 cups
1 quart = 2 pints
1 gallon = 4 quarts
1 gallon = 231 cubic inches
1 pound = 16 ounces
1 ton = 2000 pounds
1 cubic foot ≈ 7.5 gallons

U.S. Customary to Metric
1 inch ≈ 2.54 centimeters
1 foot ≈ 0.3 meter
1 mile ≈ 1.6 kilometers
1 quart ≈ 0.95 liter
1 gallon ≈ 3.79 liters
1 cup ≈ 237 milliliters
1 pound ≈ 0.45 kilogram
1 ounce ≈ 28 grams
1 gallon ≈ 3785 cubic centimeters

Time
1 minute = 60 seconds
1 hour = 60 minutes
1 hour = 3600 seconds
1 year = 52 weeks

Temperature
$$C = \frac{5}{9}(F - 32)$$

$$F = \frac{9}{5}C + 32$$

Metric
1 centimeter = 10 millimeters
1 meter = 100 centimeters
1 kilometer = 1000 meters
1 liter = 1000 milliliters
1 kiloliter = 1000 liters
1 milliliter = 1 cubic centimeter
1 liter = 1000 cubic centimeters
1 cubic millimeter = 0.001 milliliter
1 gram = 1000 milligrams
1 kilogram = 1000 grams

Metric to U.S. Customary
1 centimeter ≈ 0.39 inch
1 meter ≈ 3.28 feet
1 kilometer ≈ 0.6 mile
1 liter ≈ 1.06 quarts
1 liter ≈ 0.26 gallon
1 kilogram ≈ 2.2 pounds
1 gram ≈ 0.035 ounce
1 cubic meter ≈ 264 gallon

Surface Area and Volume

Prism

S = areas of bases + areas of lateral faces
$V = Bh$

Cylinder

$S = 2\pi r^2 + 2\pi rh$
$V = Bh$

Pyramid

S = area of base + areas of lateral faces
$V = \frac{1}{3}Bh$

Cone

$S = \pi r^2 + \pi r\ell$
$V = \frac{1}{3}Bh$

The Coordinate Plane

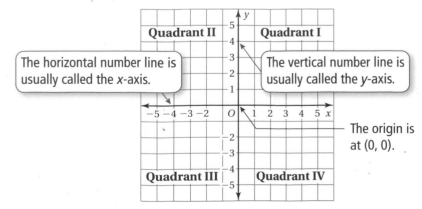

The horizontal number line is usually called the x-axis.

The vertical number line is usually called the y-axis.

The origin is at (0, 0).

Quadrant II   Quadrant I
Quadrant III   Quadrant IV

NCTM Curriculum Focal Points

K

FOCAL POINT   Represent, compare, and order whole numbers and join and separate sets.

FOCAL POINT   Describe shapes and space.

FOCAL POINT   Order objects by measurable attributes.

Connections

Algebra • Data Analysis • Geometry

1

FOCAL POINT   Develop understandings of addition and subtraction and strategies for basic addition facts and related subtraction facts.

FOCAL POINT   Develop an understanding of whole number relationships, including grouping in tens and ones.

FOCAL POINT   Compose and decompose geometric shapes.

Connections

Algebra • Data Analysis • Measurement • Number and Operations

2

FOCAL POINT   Develop an understanding of the base-ten numeration system and place-value concepts.

FOCAL POINT   Develop quick recall of addition facts and related subtraction facts and fluency with multi-digit addition and subtraction.

FOCAL POINT   Develop an understanding of linear measurement and facility in measuring lengths.

Connections

Algebra • Geometry • Measurement • Number and Operations